TALK SHOW

On the Couch with Contemporary Writers

Hosted by Jaime Clarke

Illustrations by Danny Jock

Also by Jaime Clarke

We're So Famous

"This first novel is plastic fantastic . . . Sad, sassy and salient."   *- Elle Magazine*

"Clarke keeps the satire sharp . . ."   *- Spin Magazine*

"Clarke captures that unsatisfyingly minidonut flavor of entertainment culture . . . [and] finds ways to make poetry out of puff."   *- Village Voice*

"The satire works, sliding down as silvery and toxic as liquid mercury . . ."   *- Entertainment Weekly*

Vernon Downs

"Vernon Downs is a gripping, hypnotically written and unnerving look at the dark side of literary adulation. Jaime Clarke's tautly suspenseful novel is a cautionary tale for writers and readers alike – after finishing it, you may start to think that J.D. Salinger had the right idea after all."   *–Tom Perrotta*

As Editor

Boston Noir 2: The Classics

No Near Exit: Writers Select Their Favorite Work from Post Road Magazine

Don't You Forget About Me: Contemporary Writers on the Films of John Hughes

Conversations with Jonathan Lethem

Talk Show

PFP, INC
publisher@pfppublishing.com
144 Tenney Street
Georgetown, MA 01833

September 2013
Printed in the United States of America

First PFP edition © 2013

ISBN-10:0989237230
ISBN-13:978-0-9892372-3-9
(also available in eBook format)

Some of this material originally appeared in
Fanzine magazine - www.thefanzine.com

Cover Design:
Josephine Bergin Design
www.josephinebergindesign.com

For Pete Hausler

Welcome to *Talk Show* . . .

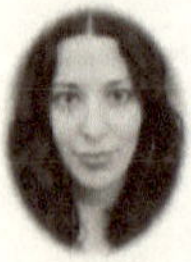

Elisa
Albert

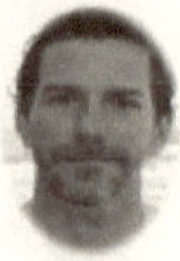

Mike
Albo

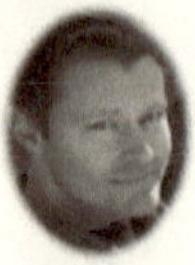

Will
Allison

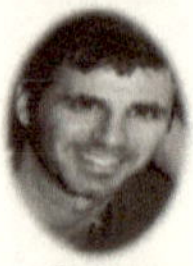

Steve
Almond

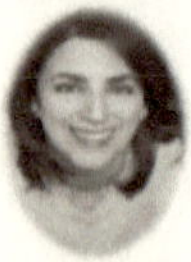

Allison
Amend

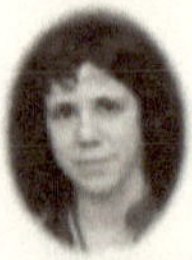

Jami
Attenberg

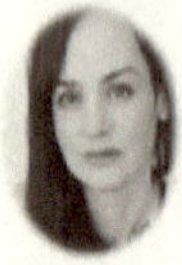

Julianna
Baggott

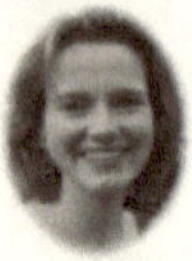

Daphne
Beal

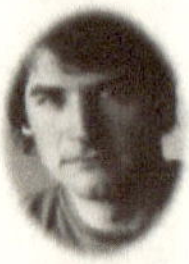

Thomas
Beller

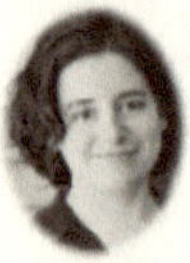

Aimee
Bender

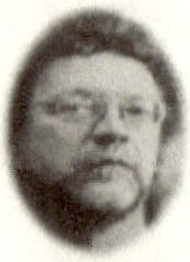

Sven
Birkerts

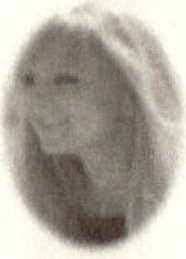

Jenna
Blum

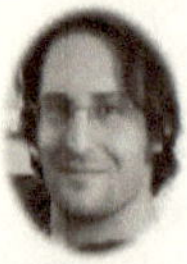

Charles
Bock

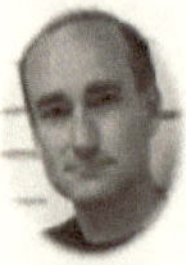

Chris
Bohjalian

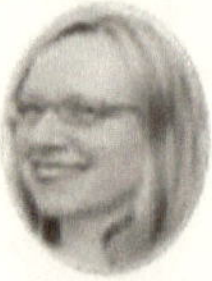

Lisa
Borders

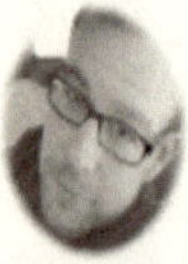

Christopher
Boucher

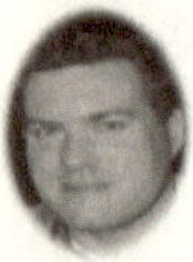

Ryan
Boudinot

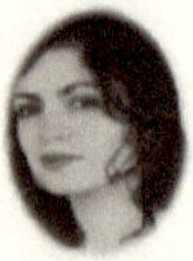

Sarah
Braunstein

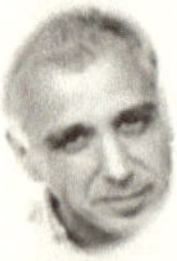

Adam
Braver

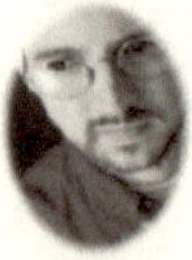

Kevin
Brockmeier

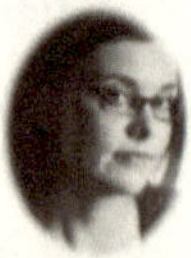

Kiara
Brinkman

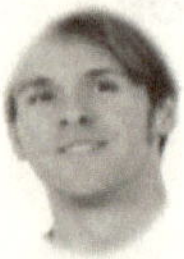

Blake
Butler

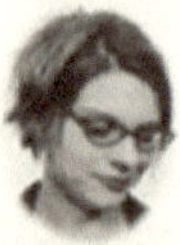

Maud
Casey

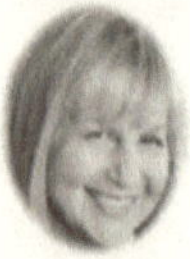

Susan
Cheever

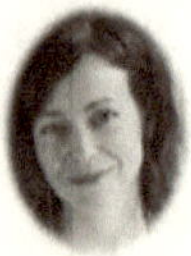

Emily
Chenoweth

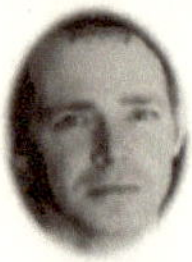

Brock
Clarke

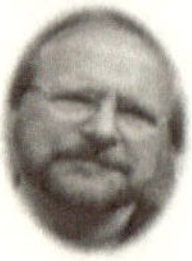

Jon
Clinch

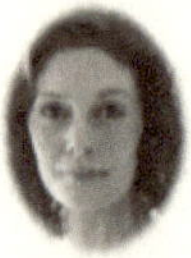

Leah
Hager Cohen

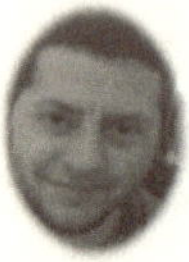

T
Cooper

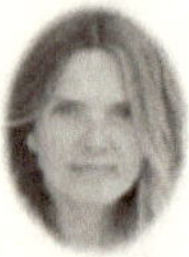

Elizabeth
Crane

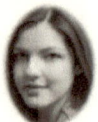
Sloane
Crosley

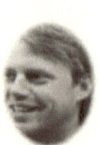
Michael
Dahlie

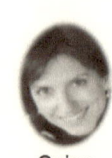
Quinn
Dalton

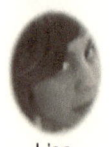
Lisa
Selin Davis

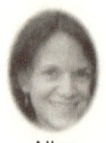
Nina
de Gramont

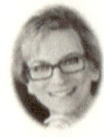
Anita
Diamant

... featuring Special Guests:

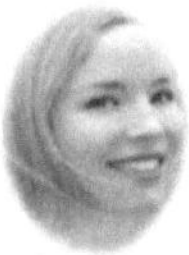

Rebecca Donner	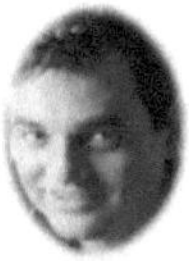 Tony D'Souza	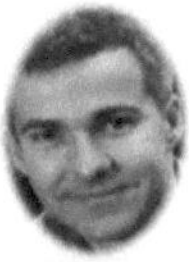 David Ebershoff	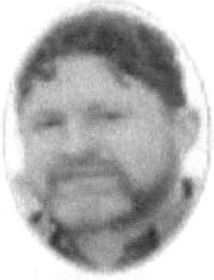 Brian Evenson	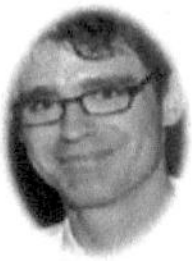 Joshua Ferris	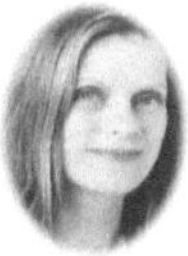 Maria Flook
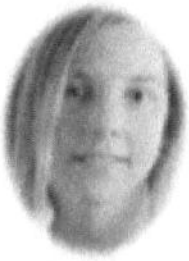 Emily Franklin	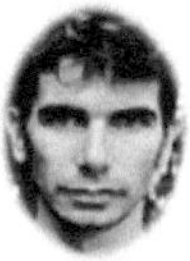 Joshua Furst	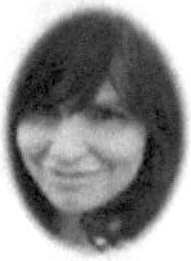 Lisa Gabriele	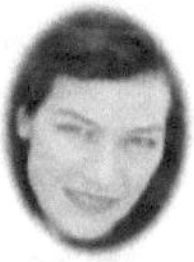 Elizabeth Gaffney	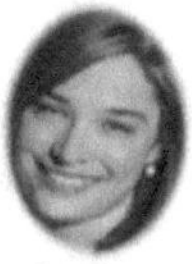 Sophie Gee	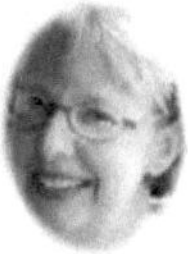 Julia Glass
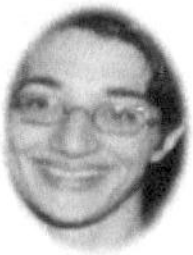 Myla Goldberg	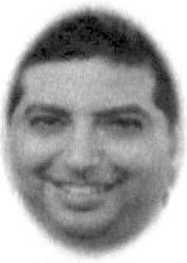 Tod Goldberg	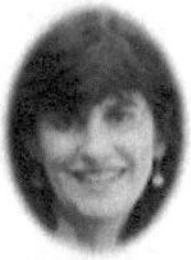 Elizabeth Graver	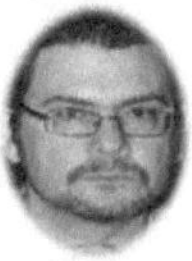 Ben Greenman	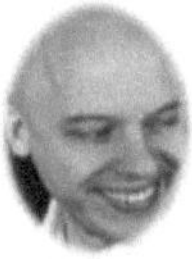 Lev Grossman	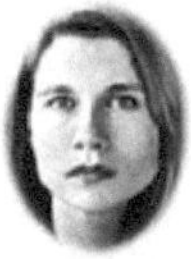 Jennifer Haigh
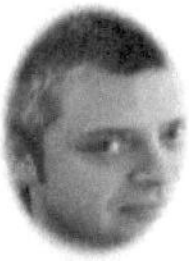 Paul Harding	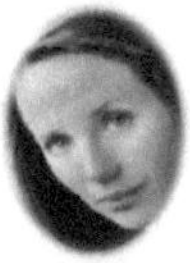 Sheridan Hay	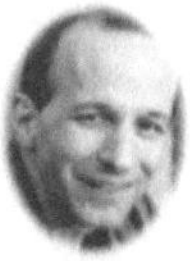 Joshua Henkin	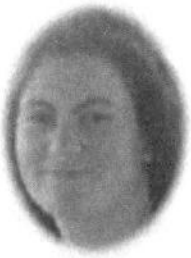 Nellie Hermann	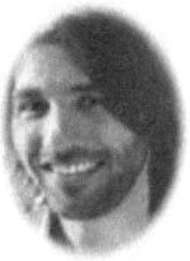 David Hollander	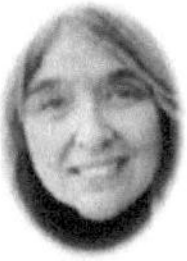 Ann Hood
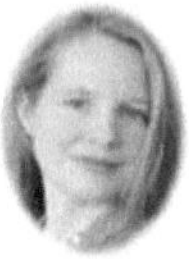 Samantha Hunt	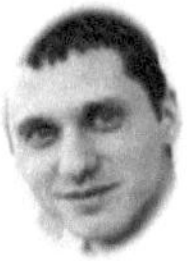 Karl Iagnemma	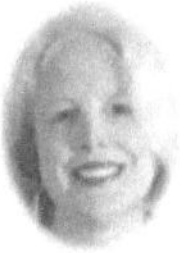 Perrin Ireland	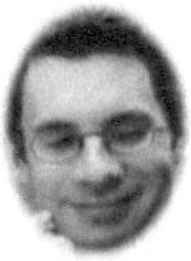 Bret Anthony Johnston	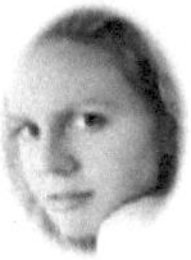 Molly Jong-Fast	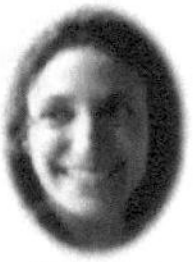 Rachel Kadish

 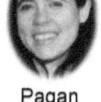 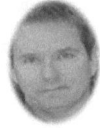 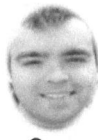 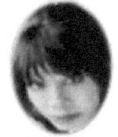 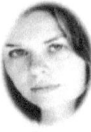

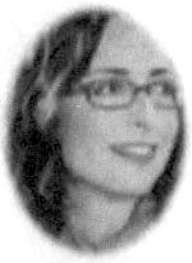

Daphne Kalotay	Pagan Kennedy	Dave King	Owen King	Binnie Kirshenbaum	Aryn Kyle

Welcome to Talk Show...

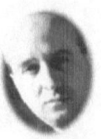

Adam
Langer

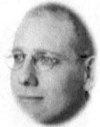

David
Leavitt

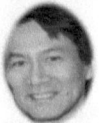

Don
Lee

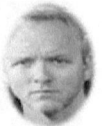

Dennis
Lehane

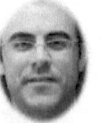

J. Robert
Lennon

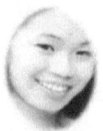

Francie
Lin

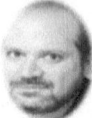

Sam
Lipsyte

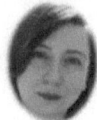

Ellen
Litman

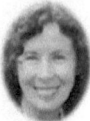

Margot
Livesey

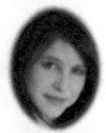

Yael Goldstein
Love

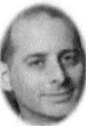

Michael
Lowenthal

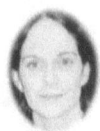

Allison
Lynn

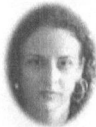

Fiona
Maazel

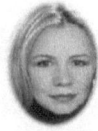

Amy
MacKinnon

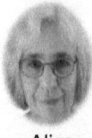

Alice
Mattison

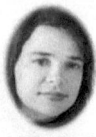

Elizabeth
McCracken

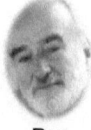

Ron
McLarty

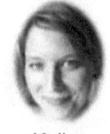

Kelly
McMasters

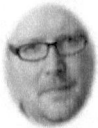

John
McNally

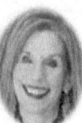

Mameve
Medwed

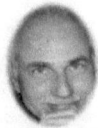

Askold
Melnyczuk

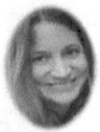

Kirsten
Menger-Anderson

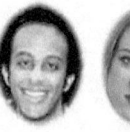

Dinaw
Mengestu

Adrienne
Miller

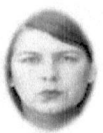

Lydia
Millet

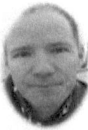

Rick
Moody

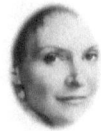

Antonya
Nelson

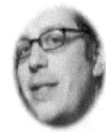

Joshua
Neuman

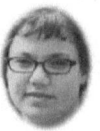

Thisbe
Nissen

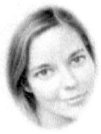

Alix
Ohlin

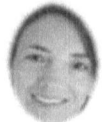

Ann
Packer

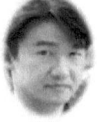

Ed
Park

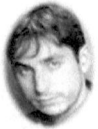

Matthew
Pearl

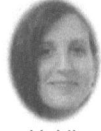

Heidi
Pitlor

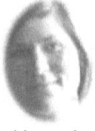

Hannah
Pittard

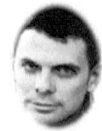

Mark Jude
Poirier

...featuring Special Guests:

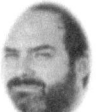
Neal
Pollack

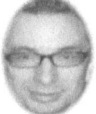
Dan
Pope

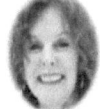
Melissa
Pritchard

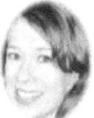
Margo
Rabb

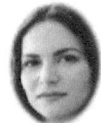
Nelly
Reifler

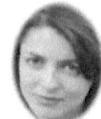
Irina
Reyn

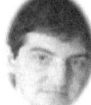
Nathaniel
Rich

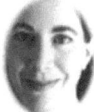
Stacey
Richter

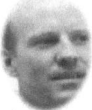
Lewis
Robinson

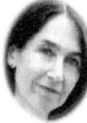
Roxana
Robinson

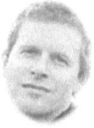
Peter
Rock

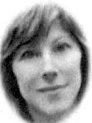
Elissa
Schappell

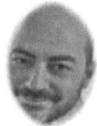
Ben
Schrank

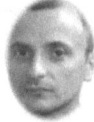
Salvatore
Scibona

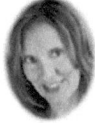
Elizabeth
Searle

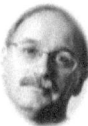
Jim
Shepard

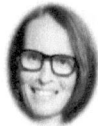
Karen
Shepard

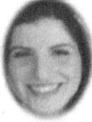
Rachel
Sherman

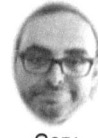
Gary
Shteyngart

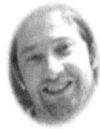
Robert Anthony
Siegel

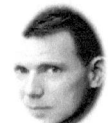
Christopher
Sorrentino

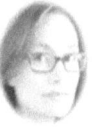
Dana
Spiotta

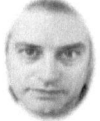
Wesley
Stace

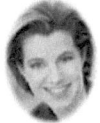
Alix
Strauss

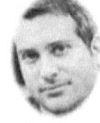
Darin
Strauss

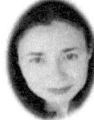
Felicia
Sullivan

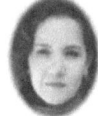
Hannah
Tinti

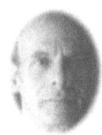
Peter
Trachtenberg

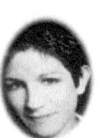
Jen
Trynin

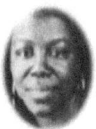
A.J.
Verdelle

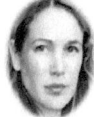
Vendela
Vida

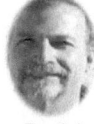
Daniel
Wallace

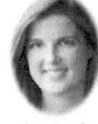
Amanda
Eyre Ward

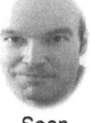
Sean
Wilsey

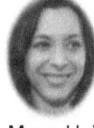
Moon Unit
Zappa

TABLE OF CONTENTS

Introduction

When the online culture magazine *Fanzine* approached me about contributing, my idea was to host a series of in-depth interviews with writers I admired. I envisioned immersing myself in an author's oeuvre, emerging with diamond sharp questions meant to elicit astoundingly deep answers. I relished the self-assignment and set about selecting my first subject. But then a triangulation of events occurred: My wife and I bought an independent bookstore, I began to assemble my last issue of *Post Road*, the literary magazine I cofounded, in preparation for its transition to Boston College, and I revisited the archive of excellent *Paris Review* interviews. Both the bookstore acquisition and *Post Road*'s transition promised separate but equally demanding sets of daunting responsibilities. I worried that I wouldn't have the stamina to bring off the type of interviews I'd imagined. In the *Paris Review* interviews, I realized with a mixture of chagrin and relief that what I wanted to do had already been done — well and comprehensively.

And so I was free to re-imagine my pitch to *Fanzine*. A residual and reflexive contrarian reaction (which is my personality, to be frank) to the *Paris Review* interviews was the (maybe original) idea to ask writers only non-writing questions, to in effect give them a spot on an imaginary late-night couch. Which is how *Talk Show* was created.

Once the concept took hold, there was infinite joy in dreaming up the topics and corresponding questions, which divide into two categories: the speculative and the biographical. I recognized that the questions in both categories were weighted to elicit confession — maybe even folly — and I worried about a general reluctance on the writers' part to expose their personalities (well, I didn't worry about them *all*), but I was pleasantly surprised at the ready answer to this call to arms by over a hundred writers, as well as the scores of writers who begged to know the topics as they were announced, hoping to contribute. We'll never know the answers from those that were lost, but the pages that follow offer a unique glimpse into the minds of some of today's brightest and best writers, as well as straight answers to these burning questions:

- *What was Rick Moody's first concert?*
- *Which movie would Neal Pollack remake?*
- *Who was Molly Jong-Fast's first kiss?*
- *Who is T Cooper's childhood hero?*
- *What historical event does Myla Goldberg wish she had witnessed?*
- *What was Hannah Tinti's first day of school like?*
- *What pop culture moment does Antonya Nelson consider to be the most significant?*
- *What family myth haunts Thisbe Nissen?*
- *Where would Moon Unit Zappa never go?*
- *What was Brock Clarke's worst job?*
- *What was Sean Wilsey's first car?*
- *What is in Owen King's time capsule?*
- *What lie did Fiona Maazel get caught telling?*
- *What does Jim Shepard consider to be his generation's defining moment?*
- *Who from history would Sloane Crosley like to talk to?*
- *What technology changed Salvatore Scibona's life?*
- *What happened when Margot Livesey hitchhiked across America?*
- *What happened on Chris Bohjalian's first date?*
- *What does Roxana Robinson doubt?*

- *What is Ron McLarty's most embarrassing moment?*
- *Where in time would Adrienne Miller like to travel?*
- *What is Ed Park's favorite cartoon?*
- *What does Julia Glass consider to be over-rated?*
- *Where was Joshua Ferris's first apartment?*
- *What is Gary Shteyngart's irrational fear?*
- *What was Dennis Lehane's first favorite album?*
- *What thing from the past would Charles Bock bring back?*
- *What blue ribbon did Thomas Beller win?*

And on and on. The responses to these questions by all the writers who took a seat on the fictional couch are startlingly original and memorable. (You'll find yourself clapping when you smell skunk thanks to Elizabeth McCracken, for example.) So dial up an episode and enjoy the surprise candor and outright laughs under the klieg-lit glare of our little show, commercial-free.

- Jaime Clarke

Episode 1: *First Concert*
with Tod Goldberg, Paul Harding,
Pagan Kennedy, Rick Moody,
and Elizabeth Searle

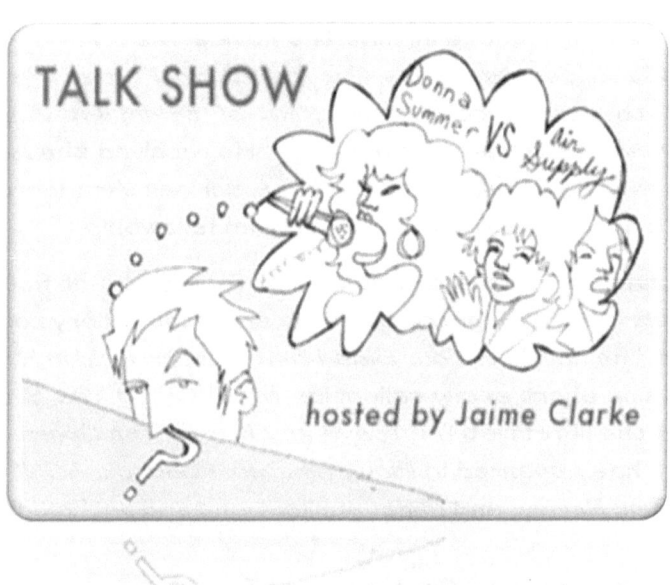

TALK SHOW — Donna Summer VS Air Supply

hosted by Jaime Clarke

Tod Goldberg is the author of several books of fiction including the novels *Living Dead Girl*, *Fake Liar Cheat* and the popular *Burn Notice* series; and the story collections *Simplify* and *Other Resort Cities*. His work has appeared in the *Los Angeles Times*, *Salon*, the *Wall Street Journal* and others.

Paul Harding is the author of the novels *Tinkers*, which won the 2010 Pulitzer Prize for Fiction, and *Enon*. He has received a Guggenheim Fellowship as well as the PEN/Robert Bingham Fellowship for Writers.

Pagan Kennedy's fiction includes the novels *Spinsters*, *The Exes*, and *Confessions of a Memory Eater*, as well

1

as the short story collection *Stripping*. She has also published several nonfiction titles. Her work has appeared in the *New York Times Magazine*, the *New York Times Book Review*, the *Village Voice*, *Playboy*, the *Nation*, the *Boston Globe Magazine* and others.

Rick Moody's books include the novels *The Four Fingers of Death*, *Garden State*, *The Ice Storm*, *Purple America* and the story collections *Ring of Brightest Angels Around Heaven* and *Demonology*. He received the Addison Metcalf Award from the American Academy of Arts and Letters and a Guggenheim fellowship.

Elizabeth Searle is the author of four books of fiction: *Celebrities In Disgrace*, a novella and short story collection; the novels *A Four Sided Bed* and *Girl Held in Home*; and the short story collection *My Body To You*. She is also the librettist for *Tonya and Nancy: The Opera*. Her work has appeared in *Ploughshares*, *Redbook*, *AGNI*, the *Kenyon Review*, and other publications and anthologies.

* * *

- What was your first concert?

Goldberg: My first concert was either Donna Summer or Air Supply — neither of whom I'd consider myself a huge fan of, but, as I recall, the tickets to both were free, courtesy of the newspaper my mother worked for. My sister Linda tells me that it was Donna Summer. My brother Lee tells me it was Air Supply. In any case, I was nine and really, really drunk and had been snorting coke off and on for, like, ten years, so the memories of both sort of meld into each other. What I remember about both shows was the shrieking diva in the middle of a stage, which is no help at all, I know. And since we had the exact same seats for both shows, it's even more confusing.

Harding: Def Leppard. The band was on tour for its third album, *Pyromania*. The opening acts were the Dutch metal band

Krokus, which was touring for its album called *Headhunter* and had a single called "Stayed Awake All Night," and the guitarist Gary Moore, whose music I didn't know but with whom I was impressed anyway because he had Ian Pace, from Deep Purple, playing drums for him.

Kennedy: I can't quite remember whether my first concert was 'Tull, Floyd or Heart, but I'm going to say Heart simply because that's the one that was most memorable. Why? Because I learned a valuable life lesson: If you're female, you should never drink a six of Miller and then go see a chick-oriented hair band. I arrived at the Capital Center in Largo, Maryland, so full of beer that I thought I was about to pee blood.

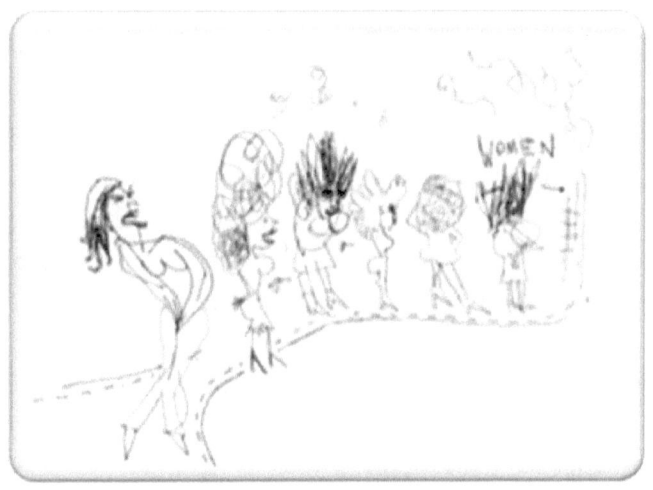

(By the way, the Capital Center would later be immortalized by my friend Jeff Krulik in underground cult film *Heavy Metal Parking Lot.*) So we found our seats down front, and I tried to ignore the bleeting of my bladder, but before the warm-up band was done, I had no choice but to head to the bathroom. There I found a line of women going out the door and all the way down to the Capital Center popcorn stand. Heart fans, I learned, had big hair. Giant cotton-candy like tufts of black and blonde ringlets. And they had to maintain that hair, so they lined up eagerly to get to the mirrors and the stalls, where they could spritz and spray and primp. I spent the whole concert waiting in line for a toilet.

Moody: Frank Zappa/Mothers of Invention, the Palladium, New York City, Halloween, 1975. At least I think it was 1975. It might have been 1976.

Searle: Elton John.

- What made you want to go?

Goldberg: When you're nine, want is a relative thing. What I recall is that my mother had four free tickets to the concert(s) at the Concord Pavilion — an outdoor concert venue not far from our home in Walnut Creek — two in the grass, two on the floor and that originally my older siblings, Lee and Karen (at the time eighteen and sixteen), we were going to take the floor seats and then they were going to give the grass seats to their friends. Well, that just wasn't going to fly. At age nine, I knew well enough that these were prime tickets and that the opportunity to see a legendary act like Donna Summer — or Air Supply — wouldn't come along again in this lifetime, so I think I cried until my mom made Lee and Karen take me and Linda, then eleven, to the show with them.

Harding: I was fourteen years old and had finally harassed my father into getting tickets to a concert for me, an almost unimaginable luxury. I asked him to get seats for U2 at the Orpheum Theater in Boston, for their War tour, but the show sold out before he could buy any. So instead I told him I wanted to go see Def Leppard. I liked their music and had *Pyromania* and their previous albums *On Through the Night* and *High and*

Dry. I thought *On Through the Night* was a lousy album, but I liked the other two, both of which had been produced by Mutt Lange, who everyone knew was the man because he had also produced AC/DC's *Highway to Hell* and *Back in Black* albums.

Moody: I'd been a big fan of Zappa's for about six months, especially a fan of the salacious, tragicomic stuff that was found on *Apostrophe* and *Over-Nite Sensation.* I was fourteen at the time, which is sort of the perfect age for Frank Zappa, at least the Frank Zappa of that period. (However, I still like a lot of his music, even though I'm now forty-five.) Also, I'd never been to a concert and was eager to experience the medium.

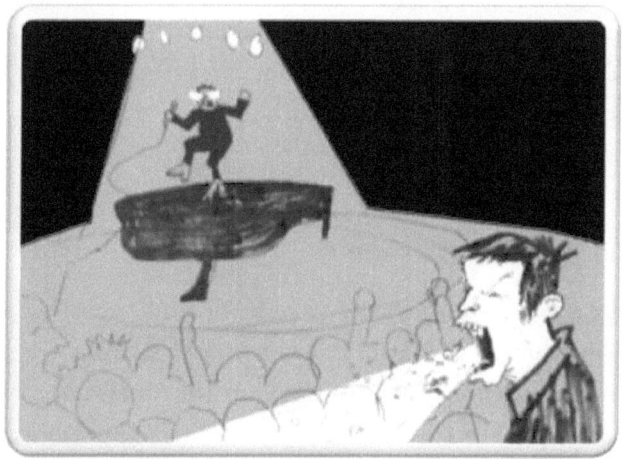

Searle: My brother. He and his friends took me to see Elton John in South Carolina; it was such a non-memory — Elton danced on the piano; someone in our party threw up, but I forget who — that for the purposes of these questions I'd like to fast-forward to my First Concert DATE. This was Tori Amos, before she became so big they made her play stadiums. What made me want to go? My date and I were both total Tori fans — and (read below) because of the concert in question, my then-date now-husband even wound up 'appearing' on a Tori CD . . .

Talk Show

- Where was the concert held?

Goldberg: The Concord Pavilion, an outdoor venue in the Bay Area.

Harding: The Cape Cod Coliseum, which no longer exits. It was essentially a warehouse where concerts were held, in South Yarmouth, Massachusetts.

Moody: The Palladium, which later became a night club. Sort of a medium-sized venue, I think, like the Beacon Theater on the Upper West Side.

Searle: Saunders Hall in Harvard Square in Cambridge, Mass. Just Tori and her piano and a crowd of two hundred or so packed into the theater's wood church-pew style seats . . . The all-wood arena made a wonderful thumping mega-sound when we all stomped our feet in Tori-love . . .

- How did you get there?

Goldberg: In the back of a blue Ford Fairmont. In later years, that same blue Ford Fairmont would be used to drop me off a mile from the Concord Pavilion for much cooler shows where a Ford Fairmont would not have been appreciated. Like, you know, Rick Springfield. Or Berlin, except that I didn't actually see Berlin, I just hung out in the parking lot trying to look cool at age thirteen. But definitely for the Thompson Twins.

Harding: My father took my best friend and me to the show. My friend liked Def Leppard, too, but had a much more sophisticated taste in music than I did at the time. He also already grew and smoked his own pot. So he showed up for the ride down to Cape Cod good and baked. My pretty straight laced dad clearly knew something was awry, but didn't say anything about it and went so far as to lie about thinking that pot should be legalized when my stoned friend brought the subject up. My dad wore a collared shirt and a cardigan sweater and pants that were called "slacks."

I think the usual drill at the Cape Cod Coliseum was that every kid from the Cape and the South Shore drove there whenever there was a show and got loaded all day in the parking lot. When the doors opened, everyone just stampeded in and kept the party going. All of the shows were general admission and I don't think that tickets were checked very closely at the door.

Moody: My sister must have driven us. She was older and had her own car. Or a series of cars, because she crashed at least one of them. She took me and my boarding school roommate, Andy.

Searle: Hmm . . . We must've driven and parked and then hiked several miles to the theater . . . Do not recall being drunk . . . I think we wanted to keep our heads clear for maximum Tori Rush . . .

- What was the show like?

Goldberg: Well, as it turns out, a nine year old can get stoned if he inhales enough secondary smoke from the disco survivors and soft-rock aficionados that peopled the grass section of the Concord Pavilion, so my memories of both shows are that they rocked big time. The deal we made was that the four of us would split the show in half, so during the first half of the Donna Summer/Air Supply show, my sisters had the seats and my brother and I had the grass and then, at an appropriate time, we exchanged spots. What I recall about Donna Summer was that when she sang "Hot Stuff" the crowd lost all control and began dancing like it was Studio 54. What I remember about Air Supply is that they had an elaborate laser show at the opening of the set for a song called, ironically, "I Can't Get Excited," and that people in the grass section were playing some hard core air guitar to it, which, upon listening to it moments before writing this, makes me think that people in 1980 didn't have a strong sense of what songs were worthy of air guitaring.

Harding: From the time we found seats in the last row, to the right side of the stage, until the concert was over, kids more or less continually lobbed and launched every manner of fireworks into and across the crowd and at the stage, including what must have been M-80s and cherry bombs, because among the fizzing and popping of firecrackers and bottle rockets, there was an occasional, violent clearing of a circle in the crowd where what looked like a concussion grenade and sounded like a howitzer being fired, detonated on the bare concrete floor. Everyone cheered and the circle closed with kids and the mushroom cloud from the explosion rolled up into the foggy rafters and another volley of bottle rockets zinged from one side of the bleachers to the other. I don't know if the fireworks were normal for all shows or particular to this one because Def Leppard's album was titled *Pyromania*.

Moody: It was great, I think. What I can remember of it was great. He played a lot of material from *Lather*, which was his quadruple album that Warner Brothers had rejected that year. A lot of this stuff later ended up on *Live in New York* (and *Sleep Dirt* and *Studio Tan* and *Orchestral Favorites*), which was recorded at that show and others. I remember that Frank unfurled a banner saying "Warner Bros. Record Company Sucks" at one point. And Don Pardo did some announcing.

Searle: Sexy and intimate — like she was singing all these fabulous dirty songs just for us I remember getting teary-eyed over her cover of the recently-deceased Kurt Cobain's "Smells Like Teen Spirit." I also remember when Tori first burst out onto stage, some nut yelled 'you're not beautiful' and someone sane yelled back: 'BULLSHIT!' and the crowd erupted: the first of countless ovations for Tori that night . . .

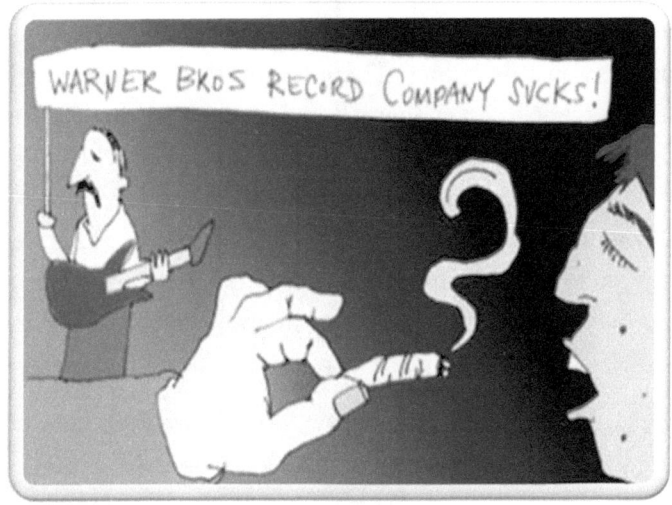

- What are your lasting memories?

Goldberg: That I knew this wasn't in any way cool, no matter which show it was that came first. That Air Supply had cool lasers. That I really liked that song "Sunset People" by Donna Summer. That I own both Donna Summer's and Air Supply's greatest hits CDs, but have no memory of ever listening to them, which makes me think they date back to a time when Columbia House allowed me to steal CDs from them using several different aliases. That the first really cool concert I went to wasn't for another five years, at least, and, in looking back, I don't know how cool Depeche Mode really was, but I sure did like their hair. That my mother was highly irresponsible in letting us go to a Donna Summer concert, what with the lasting effects disco has on young children.

Harding: I don't remember much of the opening acts. The real impression that I still have is of experiencing for the first time the house lights going down and the crowd roaring and the first guitar chords thundering out of the monolithic sound system piled up on either side of the stage. I can't remember if Gary Moore sang or had a singer. I think he might have just played instrumentals. I remember confirming that Ian Pace was a very, very fast drummer. There was nothing to remark about Krokus, except the fact that my father thought the lead singer was a woman because of his high voice, so that when the guy tore his shirt off as the band came out of the breakdown and back into the last chorus of their hit single, my father feared there would be even more bare breasts than those being revealed by the girls in the audience, in appreciation of the music. My father clapped after every song.

Moody: Well, besides the music, Andy threw up during the encore. The guy seated next to him, a stranger, gave him some pot to smoke which must have had PCP in it or something. We also drank quite a bit, even though we were underage. Anyway, Andy threw up, and the people around us scattered. He seemed okay after that, however.

Searle: At the end of Tori's great underrated "I Want To Kill This Waitress," my date, John Hodgkinson, let loose his piercing patented two-fingers-in-the-mouth whistle. His distinctive — and deafening — siren whistle is CLEARLY AUDIBLE on Tori's 'live' *Under the Pink* CD version of "I Want To Kill This Waitress" . . . just hearing John's joyful high-C whistle-pitch, preserved forever, brings back the whole night to me . . . It was John's most memorable concert-moment as well, followed by him yelling "I love you" to Joni Mitchell onstage and her yelling back to him: "What?"

Episode 2: Movie Remakes
with Steve Almond, Emily Franklin,
Ben Greenman, Lydia Millet, and Neal Pollack

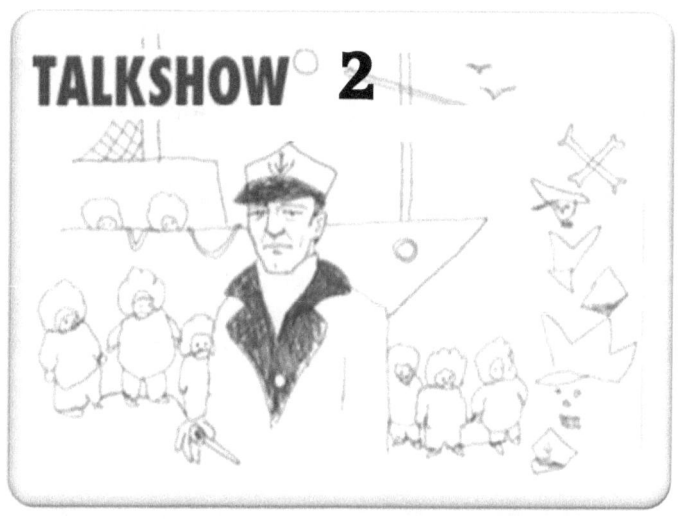

Steve Almond is the author of several books, most recently the story collection *God Bless America*. Other works include: *Candyfreak: A Journey through the Chocolate Underbelly of America*, *Rock and Roll Will Save Your Life: A Book by and for the Fanatics Among Us* and *My Life in Heavy Metal*.

Emily Franklin is the author of the novels *Liner Notes The Girls' Almanac*, and *The Other Half of Me* and a seven-book fiction series for teens, *The Principles of Love*. She edited *It's a Wonderful Lie: 26 Truths about Life in Your Twenties* and *How to Spell Chanukah: 18 Writers on 8 Nights of Lights* and co-edited *Before: Short Stories about Pregnancy from Our Top Writers*.

Ben Greenman is an editor at the *New Yorker* and the author of several acclaimed books of fiction, including *Superbad, Please Step Back, What He's Poised To Do* and *The Slippage*.

Lydia Millet is the author of several novels, including *Oh Pure and Radiant Heart, Magnificence, How the Dead Dream, Ghost Lights, Everyone's Pretty* and *My Happy Life*, which won a PEN Center USA Award for Fiction.

Neal Pollack is the author of the memoir *Alternadad*, and also several books of satirical fiction, including *The Neal Pollack Anthology Of American Literature* and the rock-n-roll novel *Never Mind The Pollacks*. Other books include: *Stretch: The Unlikely Making of a Yoga Dude, Downward-Facing Death* and *Jewball*. He is the founder of www.offsprung.com, a humor web site for parents.

* * *

- Name a movie you'd remake.

Almond: *Fatal Attraction.*

Franklin: I'm torn here. Part of me says remake a personal favorite: *The Philadelphia Story* with George Clooney as CK Dexter Haven and Kate Winslet as Tracy Lord (not the porno girl, the Katherine Hepburn role). Parker Posey would be the female reporter with one of the bright young males out there (Jake Gyllenhaal, Tobey Maguire, etcetera) in the dorky but endearing Jimmy Stewart role. Abigail Breslin as the precocious Dinah Lord. HOWEVER . . . why mess with a great thing? I can't make it better. So why not pick something hiding from current audiences. Something like *Little Darlings* — the teen camp romp with heart.

Greenman: I'd remake *Putney Swope*, Robert Downey Sr.'s satire about media culture, racial identity, masculinity, and corporate America from 1969. It seems more relevant than ever, and back in 1969 it was already fairly relevant. There are many theories that enter your head in college and slightly afterwards, theories about Brechtian alienation and negative affirmation and the impossibility of criticizing a system from within. Well, take all those theories, write them down, crumple up the paper you've written on, light it on fire, use the flaming paper to light a cigarette, and then smoke it while you watch *Putney Swope*.

It's about a traditional ad agency that's taken over, first by democratic vote (though a democratic vote worthy of *Dr. Strangelove*) and then by coup, by *Putney Swope* (Arnold Johnson), a minor executive from the music department who proceeds to make the agency in his image, hiring a staff full of black radicals. Except that they're not radicals at all: they're self-serving nihilists. Except that they're not self-serving nihilists: they're visionaries. The commercials they make follow no rhyme or reason, except for short-sighted profit, and as a result of that they start to succeed. Wool is pulled over eyes. The emperor's skin is taken along with his new clothes. Iconoclasm is smashed too.

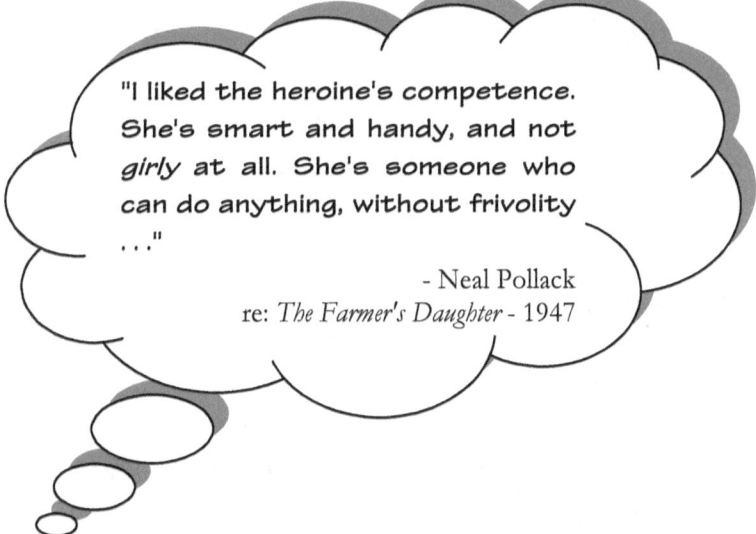

"I liked the heroine's competence. She's smart and handy, and not *girly* at all. She's someone who can do anything, without frivolity . . ."

- Neal Pollack
re: *The Farmer's Daughter* - 1947

Millet: No remake in the world could be as good as making an original feature out of Karl Capek's visionary book, *War With the Newts*, a hilarious and poignant '20s sci-fi allegory about the discovery of a race of giant newts that eventually takes over the world.

Pollack: There's this comedy called *The Farmer's Daughter* from the 1940s, starring Loretta Young and Joseph Cotten. It's about a Swedish farm girl who heads to the big city to go to nursing school, but gets robbed and ends up being the house-keeper to a congressman. Anyway, it turns into a big political parable and she winds up going to Congress because she's so straight-talking and sensible and the politicians are all so corrupt. I'd like to see this get remade today, maybe as a Mexican-American comedy. The themes are still relevant.

- Who would star and why?

Almond: Laura Linney, because I've yet to see her dig deep into her insane sexual energy/ambition. The woman is the finest actress of her generation, but she needs to make it bleed.

Franklin: See above for the first idea. Perhaps for *Little Darlings* we could have two fresh-outta-rehab girls. Or better, do a major casting call for one city girl — harsh around the edges but longing for love — and a rich girl with longings. Film the casting calls, make it into its own reality show/PR vehicle. Plot's the same — two girls at camp bet who will be the first to be deflowered. Then shove Dave Duchovny in the professor-*ish* role and Ralph Macchio (he still looks young, right?) in the city tough-boy role.

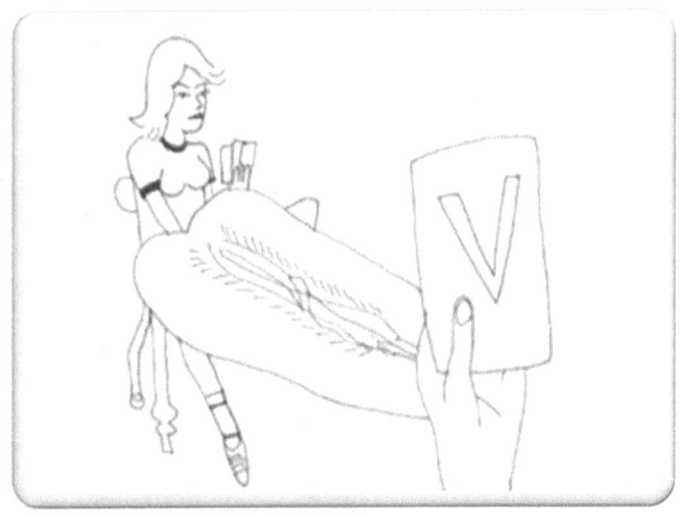

Greenman: Well, this is a weird question right off the bat, for a weird movie. The main character is the title character, who is played by Arnold Johnson. Johnson was an actor who later appeared on *Sanford and Son*, and in a small part in *Rocky*. In *Putney Swope*, he gave a great performance: great because he was terrible. He couldn't remember any of his lines, which meant that the director, Robert Downey, had to dub all his dialogue. That gives the movie, already obsessed with issues of corruption and authenticity, another layer of falseness over its truth, another layer of soullessness over its soul. Oh, right. The question. Who would I cast? I suppose it doesn't matter at all, and at the same time that it's one of the most central issues in the remake. Let's say that we're casting Don Cheadle, with a big beard, and that John Hamm will dub his lines after receiving the dialogue exactly one minute before dubbing.

Millet: Stellan Skarsgard could star as the drunken, opportunistic Dutch sea captain who discovers the newts and starts trading them as slaves.

Pollack: I'd need to get an attractive Hispanic actress with good comic timing. Anyone know any of those? I suppose an open casting call would work. I don't know. Gael Garcia Bernal in drag? The Joseph Cotten role could be played by any one of a dozen guys.

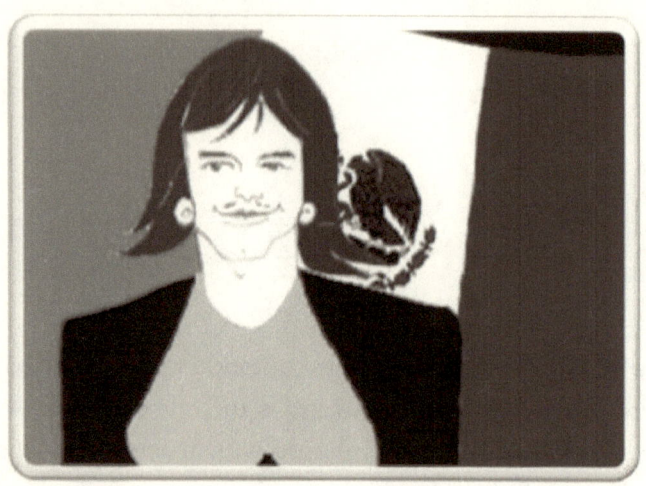

- Who would direct and why?

Almond: Brigitte Rouan. She directed this awesome French film, *Post Coitum* in 1997. I'd select her because she has a precise eye for female sexual abandon. Her heroine was destructive and tragic, without ever seeming absurd.

Franklin: Um, George Cukor if he were able. But failing that, Wes Anderson for *The Philadelphia Story* and Hal Hartley for *Little Darlings*. Or the reverse.

Greenman: Everyone would say that Charlie Kaufman should direct, wouldn't they? Or that some schlocky, brilliant director who has been toiling in the salt mines of the Sci-Fi channel's monster movies should step up and take a shot at it.

But I'd say, maybe, that Paul Beatty should write a new screen-play and Tom Hooper should direct. That will give it the appropriate mix of great writing and lunatic disjunction. Or maybe Dave Chappelle should just do the whole thing.

Millet: Lars von Trier could direct, but with a huge block-buster budget and a strict anti-Dogma 99 mandate from the execs.

Pollack: Whoever was cheapest. This isn't a movie that needs an artistic treatment. Getting the right screenwriter is far more important.

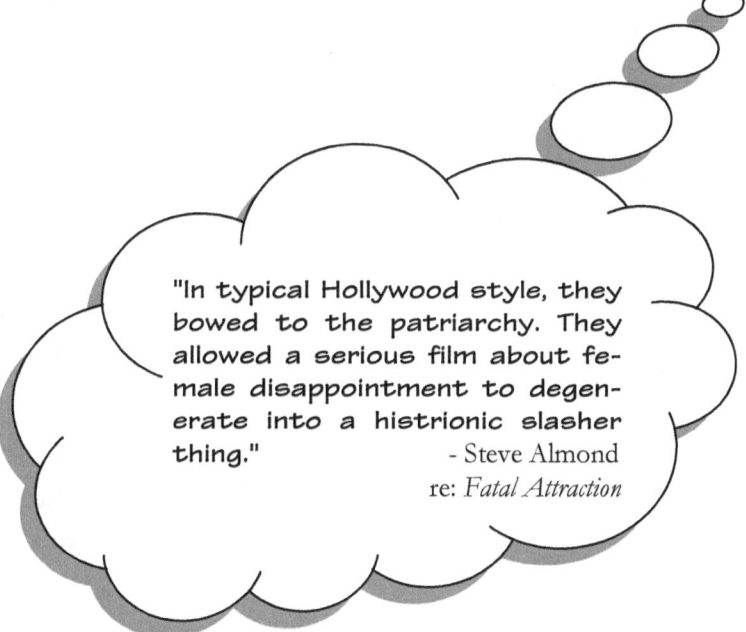

"In typical Hollywood style, they bowed to the patriarchy. They allowed a serious film about female disappointment to degenerate into a histrionic slasher thing."   - Steve Almond
re: *Fatal Attraction*

- What would you keep from the original?

Almond: Definitely the sex-on-the-counter scene. In fact, maybe extend that scene, and all the other sexual scenes. The connection is carnal and frantic and flagrant. It should play like that on-screen. Fuck the ratings system. Hard.

Franklin: The plots — they'd still stand the test of time. I'd keep the settings, too. You can't beat camp cabins and woods and certainly I'd want to revisit the estate on which most of *The Philadelphia Story* is set.

Greenman: I'd keep everything. Am I allowed to keep everything? What would you lose? And also, by not losing any of it, you're reiterating the movie's central argument: the more things change, the more they stay the same. *Putney Swope*, after his accidental election to company president (everyone votes for him under the assumption that no one else will), is a new boss who's every bit as bad as the old boss. All that's different about him is that he has marginally better pants and friends (read: toadies) who look like (but never really are) the epitome of cool.

Pollack: I liked the heroine's competence. She's smart and handy, and not girly at all. She's someone who can do anything, without frivolity.

- What would you change?

Almond: Most of the early scenes are terrific. It's when Glenn Close turns all psycho and witchy that *Fatal Attraction* descends into bathos. If the film takes into account the husband's recklessness, his passive sadism, the distress of his mistress becomes more understandable, and the film far deeper. In typical Hollywood style, they bowed to the patriarchy. They allowed a serious film about female disappointment to degenerate into a histrionic slasher thing.

Franklin: Some of the music. The tag line from the 1980 *Little Darlings* ("*Two 15-year-old girls from different sides of the tracks compete to see who will be first to lose their virginity while at camp*") because, though it gets the point out there, it might not suit the thing once these directors get hold of it.

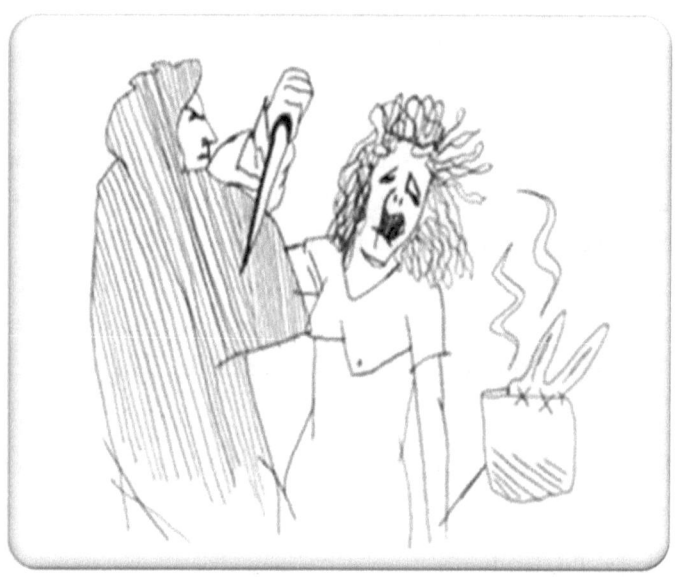

Greenman: I might update some of the commercials and products to reflect new technology, and specifically the way that people have become zombies and brain-dead servants before new metrics and the notion of "traffic" or "eyeballs." The original *Putney Swope* vowed not to advertise tobacco, alcohol, and toys. What is left in society now? And I'd have someone new do the music. Maybe Mike Patton could just sing the original music cues in his least eerie voice.

Pollack: In the original, the heroine has these big-lug Swedish brothers who come in handy when she's kidnapped by mobsters hired by an opposition politico. There's this great fight scene. I'd like to give her some good-guy cholo brothers who drive around in a low-rider and perform more or less the same function. Maybe they're more urban, though.

- If you were going to give yourself a part, what would it be and why?

<u>Almond:</u> I think we all know where this is going: I get Michael Douglas's part. And I'm happy to get myself *offed* at the end, as long as Laura's holding the blade.

<u>Franklin:</u> I'd like to consult on the music. I'd pick the soundtrack — some original work, some classic songs. And then also have a role like "woman in yellow dress" or "counselor #5". Just something to show the kids. "Look, Sweetie. There's mommy. No — not that one. Wait pause right there. See? The lady in the yellow dress. No. Not that one. The one behind her."

<u>Millet:</u> And I could never have a part in any movie, because I'm the worst actor in the world.

<u>Pollack:</u> I'd probably just be a newspaper reporter in the background of the larger scenes. That's all you'll really want me to do. Anything else would just distract.

Episode 3: *First Kiss*
with Mike Albo, David Hollander,
Molly Jong-Fast, Lewis Robinson,
and Wesley Stace

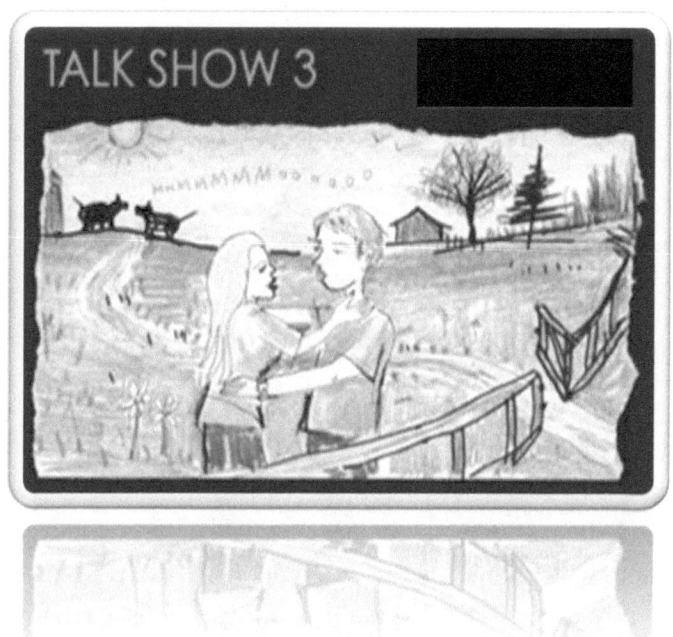

Mike Albo is the author of *The Junket, Hornito: My Lie Life* and, with Virginia Heffernan, *The Underminer: or, The Best Friend Who Casually Destroys Your Life.* A writer and performer, Albo lives in New York City.

David Hollander is the author of the novel *L.I.E.* His work has been adapted for film and frequently anthologized. Hollander teaches at Sarah Lawrence College and lives in the Hudson Valley with his wife, the writer Margaret Hundley Parker, and their two children.

Molly Jong-Fast is the author of the novels *Normal Girl, Girl Maladjusted* and *The Social Climber's Handbook.*

Her work has appeared in the *New York Times*, *Harper's Bazaar*, *Cosmo*, *Marie Claire* and others.

Lewis Robinson is the author of *Officer Friendly and Other Stories*, winner of the PEN/Oakland-Josephine Miles Award and the novel *Water Dogs*. He teaches in the Stonecoast MFA program at the University of Southern Maine.

Wesley Stace is also known as the musician John Wesley Harding. His novels include *Misfortune*, *by George* and *Charles Jessold, Considered as a Murderer*. He has released more than sixteen records and is the artist-in-residence at Fairleigh Dickinson University.

* * *

- Name the year and place of your first kiss, and with whom.

Albo: I am assuming you mean real kiss with passion and meaning, which would be with a guy, which would be when I was seventeen in 1987. I think it was in my bedroom (how the hell did I get him up there?)

Hollander: Well, the first kiss was no doubt administered by my dear mother, mere moments after my unfortunate birth in 1969. But my first romantic kiss came embarrassingly late in life, in 1986 at the overripe age of sixteen. This kiss took place (like so many first kisses) in a drainage ditch, or "sump," during a typically awful Long Island heat wave. There on the sandy slopes, blinded by a miasma of raw sewage and toxic runoff, I kissed Vanessa Vega. Redhead, my age-ish, cousin of a friend.

Jong-Fast: He was called Teddy and we were in third grade. I had such a crush on him. He was just the nicest guy. I'm pretty sure it was against his will; I just sort of fell on him. I'm sure it was horrible for him, but I was sort of a hero for doing it.

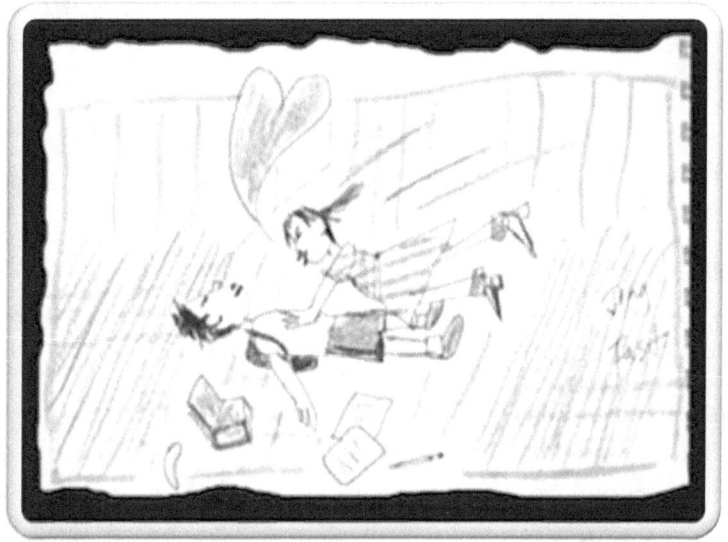

Robinson: 1983, in the Yarmouth (Maine) Junior High cafeteria. Late fall, school dance. There were these French Canadian girls who I was obsessed with, but I'd never talked to. Danielle Paquet was the ringleader, but it was her quiet sidekick — Jackie Roux — who was truly amazing. Black feathered hair to her shoulders, Motley Crue T-shirt under a green and blue plaid flannel.

Stace: I'm afraid that I can't actually remember the precise first kiss, though it was certainly in Hastings with a girl called Caroline, whose brother was in the church choir and liked Ian Dury and Chuck Mangione. I was twelve, perhaps thirteen. The year: 1977. There was some form of grappling with Caroline and a lot of work with little reward — by which I don't mean physical contact (not that there was much of that — I'm not even sure about tongues, in retrospect) but a twelve-year-old's idea of emotional fulfillment. There is a possibility that she simply didn't want to be my girlfriend. So I'm settling for the proper first kiss — the one that meant something. It was in 1979 with Rebecca on Cadborough Cliff in Rye, East Sussex.

- Describe the circumstances leading up to your first kiss.

Albo: This is all painfully detailed in my "novel" *Hornito*, which isn't a memoir, or is, as much as any book named "memoir" these days.

Hollander: I had it all planned out. See, there were rumors going around that Vanessa had done it with Jack Inzerillo (a neighborhood tough) on a cardboard platform strategically placed on the steep walls of the sump. (This turned out to be patently untrue; Vanessa later revealed to me that Jack was a prude and terrified to do anything more than touch her ass with uncommon frequency.) So when Joe Patolano told me that his cousin Vanessa "liked me," my fantasies leapt straight for fornication, though I understood that a first kiss would likely (though not necessarily) precede that Great And Holy Moment Of First Penetration. I had only a rudimentary knowledge of how sex might work, based on the scrambled images received via The Playboy Channel, before which images I knelt in scrutiny on countless evenings whilst the parentals were elsewhere. So . . . we walk to the sump together, right? It's Long Island summer. 900% humidity. We should've been wearing scuba gear. We strolled the ten blocks holding hands, waiting for the sun to set in a fury of color over the shit-stench of the drainage ditch, which itself sat at the center of our housing development like the black hole around which galactic matter spins.

Jong-Fast: We were at wood shop at the Dalton school in Manhattan. I feel like someone was daring me but I could be wrong.

Robinson: We did the group dance thing for a while, then Jackie and I paired off for "Free Bird." I didn't ask her to dance — we were just standing side by side when the song started. And it took a minute to get our arms around each other. I don't remember even looking her in the eye. Neither of us seemed to have a plan. I think it was just two twelve-year-old bodies being pulled sleepily toward each other. We didn't kiss during "Free Bird" — the tempo of the song sped up before I could get my mouth up next to hers — but I knew not to make the same mistake during "Stairway to Heaven," which was, of course, the last song of the night.

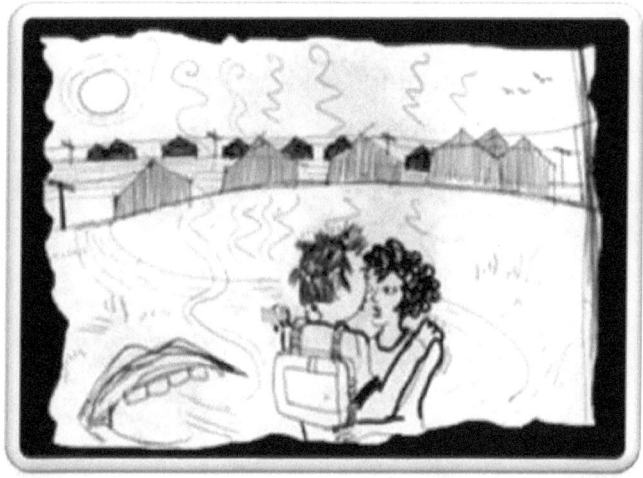

Stace: I was in the unique and very happy position of being the only male employed at my grandmother's tea shop, Fletcher's House (birthplace of playwright John Fletcher) in Rye, just around the corner from Lamb House where Henry James lived and wrote. It was a situation with boundless potential, if only in my mind. (Fletcher's is glimpsed in episodes of *Mapp and Lucia*

— the TV version of E.F.Benson's books, starring Geraldine McEwan and Prunella Scales: highly recommended.) Actually, Rebecca, who was terribly good-looking and had a lovely voice, didn't work there — she worked at another tea shop (there were hundreds of them, many owned by my family) — but knew someone who did. Having paid court to her friend Sally, I asked Rebecca out (probably for tea) and when we parted, I (being well brought up) shook her hand. Apparently, she hadn't been sure about me before then, but this gallantry sealed the deal. A few days later, we went for a walk, on the steep hills behind the back of my grandmother's old house on Cadborough Cliff. We walked with purpose. I remember helping her over a stile, or perhaps through a gate.

- What are your outstanding memories of the kiss itself?

Albo: He was seventeen too, and smoked. To this day I kind of get a thrill kissing a smoker.

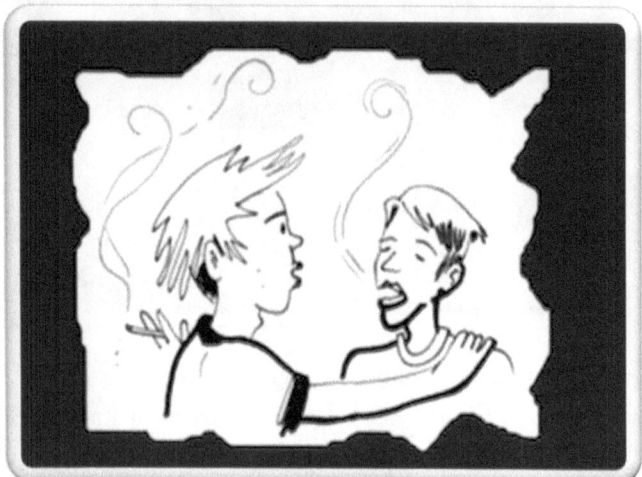

Hollander: First off, thank all that is holy that Vanessa knew that I might need a little prodding. If she hadn't turned to face me and looped her arms around my neck in a style familiar to prom-dancers everywhere, I might still be waiting on my first kiss. Don't get me wrong, I'm sure I was trying to affect an air of confidence and familiarity. Somehow or other our mouths locked together in a way that created a vacuum seal, so that when we eventually separated there was the same *thwuck* you'd expect when opening a new jar of peanut butter. But right, right . . . the kiss itself: our tongues swirled in an impressive clockwise syncopation, rolling over each other once every third rotation. My belly was doing flips and I had an instant hard-on, which made the fact that I'd chosen sweatpants for this momentous occasion unfortunate. Vanessa smiled when we broke for air, and we continued in this manner for maybe fifteen minutes, sometimes achieving the *thwuck* effect, sometimes not. I felt like sex must somehow be imminent.

I remember thinking anatomical thoughts, wondering how to arrange ourselves for communion in that canted pit of filth. It's a nice memory, mostly. The really embarrassing part is that eventually we slunk down to the sand itself, as if we were lovers on some tropical beach, and mind you all this time the sheer stench of that sewage was searing our nasal passages to ash, and I reached under her shirt and pinched her nipple through her bra, basically borrowing my moves from those strips of images I'd seen on the dirty cable channel. And she was sort of moaning in some pantomime of her own, maybe she'd seen the same films, and the sun was indeed going down and everything was so sexed up and my erection was just out of control, dire and excruciating. Which is when I, um . . . climaxed in my sweatpants. It was like the culminating fusillade of some terrible warfare. I pretended I was tired of kissing and touching and etcetera, that I had to get home . . . I think I told her I had to feed my dog. Maybe I thought this would sound noble. We held hands on the return trip and I invented stories about my intelligence and athletic prowess.

Jong-Fast: I remember it being very short and afterwards there was a look of horror on his face, not the look I was going for.

Robinson: I was worried about our noses banging together. I wasn't sure how the mechanics of it were going to work. So when I moved toward her, I ended up kissing just the corner of her mouth. It was almost a cheek kiss, but I definitely hit lips. She was totally shocked. Luckily, Robert Plant and Jimmy Page took over, and we group-danced the last part of the song.

Stace: We were sitting on the fields behind Cadborough Cliff, as though we had packed a picnic. There was probably wildlife near. The kiss tasted good, and I was surprised at how less messy it was than it looked — I don't know quite how much saliva I had experienced before, or expected, but we seemed to kiss very neatly. She had long, quite thick, pre-Raphaelite blonde hair. (I have never dated a blonde since, strange to say, so perhaps this flaxen 'do was irreplaceable.) Her body was surprisingly womanly. I remember thinking it was much too soon for my hands to stray elsewhere — and she later confirmed that if I had, she would have been "disappointed". Besides, her duffel coat was in the way. We chatted and walked back, and I think it was then that I took photos of her jumping over the bollards outside the Ypres Tower by the Gun Garden.

- If you could go back and do it again, what would you change?

Albo: I wouldn't have tried to "set the mood" by playing hideous late '80s New Age music and (God, this is embarrassing) placed a bowl of strawberries beside the bed so we could do the "erotic" playful things that seem so nauseating to me now.

But this was just my way of mimicking the culture, I guess, because it was the height of AIDS education, when "We Don't Have to Take Our Clothes Off" was a popular song and everyone was trying really hard to rescue passion, straining and saying "Safe Sex is sexy!"

"I'm pretty sure it was against his will, I just sort of fell on him. I'm sure it was horrible for him, but I was sort of a hero for doing it. . .

. . . I remember it being very short and afterwards, there was a look of horror on his face, not the look I was going for."

- Molly Jong-Fast
re: her first kiss

Hollander: Um . . . probably the premature ejaculation into my Bellport High School (Go Clippers!) sweatpants. And maybe instead of a *fucking sewage pit* I might choose, oh, I don't know, a landfill or a mortuary. And maybe instead of being totally devastated and ashamed by the force of my orgasm, thereby refusing to arrange any subsequent romantic activity with Vanessa, maybe instead I would have realized that orgasm is terrifying by its very nature, and that it did not imply that I had the wrong type of feelings for Vanessa and that I therefore should not seek to fuck her. What I mean is, I was really confused by what it all meant, and I wish I hadn't been, because she would have been nice to kiss again and to explore the whole sexual smorgasbord with. If only I'd known *anything* about girls. I wish Vanessa Vega were here right now. I don't want to change what *happened* then, but what's happened *since* then. I'd like another shot at Vanessa. I can still taste her tongue, smell her fruity smell, strawberryish . . . ah, nostalgia, you truly are a sadistic motherfucker.

Jong-Fast: Nothing. For third grade I thought I was very suave.

Robinson: Nothing. I was terrified, but that made the accomplishment feel all the more heroic. I had very little physical contact with girls for the next few years. It wasn't until I was sixteen, when we moved from Maine down to Massachusetts, that I had an actual make-out session with a girl. I was the new kid at school, and someone had a house party the second or third weekend after classes started. We were all in the basement, drinking vodka. We started playing the game where you stand in a circle, alternating boy-girl-boy-girl, and pass a single playing card from one mouth to the next by sucking air in against the card when you want to hold onto it and then exhaling when you want to release it to the kid next to you.

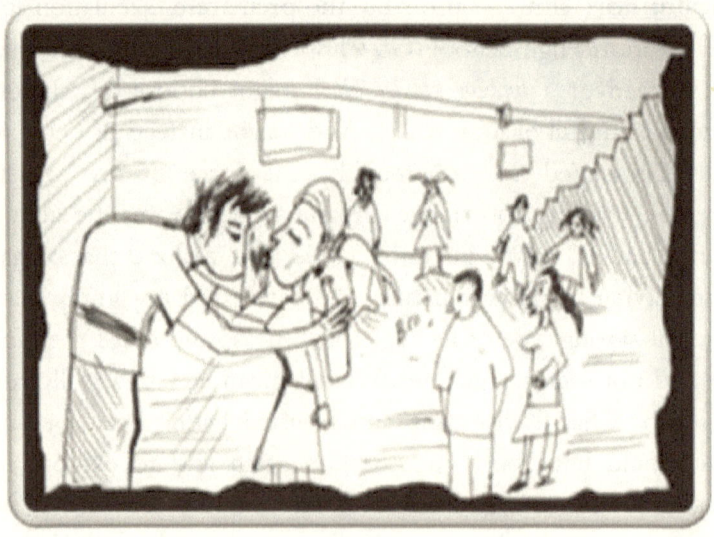

The girl on my right was nine or ten inches shorter than I was, and I had to grab onto her when I bent down to take the card. Soon we were holding hands, and then, in front of everyone, we were kissing. We hadn't waited for the card to come around again. We just took a short step out of the circle and started making out. I knew maybe three people at the whole party, so I didn't really care. What I remember is that my teeth kept hitting hers, and we kissed for what seemed like days. I kept my eyes open, but hers were closed. We didn't stop until someone flipped on the lights. I said goodnight to the girl.

Outside, I found the guy who'd given me a ride — a kid named Rich — and as we were getting into the car I asked him, "That girl, who was that?" Rich thought this was hilarious. Here was the new kid, blowing into town, ravishing girls he didn't even know. It became this big story that circulated the school. I had just wanted to find out the girl's name, so that if I saw her in the halls I wouldn't seem like a total idiot. High school was such a pain in the ass!

Stace: I guess we needn't have necessarily been in a field on which things grazed. We probably had to pick the precise spot to sit quite carefully. But other than that, I can think of nothing worth changing, and in fact I wasn't worried about sheep crap at the time, so why worry about it now? We had quite an enthusiastic epistolary relationship after this — but being away at school is hard on an early teen relationship. I don't know what she does now, but when we broke up — I can't remember how — she started going out with a guy from her school called Ronald, and I heard that they got married, had children, and lived happily ever after. I should Google her and find out. On the other hand, what if she Googled me and found this?

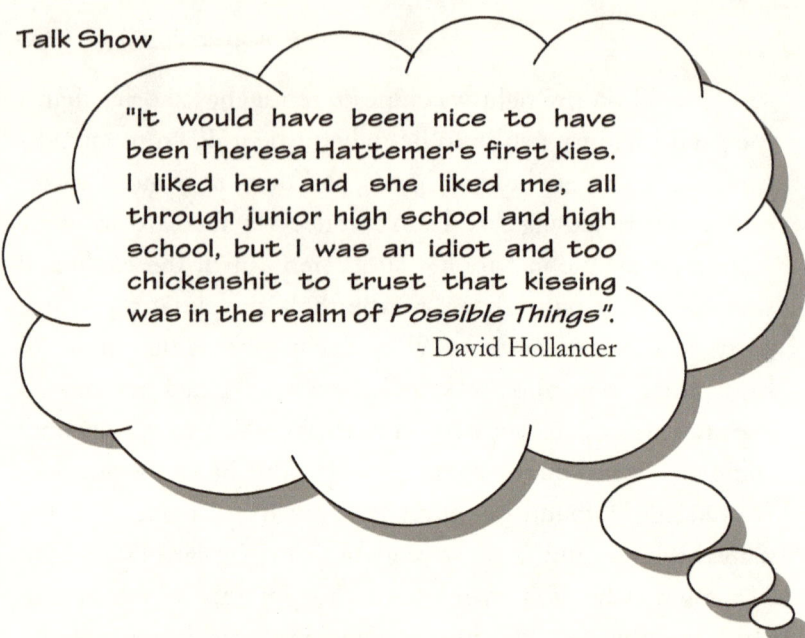

"It would have been nice to have been Theresa Hattemer's first kiss. I liked her and she liked me, all through junior high school and high school, but I was an idiot and too chickenshit to trust that kissing was in the realm of *Possible Things*".
- David Hollander

- If you could go back and be someone's first kiss, who would it be and why?

Albo: This beautiful, crazy poet boy who worked on the high school literary magazine with me. He lived near me. I would pick him up in my '79 Maverick (previously owned by my tinkering Grandpa, it lasted about six months under my rule) and we would go sit in parks and at the train tracks at night. He was a fantastic writer. He knew so much about contemporary poetry, and introduced me to "For the Union Dead," "45 Mercy Street," and "Ariel."

I owe him so much, now that I think about him. He and his language were so free and scraping. We would do these free writing exercises together with this heavily intelligent, possibly Jewish girl with blue spellbinding eyes. The poet boy was pale and had a long Italian nose and a thinly defined body. One time under a tree at night in one of our parks, it started raining hard and he came up and put his head on my chest and his arms around me. I don't know why we never ended up kissing, but now I have a well-equipped post-production facility that reanimates and reworks my past all the time, so I have revised the memory, and under that tree I put my hands in his hair and kiss him.

Hollander: You're not asking who I wish I'd kissed, but who I wish had kissed me, right? In this scenario, the kiss isn't necessarily *my* first, but hers. It would have been nice to have been Theresa Hattemer's first kiss. I liked her and she liked me, all through junior high school and high school, but I was an idiot and too chickenshit to trust that kissing was in the realm of "Possible Things." Mostly I just poked her at random intervals. If I had been *experienced*, then maybe it would have been nice to introduce someone else to kissing, in a sweetly romantic way that I imagine characterizes someone else's adolescent experience. But since I was a buffoon, at least until well beyond the age of normal first kisses, all I could ever do was fantasize and masturbate and wonder. To be someone else's first kiss in this unfortunate reality would only have meant to confuse them, as I no doubt did Vanessa, with my shame and uncertainty. So I guess it's a good thing, after all, that I was never anyone's *first* kiss. Or first anything. I've lived my life way behind the curve. And that, my friends, has made all the difference.

Jong-Fast: I think it would have been cute to have been my husband's first kiss but when he was thirteen, I was a *negative 1*, so I don't think it would have been such a great idea.

Robinson: Cate Blanchett. On a quiet little cobblestone street in Melbourne. She's sixteen, I'm fourteen. A cab is idling at the curb, ready to take me to the airport. "You're going to be a star," I'd say, and then I'd plant one on her.

Stace: I think this is an almost unanswerable question, unless you remember someone you never got to kiss, prior to your first case. In that case, the answer is Juliette Gaffney, who seemed nice when we were both nine. Otherwise, if you're looking for a hindsight kiss with someone you met later, you have to visualize them at thirteen or fourteen, which is weird, unless you want them unkissed at eighteen or twenty-one, which seems unnecessarily repressive. At the time of my first kiss, the answer was almost certainly Rebecca, whose first kiss it wasn't. Now, the answer would be my wife, Abbey — but in fact I'm quite happy with the way things turned out, and I'm glad that we didn't meet any earlier. So, on a wing: Carole Lombard, the most beautiful woman in black and white. It needn't have been her first kiss, however; could have been the last, or any number in the middle.

Episode 4: *Childhood Hero*
with T Cooper, Lisa Selin Davis, Ellen Litman, Elissa Schappell, and Amanda Eyre Ward

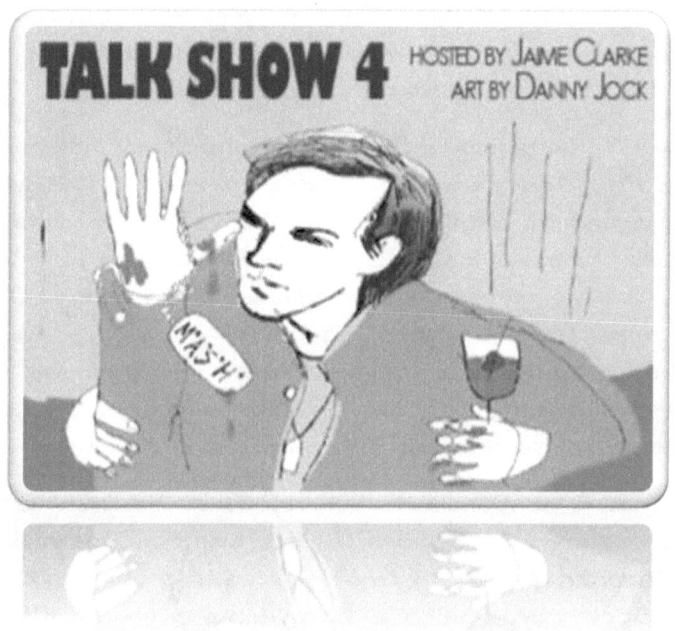

T Cooper is the author of the novels *Lipshitz Six, or Two Angry Blondes*, *Some of the Parts* and *The Beaufort Diaries*, as well as co-editor of an anthology entitled *A Fictional History of the United States with Huge Chunks Missing*.

Lisa Selin Davis is the author of the novel *Belly*, and has written about the environment, architecture, real estate and film (and lots of other things) for the *New York Times*, *House & Garden*, *Paper*, *Salon.com* and many other publications.

Ellen Litman is the author of *The Last Chicken in America: A Novel in Stories*. Her fiction won first prize in an *Atlantic Monthly* Fiction Contest, and she's been awarded a Rona Jaffe Foundation Writers' Award, as well as fellowships at the University of Wisconsin-Madison and the Fine Arts Center in Provincetown. Her stories have appeared in *Best New American Voices*, *Best of Tin House*, *Ontario Review*, *Triquarterly*, *Ploughshares*, and elsewhere. She teaches at the University of Connecticut.

Elissa Schappell is the author of the story collections *Blue Prints for Building Better Girls* and *Use Me*, which was a finalist for the PEN/Hemingway award. She co-edited the essay anthologies *The Friend Who Got Away* and *Money Changes Everything* with Jenny Offill. Schappell is a contributing editor at *Vanity Fair*, a founding editor and editor-at-large of *Tin House*, former senior editor of the *Paris Review*, and a frequent contributor to the *New York Times Book Review*.

Amanda Eyre Ward's first novel, *Sleep Toward Heaven*, was optioned by Sandra Bullock and Fox Searchlight. Her second novel, *How to Be Lost*, was chosen as a Target Bookmarked pick and has been published in fifteen countries. Other books include: *Forgive Me, Love Stories in This Town*. and *Close Your Eyes* - named a *Kirkus* Best Book *and winner of the Elle Magazine Fiction Book of the Year*.

* * *

- When and how did you first discover him/her?

Cooper: My first awareness of television as a small child involved *M*A*S*H*, (well, also *The Electric Company*, but there were, to be sure, no childhood heroes to be adopted from that show). I was born one month after the *M*A*S*H* television pilot went on the air in September 1972, and I would say that my deep, abiding love for Benjamin Franklin "Hawkeye" Pierce, developed somewhere during the program's fifth or sixth season. I watched the show religiously, both through the two-and-a-half hour series finale in 1983, and in re-runs throughout my high school and college years. (To this day — in addition to owning every season on DVD — I will pretty much always stop and watch an episode on the Hallmark Channel or TV Land whenever I'm flipping through the channels and see it on. And as much as I appreciate all of the characters, the writing, the politics — pretty much everything about that show — it always has been and always will be about Hawkeye for me.)

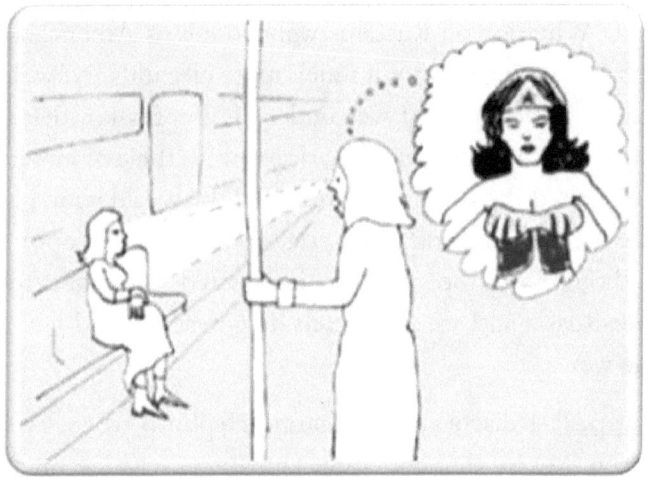

Davis: The first childhood hero I recall is *Wonder Woman* — not the 2D comic version, but Linda Carter with her tremendous cleavage and strong thighs: so powerful, and yet wearing a tiara! I'm not sure where I saw her, since we were a TV-free household until I entered third grade. But I loved her in that little girl, secular crush kind of way. When I think about it now, those kick-ass chicks — *Charlie's Angels, Bionic Woman* — were a thousand times more compelling than the painted and catty women on, say, *Dynasty* or *Dallas.* Although I supposed I was interested in them, too. All that mauve blush! That blue eye shadow! For a hippie kid, it was fascinating stuff.

Litman: It was sometime in the spring/summer of 1983. I was nine, finishing second grade. She was a year older — delicate, pretty, with long brown hair and that crackling smile everyone was so crazy about. She looked good in any clothes. She looked good with pigtails and in a forage cap of Young Pioneers. Most importantly, she was American. Her name was Samantha Smith and that spring she was all over the Soviet papers and also on TV. In case you don't remember (and most people don't anymore), she was the girl who wrote the letter to the Soviet Secretary General (Andropov), something along the lines of "Why do you Russians want to kill us Americans?" — though, of course, she put it much more elegantly. Now, like all normal Soviet children, I was under the impression that it was the other way around, that Americans were the evil imperialists who exploited the poor and threatened the world with a bomb. So clearly, this Samantha girl was confused. Andropov must have thought so too, because he invited Samantha to visit Mother-Russia and see for herself how peaceful and fair Soviet people were.

Schappell: I discovered Katharine Hepburn when I was ten or eleven. My mother and sister and I were visiting my grandparents, and I couldn't sleep, so I went into the room where my mother was sleeping, and crawled into bed with her. She was watching *The Philadelphia Story*. I wasn't allowed to watch much television, and certainly not in bed, so it was all very exciting for me. About five minutes in I thought, "I want to be her." She was so unlike any other actress I'd ever seen. She was so funny, but unlike the "funny" actresses I knew like Goldie Hawn or TV-personality Suzanne Somers, she was witty, and sharp. While she could be daft and goofy, she was never stupid. She was making the joke, or in on the joke, but she herself was never the joke. In movies like *The Philadelphia Story* and *Bringing*

Up Baby, which required her to do physical comedy (and always she did her own pratfalls because she said her stunt doubles could never capture her carriage) she was in control. And unlike other funny women — Gilda Radner, Madeline Kahn, Cloris Leachman — she was beautiful. With her red hair and killer accent (I was always working on an accent of some sort) she wasn't like anyone else I knew.

<u>Ward</u>: When I was in junior high, I saw a cool girl at the mall wearing a FREE MANDELA T-shirt. I just wanted the shirt. I thought some of this girl's magic might rub off on me if I could just dress like her. I was a nerd in beaded barrettes and parachute pants. The striped legwarmers didn't get me a second glance, so I pinned my hopes on the shirt. It was red. Some of the cool girls at school shopped in the Village (the East Village of NYC . . . we lived in the suburbs). I figured I had to get to the Antique Boutique, and then I could buy a FREE MANDELA shirt and get a metal button that showed I had been to The City. I went on a mission with my cousin, but we got lost. We ended up in Chinatown and it got dark and we took a cab back to her apartment and the cab fare cost all my babysitting money. I read about Mandela instead.

"She was so unlike any other actress I'd ever seen. She was so funny, but unlike the "funny" actresses I knew like Goldie Hawn or TV-personality Suzanne Somers, she was witty, and sharp. While she could be daft and goofy, she was never stupid. She was making the joke, or in on the joke, but she herself was never the joke."

- Elissa Schappell
re: Katherine Hepburn

39

- How did you try to emulate him/her?

Cooper: When I really started understanding the political mission of *M*A*S*H*, I tried to learn everything about the Vietnam War, because at one point I think I heard an adult talking about how the TV show was really a commentary on Vietnam . . . It was years until it clicked that it was in fact set during the Korean War, so then I tried to learn about that particular war, (I mean, "police action"). In addition to all of this, in school I tried to make Hawkeye-like wisecracks as often as possible, and I think I can credit him with teaching me what sarcasm is. (That is, assuming that I do in fact know what sarcasm is.) I also remember going to the Army-Navy supply store and getting an green hat from the Korean War era and wearing it as much as possible.

Davis: Always, there was a question when it came to these buxom and brave women I admired: did I want to be them, or, I don't know, have them somehow. Was emulation the goal? In my early meekness and shyness (both of which I've largely shed), I wouldn't have been able to imagine myself lassoing a criminal, whisking him off in my invisible plane. I don't think I wanted her powers. I wanted her romance. I wanted to be admired and feared, maybe. And beautiful. And rich. And bejeweled. And loved. I don't think I felt much of any of that in my childhood, save for occasionally loved (the best of the bunch, of course). I wanted Steve to love me.

Litman: In the youth magazine *Pioneer*, Samantha Smith was photographed sitting on the steps of her parents' house in Maine. She was dressed in a turtleneck and a pair of jeans. They way I remember it, the house was on the edge of some fields, and there was maybe a dog nearby — Samantha's dog. The accompanying article revealed that she wanted to become a veterinary doctor. Unlike her, I had no turtlenecks, no jeans, no dog, no steps to sit on, and no idea what I wanted to be when I grew up. In short, I lacked direction. That summer, while Samantha traveled through Russia and visited the best summer camp in the country (Artek), I languished at the dacha we rented every year. While she was doing press conferences and fighting for world peace, I was learning the multiplication table. And while she swam in the Black Sea, I waited for the weather to improve enough so that I could splash for five minutes in a nearby lake. But not all was lost. At Artek, Samantha befriended a Russian girl who could speak English. This gave me an idea. I whined and begged, and in the fall my parents signed me up for private English lessons. Within a few months, I could do a little speech, which I demonstrated repeatedly to all our relatives and friends. It sounded something like this: *I have a big family. I have a mother. I have a father. I have a sister. I have a grandfather. I have two grandmothers.* It wasn't much, but then again, I didn't think Samantha could speak much Russian either.

Schappell: Well, at first I tried to mimic her accent, but failed miserably. It did occur to me at some point — perhaps seeing her on a talk show — that she would think it very lame that I was trying to be her, when what I admired about her was her insistence on being so fully herself, and never apologizing for it. I aspired to the sort of bantering she shared with co-stars like Spencer Tracy in *Woman of the Year*, and Cary Grant in everything they ever did together. I tried to style my own flirtatious interactions with boys after her. From the way she wrinkled her nose, to her way she slapped the faces of men who offended her. And she did get offended a lot. A few years ago a small cabal of unhappy under-published writers and "anarchists" tried to disrupt a reading I was a part of. When they started heckling I started to panic, then I thought, "What would Kate do?" What I came up with was, Well she wouldn't back down. She wouldn't whine or complain. She wouldn't look to someone else to fight her fight. She would compose herself, lift her chin, and while appearing one hundred percent a lady defend herself with slashes of humor, and colorful language. I felt my backbone stiffen, I gripped the podium, ordered a martini, downed it, and delivered a few choice words. I didn't do nearly as well as she would have, but I did my best.

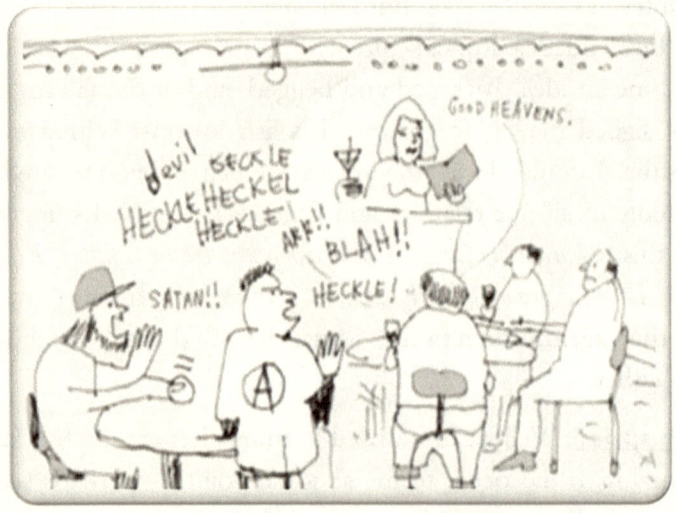

Ward: I asked my mom why there were no blacks at the golf club, and for that matter, why there were no Jews. (I didn't know about Hispanics; we didn't have them in suburban New York and we didn't have tacos either.) She told me life was complicated, so I sulked around the tennis courts, feeling morally superior.

- Did you friends share your hero worship?

Cooper: I don't think anybody understood my worship, nor my quest for *M*A*S*H* action figures in lieu of the requisite

Star Wars figures and spaceships that everybody else coveted. I have no idea what happened to all of my *M*A*S*H* action figures, but a few years ago I remember winning a Hawkeye figure on eBay, but I don't know where it is, and actually, this whole discussion reminds me that I need to locate that thing and put it on my desk where I can see it every day for inspiration and to remind me to try not to lose my sense of humor.

Davis: What little girl did not love *Wonder Woman?* Even her name, the invocation of wonder, which is sadly such a childhood phenomenon — think how many people lose their sense of wonder as they age. But, no, I can't remember bonding with any little girls over *WW*. Perhaps, more likely, little boys.

Litman: I didn't have many friends at that age. There was one who lived on the other side of Moscow (she went to a special English school and kind of looked like Samantha) and another who lived in Ukraine. I can't remember for sure, but I think they must have liked her. How could they not? That girl was everywhere. There was some talk among adults that it was her parents who wrote the letter, that she was maybe a CIA agent, and wasn't it altogether too convenient that she turned out to be so perfect and pretty, like a paid advertisement for America? But what did they know!

Schappell: Heavens no. They didn't understand why I'd be enamored of an actress that they only knew from later movies like *On Golden Pond*. If I'd told them how I admired her outspokenness and ability to articulate herself when she was angry, the way she got up in peoples' faces and challenged them — calling them on their hypocrisy like in, *Guess Who's Coming to Dinner?* they'd have shaken their heads in complete wonder, in part no doubt because I'd have been inarticulately raging in a bad Bryn accent.

Ward: No. Most of my classmates worshipped a girl in tenth grade because she had appeared in a tampon commercial.

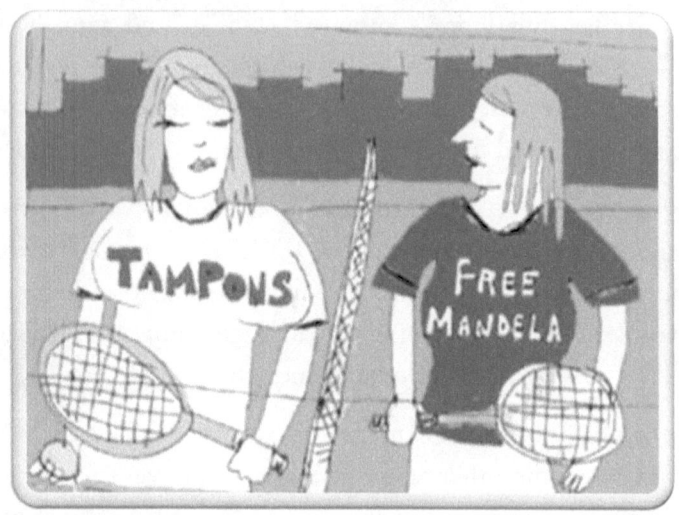

- Ever get a chance to meet/communicate with your hero?

Cooper: At a Jewish Book Council event in Washington D.C. a couple years back, I did meet Alan Alda's wife Arlene, who writes children's books and was there, like me, pitching her book and her services as a speaker to Jewish book fairs across the country. I introduced myself and briefly considered telling her how much I love her husband and his politics and his creativity; and also that I'd recently read and enjoyed his memoir, *Never Have Your Dog Stuffed and Other Things I've Learned*, and how I think it was really cool that he came out so publicly in favor of the ERA way back when, even though he took so much shit for it. But in the end I decided simply to shake her hand and look her directly in the eye and try to wordlessly communicate my respect for her and her husband in a more dignified (well, sane) manner.

Davis: Once, I saw a woman on the subway who looked so much like her. Actually, I saw her twice, and stared and stared. I know Linda Carter wouldn't ride the subway. No, no contact. I don't even think I wrote her any fan mail. I did, however, watch a TV movie with her and Loni Anderson, where they both were spies or something, sometime in the late '80s. Now that's loyalty.

Litman: At the end of the summer, Samantha went home. She changed her mind about being a veterinary doctor and decided to become an actress instead. It proved to be a fateful decision. A couple years later she was killed in a small-plane crash, while returning from filming some silly TV show. Some people in Russia said it was CIA's work. Far-fetched? Probably. I suppose I could've written her a letter in those two or three years between her visit and her death. But I was never the type to write fan letters. Besides, what could I have written back then? *I am a schoolgirl. I am ten. I have a big family.*

Schappell: No. Though I did find out a few years ago that a friend of mine's sister had worked for her until she died. She was her companion, she ran errands for her, and took her for drives. She said Kate really loved tooling around in her sister's beat up little Toyota, and that she kept her wits, sense of humor and independence until the end.

Ward: Not yet! My obsession with Mandela grows. I went to Cape Town last year to research my novel set in South Africa, and asked everyone I could find what they thought of him. I've watched dozens of documentaries about him and read countless books. All ironic detachment aside, I think he is an inspiration. I cannot imagine an American leader who even compares.

45

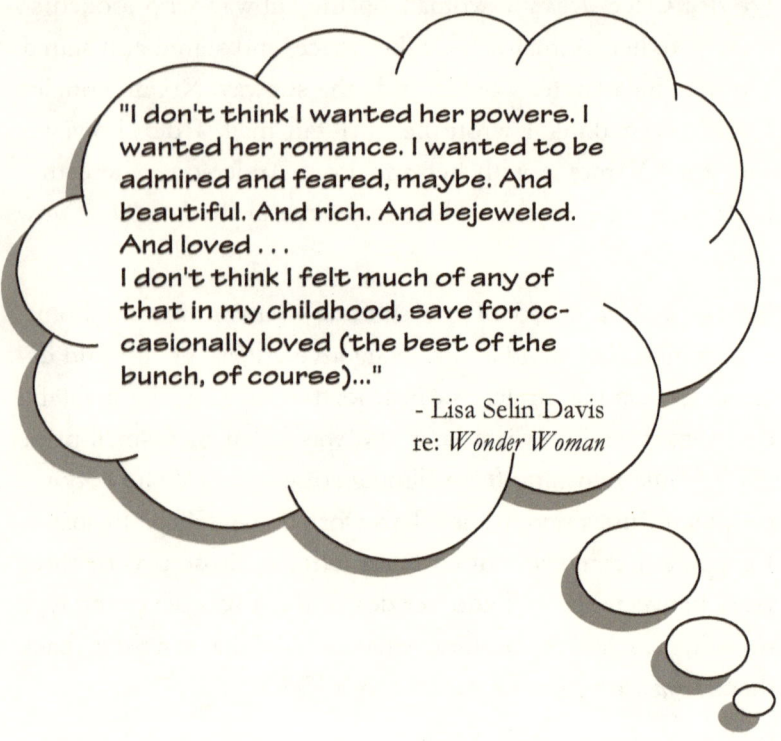

"I don't think I wanted her powers. I wanted her romance. I wanted to be admired and feared, maybe. And beautiful. And rich. And bejeweled. And loved . . .
I don't think I felt much of any of that in my childhood, save for occasionally loved (the best of the bunch, of course)..."

- Lisa Selin Davis
re: *Wonder Woman*

- If you could say something to him/her now, what would it be?

<u>Cooper</u>: I think I kind of already tried to say something to him a few times in recent years . . . On page 241 of my first novel, a "fictional character" goes on and on about how handsome and generally excellent Alan Alda is, and shortly after the book came out in 2002, I might've sent a copy of it to him through his agent in New York. (No, I didn't hear back, and further didn't even get a signed photo in return. But it's okay, because in *Never Have Your Dog Stuffed and Other Things I've Learned,* I found out that around the time my book would've arrived, Alda had been going through a life altering, near-death experience with a mechanical intestinal obstruction while

shooting *Scientific American Frontiers* in Chile, and shortly thereafter decided to go on anti-depressants. So it was a hectic time for the guy.)

Furthermore, *M*A*S*H* is also mentioned in a short story of mine that appeared in a recent issue of the *New Yorker*, and secretly, I've been thinking that out of all of the publications out there, I think of Alan Alda as someone who probably has a subscription to and reads the *New Yorker* regularly, so I've been quietly hoping that he by chance came across my story and saw the reference, and that a letter to me is on its way through my agent right this very moment. It could happen. And when it does, I'll totally be sending him a signed photo in return.

Davis: I suppose I'm curious to know if she felt she was furthering the feminist cause somehow. She and her TV powerful/beautiful sisters: were they busting doors down for the next generation, allowing us the freedom to be strong, tough, calm in all weathers? Or were they saying: you have to do everything men do, and as well, but wearing makeup and heels (like the Ginger Rogers quote)? Maybe that was the beginning of the superwoman phenomenon (perhaps we should have called it *Wonder Woman* phenomenon), whereby you were "free" to have both families and careers, but slowly women have been finding that it's a hell of a lot of work to have both. Most of us still want to be powerful and domestic. I haven't figured out how.

Litman: If I could go back in time? Maybe I'd say, *Hey, Samantha, I've been living in America for fifteen years now, and this whole TV business is totally insipid, you know? You're better off treating sick animals.* Though, let's face, the girl was photogenic as hell and clearly meant for public life. So who am I kidding?

Maybe instead I could tell her how it would end – not the plane crash, but the whole Soviet saga, the Cold War, and everything that would follow. On the other hand, that's a lot to tell, and I tend to get self-conscious and tongue-tied, especially around people of importance. Maybe I could just tell her not to get on that plane.

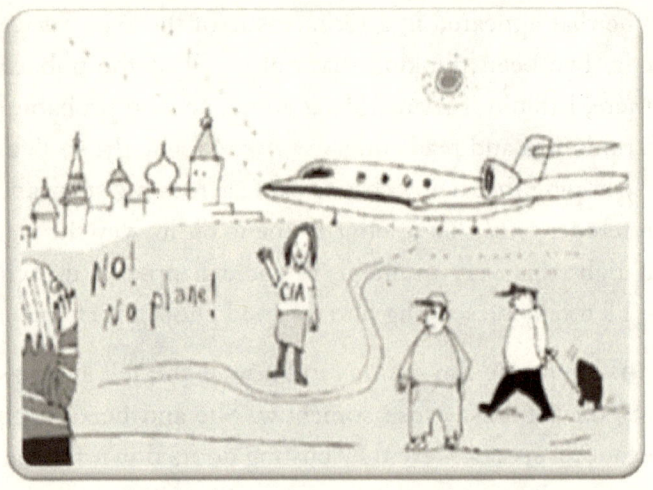

Schappell: Oh Kate, you were *yar*. And you were right, "If you obey all the rules you miss all the fun."

Ward: Nelson, who was *your* childhood hero?

Episode 5: _Witness to History_
with Maud Casey, Myla Goldberg,
Karl Iagnemma, and Christopher Sorrentino

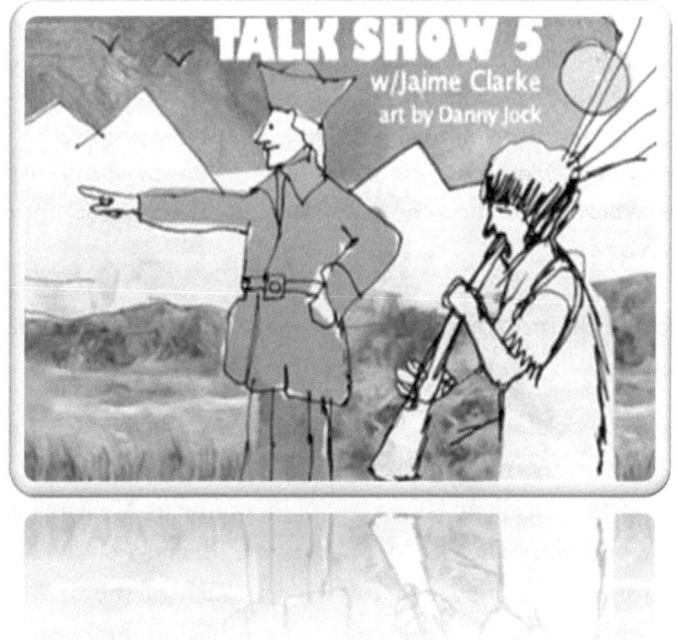

Maud Casey is the author of two novels, _The Shape of Things to Come_, a _New York Times_ Notable Book of the Year and _Genealogy_, a _New York Times_ Editors' Choice Book; and the short story collection, _Drastic_. She teaches at the University of Maryland.

Myla Goldberg is the author of the novels _Wickett's Remedy_, _The False Friend_ and _Bee Season_, a _New York Times_ Notable Book. Other books include the children's book _Catching the Moon_ and the essay collection _Time's Magpie_. Her work has appeared in _McSweeney's_, _Harper's_, the _New York Times_ and other publications.

Karl Iagnemma, a roboticist at MIT, is the author of the story collection _On the Nature of Human Romantic In-_

teraction and the novel *The Expeditions.* His short stories have appeared in the *Paris Review, Tin House, Zoetrope,* the *Best American Short Stories* and elsewhere.

Christopher Sorrentino's books include: *Sound on
Sound, Trance* - a finalist for the National Book Award,
American Tempura, a collaboration with artist Derek
Boshier and *Death Wish,* a critical analysis of the
Charles Bronson film. His writing has appeared in *Es-
quire, Harper's,* the *New York Times, Playboy,* and other
publications. He teaches writing at The New School in
New York City.

* * *

**- Name a historical event you wish you would've
witnessed/participated in and why.**

Casey: I would like to drop in *Quantum Leap* style (or maybe
Journeyman is the more current TV reference, though I can only
think of the excellent Kevin McKidd as Lucius Vorenus and I
keep wondering whether McKidd as the Journeyman will travel
back to himself, but I digress . . .) on much of the middle-to-
late part of the 19th century in France to watch the burgeoning
psychiatric culture, well, burgeon. More specifically, I would
like to attend one of the Tuesday Lessons held by Jean-Martin
Charcot at the Salpetriere Hospital in Paris and, more specifically still, I'd like to attend the one he gave on February 7, 1888
titled "Hysteroepilepsy: A Young Woman With a Convulsive
Attack in the Auditorium." For those not obsessed with the
history of psychiatry, the Tuesday Lessons were the weekly
public lectures Charcot gave on various illnesses, though hysteria became a frequent and major subject.

He would hold the lectures in the amphitheater of the hospital and he would have a patient there to, essentially, perform
the illness up for discussion. In the transcript of the February
7, 1888 lecture, Charcot writes, "Isn't there something immoral

about waiting and provoking such crises?" This is, in fact, what he goes on to do. He instructs, for example, an intern to touch the woman's "hysterogenic point," located conveniently under her left breast, in order to trigger the "epilleptoid phase" of hysterioepilepsy. Then he instructs the intern to compress the woman's "ovarian region" with an "ovarian compressor belt." Like so many trailblazers doing really weird things, Charcot kept elaborate records, so drawings of an ovarian compressor belt, as well as pictures of women in the Salpetriere amphitheater, in all stages of hysteria and hysterioepilepsy, are easy to find should you care to check it out.

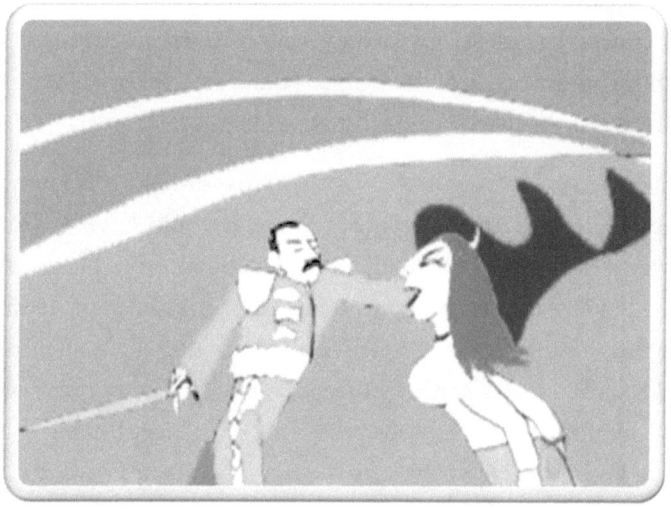

It's all a bit grim — and my desire to be there may seem akin to wanting to see a bullfight in which the bull is replaced by a mentally ill woman — but the patient's performance, its freak show aspects aside, is moving to me because it was exactly that, a performance, and as a performance, it was hers to perform. To look at the drawings and photographs of women whom Charcot had assigned this diagnosis is to see women translating their messy, amorphous pain (usually exacerbated by living in the Salpetriere) into something legible.

Goldberg: The electrocution of Topsy the elephant by Thomas Edison at Coney Island's Luna Park in 1903. My motives for wanting to be there are kind of schizophrenic. The do-gooder time traveler in me wants to be there to let everyone there know what Edison's true motives are for the electrocution, which I'd like to think would have had potentially far-reaching implications. I have no illusions about being able to save Topsy herself, but it would have been nice if her death could have revealed Edison's black heart to the general public and brought recognition to Nikola Tesla, overlooked genius of the twentieth century. The wistful-tourist time traveler in me wants to be there because, either before or after the elephant goes down, I could enjoy Coney Island in its heyday. I've seen old films and postcards of Coney Island in the early 1900s and it was clearly the most beautiful amusement park ever.

Iagnemma: I would have loved to have been a member of the Lewis and Clark expedition. Since I would have been useless as a hunter, canoeman, naturalist, or cook, I suppose I might have been Meriwether Lewis' personal assistant. It would have been great for so many reasons: seeing the western US before it had been settled, interacting with Lewis (who was a great explorer and, by all accounts, an exceptionally smart man). Even hearing Thomas Jefferson's stories, secondhand from Lewis, would have been wonderful.

Sorrentino: Not to derail the entire spirit of the thing, but I've never been more conscious of actually inhabiting history. "Interesting times," etcetera. It makes me despair a little — a writer is in a better position than maybe anybody else to lodge a coherent protest, but it's looking obvious that few people are interested in coherent protests or the action that should flow from them. There's all this awareness of what's going on politically, socially, economically, environmentally, and there seems to be very little way to participate other than as a willfully blind accomplice. Our participation begins and ends with *The Daily Show*.

- When and how did you first become interested in this historical event

<u>Casey</u>: Charcot is one of those larger-than-life characters; he's almost a parody of himself. I'm interested in the history of psychiatry and he looms large there. He was the first Professor of Diseases in the Nervous System and was at the forefront of neurology (it was just emerging when he started school). He was a plump fellow with no facial hair, often compared to Napoleon. He had a pet monkey who, I believe, dined with the family. His son fled an internship at his father's hospital to sail a ship — the aptly named *Porquoi Pas* — on an exploration of the Northern seas, where he eventually sank near Iceland. There's an island named after him (Charcot Island). So, Charcot Senior was the kind of father who inspired his son to go really, really far away from him and die doing dangerous things. He was not a simple guy and the combination of wanting to help (*let's study the problems of the mind*) even as he's treating his patients a bit like circus animals (*let's get really famous and lose track of the original, honorable goal*) is, let's face it, not so unusual.

Interesting people doing groundbreaking things are, often, compelling complicated assholes. And then there's the patient. Again, this notion of someone with anguish they can't describe aiming to please a doctor in order to get help or attention or love is heartbreaking to me. The woman who was the "young woman with the convulsive attack in the auditorium" says at one point during that particular Tuesday lesson, "Mother, I am frightened."

Charcot's response? "Note the emotional outburst."

But the woman's performance in all of this is also strangely heartening. She's doing whatever she can to get something.

Goldberg: I was watching a collection of Edison's early films and one of them documented Topsy's execution. I'd already known about the golden age of Coney Island, but hadn't known that Luna Park's debut year included the execution of an elephant as a publicity stunt. It wasn't until years later that I learned the undercurrents of jealousy and greed that were the event's secret motivating factors.

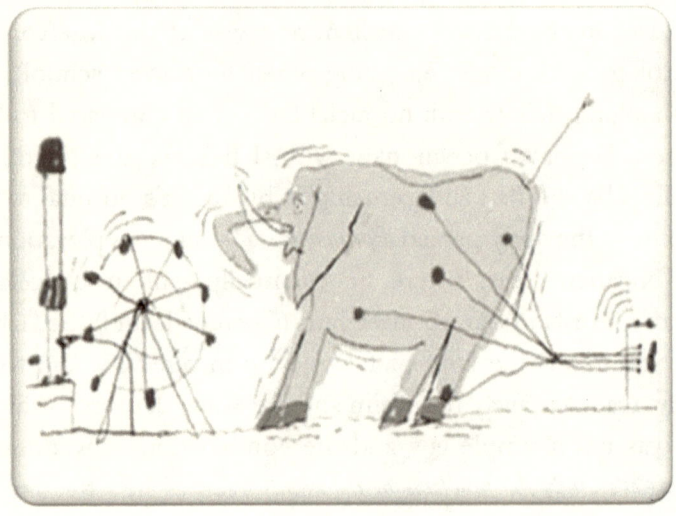

Iagnemma: Probably after reading Stephen Ambrose's *Undaunted Courage*, which is a very engaging treatment of the expedition. Somehow I missed the PBS love-fest from a few years ago.

Sorrentino: Around the time that I heard a TV commentator in the days after the 2000 presidential election ask some expert or another whether he thought that Al Gore would "take the high road" and concede the election to Bush — there was something so marvelously Orwellian about the language, the sinuous suggestion that to contest the vote would be a ploy, a selfish act not in the interest of the American people or democracy. And of course this "expert" didn't object; didn't protest that there was nothing subversive or unsportsmanlike in letting the democratic process play itself out. It became clear to me that protofascism had at last established the kind of foothold it likes best: quietly persuasive, almost homespun, declaiming what Roland Barthes witheringly calls "the perfect intelligibility of reality." The unchallenged use of that sort of language managed in two seconds to do what a loudmouth like Rush Limbaugh hasn't done in twenty years.

- Name a player in the historical event whose motives aren't clear and speculate about what the motives might be.

<u>Casey</u>: Everyone's motives are murky here. Charcot's, the patient's, and the audience. My own desire to crash this wacked-out party. The Tuesday Lessons were spectacle as much as science, a freak show like any other. *Come see the woman cower in a corner! Come see the woman arch her back! Come hear her beg for her mother!* Charcot's lectures and these live experiments with patients were about the emerging field of neurology, about scientific discovery and inquiry, about Charcot's career (not surprisingly, his focus on hysteria has overshadowed a lot of the genuine progress he made) and his increasingly rotund ego. It's unclear who this "young woman with the convulsive attack in the auditorium" was before she was that, but it's likely her life was pretty rough at the overcrowded, unsanitary Salpetriere. Was this moment "onstage" a small moment of relief? Of rare attention? When I read the stages of hysterioepilepsy Charcot induces, I imagine someone dancing faster and faster on a table as the applause grows louder and the crowd in the bar shouts

for more. I'd like to see her face — not her photographed face or her drawn face, her actual face. Charcot wants something from her and she's providing it. Is she getting something in return? At another point, she says, "Oh! Mother."

Goldberg: While Edison's true motives weren't general knowledge at the time, they were certainly clear to anyone working with him. I wish I could interview Topsy. She was executed after killing three of her handlers in three years. Considering that the last of these guys, J.F. Blount, had tried to feed her a lit cigarette, I suspect that the previous two were equally enlightened in their behavior toward animals. After J.F. tried to pass off his cigarette as a peanut, Topsy picked him up with her trunk and then threw him to the ground, killing him instantly. She didn't run at him or knock him over; she did something much more deliberate. I love that. And I wish I could take her to a peanut bar, treat her to a pound of salted, and talk with her about it.

Iagnemma: Most historians seem to agree that Meriwether Lewis committed suicide in 1809, three years after the expedition's conclusion, but there are still some who suggest that he might have been murdered. Lewis was a depressive, who had previously attempted suicide, but he left no clue about what happened that last night. Some commentators seem amazed that a man so rugged and accomplished could have committed suicide; but of course accomplishments don't mean anything to a person suffering from depression. Lewis was probably just exhausted by life.

Sorrentino: Wouldn't it be nice, or at least vaguely hopeful, if our current situation were rife with ambiguity, ironic Sophoclean trials of character, and Shakespearean doubt and uncertainty?

- If you could affect the outcome of the historical event, what would be different?

Casey: Though I know it's against all the *Quantum Leap, Journeyman, Back to the Future* rules, ideally I'd like to rescue the young woman from a life of misery, bring her into the future where she could cast off the ovarian compressor belt and take a warm bath and some Valium. Though — and this is why I'm interested in this particular event to begin with — the impulse to diagnose is as potent here in the 21st century as it was in its nascent form back then. Who knows what kind of too-tight sweater her messy story would be stuffed into now? In Freud's obituary of Charcot in 1893, he described him as Adam, the great namer of things. You, my dear crazy lady, are a hysteric. There's a label to contain you and your wild contortions. A similar yearning exists these days to contain the wild, mysterious mish-mash of emotion, experience, neuroscience, to name it. And the flip side: to be contained, to be named.

Goldberg: I wish I could have been a small voice in the crowd watching Topsy go down. I wish I could have said, "You know why Edison's making a big deal out of using alternating current to kill off this beautiful elephant? Because he didn't invent it: his former employee, Nikola Tesla, did. Edison stiffed Tesla out of a $50,000 bonus for completely redesigning the company's generators and then refused him a raise. Edison wants you to think that Tesla's alternating current is dangerous so that you'll continue using direct current, which is his much lamer invention."

Iagnemma: If Lewis was murdered, then obviously this is the aspect that would change. If he wasn't . . . it's tempting to say that his suicide could be changed, but that doesn't make a lot of sense. It would have been nice if Clark hadn't been treated so poorly by the federal government. Aside from that it's difficult to imagine what I'd change about one of the most successful expeditions in American history.

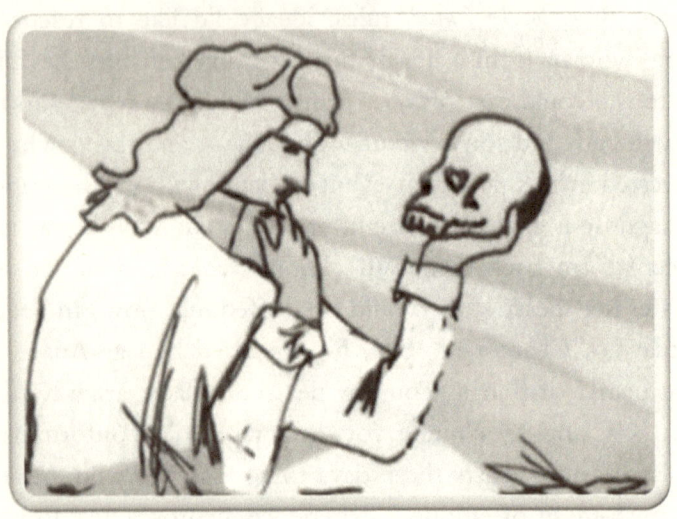

Sorrentino: What would be different, but alas won't be, would be if the issues the current and all future national campaigns will address aren't left for the candidates and their consultants to delimit. They fall into the deep sleep of their comfort zones and nobody in the press can bear to pull the comforter off them. Looking at all the wreckage George Bush has left in just seven years, I can't believe that he and Al Gore spent the entire 2000 presidential campaign grappling over social security.

- What aspect of the event do you consider either overblown or under-appreciated?

Casey: Charcot and his Tuesday Lessons are very much appreciated and discussed and criticized. They have been dissected, deconstructed, and otherwise fed through many an academic shredder. I first read a book about Charcot, specifically the photographs that were taken of the "hysterical" women he studied, in a class in college. The take home message was that Charcot was pure patriarchal monster, another too-tight sweater.

The truth is I don't think I'd like Charcot much. I'd be rooting for the woman dancing faster and faster on the table. It would be hard to watch, this Tuesday Lesson on February 7, 1888, but I'm interested in the glimpse of relief the woman might have felt in being watched, in having her mysterious pain anointed with a name. Diagnoses are, after all, stories, and in its screwy way, the Tuesday Lesson was a story about her. Maybe not her story but a story in which she had a leading role, which is sometimes better than no story at all.

Goldberg: Nikola Tesla was a celebrity in his day, but his name has been largely forgotten. He not only invented alternating current — which despite Edison's national smear campaign became the international standard — but vied with Marconi for inventing the radio and was a pioneer in the development of radar technology.

The fact that Edison's name is so much huger than Tesla's today makes sense, given that Tesla had no business sense and was eccentric enough to fall in love with a pigeon, but in a better world schoolchildren would be singing his praises and Tesla's later vision of a system of free, wireless electricity for all would have made Thomas Edison's name the quaint, historical footnote.

lagnemma: The expedition has been written about so exhaustively that it's tempting to say that it's all a bit overblown. But what seems somewhat unappreciated (or at least less overblown?) is the scientific nature of the journey. Mostly this was

Lewis' work, collecting botanical and mineral specimens, and it completes the picture of Lewis as a writer / adventurer / scientist, the sort of man that seems to have only existed in the 19th century.

Sorrentino: September 11th is certainly overblown, or at least distorted. It's become National First Responders Day. Whatever's underappreciated will get its due, when we're paying for it.

Episode 6: *First Day of School*
with Susan Cheever, Rachel Kadish, Daphne Kalotay, Mameve Medwed, Hannah Tinti, and Vendela Vida

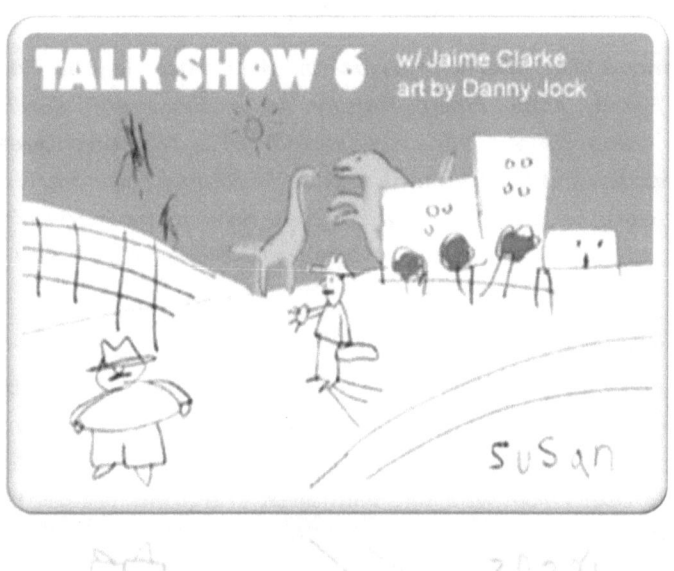

Susan Cheever is the author of twelve books. These include the novels *Looking for Work*, *Elizabeth Cole* and *A Handsome Man*; memoirs entitled *Home Before Dark*, *Treetops* and *Note Found in a Bottle* and a biography of Louisa May Alcott. Cheever teaches at the Bennington Writing Seminars and at the New School.

Rachel Kadish is the author of the novels *From a Sealed Room* and *Tolstoy Lied: a Love Story*, as well as numerous short stories and essays. She has been a fellow of the National Endowment for the Arts and a writer-in-residence at Stanford University. She teaches writing in Lesley University's MFA program.

Daphne Kalotay is the author of *Calamity and Other Stories*. Her novels include *Sight Reading* and *Russian Winter* - published in twenty one foreign editions and winner of the Writers' League of Texas Fiction Award. She has received fellowships from the MacDowell, Christopher Isherwood and Bogliasco Foundations.

Mameve Medwed is the author of the novels *The End of an Error, Mail, Host Family, How Elizabeth Barrett Browning Saved My Life*, (winner of a Massachusetts Honor award for Fiction) and *Of Men and Their Mothers*. Her stories, essays, and reviews have appeared in *Yankee*, the *Boston Globe, Missouri Review, Newsday* and the *Washington Post*.

Hannah Tinti is the editor of *One Story* magazine. Her short story collection, *Animal Crackers*, has been translated into more than a dozen languages and was a runner-up for the Pen/Hemingway award. Tinti's novel, *The Good Thief*, was the winner of the John Sargent, Sr. First Novel Prize and an ALEX Award.

Vendela Vida is the author of the novels *And Now You Can Go, Let the Northern Lights Erase Your Name*, and *The Lovers*. Her first book, *Girls on the Verge*, was a journalistic study of female initiation rituals in America. She is a co-editor of *The Believer* magazine, the editor of *The Believer Book of Writers Talking to Writers*, and a founding board member and teacher at 826 Valencia, a nonprofit youth writing lab.

* * *

- When and where was your first day of school?

Cheever: My first day of school was sometime in the 1940s when there were still dinosaurs in Central Park and all the men wore hats and some of them were still in uniform from World

War Two, which had ended recently. It was a nursery school called Walt Whitman that my bohemian parents (in those days that meant left wing, not hailing from a province of Czechoslovakia) thought was cool — although they wouldn't have used that word either. Did we even speak English back then?

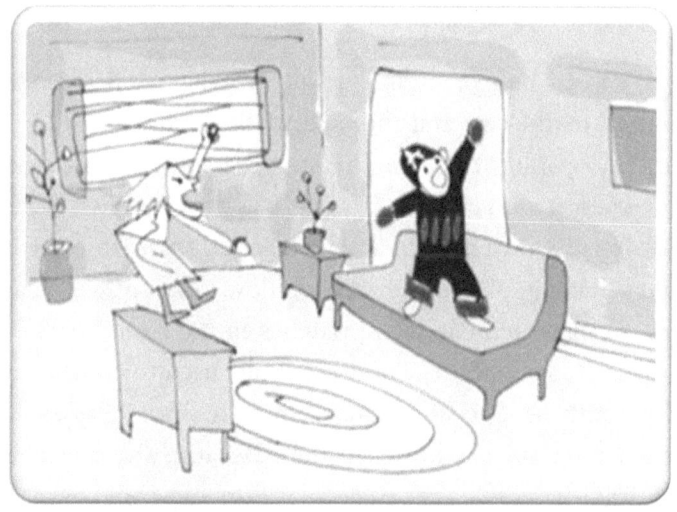

Kadish: September 1974, kindergarten in a tiny Jewish day school in a suburb of New York. Solomon Schechter Schools are now a big movement offering top-notch everything . . . but back then the school was a tiny startup. Most grades had eight to fifteen students. If you were chided by a teacher or had the hiccups during morning prayers, the entire school knew it in milliseconds.

Kalotay: If we're counting preschool, then Madison, New Jersey, at the Methodist church, where my mother dropped me off and left; and though I'm sure she must have prepared me for weeks ahead of time, telling me what was going to happen, I remember thinking, "You're just *leaving* me here?" It was a very frustrating place because for arts and crafts they would give us used, flattened cardboard containers to paint on (toothpaste boxes, for instance), and the paint would never stick to the coating. I also have a very powerful memory of going to the water fountain when I was three, and the girl ahead of me in line was from the other class, which meant she was *four*, and bent down and tied her shoe-lace all on her own; I was incredibly impressed.

Medwed: In Bangor, Maine at the Abraham Lincoln School sometime in the last millennium. In the middle of the playground, a couple of squares of unimpressive asphalt, stood a house where a whole family lived. It was as if a Fisher-Price toy had dropped out of a truck and just landed there. It looked like a child's drawing of a house with window boxes of weeds and a couple of dispirited dandelion patches in the front "yard." The only kid who lived there, Toothie Ruthie, used to come out and play tag with us. She was huge, with coke bottle glasses and a constant river of drool on her chin. Because she was considered "off," she didn't have to go to school but could participate in recess throughout the whole school day. We envied her. By force of size and strength, though not speed, she always managed to be "it."

Tinti: My first day of school was at Harborlight Montessori in Beverly, Massachusetts. I'm not sure of the year. I think I started when I was three, so that would make it fall 1976. I stayed there until I was five and graduated kindergarten.

Vida: My first day of school was at Katherine Delmar Burke's, an all-girls' school in San Francisco. I had never gone to preschool or anything like that so I was incredibly excited, and, also, totally terrified of being late. I woke up at 4 a.m. that morning to get dressed and then waited until the sun came up to wake my parents.

- What did you wear?

<u>**Cheever**</u>: Probably some kind of pinafore, which is what they called a skirt with an attached top. That's what three-year-olds wore in the days before Baby Phat and Osh Kosh B'Gosh.

<u>**Kadish**</u>: This was the '70s, so you can imagine. Probably something velour. It wasn't my fault. I wasn't yet picking my own clothing.

<u>**Kalotay**</u>: Bellbottoms. But starting in kindergarten I always wore a skirt to the first day of school. It was the only time all year I wore a skirt, which usually came from Sears.

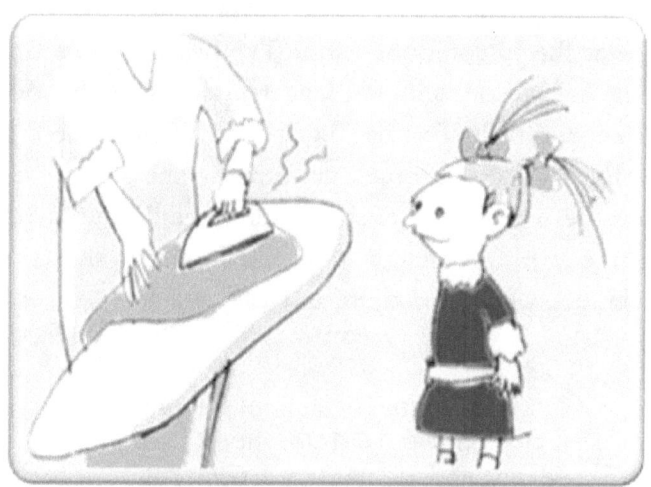

<u>**Medwed**</u>: Pigtails with big bows, beautifully ironed dresses (my mother prided herself on her ironing skills) white anklets and laced Oxfords that were good for your foot development. (though I had patent leather Mary Janes for party days). I also had hand-knit sweaters with silver buttons and hearts and snowflakes all over them. During the winter, I wore three pairs of socks and stiff rubber boots (it was COLD, then) which

rubbed raw red stripes on my legs. I was much too well dressed for Maine and longed for faded corduroy overalls and wrinkled misbuttoned plaid shirts like everyone else.

Tinti: I have no idea, but seeing as it was 1976, there was probably corduroy involved. I'm guessing corduroy pants, and a thick Irish sweater with wooden buttons. My family went to Ireland when I was around that age, and I had one of those sweaters, and I wore it all the time.

Vida: We had a uniform. A green plaid dress that we wore over a short-sleeve white blouse, and under a green cardigan with big white buttons. Green knee-high socks (that we had to keep pulled up) and brown leather lace-up shoes that everyone bought at the Junior Boot Shop. (I've heard rumors that the guy who sold us our shoes in kindergarten still works there.) I didn't know this the first day, but I quickly learned all the girls wore shorts underneath their uniforms so they could step out of their dresses for gym class and run around in what has got to be the world's worst workout outfit: shiny shorts and a white blouse, wool knee-highs, and leather shoes.

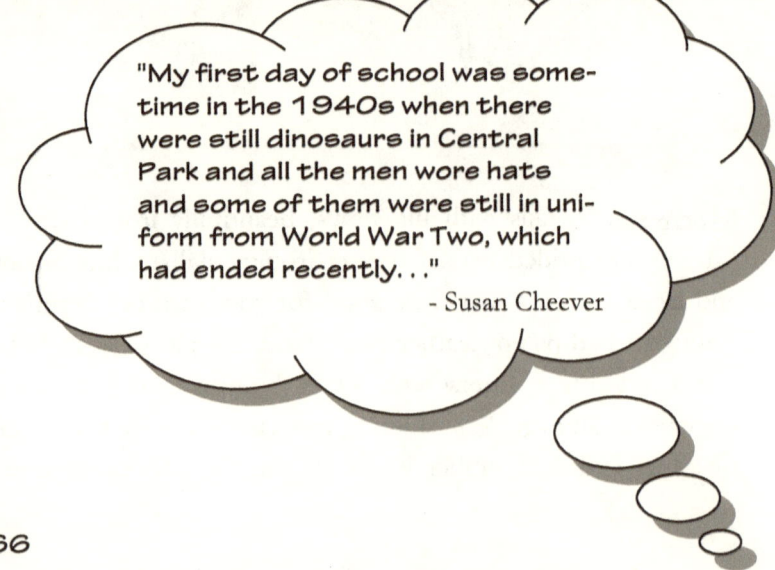

"My first day of school was sometime in the 1940s when there were still dinosaurs in Central Park and all the men wore hats and some of them were still in uniform from World War Two, which had ended recently..."

- Susan Cheever

- Who was your closest friend in kindergarten and were you still friends at the end of the school year?

<u>Cheever</u>: I had one great friend, Sally Belasco was her name. By kindergarten I had two other friends, Mitten Mittendorf and Connie Morrow, who is now a student of mine at Bennington! Sally and I were so close that I inherited a hamster from her which I named Algernon Belasco. The tragedy of my young life was moving to the suburbs, I had to leave my friends behind — but Algernon came with us.

<u>Kadish</u>: I think his name was David, but I'm not sure about that. I'm sure that he liked to play *Captain America* and let me pretend to be some other superhero, and at his house we jumped off a lot of furniture that I wouldn't let my kids jump off today. And, he had a miniature orange tree and it had one orange on it. That's all I remember, except that this was his last year in the school, and also that each of us was teased for having a best friend of the opposite sex, and I think that by the end of the year the teasing had put an end to our playdates.

<u>Kalotay</u>: Elizabeth, who lived not far from the school, and we're *still* friends. But my walking-to-school partner from my neighborhood, Allison, did in fact try (unsuccessfully) to come between the two of us; I can't quite remember how, but it involved a threat about eating or swallowing leaves . . . Allison was great to walk home with because I would stop off at her house and we would eat marshmallows with peanut butter on top. But pretty soon after that she went to private school and I didn't see her anymore.

<u>Medwed</u>: My husband, whom I met in nursery school (he was a couple of years ahead, but we have a photo of the two of us sitting across from each other at a birthday party. He was

wearing short pants and a wide tie; I, a pinafore and ribbons in my hair) swears he completely remembers every single detail of me in kindergarten, my finger-painting skills, my peg-hammering abilities, my eraser-clapping technique — even though he would have been in second grade at that time and much more advanced. Despite our age gap, he insists we were soul mates back then. I don't remember him for one minute. I doubt we ever spoke. Still, I must admit this romantic construct does make a good story — even if it isn't true. My best friend was Natalie Burnett and we stayed friends through most of grammar school. Her mother was a nurse, her father was a policeman and she had a mass of curly red hair which she hated and I envied. My hair was thick and unruly. My mother used to thin it by lifting the top layer and hacking the underbrush to the scalp. That was fine for two days until my hair started to grow in, turning the outer surface into craters of the moon.

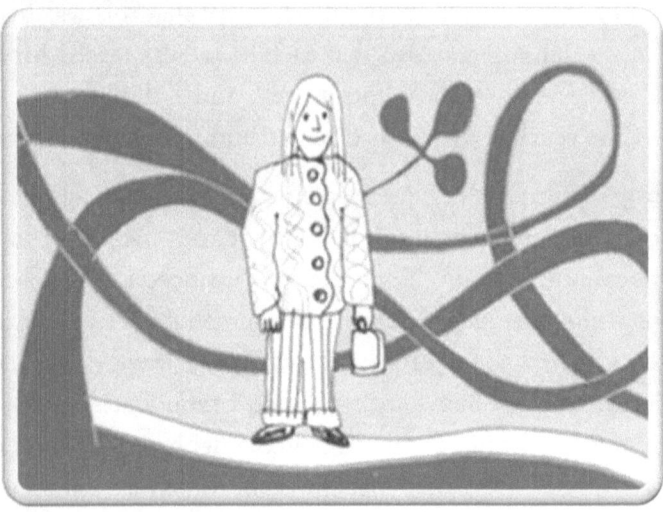

Tinti: I have a vague memory of a boy named Sebastian, but I don't know what happened to him. I am still friends with another kid named Mike Scagliotti, who was in my carpool, and who always got bloody noses.

Vida: My closest friend was a striking-looking girl with dark brown hair and light blue eyes named Aimee. I don't think either of us were trouble-makers on our own, but something would happen when we got together and we'd get into a lot of . . . mischief. We went to that girls' school for nine years, and never once were we placed in the same classroom. I think word got out that it was best to let us mingle in our own free time. We tap-danced together when we were young, and when we were ten or eleven we started a local chapter of the Robert Downey, Jr. fan club — we would write letters to Downey and watch *Tuff Turf* over and over. When we were in the eighth grade we had slightly more unconventional ways of showing our affection for boys, including an incident in which we threw a glass bottle through the window of a crush's house. We succeeded in getting the attention of his parents and the police. Aimee and I still see each other around San Francisco sometimes. All she has to do is laugh and I laugh too.

"...he would have been in second grade at that time and much more advanced. Despite our age gap, he insists we were soulmates back then. I don't remember him for one minute. I doubt we ever spoke. Still, I must admit this romantic construct does make a good story — even if it isn't true."

- Mameve Medwed

- What was your teacher's name, and what do you remember most about her?

Cheever: I don't remember a teacher until second grade. Maybe we all ran wild!

Kadish: I am so very glad you asked this question. My kindergarten teacher's name was, and I am not making this up, Mrs. Eisenbach . . . pronounced *Eyes-in-back*. She told us she had eyes in back of her head and could see what we were up to. Call me credulous, but I will swear this was true. Nobody pulled one over on Mrs. Eisenbach.

Kalotay: Mrs. Rendall! I loved her. She was old — about to retire, in fact — and drove a big Cadillac to school. According to my mother I would come home saying things like, "Everything's just topsy-turvy." Outdated expressions like that.

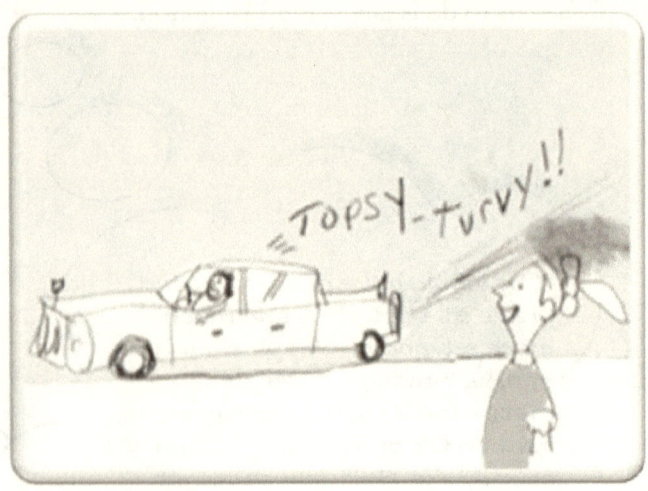

Medwed: Miss O'Conner. She was strict. She had taught both my parents. And considering my father was twelve years older than my mother, Miss O'Conner had staying power up the kazoo. She liked orderly lines and would smack you if you stepped out of yours even a foot. She wielded a mean ruler, ready to snap it against your fingers if you smeared your crayons or splattered your ink. Unlike me, my parents had been exemplary. She never stopped comparing us. They were always smarter, more industrious, better behaved and towed that line far better than their offspring.

Tinti: We had two teachers, Linda and Debbie. Linda had dark hair, and Debbie had short blondish brown hair.

Vida: My teachers were Mrs. Van and Mrs. G. I don't remember much else about them except one of them had curly hair while the other one had straight hair. We also had a hippie music teacher come in and sing to us with a guitar. Her favorite song was "Little Boxes," the song about how all the houses are the same, and all the people who live in them are the same. She'd make us practice the song, and then tell us that in our uniforms we were just like those houses, and that none of us had any individuality. We were only five but we knew she was a bad, bad person.

"A girl named Randy asked me whether I kept kosher. All the kids were standing around the swingset. I had no idea what a kosher was, or whether we had one, or where in our house my parents might keep it. But all the other kids seemed to keep one, so I said I did too."

- Rachel Kadish

- What are your outstanding memories from kindergarten?

Cheever: I went to a very special kindergarten at The Brearley School, a school which even then was hard to get into (believe it or not as a three-year-old my intellect was quite impressive). Brearley provides an identity for its students even now and I reveled in that identity. I was a Brearley Girl down to my special rhythm shoes and when we moved to the suburbs I continued to wear my Brearley uniform until it fell apart.

Now, many years later, I live across the street from the Brearley School.

Kadish: A girl named Randy asked me whether I kept kosher. All the kids were standing around the swingset. I had no idea what a kosher was, or whether we had one, or where in our house my parents might keep it. But all the other kids seemed to keep one, so I said I did too.

Kalotay: Having our photographs taken outside by the jungle gym. In my recollection, the principal was the one taking the photos, but this seems odd now (although I know that when, a few years later, one of the lenses came out of my glasses, I immediately went to the principal's office because I was sure that he would be able to fix them — which he did.) I also remember that we made some kind of food for each letter of the alphabet. *A* was applesauce, *B* was butter. I don't recall *C*, but *D* was fried donuts.

I was especially lucky because when it was my turn to eat a donut, the one I got was sort of runty and small, so the teaching assistant gave me an entire other one, too!

Medwed: They mostly involve Miss O'Conner. My father used to drop me off at school early on his way to the office. As a result, there was plenty of time for Miss O'Conner to take me to mass at St. John's Catholic Church. I learned a lot — how to click the rosary beads, all the words to "Ave Maria," when to kneel. I was quite fond of the hush in that particular cathedral. I brought my Raggedy Ann doll along with me. She liked it, too. That I was Jewish was irrelevant.

My Catholic kindergarten ended, however, when I walked by St. John's with my father and I crossed myself.

Tinti: I remember making a solar system out of construction paper, using different sized coins to trace the planets. A silver dollar for Jupiter, a quarter for Saturn, a dime for Pluto, a nickel for Earth.

But, my outstanding memory happened in my last year, when I was five. Harborlight was in the basement of a church, and we played in the graveyard for recess. It was an old New England graveyard, with black slate markers, which are very sharp when they splinter and break. One day I was running through the graves and I fell on one and it went through my left wrist, severing the artery. I was rushed to Salem Children's hospital in a police car. But when I got there they couldn't operate on me, because they didn't have parental consent, and my mom and dad were at a Red Sox game. Again, this was the '70s — no cell phones. So there was a lot of mayhem with the doctors. I remember a drawing of Snow White and the Seven Dwarves on the wall. They finally got the OK from a friend of the family and stitched me up. I still have a pretty bad scar there. And my mom never went to another Red Sox game.

Vida: One day, two hamsters were brought into our classroom in a cage. We had a wedding for them — white dress on one, black top hat on the other — and waited for them to have babies. After a few months, when no offspring appeared, we learned they were both male. Many parents made jokes about this being San Francisco, after all, but none of us understood what they were talking about.

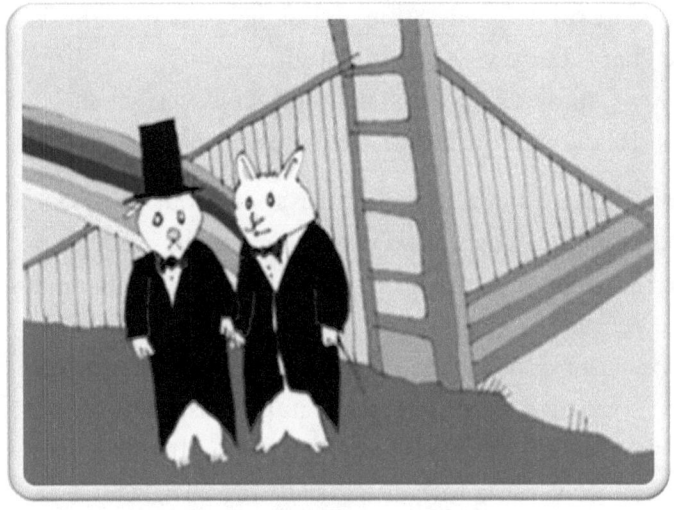

Episode 7: *Monumental Pop Culture* with Julianna Baggott, Lisa Borders, Maria Flook, Antonya Nelson, and Darin Strauss

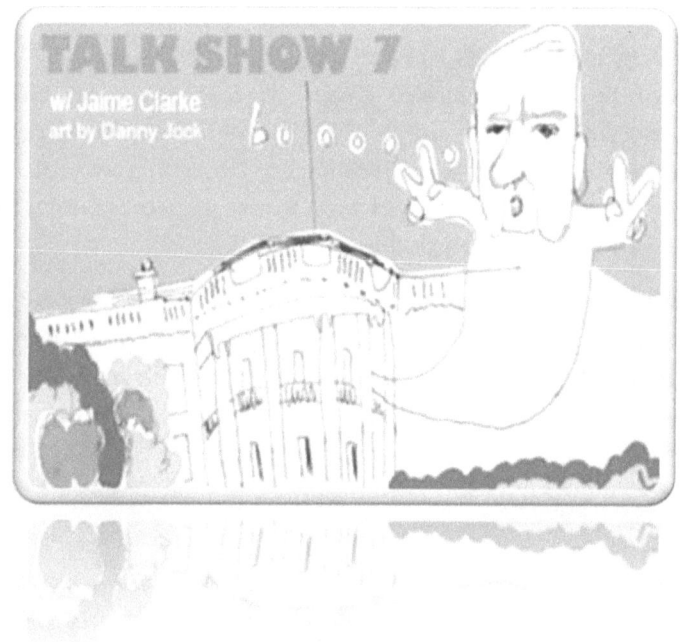

Julianna Baggott has published novels, children's books and three volumes of poetry. She also writes under the pen names N.E. Bode and Bridget Asher. Her books include *The Miss America Family, Girl Talk, The Ever Breath, The Madam, Mr. Magorium's Wonder Emporium, The Prince of Fenway Park, Pure* and *Fuse*. Baggott teaches at Florida State University and is the founder of the nonprofit Kids in Need - Books in Deed

Lisa Borders' first novel, *Cloud Cuckoo Land*, was chosen by Pat Conroy as the winner of River City Publishing's Fred Bonnie Award for Best First Novel. Her second novel is entitled *The Fifty-First State*. Borders has been nominated for a Pushcart Prize and her short stories have appeared in *Kalliope, Washington Square, Black Warrior Review, Painted Bride Quarterly, CrossConnect* and other publications.

Maria Flook is the author of two works of nonfiction, *Invisible Eden: A Story of Love and Murder on Cape Cod* and *My Sister Life, The Story of My Sister's Disappearance*; three novels, *Open Water, Lux* and *Family Night* (which received a PEN/Hemingway Foundation Special Citation); a collection of short stories, *You Have the Wrong Man* and two poetry collections. She teaches at Emerson College.

Antonya Nelson is the author of several books of fiction, including the story collections *Some Fun, Female Trouble, Nothing Right, In the Land of Men* and *The Expendables*, as well as the novels *Bound, Living to Tell, Nobody's Girl* and *Talking in Bed*. Winner of a REA Short Story Award, Nelson teaches at the University of Houston.

Darin Strauss is author of the novels *Chang and Eng, The Real McCoy* and *More Than It Hurts You*, as well as the memoir *Half A Life*. His work has been translated into fourteen languages. Strauss is a winner of an ALEX and National Book Critics Circle award. He teaches at New York University.

* * *

- Name the most significant pop culture event in your lifetime.

Baggott: I certainly can't be responsible for a task of such magnitude. I'm barely allowed to drive a car. I've never even been chosen as secretary at our departmental meetings because I'm prone to hyperbole. (But, later, when pressed, I'll cough up a Red Sox moment. Scroll down.)

Borders: *The Partridge Family* — the TV show, the prefab pop band, and, most importantly, the show's star David Cassidy, he of the shaggy mane and puka-shell necklaces, the ruffles and red velvet. You have to respect a guy who can pull off ruffles and red velvet while playing a character named Keith Partridge.

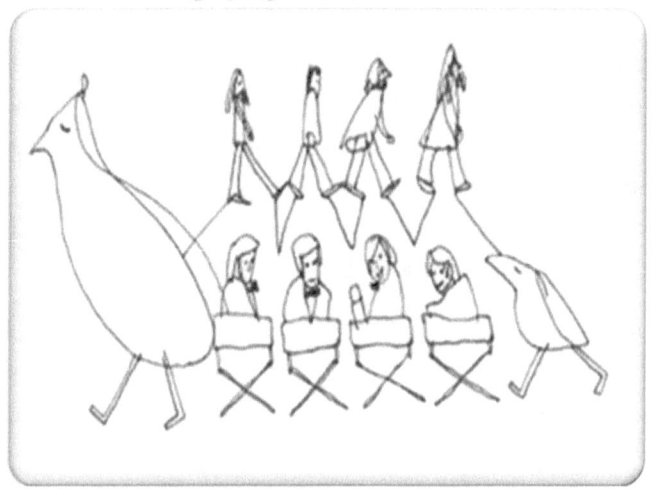

Flook: Seeing Janis Joplin at Newport Folk Festival, 1968.

Nelson: I wonder if Watergate counts as pop culture? Certainly it was the only show we watched, one dull summer. My parents were so into it — they who disdained television and soap operas, tuned in like any bored housewife, ready to see what was going to come out of those people's mouths next.

Strauss: Unfortunately, the release of Michael Jackson's *Thriller*. The album was neither as bad as is claimed by its embarrassed ex-devotees (everyone, basically), nor good enough to have caused the stir it did. A cultural phenomenon, like any whirlwind, is hard to predict. Some products, like local cloud systems, just drift over the country. You can't forecast which stories might gather force and momentum, which Airstream will go squally and funnelform until it tornadoes out into national attention.

-Where were you when you experienced this event?

Baggott: Since I got this assignment a few days ago, my husband will randomly shout out things like: *the death of Princess Diana and the costume malfunction of Janet Jackson and OJ's white Bronco on the LA freeway?* And I've come to realize that I live in Baggottland — just south of *Jungleland* — and I receive dispatches from the real world via the wobbly negotiations of something like a carrier pigeon or singing telegram. "I don't know where I am at any given moment," I say. "I'm in my head, I think." And this is sad, sad, sad.

Borders: The year was 1970; I was seven years old and living in Keyport, New Jersey, a 1.4-square-mile parcel of swampland. I'd had crushes before — on Davy Jones, on Batman's sidekick Robin, and even, strangely enough, on the cartoon character Underdog. But nothing could have prepared me for what David Cassidy and the *Partridge Family* were about to do to me — emotionally, hormonally, music-fanatically — as they began to appear on the black-and-white TV in our living room each Friday night. (I successfully begged my parents for a color TV shortly after *Partridge* mania began.)

Flook: I was fifteen and traveled to Newport with my older hippie sister in her VW Micro bus. She had just left her husband and was doing this wild-ass reinvention thing. I was on probation for stealing cars in Wilmington, Delaware. It was this intense sister thing. We cleaved to one another! We picked up two hitchers, college boys from Kent State (two years before the shoot out), and I ended up sleeping with one of the guys in a sand dune.

I had to remove my retainer when he kissed me, and remember to put it back each time so it wouldn't get lost.

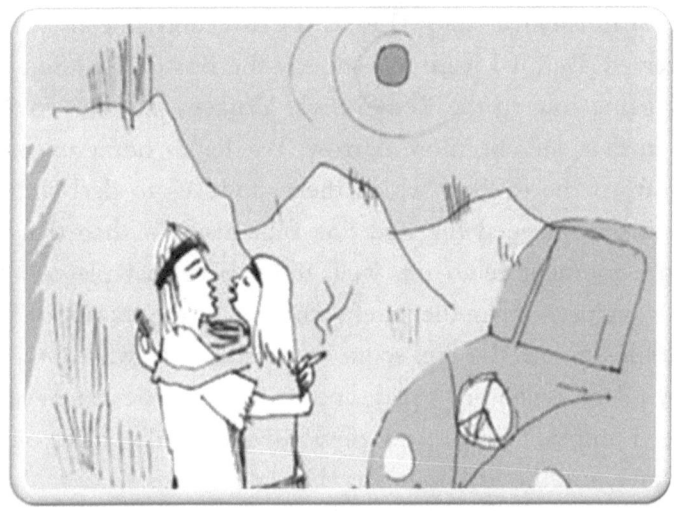

Nelson: We didn't even have a decent television or reception, then. We were in a tiny town in Colorado that got exactly one channel. On it was whatever the regional station manager declared worthy. Maybe that's why Watergate seemed so incredibly omnipresent.

Strauss: In the slow lane of a steep puberty.

- What, in your opinion, fuels the longevity of this event in pop culture?

Baggott: Well, there's a scientific hypothesis — which I heard once, but don't remember where I was when I heard it — that memory cannot exist until one memory can refer to another memory . . . something like memory only exists when it stands for another memory — basically metaphor has to exist. This is an argument the likes of *Is there thought before language*, which Helen Keller weighed in on in the category of No, there isn't. This is supposed to explain why people don't remember infancy. I think that infancy is overshadowed by an enormous haze of Existential Angst (I exist? I exist?) and little else can be perceived. But, if I were to pick, say the Boston Red Sox winning game four in the Red Sox vs. Yankees play-offs in 2004 — in fact, let's be more narrow: Big Papi's homerun in the bottom of the twelfth (which then allows us to deal with the racism that plagued the Red Sox franchise) — then that pop culture moment relies on, well, the racism that plagued Red Sox franchise — like the hateful charade of the try-out of Jackie Robinson and the Sox scout who refused to wait out a rain delay to see Willie Mays play, and the horrible treatment of the sweet Pumpsie Green. And, obviously, all of this relies on Bill Buckner, and the ball bouncing through his legs.

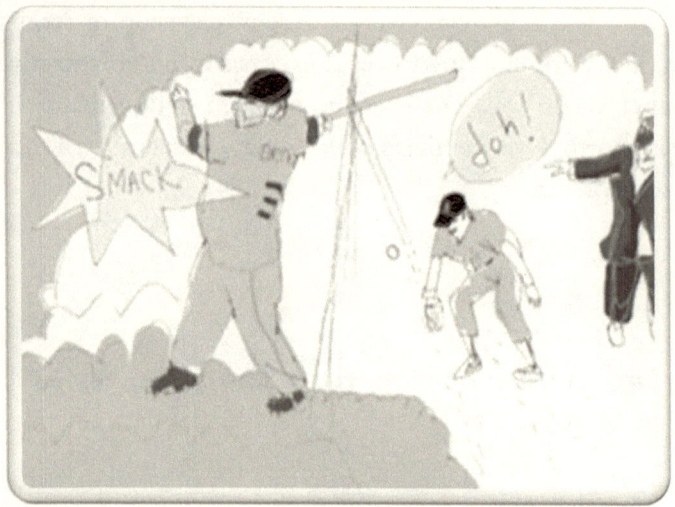

Borders: *The Partridge Family* will not die out until my generation of girls who grew up in the seventies dies out, or until Danny Bonaduce stops doing reality shows (whichever comes first). I wish I could say that the *Partridge Family*'s music would endure, that "I Think I Love You" is a classic rock song on the order of "Thunder Road" or "Smells Like Teen Spirit," but, well, it's not even "My Sharona."

Flook: I, like millions of white kids across America, had to make a choice to leave behind the past; for some it was the Beach Boys and the Association, but for me it was a lifetime of Vanguard recordings. At the Folk Festival, my sister wanted to go to the Pete Seeger hootenanny that ran at the same time Janis was supposed to perform in another arena, but for me and the Kent State boys it was Janis or bust! In truth, I hate Janis Joplin, but there was this incredible feeling that her unpleasant screeching was directly aimed at people's parents and at Nixon.

Nelson: As for why it's remained so current: it was the beginning of deep and proven suspicion concerning our government. What glee my parents expressed, hearing Nixon hang himself, again and again and again. Since then, every major news event that features shameful government behavior has been labeled *Whatevergate*. It's like people who decide they are shopaholics or chocoholics, since alcohol got the whole thing rolling.

Strauss: Not sure it's had much longevity; isn't that the thing about Pop culture — it's disposability? This album, which seemed indispensable, is almost never listened to anymore. Not by me, at least. Except for "Wanna Be Startin' Somethin,'" which — with its cool Funkadelic and Manu Dibango rip-offs — is a great compendium of funky tropes.

- What pop culture event do you think precedes it?

Baggott: If I had to really choose the most important SPORTS pop culture event, it couldn't really be that Red Sox game. It would have to be the Miracle Game — the Olympic gold medal game of the US versus USSR in 1980, mid Iranian Hostage Crisis.

Borders: I've read that *The Partridge Family* was loosely modeled on the '60s band the *Cowsills*, none of whom rocked their bell bottoms quite the way David Cassidy did. *The Monkees'* TV show (which was itself a rip-off of the Beatles' *A Hard Days' Night*) was probably the most direct television predecessor. And I liked the *Monkees*, especially the shots with their surfboards in the opening credits, but the *Monkees* were missing the *Partridges'* secret weapon: David Cassidy.

Flook: Dylan's first electric appearance at the Folk Festival.

Nelson: The event that precedes Watergate, in my mind anyway, is JFK's assassination. The two events, a decade apart, couldn't be more different in tone. The nation couldn't have responded more oppositely: one was the end of innocence, the other was the beginning of cynicism. They seem like two sides of a single coin, defining events in the center of the century.

Strauss: At the time, people were saying Elvis and the Beatles; nowadays, it seems clear that those musicians had a more lasting impact than MJ did. Not sure there was ever a pop artist who was so huge and then basically went forgotten: Bing Crosby, maybe?

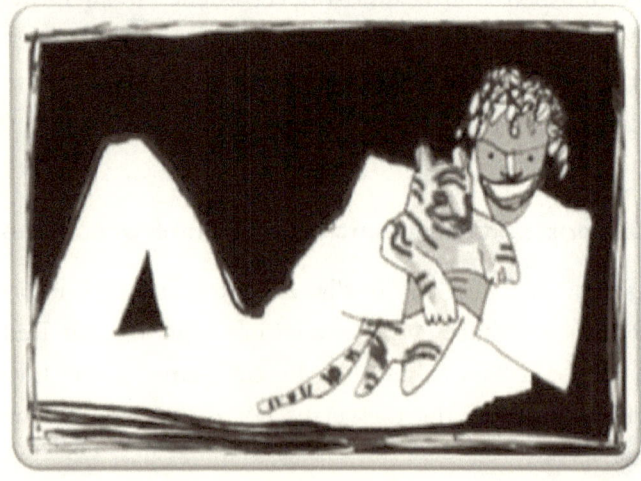

- What more would you like to know about the event?

<u>Borders</u>: Where do I begin?

As a child, I always wanted to know how Suzanne Crough landed the role of Tracy; she hit that tambourine like she was on valium, her mouth hanging open and never, never on the beat, and I knew even at age seven that I could have done better. I'd like to know what happened to Simone, the dog who was the Partridges' pet for one season and then mysteriously, inexplicably vanished (much like Tiger from the *Brady Bunch*). I'd also like to know if Susan Dey really did turn orange from eating so many carrots in an anorexic quest for extreme thinness, as urban legend and at least one behind-the-scenes, made-for-TV movie have asserted. Finally, I'd like to know if David Cassidy remembers as I do that concert at the Garden State Arts Center in 1971, the little girl in the purple dress with front row seats who nearly went catatonic when he took the stage in his white fringe jumpsuit, a little girl who must have looked so wigged that he actually uttered into the mike, *"Little girl in the purple dress, are you alright?"*

That little girl would never be alright again, for she was from that moment on conditioned to pretty much only be attracted to guys with guitars (the white fringe jumpsuits, not so much).

<u>Flook</u>: My sister went back to East Lansing, but I'd love to know what happened to the hitchhikers we spent three days with. Are they bankers? Walmart executives? or like me, did they choose literature or art, and like me, did they become totally "bent" and try to live up to their potential. Although, thanks to the retainer, my teeth are beautifully straight.

Nelson: I feel like I don't ever want to know anymore about Watergate, but it keeps being delivered, unsolicited, to me. There's always some new information, extra tapes, more footage, etcetera. Maybe Watergate was also the beginning of TMI.

Strauss: Why I spent all my money on a leather/mesh-combo jacket and flood-water pants, and why I wasted the Summer of 1984 trying to perfect my frontward moonwalk.

Episode 8: *Family Myth*
with Allison Lynn, Joshua Neuman,
Thisbe Nissen, Dan Pope,
and Rachel Sherman

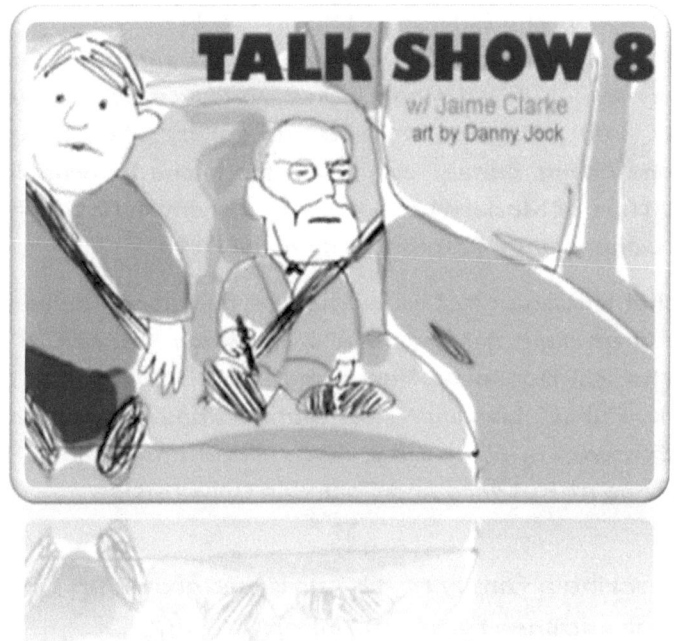

Allison Lynn is the author of the novels *Now You See It* and *The Exiles*. Her essays and book reviews have appeared in the *New York Times Book Review*, the *Chicago Sun-Times*, *People*, *Redbook*, *In Style* and others. She teaches at Butler University.

Joshua Neuman is the author of *The Big Book of Jewish Conspiracies*. He has written for *Slate*, *BlackBook* and ESPN and appeared on VH1, A & E and National Public Radio. Neuman is the Head of Programming and Editorial Director at GOOD Inc and has served as Publisher and Editor of *Heeb Magazine*.

Talk Show

Thisbe Nissen is the author of *Osprey Island*, *The Good People of New York*, *Out of the Girls' Room and into the Night*, and co-author/illustrator of *The Ex-Boyfriend Cookbook*. She was a James Michener fellow and teaches at Western Michigan University.

Dan Pope is the author of the novels *In the Cherry Tree* and *Housebreaking*. His stories have been published in *Crazyhorse*, *Post Road*, *Iowa Review*, *McSweeney's*, *Gettysburg Review*, *Witness*, and others. He is a winner of the Glenn Schaeffer Award from the International Institute of Modern Letters, and a grant in fiction from the Connecticut Commission on the Arts.

Rachel Sherman is the author of the story collection *The First Hurt* and the novel *Living Room*, chosen as one of the 25 Books to Remember of 2006 by the New York Public Library. Her fiction has appeared in *McSweeney's*, *Open City*, *Post Road* and others. She teaches at Rutgers and Columbia Universities.

* * *

- Describe a family myth that has grown up around you or another family member.

Lynn: My late grandmother, Sophie, claimed that she and my grandfather taught Bette Midler's parents to have sex. As my grandmother told it, they were all friends back in the 1930s in New Jersey — the kind of friends who would drive around together at night, the guys in the front seat talking shop, the girls in the back singing the latest hits and bopping their heads to the beat. Then, the Midlers got married, came back from the honeymoon and fessed up that they hadn't consummated their love. Because *they didn't know how.* This is where the suspension of disbelief kicks in. According to my grandmother, she took Bette's mother into one room, while my grandfather took her father into another, and they explained how to do it.

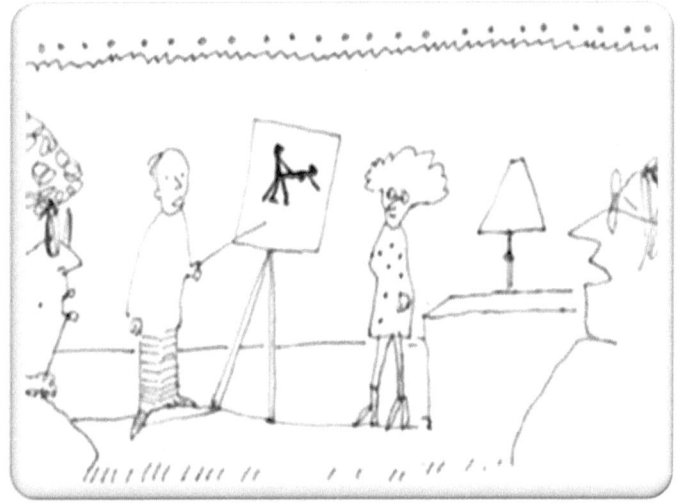

Neuman: There are people who constantly compare life to Seinfeld. Then, there is our family who has gone one step further, constantly likening Seinfeld's life to ours. We do not trace our roots to the Mayflower or to European nobility, but we do think of ourselves belonging to Seinfeld stock.

Nissen: The story, as my mother tells, goes like this: when I was little we got a cat. We hadn't had her too long when my mother came to tuck me in one night and to have a serious talk. My father, it was becoming clear, was allergic to the cat. He was having trouble breathing, sleeping, etcetera, and we were going to have to do something. It was all very sad, but Daddy and the cat just couldn't live together in the same house. I looked up at my mother earnestly from bed, eyes wide, and said: *"But where will Daddy go?"*

Pope: Around the turn of the last century, Colonel Albert Augustus Pope was Hartford's major industrialist. He founded the Columbia Bicycle Company, which manufactured about a quarter million bicycles annually in the mid-1890s, earning himself a fortune. A few years later, Colonel Pope diversified into automobile production with the Pope Motor Carriage. In 1895, he donated Pope Park to the City of Hartford for the use of his employees and city residents, a lovely piece of earth landscaped by the Olmsted Brothers. I grew up in Hartford in the 1970s, when the city still bore the legacy of this industrial giant in communal memory, and the myth in my family is that we are descendants of this Pope.

Sherman: We believed that my family was normal because we were all in therapy. We believed that families that were not in therapy were not normal. We were not in therapy together; we each went individually. But, we believed, each of our "therapies" worked to help the family at large.

- What was the genesis of this myth?

Lynn: Well, who knows, maybe it's true. If not, the genesis was completely my grandmother's imagination. She considered herself the family storyteller, and had a tendency to tell tales that just slightly romanticized her role in all sorts of situations. At the time of her death in 2004, she was writing these tales down for posterity. It's not entirely clear who she thought might be interested. Other than Bette Midler.

Neuman: It started when my mother and I saw a young comic named Jerry Seinfeld perform on *The Tonight Show with Johnny Carson*. I was probably around ten years old at the time. My mother was named after her maternal grandmother, Jennie Seinfeld, who lived from 1890-1943. The Seinfelds, my mother told me, were originally from Poland (present day Ukraine) where their last name was Stanislavaw. She wondered whether the wise-cracking comic joking about missing socks and the cereal aisle of the supermarket was related to us. Phone calls were made. Shoe boxes of old photos were excavated from attics. Family trees were drawn up. In anticipation of tracing a straight line between us and comic aristocracy, my mother let me stay up late when Jerry made his first appearance on *Late Night With David Letterman*. We taped Jerry's first HBO special and watched it over and over again. Soon after, we learned that our suspicions were correct: Jerry was one of us.

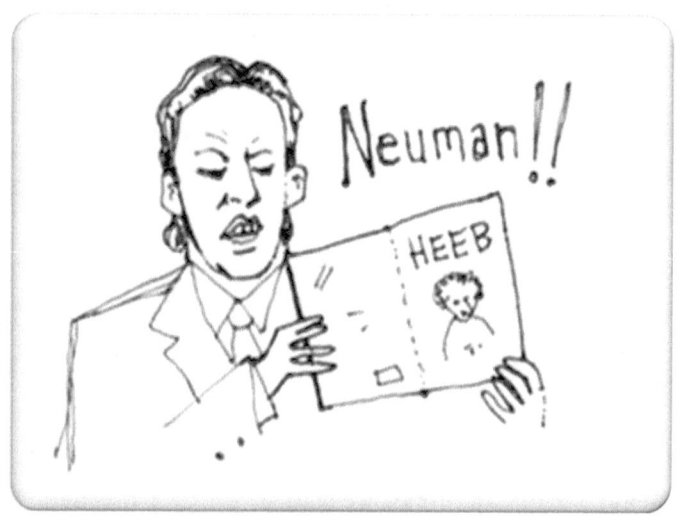

Nissen: Like many small children, I'd really wanted a pet, and a cat was the only reasonable pet to have, living, as we did, in New York City. (This because the only reasonable kinds of pets to have at all, according to my parents, were cats and dogs, and though my mother claimed to really be a dog person, not a cat person, keeping a dog in the city was cruel.) The problem was that my dad was ostensibly allergic to cats. (I say ostensibly because we'd never actually seen him around a cat, but he claimed to be allergic.) He also professed an allergy to Golden-rod, which always struck me as too specific to be legitimate. He also once told me that his favorite color was yellow, which I found out years (and many yellow Fathers' Day tie presents) later was something he'd just said so I'd stop asking him what his favorite color was. But we had some friends who had a cat named Pushkin who was a fancy breed of cat called a Korat —

a short-hair, all gray, from Thailand — who was supposed to be hypoallergenic somehow. We had Pushkin come stay with us for a weekend, and my dad seemed fine, so it was settled that we too would get a Korat.

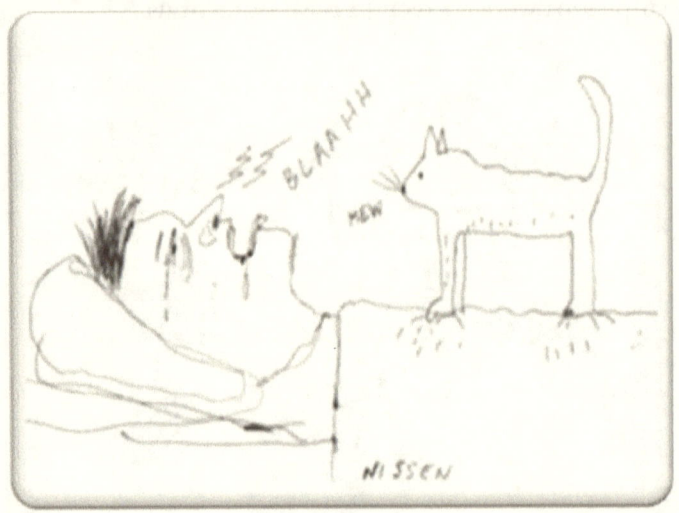

Being a fancy-bred cat, we had to go to a breeder, so we drove to some crazy cat-woman's house somewhere outside the city where she bred Korats for showing. It was Christmas time, and she had a tree up in her living room, and a million gray cats running all over the place. These cats were full-breed Korats, and they were seriously expensive, but there were two cats from a recent litter who had defects and were going for cheap. One had a white spot on her chest; that was her championship-disqualifying imperfection. She also had a cold and sneezed a lot. It was pretty cute. I thought the white freckle was cute too. Plus she'd been the runt of the litter, so she was tiny. As we watched the cat zip around the breeder's living room we came to identify her as Sneezy. About the other cat-show-reject Korat I don't recall any physical flaws, but I remember him as a gremlin of a cat, a hyperactive monster-child, a maniac in kitten's clothing. By the end of the evening he'd eaten a box of tinsel and knocked over the Christmas tree. We called him Beastie.

Perhaps it's needless to say that it was Sneezy we brought home with us that night. She got over her cold, but the sneezing continued, and her name stuck. The irony? She made my dad sneeze too.

Pope: My father, Donald Pope, referred to Colonel Pope and his descendants in the Hartford area as the money Popes, and whenever an opportunity arose in public, my father let it be known that we — my brother, sister and I — were Money Popes. My father relished the deference afforded to him by others who thought him rich and powerful, and I once heard him tell a car mechanic, in the middle of some minor dispute, Do you know who I am? *I'm Don Pope.*

Sherman: The genesis is a person. Her name is Mom. She is a Freudian psychoanalyst. The genesis is also four individual therapists, all working outside the home, unknown to one another, but existing inside our house in the forms of two parents, two children.

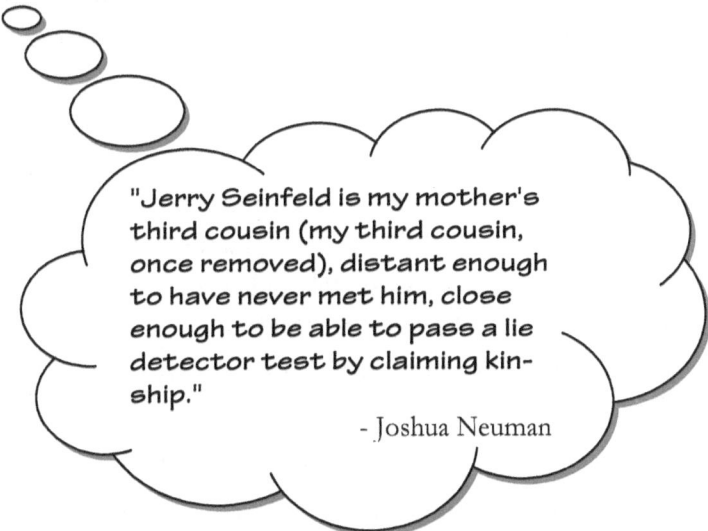

"Jerry Seinfeld is my mother's third cousin (my third cousin, once removed), distant enough to have never met him, close enough to be able to pass a lie detector test by claiming kinship."

- Joshua Neuman

– What kernels of truth are buried in the myth?

Lynn: Well, Fred and Ruth Midler did live in Paterson, New Jersey during the 1930s. Apparently my grandmother once had a slew of pictures of she and my grandfather hanging out with Bette's parents. But sometime after both Fred and Ruth (whom my grandmother hadn't spoken to in probably forty years) both passed away, my grandmother packaged up the pictures and sent them to the Divine Miss M, via her management, since she thought Bette would like to have them. To my grandmother's chagrin, Bette never wrote a thank you note. Bupkis.

Neuman: Jerry Seinfeld is my mother's third cousin (my third cousin, once removed), distant enough to have never met him, close enough to be able to pass a lie detector test by claiming kinship. My mother distinctly remembers the story of her grandmother's first cousin Sam Seinfeld (Jerry's grandfather) visiting her apartment in the Bronx when she was an infant. Apparently, Sam showed up with a bad cold, which upset my over-protective grandparents. The story was soon canonized in the annals of family hypochondria (lodged somewhere between the time my brother's friend Jeff threw up in our recreation room and when my mother discovered where I was secretly stashing the Wash N Dries she routinely placed in my brown lunch bag before school). To this day, my mother has never met Jerry Seinfeld, though she suspects that they were both named after Jennie Seinfeld (who was apparently very close to Sam). I haven't met Jerry Seinfeld either, though I do recall receiving several checks from Seinfelds at my bar mitzvah (one from Joe Seinfeld from Montreal, an eighty-year-old "bachelor" and magician).

Nissen: My mom is a former actress, and a big storyteller, and a generally dramatic human being. When she tells a story, truth is not, shall we say, her first priority. It's about drama. Truth she's willing to sacrifice for the sake of the story. (And we wonder how I become a fiction writer!) There is, in fact, a great deal of fact in her story of Daddy and Sneezy. Up until a point.

Pope: The myth is a total lie. In fact, we were not descendants of Colonel Pope. My father was born Dominic Roberto Papa, the son of Carlo Angelo Papa, a poor Italian who immigrated to this country in 1898. Soon after my father graduated high school, he legally changed his name, Americanizing it, to the WASP-ish Donald Robert Pope. (Papa means Pope in Italian, so the change came naturally.) He liked that his initials, DR, would make some think he was a medical doctor (he was, in fact, a general contractor). Perhaps this change of identity provided my father with a buffer against any anti-Italian sentiment of the times circa the 1940s, when during wartime Italian-Americans were required to register with the FBI and some Italian families were even relocated to internment camps. But, mainly, my father had a waggish quality, and he liked fooling people and being considered a big-shot.

Sherman: That therapy is probably good for some people, but not for every person; that being in therapy might help you read other people, but that it might not be the best thing to help you know yourself; that if your mom is a therapist, then you probably need therapy anyway; that if you are in a family, trying to work within your family, you should probably just move out; that therapy can reach a saturation point.

- How has the myth evolved over the years?

Lynn: In 1987, Bette had a daughter, and named her Sophie. My grandmother used to say that Bette might have named the girl after her. I can't imagine any woman doing this: naming her child after the woman who taught her parents to have sex.

Neuman: When Jerry Seinfeld became a national icon, my family started referring to him as "Cousin Jerry." We started wildly speculating that the character Newman was an allusion to us (even though my father's side spells its name "Neuman" and has absolutely no relationship with any Seinfelds). When I became the editor of *Heeb Magazine*, my grandparents gloated that both Jerry and I had made it in "show-biz." Apparently, my mother's cousin Stewie from Huntington, Long Island (an arms dealer at the time) attended one of Jerry's performances in the Catskills to introduce himself and officially welcome him to the larger family. Unfortunately, he was unable to get a word with Jerry after the show.

Nissen: I feel like the story gets shorter every time she tells it. The listener doesn't have time to think before she's there with the punch line and everyone's laughing and I'm the one standing there saying *"But wait a second . . . !"*

Pope: The myth was passed down to my brother, sister and me, and we permitted its dissemination. It was easy to pretend that we, the children of D.R. Pope, were inheritors of old-WASP wealth. We looked generically American in appearance, if a tad swarthy, and we lived in one of the better neighborhoods of West Hartford, an affluent suburb of the now-downtrodden city. I spent my high school years at prep school in West Hartford, the Kingswood-Oxford School, whose most famous graduate was Katherine Hepburn. My classmates were well-off suburban kids like me, with a few scholarship students tossed into the mix. We were required to wear blue blazers and gray slacks (except on Fridays). In school, I did not actively perpetuate the myth of my false heritage, but somehow the myth grew anyway. I let this happen because it afforded me social status among some of my classmates, these sons and daughters of doctors and lawyers, politicians and judges.

Sherman: We have all been in and out of therapy. I attempted to break the cycle at certain times, but have not fully succeeded. Other people in the family have not evolved. My myth is still their truth.

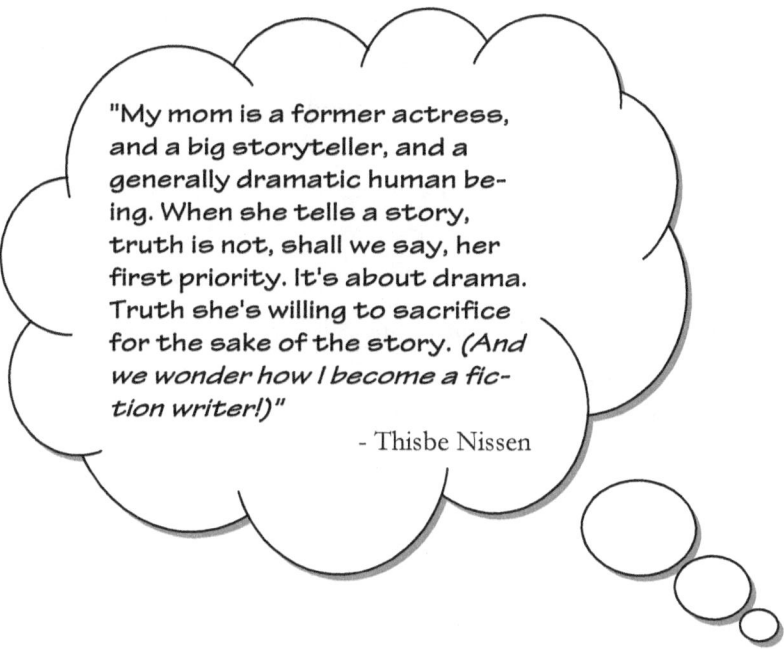

"My mom is a former actress, and a big storyteller, and a generally dramatic human being. When she tells a story, truth is not, shall we say, her first priority. It's about drama. Truth she's willing to sacrifice for the sake of the story. (And we wonder how I become a fiction writer!)"

- Thisbe Nissen

- Which part of the myth is a blatant untruth?

Lynn: Well, the naming bit. I mean, my grandmother seemed not to notice that Sophie, as a name, was quickly coming back into vogue in the late '80s. The name has become so ubiquitous that it would have been shocking if Bette had named her child anything *but* Sophie. As for the rest of the myth, it's curious that my grandfather, who outlived my grandmother by a year, always kept oddly silent when she told this story (which was often). After she died would have been the time to get his side of things, but I never asked. Honestly, I loved my grandfather, but the idea of talking sex (even Midler sex) with him seemed pretty unappealing.

Neuman: At one point, an apocryphal feud was posited between the "Newmans" and the Seinfelds, perhaps as a result of Sam Seinfeld coming to my grandparents' (whose last name was not even "Neuman," but Speigel) apartment with a bad cold. I guess the idea was that somehow Sam felt so rejected that he passed it along to his son Kalman, who passed it along to his son, Jerry, who somehow found out that his third cousin Janet had married someone with the last name of "Neuman." As the illogic goes, he then avenged his grandfather's hurt feelings by having America forever associate our last name with the hideous character portrayed by Wayne Knight.

Nissen: Look, I'm not going to call my mother a liar. (Can I call her a blatant un-truther? Maybe . . .) Let's just say that I find it very very difficult to imagine that I had such a fabulous, story-ready response at the time. My memory of that night when I ostensibly spoke my great one-liner is very vague — and probably really only a construction compiled from the retellings of the story — but I feel like I either recall, or have extrapolated from the context, that I was confused by what my mother was trying to tell me, talking in circles about Daddy and Sneezy, hedging her point, waiting for me to catch on. It was bedtime; certainly I was tired. I was a child! I'll concede this much: it's possible my eyes were wide. It's possible I seemed confused. It's possible I really didn't catch what she was trying to get at. I'd even say it's possible that I was trying to read between the lines and what I thought, or feared, she was trying to tell me was that Mommy and Daddy were getting divorced, and she was couching the whole thing in some mishigas about cat allergies, hoping I'd think Daddy was leaving because of Sneezy, not because of Mommy.

As it turned out, no one was leaving. Not Daddy, and not Sneezy either. Daddy seemed inclined to stick it out, (though he never did have much of a relationship with Snee, who remained a sneezer all her life, and for much of it was a big barfer too. Those full-breeds — not the strongest constitutions . . .) and Dad's allergy (of which I, for the record, have no tangible recollection) just seemed to dissipate after a while. Sneezy lived and sneezed and vomited expensive cat food for many many years. And was then replaced by Clementine, until she passed on, and then by Albert, who was the feline love of my mother's life but who lived only six months longer than my father in the end. They both died last year, and my mom's alone now. They may have gotten Sneezy for me all those years ago, but she was always my mother's cat. She never has had a dog. Nor will she, I don't think, have another husband. But she'll have another cat. Of this I am sure. And she'll continue to tell the story of that night in my childhood when I was ready to trade my father for a defective Korat who probably had more allergies than my father did! I never saw him sneeze . . .

Pope: The entire myth was a blatant lie, but it was easy to fool everyone. People assumed I was a descendant of the Popes of Hartford because of my aunts' mansion.

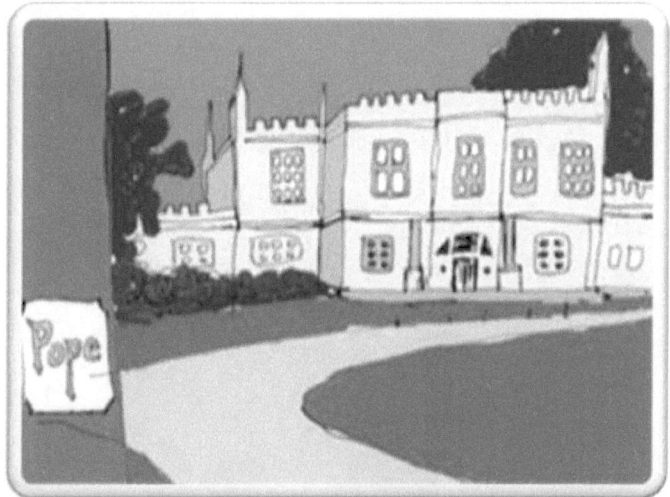

My grandfather, a stonemason who worked tirelessly his whole life, saving his dollars with a Depression-era thriftiness, in his later years purchased an enormous Tudor mansion on Prospect Hill, the premier neighborhood in Hartford, where the descendants of the old-rich did, in fact, reside in a row of outsized, Gilded Age architectural wonders overlooking the city of Hartford, culminating in the Governor's Mansion, the last house on the street. Next door to my grandfather's house was an 18th century brick mansion, which had once been an inn where George Washington stayed the night.

After my grandfather died, my four spinster aunts remained in the mansion, with the name POPE proudly displayed on the mailbox beyond the outlying gates for all to see.

Sherman: That therapy is a lifestyle choice.

Episode 9: *Places You Would Never Visit* with Jami Attenberg, Adam Braver, Nina de Gramont, Ann Hood, and Moon Unit Zappa

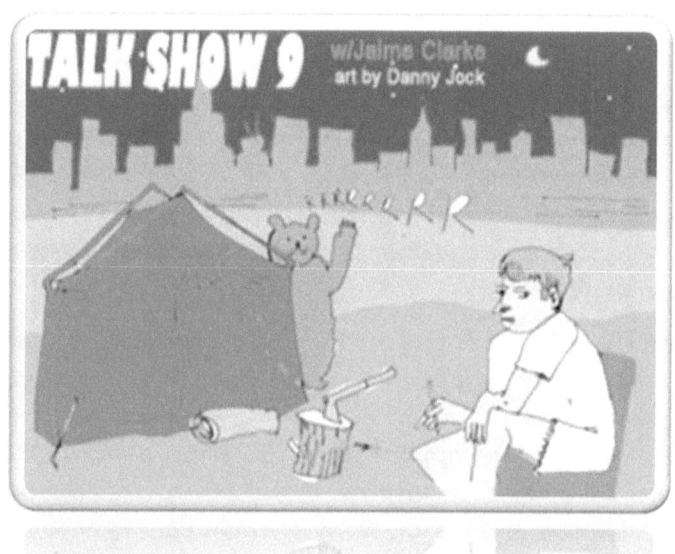

Jami Attenberg is the author of the story collection *Instant Love,* and the novels *The Kept Man, The Melting Season* and *The Middlesteins.* She has written for *Jane, Print, Nerve, Nylon, Salon,* the *San Francisco Chronicle* and others and is the fiction editor of *Maura Magazine.*

Adam Braver is the author of *Mr. Lincoln's Wars, Divine Sarah, Crows Over the Wheatfield, Misfit* and *November 22, 1963.* His work has appeared in *Daedalus, Ontario Review, Cimarron Review, Water-Stone Review, West Branch,* and *Post Road.* He teaches at Roger Williams University and is a writer-in-residence at the New York State Summer Writers Institute.

Nina de Gramont is the author of a short story collection, *Of Cats and Men*, a novel, *Gossip of the Starlings* and the YA titles *Every Little Thing in the World* and *Meet Me at the River*. She is co-editor of the anthology *Choice*. Her work has appeared in *Isotope, Nerve, Post Road, Seventeen, Harvard Review* and others.

Ann Hood is the author of several novels including *The Obituary Writer, The Red Thread, The Knitting Circle* and *Somewhere off the Coast of Maine*. She has also published a short story collection, *An Ornithologist's Guide to Life,* and the memoirs, *Do Not Go Gentle: My Search for Miracles in a Cynical Time* and *Comfort: A Journey through Grief.*

Moon Unit Zappa is the author of the novel *America the Beautiful.* Her work has been published in *Details, Harper's Bazaar* and the *New York Times* As an actress, Zappa has appeared in the films *National Lampoon's European Vacation* and the *Spirit of '76*, as well the television shows *Curb Your Enthusiasm, How I Met Your Mother, Roseanne, Grey's Anatomy* and others.

* * *

- Name a place you have no interest in visiting and why.

Attenberg: Thailand. First off it's a super long flight. I know everyone says just take a sleeping pill and you'll be fine, but I will NOT be fine. I can barely make it on a flight to the west coast without losing it. And I know a great deal of their economy is dependent on the tourist industry and that kind of environment usually does not appeal to me. I think the child prostitution problem there might depress the hell out of me as well.

Braver: Anywhere that involves camping and the outdoors — more specifically, I never want to be anywhere that isn't within about thirty minutes of a metropolitan area. And by thirty minutes, I mean thirty minutes by car (although I suppose there could be an exception made if an emergency services vehicle could be on the scene during that same thirty minute window).

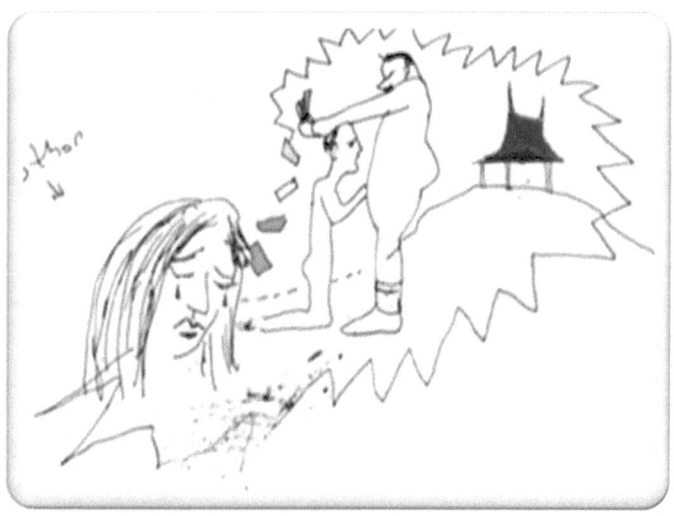

de Gramont: Israel. It's not that I have no interest in visiting Israel. How could I not want to visit Israel? I would dearly love to see Bethlehem, and Jerusalem, and pay my respects at Yad Vashem. I would love to spend a summer on a kibbutz; I see myself in a garden, wearing a kerchief, living off the earth in strength and cooperation with others. But every time I look at a map of the Middle East I see Israel — this teeny tiny country surrounded by enormous countries that hate it. The only protection is its fierce, well-organized army and its far away big brother, the U.S. Looking at a map of the Middle East makes me sad, and makes me think: I would never, ever go to Israel.

Hood: The night I met my future husband Lorne, he tried to impress me by describing his trekking in Nepal. After I listened to descriptions of the freezing temperatures, bad food, altitude sickness, stomach problems, and dirty accommodations, I said:

"If that's your idea of fun, this will never work out."

He then tried to tell me how easy it was, how beautiful the views were, how exhilarating an experience it was. But here's the truth, I don't hike, trek, or climb. Anything. Anywhere. I am so afraid of heights that I can't even climb the stairs in the Eiffel Tower. I admire Italy's Duomos from the piazzas below. I don't mind rough travel, or exotic travel. In fact, I love exploring Cambodia, Peru, China, anywhere that does not require special equipment or extra oxygen. Since that night sixteen years ago, Lorne has climbed mountains in Africa, Russia, Japan, and Chile. Alone. Each time he invites me along and each time I say no. He has tried to convince me to go by talking about stopovers in Moscow or a Kenyan safari.

Zappa: I have several places I have no interest in ever visiting — India, Mexico, anywhere by car, plane or sea, a bad guy's lair, twister alley, anywhere flat, anywhere too switch-backy, jail, any courtroom where I would have to testify, and my in-laws'. But I think I'll go with outer space as my top travel destination to avoid. Mainly because you'd be solely at the mercy of the government. The irony of that much space and no privacy. Nothing of comfort, nothing of any aesthetic value (besides a landscape you can't really interact with without a mechanical device and an audience). Plus you'd wear diapers and asteroid/atmospheric turbulence seems like a motherfucker.

- What are your preconceptions about this place?

Attenberg: Beautiful beaches, decadence, and wandering souls. There are all those stories about sweet young English women visiting Thailand and getting caught smuggling heroin in their private areas because some hot guy told them to, and then being sent to jail for five hundred years. Also, I feel like it's the kind of place where you would be sitting on a beach having a peaceful moment and then some vaguely European dude named Corazon with white guy dreadlocks and scabs on his arms would come up and want to talk about living off the earth and then try to sell you weed. Basically my fear is that I would end up meeting annoying travelers who are living there because it's so cheap and I would have to pretend I liked them when I didn't.

Braver: It seems to me that there will be an almost crazy inherent need to adapt to some model of survival living. For example, in terms of medical emergencies, I have very little interest in the First Aid kit — particularly the wilderness version that has the snake bite kit. Besides having no desire to see a snake (especially a biting snake), I have even less interest in making small incisions into a friend's leg, and orally vacuuming out venom in tandem with a gray rubber suction cup. My preconception is that one will get caught up in the gestalt of the survival experience, when, for example, a hospital would seem much more practical and wise.

de Gramont: That it's dry and dusty, and filled with the most sacred and magical history. That I would be welcomed as a citizen because my mother is Jewish, and that there would be terrorists around every corner wanting to kill me.

Hood: The aforementioned freezing temperatures, bad food, altitude sickness, stomach problems, and dirty accommodations.

Zappa: That we've never really been there and if we have, all we do is put missiles and spy satellites in space aimed at the rest of the places on the planet right wing Republicans want to control and/or make money from. Yunno, Big Brother HQ.

- What would it take to convince you to visit?

<u>Attenberg</u>: I would go if Anthony Bourdain would come with me and take me on one of his magical food tours. Whenever I visit a new city and am hungry I always ask myself, "What would Tony do?"

<u>Braver</u>: I think it would take a well-crafted, very convincing lie. Maybe something about the harmony of nature. Or the freeing experience of the mind. Or maybe that we're going to Paris.

<u>de Gramont</u>: The Jews and the Arabs would realize that they are the same people, and they would make peace with each other. The bombings would stop, the PLO would disband, and Palestinians and Israelis would be happily living in the same neighborhoods, and working together on that kibbutz.

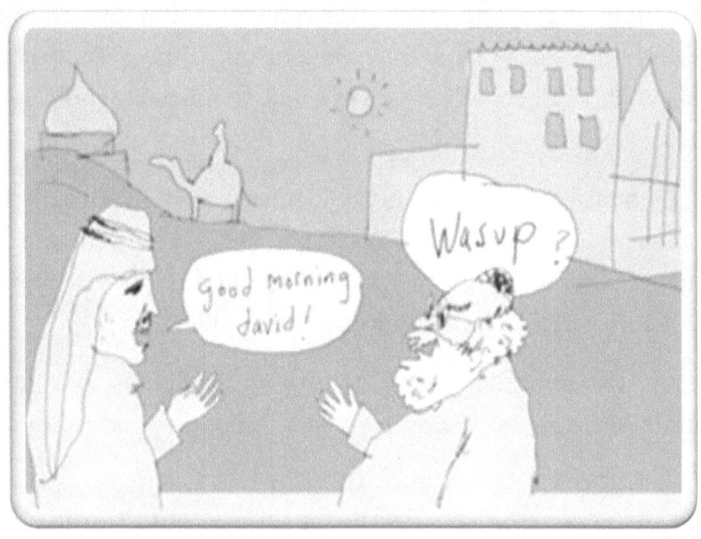

<u>Hood</u>: I can't think of anything that would get me on a mountain top.

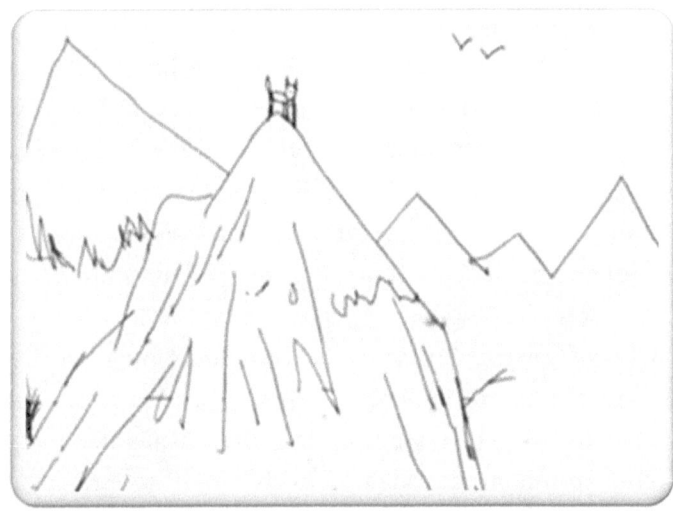

Zappa: If my family could come with me I'd go. Anywhere our daughter Mathilda is is where I'm always happy to be. I'd need some great books, internet access, freeze-dried earl grey tea with milk and two sugars, a kickass sound system with my favorite music, plus the shows I'd be missing on DVD and a lotta Xanax for the ride up and back.

- What do you imagine would happen if you did visit?

Attenberg: My boyfriend went there last year to work on a documentary where they brought Katrina survivors to meet tsunami survivors. He hung out with lots of amazing Thai people and would go to these small fishing villages where he and his group would be greeted by songs and feasts. It was really a beautiful and important experience for him. But I always attract the Euro hippies, no matter what I do, so I would probably not have the same experience.

Braver: I'm almost certain that I would never sleep. During the day, I might believe the lie that got me there, convincing myself how fortunate I am to be in nature, intellectualizing a rationale about simpler times where all one had was the land, the solitude of spending my days among lakes and trees without the confines of the modern world. And for the most part I suspect that could be true. But night would be a different story. Never mind the blow-up mattresses that lose their air by the middle of the night. Or negotiating the cold air with the inferno heat of the sleeping bag (*or just the sleeping bag!*).

Mostly, I imagine laying awake all night, hoping that I don't have to go the bathroom, because should I need to go, it would mean having to get dressed, finding the flashlight, unzipping the tent, stumbling through a pitch black forest, stealthily avoiding hungry bears, walking in a way where every footstep sounds as though it echoes throughout the entire woods, before getting to a flickeringly fluorescent bathroom where the urinal cakes smell of piss, where there are shivering snakes in the stalls, or, where leaned up against the sink and staring at the ceiling, is a man who is contemplating leaving his family.

de Gramont: I imagine that I would die or witness some terrible, life-altering violence. Or else I would just be worrying about that happening every minute. When I hear about people bringing their children to Israel I think they must be crazy. It may very well be the last place on earth I would ever bring my child, which is sad, because I'd love for her to see it. I'd love to see it myself.

Hood: Katmandu sounds exotic, even exciting. But I imagine that if I went to Nepal and trekked, I would fall from the Himalayas to my death. No. I don't *imagine* that would happen. I'm *certain* it would happen.

Zappa: That once I was debriefed, I'd be on every talk show and asked A LOT of questions I couldn't answer truthfully, to the point I'd be more famous than the sun, more famous than Posh and Beckham even, but as internally conflicted as the Middle East. At that point, at least I'd be known as an ambassador — no, better — emissary of Earth and I could retire on the spin-off merchandise, bio pics, and endorsements.

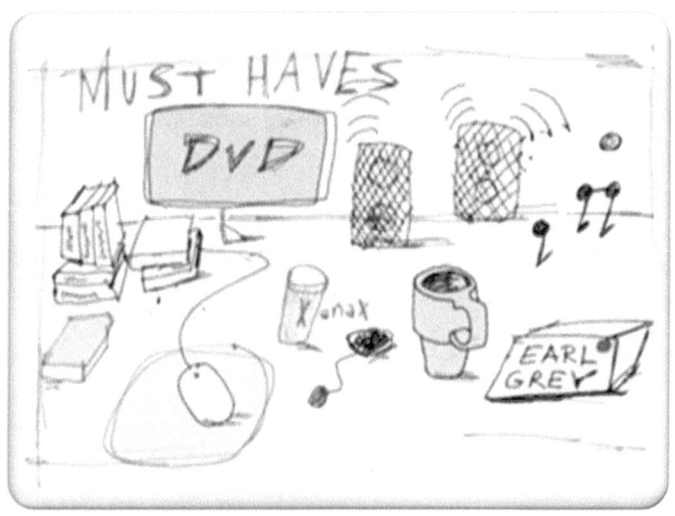

- What advice would you give this place to attract people like you as tourists?

Attenberg: I probably should be their target demographic already. A lot of my friends have gone and rented a hut on a beach for, like, a nickel, and totally loved it. The Thailand tourism folks are doing everything right. It's just my problem.

Braver: My first instinct is to make a laundry list that includes getting rid of the bugs and the creepy reptiles, installing an emergency response system, perhaps building a hospital, a bakery with fresh bread would be nice — although I'd settle for a place that served a good cup of coffee before 8 a.m., access to a bathtub, a little noise — but not the noise of generators and battery-powered TVs and Winnebagos, maybe a few less ghost stories, food not cooked and eaten off sticks, and, and . . . I could keep on with the list, but I realize I'm only making the outdoors into my home, and if the outdoors is my home, then there are no outdoors for me to escape to. Even if I never want to go there.

de Gramont: Peace. Peace. Peace.

Hood: I suppose the Nepal tourist bureau could get me there for a trek if they announced that, inexplicably, Nepal had dropped 15,000 feet and it was now possible to visit Katmandu and trek in its lovely valleys.

Zappa: Downplay the re-entry turbulence and mechanical defects. More footage of the fun to be had with gravity.

Episode 10: *Worst Job*
with Christopher Boucher, Brock Clarke, Elizabeth Gaffney, Felicia Sullivan, and Jen Trynin

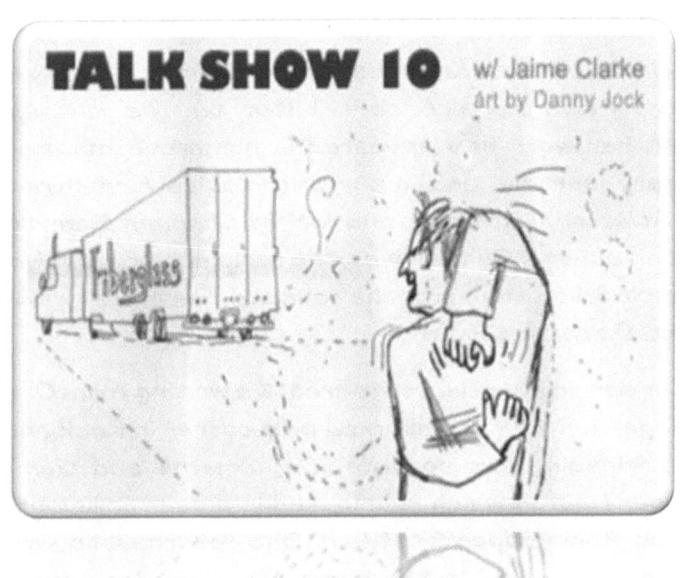

TALK SHOW 10 w/ Jaime Clarke
art by Danny Jock

Christopher Boucher is the author of the novel *How to Keep Your Volkswagen Alive*. He teaches writing and literature at Boston College where he is also the Managing Editor of *Post Road Magazine*. In his free time, Boucher plays banjo in a bluegrass band.

Brock Clarke's fiction includes the novels *An Arsonist's Guide to Writers' Homes in New England*, *The Ordinary White Boy* and *Exley*, and the story collections *Carrying the Torch* and *What We Won't Do*. He teaches creative writing at Bowdoin College.

Talk Show

Elizabeth Gaffney is the author of the novels *Metropolis* and *When the World Was Young*. She was an editor at the *Paris Review* and *A Public Space* and has translated three books from German. Her work has appeared in *Epiphany*, the *Colorado Review*, the *North American Review* and others. Gaffney teaches at the New School.

Felicia Sullivan is the author of the memoir *The Sky Isn't Visible From Here*. A contributor to *The Huffington Post*, her work has appeared in numerous magazines, literary journals, and in the anthologies *Homewrecker: An Atlas of Illicit Loves* and *Money Changes Everything*, among others. Sullivan was the recipient of a *Tin House* memoir fellowship, and she founded the literary journal *Small Spiral Notebook*.

After earning her degree in creative writing from Oberlin College, Jen Trynin embarked on a career in Rock and/or Roll, releasing two records (*Cockamamie* and *Gun Shy Trigger Happy*) which culminated in a near collision with full-on Rock Super Stardom. She returned to writing prose and played in the band, *Loveless*. Jen's memoir, *Everything I'm Cracked Up to Be: A Rock & Roll Fairy Tale*, is based on her experiences in the music business.

* * *

- What was the worst job you ever had?

<u>Boucher</u>: Given my upper-middle class upbringing, I'm not sure I can gripe about my worst job. I've done my share of less-than-glamorous work — changing oil and tires at an auto repair shop, various home-renovation grinds (which often included demolition or working in insulated attics in the middle of summer, and once required me to help knock down a three-story chimney with a sledgehammer) — but my worst day on the job is very likely someone else's average day.

There is one job, though, which stands out from the rest.

My Dad has a part-time business renovating houses, some to rent out and others to flip. I began working with him in college, and my role grew more prominent with every project. When my grandfather died in late 2001, my Dad proposed that he and I buy my grandfather's house — a one-story ranch in Wilbraham, Massachusetts — and renovate it. I thought it sounded like a great idea. It would turn out to be the worst job I ever had.

Clarke: The worst job I ever had was working at a fiberglass plant, where I sanded fiberglass shells and then loaded them onto trucks and then itched and itched and itched and then did it all over again.

Gaffney: I worked cleaning instruments at a dentist's office in Munich, right around the time that the Wall came down in Germany. I had to wear a little white coat, so I looked like a hygienist or something, but I was just a foreign graduate student who couldn't find a better job. My main duties were sterilizing the instruments and cleaning the equipment in the office and a little filing. The instruments were repulsive — coated with little bits of plaque and scum. I had to put them in an antiseptic bath, scrub them, rinse them, and then run them through a giant dental dishwasher. The worst were the sharp blades they called curettes. They were like tiny scythes, and they always had shreds of flesh dangling from them. They were so sharp they would slice right through my gloves and my skin in an instant if I wasn't careful. But come to think of it, the grossest thing may have been cleaning out the molds for the dentures. The impressions of the patients' original teeth were made in a red rubbery material held in a form that fit the patient's jaw. After the dentures were made, the forms would be dropped into some sort of solvent, so there was this huge tub of viscous red chemicals that seemed like it would be perfect for use on the set of a slasher movie. I had to fish around in there to find the molds, and them scrub them out.

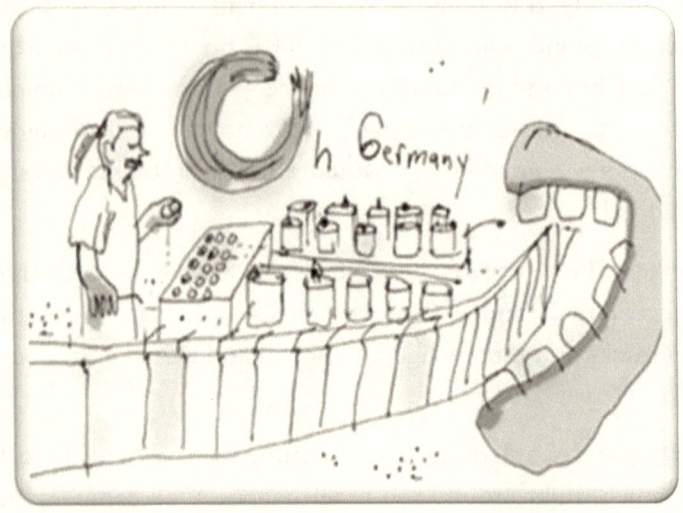

Sullivan: Two years ago I worked for six months as an Associate Editor at a children's publishing house. I was thrilled with the opportunity — who wouldn't want stuffed Strawberry Shortcakes in their cubicle? Glitter pens and a carpet printed with empowering mantras! However, all of my excitement overshadowed the fact that I was about to work for an anorexic, obsessive-compulsive control freak who managed to alienate her whole department to the point that they moved her to another floor.

She had many phobias — subways, submarines, or any means of underground transportation. She also feared sudden noises, blue ink and food. Since I had a background in finance, I was used to unhinged people; however, her behavior was borderline insane. I fell victim to her passive-aggressive tirades, sudden mood swings, her snide remarks about my lunch, and ultimately the theft of my ideas and work (after she had ridiculed my ideas in front of my coworkers). I still have nightmares about the possibility of running into her.

Trynin: It was the summer of my senior year of high school, 80's New Jersey. I was the only assistant to this guy, Phil, who, to the best of my retrospective knowledge, did two things: chiefly — and this is what I "assisted" in — Phil was a central conduit between New Jersey-area rock clubs and the myriad of local newspapers concerning the clubs' weekly gig listings. The second thing he did was less clear, but entailed much phone talking which elicited the kind of loud laughing that resulted in much spittle on the clunky old phone receiver — spittle that I was later responsible for wiping clean. He had a big belly that

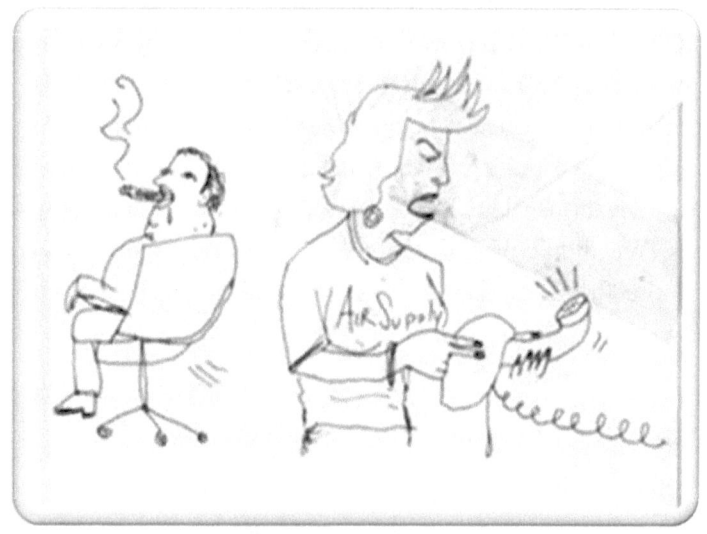

strained his stained buttondowns, dark New Jersey-coifed hair, and a heavy way of breathing what was surely his sour breath. I had my own office which was simply the maintenance closet in the small hallway that led to Phil's main office. In the closet was a small square table, a phone, Phil's Rolodex, and a dull metal rod that spanned the length of the "room" up by the ceiling. My main responsibilities were keeping his Rolodex organized, answering the phone, and pursuing the delinquent rock clubs to get us their listings ON TIME! Mostly, I sat there, staring at the windowless walls, thinking about pizza, sex, or getting wasted — sometimes concurrently.

- What made you seek the job out in the first place?

Boucher: My grandfather died in December, during my third year of graduate school. At the time, I had tentative plans to move back to western Massachusetts the following summer and begin teaching in Boston that fall.

On paper, this renovation seemed like the perfect project. I'd been close to my grandfather, and I'd known that house my entire life. This job would give me the chance to say a proper goodbye. Plus, the renovation itself seemed pretty straightforward. The house had good bones, a new roof and new windows. We didn't plan to do much to it: we'd paint the walls, sand the floors, update the kitchen and add a half-bathroom and a deck in the backyard. We thought that we could do all of this by September 1st.

Clarke: Really the only reason anyone ever seeks out that kind of job: I needed the money.

Gaffney: I didn't have working papers, and so it was really hard for me to find a job. I only had just enough money to pay my rent and school fees, and I needed to earn money for food if I didn't want to go into credit card debt. That year, I ate a lot of thin leek and potato soup that I made with my equally broke German roommates and lost a good bit of weight. I started out looking for waitressing jobs, and then for some reason my dream job was to be a bakery salesgirl. I guess because I was hungry, I wanted to work around food, but also, I had done restaurant and food service work in the US, summer jobs during high school and college. I tried to get work teaching English, too, but again, no one would hire me, so I started looking in the classified section of the paper. At the time, I was having some tooth pain, and since I couldn't afford to go to a dentist, this job at a dentist's office caught my eye. It was right near my apartment, and I was hoping maybe it would be a way to get my cavity filled.

Sullivan: I had left a comfortable job as a project manager to complete my memoir which I had just sold to Algonquin Books. Inevitably, my financial cushion disappeared and I became desperate for employment. The job was promising because it combined two things I valued: books and the ability to pay my rent.

Trynin: Right up against my aforementioned worst job was my best job: assistant in a recording studio, a job I began at the beginning of my senior year, which, at seventeen, was about the coolest thing known to man. Not only did I work there during the school year, but I somehow convinced my silly high school to allow me to do my Independent Study Project (my ISP) at the studio, which translated into my final three months of high school taking place in a dark carpeted room with lots of smoking, various drugs, and older guys in tight pants and lip gloss. I got my worst job through the owner of this recording studio, who was Phil's friend.

- Anything remarkable about the application / interview?

Boucher: There wasn't an interview, but I remember my first day on the job very clearly. My grandfather had died in his home the previous winter, and the house went untouched that entire spring. When I walked into the house that first day, everything was exactly where he left it the day he died: his coffee cup in the sink, his shoes by his bed, his glasses on his desk.

My first task was to clear out the house, which meant throwing away all of his belongings. I shoved all of his clothes into plastic bags. I removed rusty pulleys from the basement ceiling (which he'd put up for me when I was a kid so that I could run an elaborate, and meaningless, system of ropes). We gave away the steel printing press in his basement to the first person who responded to our craigslist ad. All of this felt like a grand betrayal.

Clarke: I don't remember there being any. It's as though I woke up one day, covered with fiberglass dust and fiberglass pitch and realized that I worked in a fiberglass plant.

Gaffney: I remember feeling horrified at the interview, not really believing I was going to do this job. The receptionist was the dentist's wife. She was sickly sweet but at the same time very rigid and uptight. I decided to think of myself as a sort of a spy, and that I would learn something essential about Germanness from watching them. The whole thing was trippy, like I was a fly on the wall, not really there but watching my own experiences. I found that living abroad was often like that. Everything was surreal because I was living my life in German without being fully bilingual. I never knew exactly what I or anyone else was saying. It must be what it's like to be a young child who is just acquiring her first language. 'Till I could really communicate, the world just sort of seemed to happen to me, with varying degrees of my own participation. And as a result, I learned German fast.

Sullivan: It's remarkable that I didn't flee the interview when I heard that three people had resigned from the position within eight months. Or the fact that over lunch the current Associate

Editor delivered this piece of sage advice: *"Don't do it. Don't take the job."* Rent and the possibility of being homeless clouds judgment.

Trynin: There was no interview for my worst job. I walked in with the recording studio guy, and Phil just looked me up, then down, then up again, shrugged, and said, *"So this is her?"*

- Was there anything pleasurable about the job at all?

Boucher: I have a lot of good memories from that summer. My Dad was still working his full-time job as a high-school teacher then, but he'd often drive out to my grandfather's house after work with two cans of beer and a grinder for us to share. And when I was at the house alone, I used to listen to the Red Sox games on the radio. Ted Williams died that summer, and I remember listening to the broadcast the night he died — "Noma" (Nomar Garciaparra) was invited into the broadcast booth, and he teared up as he spoke about his rapport with Teddy Ballgame.

Clarke: Only the stories that came out of it afterward.

Gaffney: I had to clean the spots of tooth decay and feck off the big equipment with orange oil on cotton balls. I don't know why they used that rather than something more fiercely antiseptic, but it smelled really good. Also, one time the hygienist dropped the box of silver caps, and I spent a very zen, quiet day sorting hundreds and hundreds of tiny hollow silver teeth by size and putting them back into the correct compartments in their box. Clink clink clink. That was pleasant, in a way.

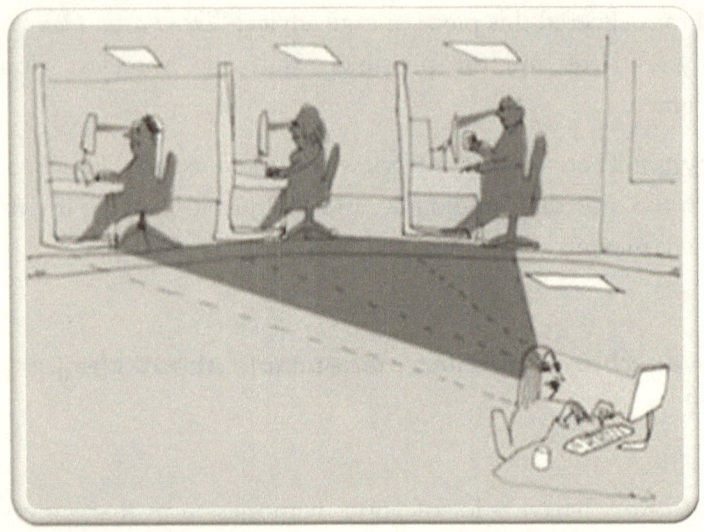

Sullivan: A weekly paycheck and the easy commute.

Trynin: Phil had lots of porno magazines under his sagging couch and he often left for hours at a time, during which I did, well, nothing to speak of.

- What was the first sign that things were going south?

Boucher: The renovation was fraught with difficulty from the get-go: Even with three coats, the cheap paint we bought didn't cover the 1960s pastel colors. We ran into trouble with old wiring, the old oil tank, the leach field in the backyard. The tiles on the kitchen floor wouldn't lift up without breaking into half-inch shards — we had to chip the floor off with a hammer and chisel. The cast-iron baseboard heater had to be cut and reconfigured by a master plumber. The backhoe operator we hired caught his truck on the cable wires that ran from the house to the curb.

   It was soon clear that our timeline was unrealistic; we

weren't even close to being finished by the time I moved to Boston in mid-August. It would take us — my Dad, mostly, with me helping when I could — another year to complete the project.

We finally listed the house the following spring, and soon we'd found a buyer. But on the day of the scheduled home inspection — Friday, June 13, 2003 — my father had a massive heart attack at work. He survived, but he was unconscious for days and he'd lost his short-term memory. He was in the hospital for over a week, and he was weak for months afterwards.

During his time in the hospital, I tried to keep the sale of the house moving forward — I made calls to lawyers and realtors, and we pushed back the closing date and rescheduled the home inspection. But I was completely naïve to this part of the process. When the inspection turned up a litany of new problems, I fixed what I could and refused to fix the rest. The buyer conceded, thankfully, and we closed on the house.

Clarke: Well, the first sign was that no one wore protective masks. No one, not even the bosses. The second sign was that everyone except me smoked cigarettes while they worked, which might explain why no one wore protective masks. The third sign was that we had a half hour for lunch and the guys spent their half hour chugging beer in the parking lot and then stumbled back in and climbed right into the ovens where they baked and rolled the fiberglass, or picked up the saws which they used to cut the fiberglass. There was a guy there with one arm, although I don't think he'd lost it on the job.

Gaffney: I would say it started pretty far south, but there was one particular day when it went Antarctic. The hygienist and the receptionist and the dentist were arguing more than usual that day. I sort of think the hygienist, who was very dishy, had been having an affair with the dentist, but I can't swear to that.

Anyway, one day she quit right in the middle of a root canal. The patient was subjected to some very unprofessional invective shooting back and forth across her body, which I could hear from the next room, and then, the hygienist just threw down her coat and stomped out. What was even worse for the patient was that they called me in from my usual drudgery, scrubbing off the instruments, to fill in for her. The dentist thrust that sucking thing into my hand, the one that keeps the water and saliva from pooling in your mouth. *Suction!* he commanded, but it kept getting stuck to the back of her throat like a leech and making her gag. It's not easy, what they do, dentists. I give them that. But this dentist was a real jackass. I guess he wanted the patient, who by the way was a nun in a black habit, to think that I was properly trained to be there, because he kept shouting at me, asking me what the hell was wrong with me, and didn't I know what I was doing. Clearly not.

Sullivan: Two incidents should have warned me to get out of Dodge:

1): As I was eating a small cup of butternut squash soup and a roll, my boss eyed my lunch with disdain and said, *"You eat a lot of food."*

2): The former editor left a notepad of her ideas about launching a new series of books based on a doll *de jour*, which was immediately rejected by my boss. Three months into the job in an "idea" meeting, my boss brought up the idea of launching a series based on these dolls and acted as if the idea was her own.

Trynin: There was never a sign of anything going north.

- How did your employment end?

Boucher: In one sense, the job ended with the sale of the house. But the house wasn't quite gone from our lives: that winter, my Dad was browsing the real estate listings when he saw an ad for my grandfather's house. He called the neighbor to find out what had happened: someone had allegedly died of a drug overdose in the house, and the rest of the family had vacated. The first open house was scheduled for that weekend.

I still remember the strange feeling of walking into that house again; it looked neither like the house we'd sold nor the one my grandfather had lived in. It smelled different; the walls had been painted again; there was an ugly couch in the living room. For some reason I made a bee-line for the back bed-room — the room where, two years earlier, my grandfather had collapsed and died; where, fifteen years before that, I'd slept when I stayed over; where, twenty years before that, my uncle had slept. All of that living seemed lost — that room was no one's now. Our work, too, was lost — not erased, per se, but blended in, diffused.

As my Dad and I walked from room to room, the realtor approached and asked if we had any questions. I had a million of them: What, if anything, had we accomplished here? What was all of our work worth?

Clarke: One day, two of us were sent to do inventory at a building a mile or so away from the main building. We drove to the building, but instead of doing inventory, we smoked pot. And when we were done smoking pot, the other guy went back to work, but I didn't.

Gaffney: That night I asked the receptionist if there was any chance I could get a check up and a cavity filled for free, because I didn't want to work there another second longer if I wasn't going to get a major dental-work payoff. She seemed incredulous and suggested that if I didn't have insurance, I could maybe get a 5% discount. I never went back. In the end, I think it must have been a sinus infection that had been bothering me, because it went away without my ever going to see a dentist. From that job, I moved up to being a cleaning lady at a bead shop, which was better, because I worked at night when they were closed and could play Led Zeppelin really loud while I was vacuuming. Eventually they fired me, for disturbing the neighbors, but by that time my German had gotten good, and I found a job translating German computer manuals into English.

Sullivan: After I had learned (via email) that my boss had stolen a presentation I'd drafted — ideas of how the publisher could market themselves online, new concepts for a book series — and presented the ideas as her own, and then had the nerve to inquire that I deliver her an execution plan, I gave my two weeks' notice. Over the course of the next few days, I was terrorized with passive aggressive emails, clipped orders and her leaning over my shoulder issuing criticism over word choices. After a week of this, I left her my passcard and walked out the door.

Trynin: My employment came to a sudden end just after Phil said into the phone, "Yeah man, I know. But my luck's about to change, my friend. I got a new girl comin' in next week, and this one's a fuckin' peach. This one's like, you know, stacked, really stacked, like —" and this is when Phil looked up and saw me standing in his doorway.

Episode 11: *First Car*
with Jon Clinch, Don Lee,
Robert Anthony Siegel, Alix Strauss,
and Sean Wilsey

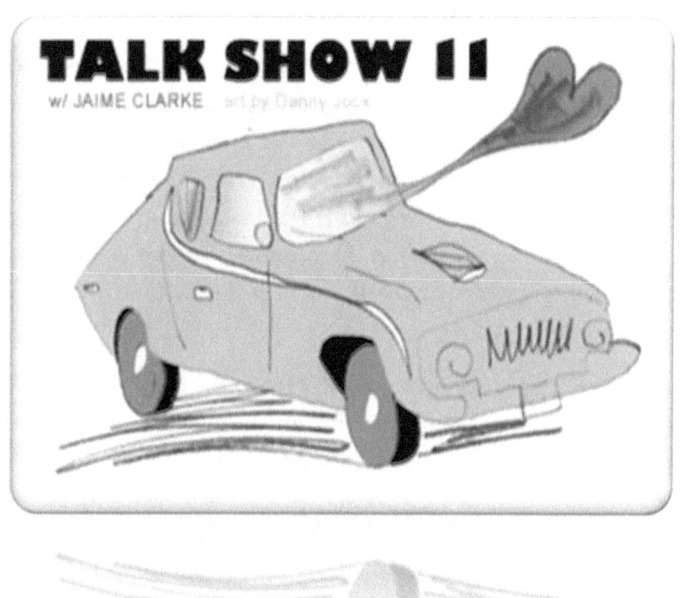

Jon Clinch is the author of the novels *The Thief of Auschwitz* , *Kings of the Earth* and *Finn* — an American Library Association Notable Book and winner of the Philadelphia Athenaeum Literary Award.

Don Lee is the author of the novels *Country of Origin*, an American Book Award winner, *Wrack and Ruin*, and *The Collective*, which won the Asian/Pacific American Award from the Asian Pacific American Librarians Association. His collection, *Yellow*, won the Sue Kaufman Prize for First Fiction. Lee is the director of the MFA Program at Temple University. For twenty years, Lee was principal editor of the literary journal *Ploughshares*.

Robert Anthony Siegel is the author of the novels *All Will Be Revealed* and *All the Money in the World*. His work has appeared in *Tin House*, *Ploughshares*, the *Los Angeles Times* and elsewhere. Seigel has received a Fulbright Fellowship and a Pushcart Prize. He teaches at the University of North Carolina Wilmington.

Alix Strauss is the author of the novels *The Joy of Funerals* and *Based Upon Availability*. Her other books include an anthology *Have I Got a Guy for You* and the nonfiction work *Death Becomes Them: Unearthing the Suicides of the Brilliant, the Famous, and the Notorious*. Strauss has been a featured lifestyle and trend writer on national shows including ABC, CBS, CNN, and *The Today Show*.

Sean Wilsey is the author of the memoir *Oh the Glory of It All*. He is co-editor of the anthologies *State by State: A Panoramic Portrait of America* and *The Thinking Fan's Guide to the World Cup*. His writing has appeared in the *London Review of Books*, the *Los Angeles Times*, and *McSweeney's Quarterly*, where he is the editor-at-large.

* * *

- What was the make and model if your first car?

<u>Clinch</u>: My first car was one of the worst ever made in this country or any other, a 1974 Chevrolet Vega. The Kammback version. "Kammback" was Chevrolet's oddball way of avoiding saying "station wagon" — a bit of euphemistic marketing-speak that I have continued to endorse by owning, by and by, such cars as the Audi A4 and A6 Avant. Station wagons the both of them. Obviously, station wagon lovers like me are in the minority and can be addressed only by indirection.

<u>Lee</u>: It was a 1975 puke-green Mercury Capri.

124

Siegel: It was a Cadillac convertible from the mid-sixties, though I can't remember the exact year. It must have been twenty years old when I got behind the wheel in — when was that, exactly? 1985? — but it had been lovingly restored by its true owner, a client of my father's named Howie Shapiro. (My father was a criminal defense attorney; Howie was a former drug addict working his way through culinary school.) But back to the car: it was white, with huge, really extraordinary fins in back, and a big chromium grill in front. It was nearly a block long, or felt as if it were, and I could barely see over the dashboard, but the engine was perfectly silent, and the steering wheel moved with the touch of a finger. The mere thought of tapping the gas pedal sent the machine gliding forward like a great white shark. Oh, and did I mention that the interior was red leather? And the radio was incredibly loud? The thing was brash, devoid of self-doubt — all the things I wanted to be.

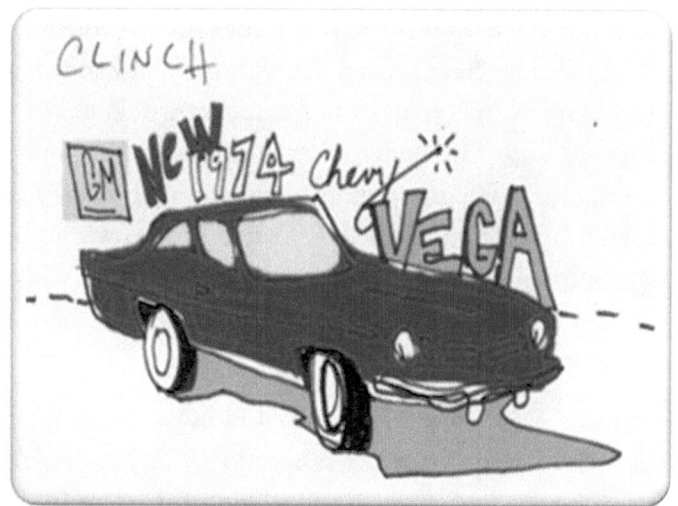

Strauss: A blue-ish gray 1986 Volvo 240DO.

Wilsey: It was a Saab 900 Turbo, one of the last ones they made before discontinuing the series in the early '90s. Color: "beryl green."

- How did this car come into your possession?

<u>Clinch</u>: My dad and I bought it brand new. He produced the down money and I handled the payments — which came, as I recall, to something on the order of $3,000. The car had a three-speed automatic transmission, a brown vinyl interior, and a 70-horse engine that looked like something stripped from a John Deere lawn tractor. My dad, who has always been a great inspiration to me, was then and is now of the opinion that when you buy a used car you're buying somebody else's troubles. So we bought a brand new 1974 Chevy Vega instead, and got $3,000 worth of our very own troubles.

<u>Lee</u>: A hand-me-down from my sister.

<u>Siegel</u>: That would depend on what "possession" means. The car was Howie's, but he had nowhere safe to park it, so my father stored it for him in the garage under his apartment building. My father may have started out with good intentions; good intentions are a family trait. In this case that would have meant keeping the Caddy safe under the tarpaulin, probably, but pretty soon he was driving it around town, and then I was driving it, too, and then Howie seemed distracted by his own problems (money, sobriety, marriage, cheese soufflé). After a while, he stopped coming by to check on it, and I didn't see him again for a long time.

<u>Strauss</u>: I grew up in Manhattan and never sat in the driver's seat until I went to Ithaca college in 1987. My best friend was from Rockville Center and was one of the few freshman with a car. Late at night, after we'd seen a movie or gone for a pizza run, she'd pull into a mall's parking lot and hand me the keys. Technically, I learned to drive in the freezing cold, in dark while listening to Rick Astley.

Wilsey: I bought it straight from the Saab factory in Gothenburg. It was me and a bunch of US Army guys stationed on bases in Germany. Saab had a deal where they'd charge no tax and ship the car home for free if you came and got it. Airfare to Sweden was a lot cheaper than sales tax back then. Also, it was defective!

- What was the first trip you took in this car?

Clinch: I drove, in the time-honored tradition of young men everywhere, to see my girlfriend in New Jersey. This was maybe a six-hour drive from my parents' place in upstate New York, and I wasn't entirely confident that the Vega was up to the rigors of the trip. I remember now (I have kept this a secret from everyone on earth, often even myself, until this very moment), that somewhere along the Northeastern Extension of the Pennsylvania Turnpike I pulled over and opened the hood so as to let the engine cool off. A state trooper, recognizing the universal symbol for engine overheating, stopped to check on me, and I told him that I was merely airing out that mighty 70-horse engine. Just in case. As Bugs Bunny would have it, *"What a maroon."* The trooper kindly refrained from shaking his head before getting back into his patrol car and zooming off.

Siegel: I took it on a camping trip, of all things, with a bunch of college friends. I didn't have a tent so I planned to sleep in the car — the front seat was as big as a couch; I could completely stretch out on it, and a friend of mine took the back seat. But during the night I kept rolling into the horn, which was unbelievably loud, the brass section of some kind of gigantic dream orchestra. No one slept too well, even the squirrels. But I wouldn't leave the car. I had latched onto the idea of sleeping in it as some kind of self-conscious gesture of cool.

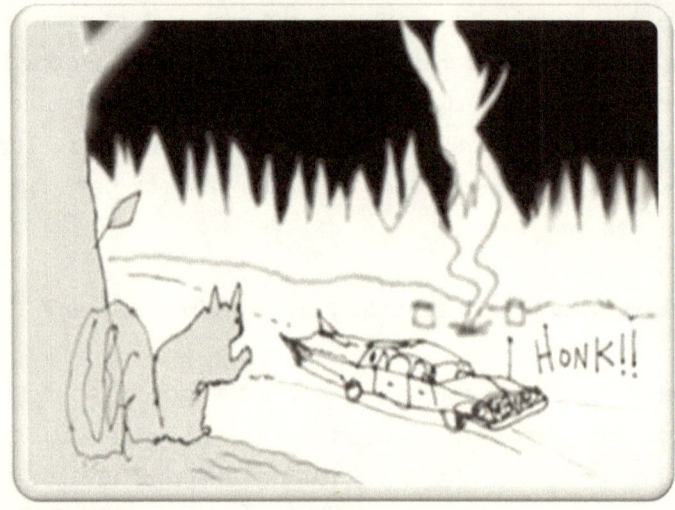

Strauss: Since we were in the middle of nowhere, going to the mall was considered a road trip. Though after college, we'd take long weekends and drive up to the Hamptons, the Berkshires, Vermont and Woodstock.

Wilsey: I drove it on the autobahn. Eventually I took it up to the maximum speed of 140 mph and tried to set the cruise control. (Not possible.) At that speed you could actually watch the gas gauge tick to the left.

- What are your outstanding memories of the car?

Clinch: My outstanding memories are of its dissolution. The 1974 Vega was a rustbucket of a very high order, and mine in particular was no match for the highly-salinated roadways of upstate New York. Its front and rear fenders rusted into lacework within a year, and they would have fallen off had my dealer not clued me in about a secret warranty program that replaced them at the last minute.

Lee: As I remember it, it was a fast car, but butt-ugly. I was living in L.A. at the time, and rode that thing to the ground.

Took a lot of trips up to San Francisco with it up Highway 1, camped in Big Sur on the way. My last year in California, just before I left for grad school in Boston, I was living in Burbank, but I had a job with a painting/construction company that had most of its business in the South Bay. So I used to leave the house at 6:30 in the morning and drive through rush-hour traffic to Huntington Beach or Manhattan Beach — fifty miles, anywhere between an hour and a half and two and a half hours, each way. I'd get home at 7:30, utterly beat. The only way I could stay awake through dinner was to lift weights (I have a photo of myself from that time, and I'm virtually unrecognizable with twenty extra pounds of muscle).

But I learned all the shortcuts, when to anticipate a slowdown and get off the freeway to Sepulveda, say, and where I could hop back on. I just tore the shit out of the car. In that one year, I had to replace the clutch three times — I kept burning them out. Toward the end, I had to change the sparks and spray the carburetor constantly just to keep the thing going.

Siegel: My sister was moving to Chicago to go to art school, and we drove her out there in the Caddy. A friend of hers by the name of Jan Chelminski did most of the driving — he would speed along at about a hundred miles per hour, with a single finger wrapped around the steering wheel. With the top down it felt like we were flying at an altitude of about one foot over the payment, a very naked feeling, both frightening and magical. I remember falling asleep in the back seat out of sheer exhaustion — an incredibly deep sleep — and then waking up, unsure for the briefest moment where I was. The wind was beating at my head and the trees were rushing by, and beyond that there was nothing but fields. It was like waking up from a dream into a different dream.

Strauss: I loved being in that car — whether I was driving or being driven. It was like a very tiny studio apartment on wheels. There was something about the freedom, the intimacy and the memories that car created for me. And if I wasn't driving, I was in charge of the music.

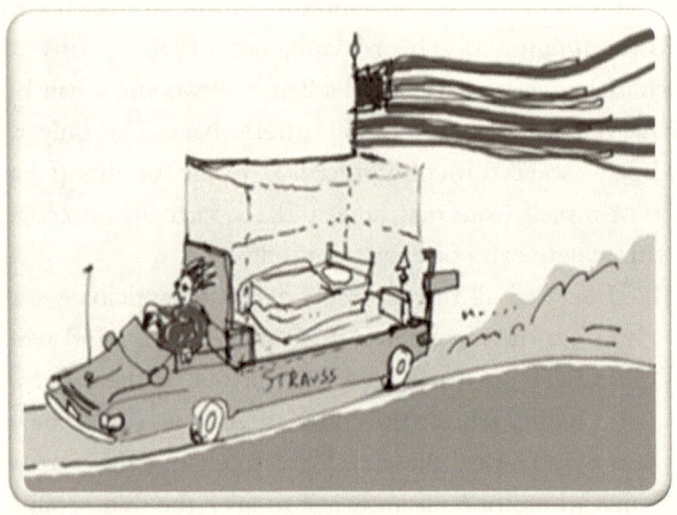

Wilsey: I was driving at night with two friends when the road in front of us disappeared. Before I could react we were flying, four wheels off the ground, having hit the top of a rise where the country road we were traveling on crossed an irrigation ditch. We landed perfectly after a solid three one thousand count.

- What ultimately happened to the car?

Clinch: I traded it in for the second-worst car ever made in this country or any other, a 1976 Dodge Aspen. Don't even ask.

Lee: A couple of days before I left, I miraculously got an offer for the car. I'd parked it on the street with a sign, and I really hadn't thought there'd be any takers. We agreed on $500. My last day, I drove it to the guy's house. He wasn't home, but his daughter gave me the cash and asked me to move the car from the driveway to the street. No problem. Except the car wouldn't start — not an unusual occurrence at that juncture. So I backed it out in neutral, and fortunately the street was on a hill, and I was able to pop the clutch and roll-start it. I parked it on the street and guiltily hightailed it out of there as fast as I could.

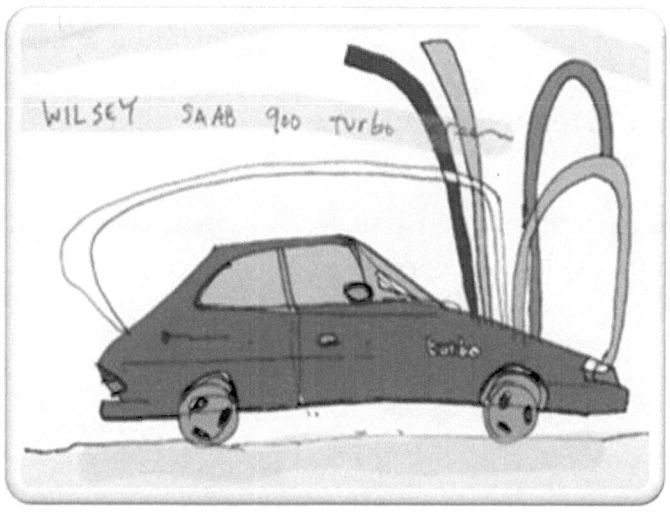

Siegel: Some years later, I was driving down the street in a car I actually owned, a Chevy Impala with a ripped up interior (I'd inherited it from my grandfather), when I recognized the Caddy up ahead — there was no mistaking that magnificent beast. The top was down and my father was behind the wheel, and next to him was a friend of his, Jim Kirk, who was dying of cancer. I knew that my father took Jim out on drives, but I'd heard it from my mother, not from him; he and I were going through a period of estrangement and hadn't spoken in a while . . . which is a way of saying that I don't know what ultimately happened to the Caddy. I ran into Howie some years after that on the street, but he looked like a junky again, wearing those mismatched clothes from Goodwill. He said hello and then darted away. My father died in 2002. It's been five years, but I still find missing him incredibly disorienting, like waking up in that gigantic white car, doing a hundred with the top down.

Strauss: Sadly, after 120,000 miles and eight years later, it was sold to a family-run business and then given to one of their employees who ended up destroying it. I still feel a slight twinge of loss when I'm picked up by my friend in her black Range Rover. It reflects the new life she has, the family she's started and how many years have gone by since our college days.

Wilsey: Sold it to a Saab dealer in Ramsay, New Jersey, and took the bus to New York.

Episode 12: *Time Capsule*
with Quinn Dalton, Owen King, Adam Langer, and Nelly Reifler

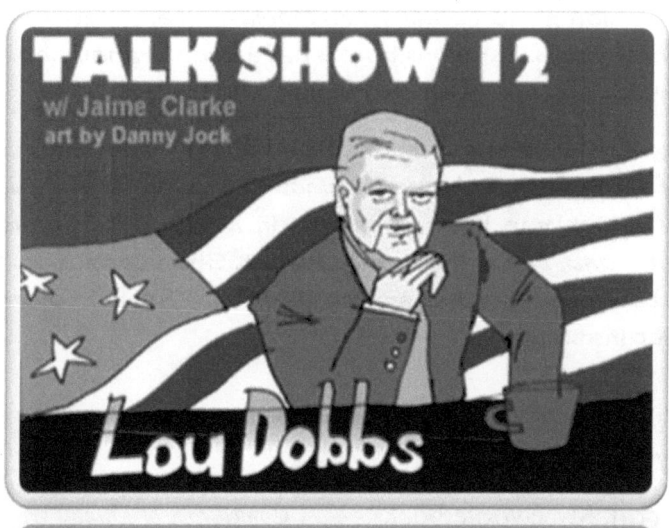

Quinn Dalton is the author of a novel *High Strung*, and the short story collections *Bulletproof Girl* and *Stories from the Afterlife*. Her work has appeared in *One Story*, *Glimmer Train*, *Indiana Review*, the *Kenyon Review* and others and has been anthologized in *Glimmer Train's Where Love is Found: 24 Tales of Connection* and in *Peculiar Pilgrims: Stories from the Left Hand of God*.

Owen King's books include *We're All In This Together: A Novella and Stories* and *Double Feature*, a novel. He is co-editor of the anthology *Who Can Save Us Now?* His work has appeared in the *Boston Globe*, the *Bellingham Review*, *One Story*, and other publications.

Adam Langer is the author of the novels *Crossing California*, *The Washington Story*, *Ellington Boulevard* and *The Thieves of Manhattan*, and the memoir, *My Father's Bonus March*. He is also the lyricist for the musical companion piece to *Ellington Boulevard* and has written several plays. Langer's books have been translated into Spanish, German, Dutch, Finnish, and Italian.

Nelly Reifler is the author of the short story collection *See Through* and the novel *Elect H. Mouse State Judge*. Her fiction has been published in *Bomb*, *McSweeney's*, *Post Road*, *Black Book* and *Jubilat*. She teaches at Sarah Lawrence College and co-directs Writers' Forum at Pratt Institute.

* * *

- What book would you include in a time capsule and why?

<u>Dalton</u>: My favorite books — *A Confederacy of Dunces* by John Kennedy Toole and *Pretty Birds* by Scott Simon. I would put both in because they so beautifully — and hysterically in the case of *Dunces*, tragically with *Pretty Birds* — capture a time and place. They're great stories. They put you on a certain street on a certain day. And readers fifty years from now should know about those streets and the people populating them.

<u>King</u>: I'm going to assume that there's a compendium version of Philip Pullman's *His Dark Materials* trilogy available somewhere and put that in. (By the way, we need to be very careful about selecting and sealing our container. For those of you who didn't see the photos: in Tulsa, a Plymouth was buried in 1957 for excavation at the 2007 Oklahoma Centennial. Awesome idea, right? Not so much. At some point that capsule had flooded, so when the Plymouth emerged from its grave it appeared to have been afflicted with what appeared to be a particularly malignant case of car-leprosy. Yuck. Even fifty years

after my own internment, I expect to look better.)

While I believe that Ian McEwan is probably our finest novelist writing in English — with Phillip Roth and Michael Chabon snapping at his heels — Pullman's fantastical young adult trilogy provides the most timeless evocation of our world that I've encountered. The series is essentially the chronicle of a war against god, a god who has abandoned his duties and dwindled to a ghastly little figure in a glass box, propped up as the standard of craven zealots of every stripe. It's a metaphor for our times, an affirmation of reason and humanity in the face of the pestilential fundamentalism that has so thoroughly infested our world.

Also, the books feature some ass-kicking armored bears. The optimist in me says that the people of the future will still recognize how awesome that is — bears wearing armor and kicking ass.

Langer: If you wanted to reflect what living in 2007 or thereabouts was like, you'd probably have to stick a memoir in there, one of those supposedly all-revealing but actually self-mythologizing books, some purported confessional or tell-all written by some guy whose name rhymes with *schrei* or even *Chronicles*, by Bob Dylan, a book I loved, though I only believed about half of it. Instead, I'd choose a book that suggested we lived in a more elegant, nuanced, and truthful world, one where subtlety reigned and indeterminacy was favored over certainty, a world where people had been so very eager to read *The Florist's Daughter*, by Patricia Hampl or *Listen*, by Wendy Salinger that they had buried those books in the time capsule instead of some more obvious choices.

Reifler: David Ohle's *Motorman* was first published by Knopf in 1972 — and then it was out of print until 2004, when it was republished by Third Bed. It's a dystopic little tome. Our hero,

Moldenke, once had a life that was "free and new green, bright suns behind him, spirals ahead." But he has been manhandled and winnowed down bit by bit, through the replacement of his one fragile human heart with multiple sheep hearts; the sacrifice of his feelings to the cause of the mock War; the loss of his woman, Cock Roberta, who has been institutionalized for her compulsive punctuating. When we meet him, he is under surveillance, forced to stay inside his quarters, harassed, constipated, addicted to drugs. He's unsure whether or not he killed a couple of humanoid jellyheads. In its own queasy way, *Motorman* is as good a portrait of its era as any of the more literal books that were its contemporaries.

But the reason I'm putting it in my time capsule is that it's also an eerily perfect picture of this moment. Or the way this moment feels to me. Sitting in my apartment on Atlantic Avenue with the monstrous condominium construction grinding outside and shaking the earth, my neighbors gingerly making their way up and down the stairs in their burkhas, the mock War thriving and mutating, everybody's hearts seeming to becoming sheep-like, I often feel like Moldenke.

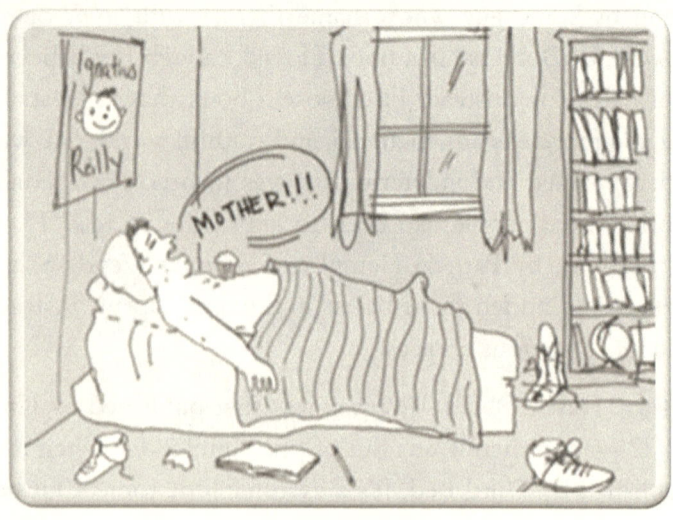

- What movie and why?

Dalton: *Bull Durham,* not because I think it's the best movie ever made (even if thought I could say such a thing about a movie) but because, like my book choices, it is a love story wrapped in a lost cause. The original Durham Bulls stadium where the movie was filmed has since been relegated to little league games and what not, just like Greensboro's War Memorial — both given up on in favor of slicker digs. The movie came out twenty years ago and already the places it depicts have ceased to exist in the same way. I saw it when I was sixteen and I thought it was such a smart comedy — I was so ready for it after the Brat Pack years (apologies, and read my homage to *Sixteen Candles* in *Don't You Forget About Me.*) Plus it's set in the south and my family had moved to Ohio a few years earlier from South Carolina. When Annie Savoy said "Oh, my," it was music to my ears. Plus, I was on a date and in love. Plus, watching it recently, I thought: no email, no texting — you only see one phone call in the whole movie. Bliss. But me loving a baseball movie? Who knew? I've never sat through an entire baseball game . . . well, I've sat through them, but not paid attention. I guess I like the idea of baseball more than the reality. In general, I love the idea of things more than the reality. And I don't think it was a baseball movie at its heart anyway. It's a good old-fashioned romance with some well-placed literary references. The quote from Walt Whitman at the end will always make me teary-eyed.

King: *No Country For Old Men* is the best movie I've seen this year, and another work of art that's representative of our age, albeit in a way that's a good deal more harrowing than the Pullman novels. This is the other side of the coin, where an apocalyptic force — the crazy-eyed Javier Bardem — cannot be understood or bargained with or stopped, ever. It's interesting to note that the film has been a box office disappointment. One of the unhappiest tendencies of our nation over these last few years is the collective shying away from the real, repugnant human cost of the war in Iraq. I say this from a position of complete guilt; I recently quit reading the newspaper, cold turkey, because it simply made me too depressed. *No Country For Old Men* might as well be page A-1 of the *Times*: good-hearted people strive, and fail, and die, for no reason.

Did I mention that this movie is not the feel-good-hit of the year?

I also want to add that it's directed by the Coen Brothers with an exceptionally novelistic eye for detail. At the beginning of the movie, Chigurh (the bad guy, played by Bardem) uses a pair of handcuffs to strangle a police officer. The camera holds on Bardem's face for an uncomfortably long time. He's pulling so hard on the handcuffs that he appears on the verge of an aneurism. When it's finally over, when the officer is still, when Chigurh is just lying there breathing, the camera slips away to show us the linoleum, which is tracked with a constellation of black scuff marks from officer's boots. It's a horrible, perfect detail. I wish I'd written it.

Langer: I've always been a sucker for the overblown movie, the book that reached out for the big brass ring and came crashing down to the ground empty-handed. The more appropriate movie for the capsule would probably be something ironic, smart, and knowing, something from the playbook of Alexander Payne or Richard Linklater, both of whom I like a good deal. But I'd prefer people in the future to think that we lived in more artistically ambitious times, that we were a more warm and open-minded people with greater attention spans. So, I'd stuff the time capsule full of the last three Wim

Wenders' movies (*Million Dollar Hotel, Land of Plenty*, and *Don't Come Knocking*), all of which are beautiful failures. I might even splice bits of them together — the lover's leap from *Million Dollar Hotel*, the final breathtaking shot of *Land of Plenty*, the exteriors in *Don't Come Knocking* — to create some crazed triple bill. And if there were room in the time capsule, I might toss in Terrence Malick's *The New World*, Alain Resnais' *Hearts*, and just about everything that Cedric Klapisch has done, to make the future think that we were watching all these movies. After all, in the future as Mike Judge's *Idiocracy* has taught us, the most popular film will be one called *Ass*.

Reifler: I always thought that if it were the end of the world, or you were about to die with a group of people, you would rise in that moment to your highest possible moral and spiritual potential. I imagined that you'd embrace the person closest to you, absolve them of what haunted them, and tell them that you loved them — even if you had never met before. I'd had a reservation to travel on United Flight 93 on September 11, 2001. I cancelled it when I got a cheaper flight on Jet Blue. Flying across country that morning we watched in real time on our little seat-back television sets as the World Trade Center collapsed, and I saw images of the wreckage of the airplane I might have been on. CNN announced that flights remaining in the air would be shot down by the military if they did not land immediately. We were not yet descending. I moved to touch the young woman next to me; we'd been chatting amiably at the beginning of the flight. She pulled away from me and pressed herself against the window, turning her face from mine. I can tell you without giving too much away that in Andrei Tarkovsky's film *The Sacrifice* we spend time with a small group of people in the hours and moments before Armageddon. But the movie is not about the apocalypse: it is about those people. They don't hug and console and absolve; knowing the world is about to end does not make them suddenly perfect. It's a beautiful movie, and it was Tarkovsky's last opus. He made it in Sweden, using some of Bergman's regular crew. I can't tell you about the sacrifice at the center of the movie because that *would* give too much away. I can say, though, that the ending fills my heart with hope . . . and that is just one of the many reasons I'm putting it in my time capsule. It would be both a warning and a hopeful call.

- What TV show and why?

Dalton: *Third Rock from the Sun* because it did such a great job of commenting on the oddities of our society through a band of aliens masquerading as humans. Because William Shatner as The Great High Head made me laugh so hard I almost swallowed my tongue.

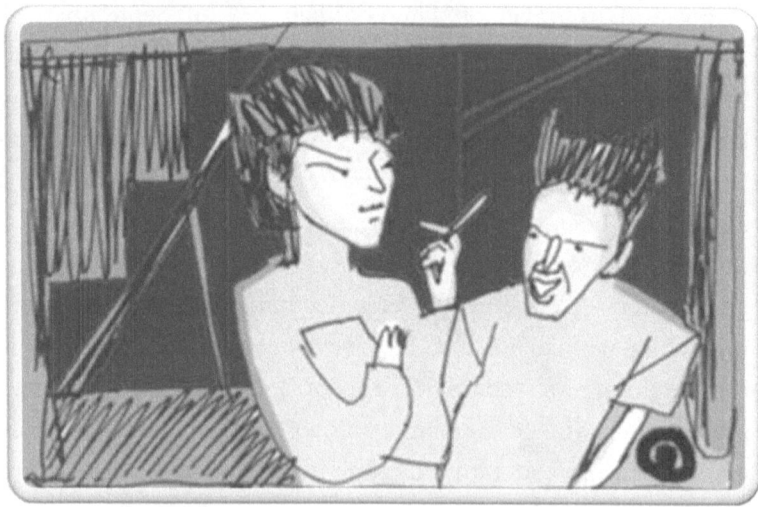

King: *Pants Off Dance Off.* This is the show on Fuse where exhibitionists shake it, and then take it off, while a music video plays on a screen behind them. What's really kind of sweet about the show is that most of the contestants aren't exactly hard-bodied. I feel like the relative success of this program is proof that our time and place isn't entirely without a certain charm: we may have irreparably fucked up the world, but we did get naked and dance. We had some merit.

Langer: I wouldn't be surprised if *The Simpsons* will still be running in 2058, so no reason to put that in the time capsule. And I'm sure *30 Rock* will still be available on DVD too. So no need to stuff that in there either. Instead, I'll burn a copy of the no-budget show *Yacht Rock*, the first and one of the funniest shows I ever saw on YouTube, which has allowed me to maintain my familiarity with pop culture without having had cable for more than five years.

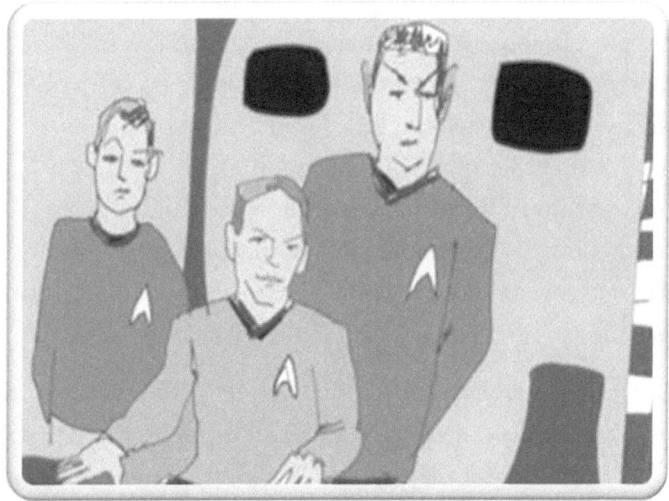

Reifler: I'd put in the original *Star Trek*. Boy, is that not how the future will turn out. But wouldn't it be cool if it did? And wouldn't it be cool for the people of 2058 to see what their great-grandparents made of outer space? All the different alien cultures, some complete with empresses in sexy costumes? All

141

the different mental afflictions you could catch from the atmospheres of various planets? Creatures that look like chilled omelets flying through the air and attaching themselves to people?

- What pop ephemera and why?

Dalton: What is pop ephemera?

King: The soul of Lou Dobbs. My thinking here is that if we could somehow extract this tiny, midnight-black moth from Mr. Dobbs, then perhaps future generations could study it, and try to determine how someone can so abruptly go completely fucking nuts. Is it a virus? Is it contagious? If Lou Dobbs's soul bit me, would I suddenly develop an irrational hatred of impoverished, brown-skinned people? Would I dream of building an impervious bubble over my entire country, a bubble made entirely of quick-drying outraged-old-man-spit, and constructed solely by industrious little angry-old-man-imps? I don't know. We don't know.

We just don't have the scientific apparatus to properly understand Lou Dobbs's soul. Put it in the capsule — and for God's sake, wear gloves while you're doing it. That thing is dangerous.

Langer: It would be nice for the people of the future to wonder if we were Luddites after all. So, I'll put in my typewriter, my .78 rpm record player, and my Sony Walkman cassette player. Just to keep everybody guessing.

Reifler: The time capsule has a hard drive, right? Into it I will download the 3.8 megabyte of Outkast's song "Hey Ya." The song is insanely infectious, and it spread like the flu for many months before it became a dormant, low-level virus. But there are reasons that this particular addictive song gets included: A) it's more complex than you might think. Beyond *"shake it like a Polaroid picture"* and *"I don't want to meet your mama, I just want to make you cumma"* is a narrator who mocks the youthful, romantic ideas about love and relationships that he once had — but who, in growing up and becoming rational and realistic about desire and emotional attachments has also become a boor. A boor who rhymes "mama" with "cumma." But more than that, I'm putting those megabytes in my time capsule because B) Outkast is a product of the highest potential and very best qualities of our culture. Andre Benjamin (Andre 3000) and Antwan Patton (Big Boi) became friends and collaborators when they were students at the Tri-Cities High School in East Point, Georgia, on the outskirts of Atlanta. It's a magnet school for the visual and performing arts, and it has a diverse student body. Andre is also a painter; Antwan is a passionate Kate Bush fan. Their influences are fantastically expansive. Outkast, for me, is the best example of popular culture in America. Even if they did get sued by Rosa Parks.

- What do you think/hope people in the year 2058 will make of your selections?

Dalton: Who can say? I'm thirty-six. I hope to be around to defend them.

King: Well, I hope they'll get a small, but accurate snapshot of our world: a world at war, a world of valiance, a world of pessimism, a world of bare-assed dancing, a world where Lou Dobbs was up to no damn good.

What do I think they'll make of the capsule? I think the people of 2058 are going to be fully aware of the consequences of our behavior, and therefore they won't have much patience for our explanations. They're the ones who are going to have to make the peace and build the levees.

Langer: The fun of burying a time capsule would be to attempt to change history — or at least to attempt to change perceptions of history. For this reason, I'd try to fill the time capsule with items that perhaps weren't popular during our time but should have been, with objects that are perhaps all too unreflective of the early 21st Century, giving those who stumble upon it the opportunity to reassess our times.

Reifler: You know what? If there are people alive on the planet in fifty years to open my time capsule, that's enough for me. Would they have my verbal explanations along with the objects? If so, I really hope they smile and shake their heads at the darkness and confusion I felt about humanity in 2008. I hope that Outkast wins.

Episode 13: *Caught in a Lie*
with Kiara Brinkman,
Bret Anthony Johnston,
Fiona Maazel, Alix Ohlin, and Margo Rabb

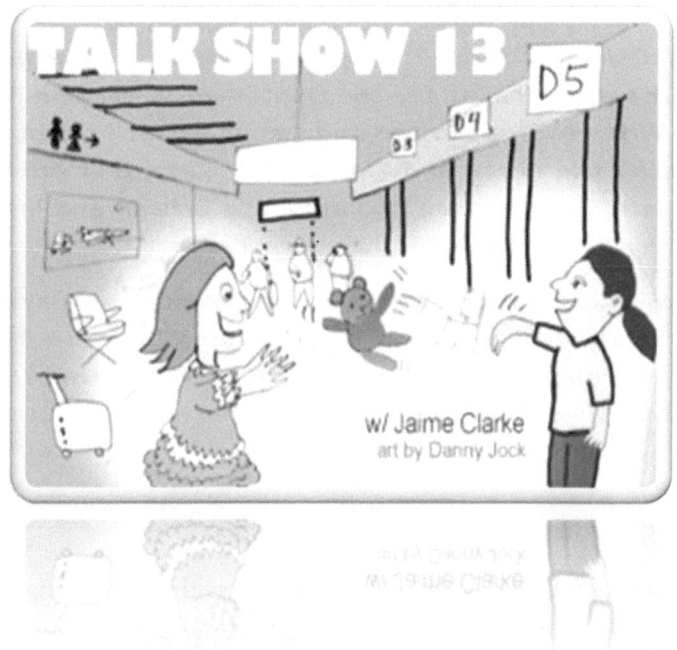

w/ Jaime Clarke

art by Danny Jock

Kiara Brinkman's debut novel, *Up High in the Trees*, was a *New York Times* Editors' Choice and a Best Book of the Year in the *Chicago Tribune*. Her fiction has appeared in *McSweeney's*, *One Story* and other journals.

Bret Anthony Johnston is the author of *Corpus Christi: Stories* and the editor of *Naming the World: And Other Exercises for the Creative Writer*. He received a National Book Foundation "5 Under 35" and a James Michener fellowship. Johnston directs the Creative Writing Program at Harvard University.

Fiona Maazel is the author of the novels *Last Last Chance* and *Woke Up Lonely*. She is winner of the Bard Prize for Fiction and a National Book Foundation "5 Under 35" honoree. Maazel teaches at Brooklyn College, New York University, Columbia, and Princeton.

Alix Ohlin is the author of *Signs and Wonders, Babylon and Other Stories, The Missing Person,* and *Inside* - which was a finalist for the Scotiabank Giller and Rogers Writers' Trust Prizes and named a best book of the year by the *Globe and Mail, Quill & Quire,* and *Amazon Canada.* She teaches at Lafayette College and in the Warren Wilson MFA Program for Writers.

Margo Rabb's novel, *Cures for Heartbreak,* was named one of the best books of the year by *Kirkus* and *Booklist.* Her short stories have been published in the *Atlantic Monthly, Zoetrope, One Story,* and have been broadcast on NPR's *The Sound of Writing.*

* * *

- Name a lie you got caught telling.

<u>Brinkman</u>: I was six or seven, traveling with my grandparents, and either our plane was delayed, or we were just super early for our flight — regardless, there was a lot of time. So, I befriended a pretty little girl, who was not much more than a toddler. We tossed her white teddy bear back and forth, and because she wasn't very good at catching, she found this game endlessly funny. I admired her blonde hair and grew somewhat jealous of her pink, ruffly dress. (Throughout my early childhood, my mother took pride in dressing me in gender-neutral clothing. That day at the airport, I was probably wearing jeans and a yellow t-shirt.) Soon, this girl and I were part of a larger group of antsy children. A parent had stopped us from tossing stuffed animals and running wild. We were now playing cards, with a deck made especially for Old Maid, and I remember the

image on the dreaded card — a cobwebby lady rotting away in a rocking chair. Anyway, the little girl, whose name I can't remember, but it could've been Katie (a favorite of mine at the time), had attached herself to me, and I enjoyed being in charge of someone. Without much thought, I told the group that Katie was my sister, and that we were from California.

Johnston: This will be a little long. Please stay with me.

I took a Bible class in high school. Long story about that, but let's just streamline that particular narrative by saying I was in South Texas. I sat by a young woman named Rebecca who looked like a free-loving hippy, but who was, in fact, a born-again Christian, the kind of girl who brought her own Bible (with her name stamped in gold cursive on its cover) to class every day. She had huge chunks of scripture memorized, and our teacher, a woman so old and frail it hurt me to look at her, regularly called on her to recite those chunks. In South Texas in the late '80s, most girls in high school shellacked their hair and squeezed into their Wranglers and wore blousy, primary-colored cowboy shirts. Not Rebecca. She had this cool and inexplicable SoHo/bohemian thing going on: bell-bottoms and henleys and platform shoes and beaded necklaces that hung to her waist.

That year, I didn't really care about anything other than skateboarding, and I came to class one morning limping from some fall I'd taken the night before. Had I done the splits on a handrail I'd been trying to boardslide down? Had I gotten hung up on the top of a ramp and smashed to the ground eight feet below? Even odds. I only know that I was limping, and when Rebecca saw me, she bowed her head and clasped both her hands behind her neck. Praying for me, I thought, and was both flattered and a little freaked out. But I was wrong. She was unclasping one of her long necklaces. She pooled it in her palm, then handed it to me. She said, "It was my grand-mother's. It'll speed up your recovery."

"Thanks," I said.

"Don't lose it," she said. "Just wear it until you feel better, then give it back."

"Okay," I said. "I won't lose it."

And I didn't lose it. I *broke* it. That night. I was helping to build a halfpipe at the skatepark and wearing the necklace when the downswing of my hammer caught the string of beads and the necklace snapped and the beads scattered like hundreds of marbles. They rolled down and behind and under the ramp, and I distinctly remember the person who was working on the lower part of the ramp and upon whom many of the beads fell (remember how Mr. Moose would rain all those ping pong balls down on Captain Kangaroo, think of that) saying, "What the shit, Johnston?"

"I just broke this girl's grandmother's necklace."

"Is she hot?" the guy said. His name was Todd, but he tried to make everyone call him "The Squad."

"She's a born again Christian," I said. "She's going to be pissed."

"I'm down with Jesus," The Squad said.

"She's going to be really, really pissed. Help me find all the beads."

"Fuck you."

By the end of the night, I'd found a handful of the beads out of maybe a hundred. I skipped Bible class for the rest of the week.

One section of the beads hadn't fallen off the string, which meant I had the pattern. Which pattern was: One ruby bead, one silver, three pearly ones, another silver, another ruby. Red, silver, white, white, white, silver, red, then repeat, repeat, repeat. The day after I ruined the necklace, I went to a hobby shop and bought the nearest approximations to the original beads. Everything looked perfect, except the rubies, which may have been antiques, according to the hobby shop worker.

("You want to sell those?" he'd asked.) Then I went back to the skatepark and asked The Squad's girlfriend to help me replicate the necklace.

She was almost done when she said, "This won't work. You're an idiot."

"I think it looks good," I said.

"The originals are antique beads. Yours are like from K-Mart. She's going to know. She's going to kick your ass."

"She's a Christian."

"Then God's going to kick your ass," she said.

"I think it looks good."

"You're an idiot."

On Monday, I told her I'd forgotten the necklace at home. I said I'd taken it off because I was helping to build a ramp at the skatepark and I didn't want anything to happen to her necklace. I managed to forget the necklace every day that week, actually. When we bowed our heads to pray, I prayed that she'd tell me to keep the necklace. The following week I mounted a campaign to buy it from her. I offered her an inordinate amount of money for the necklace — money I didn't have — and for a while she seemed to be considering it.

"Why do you want to buy it so bad? You never wear it anymore."

"I just really like it. I feel good when I wear it."

"Good how?"

"I don't know, just good."

"Does it make you feel closer to God? My grandmother was a great Christian."

"Exactly," I said. "That's exactly how it feels."

She smiled, nodded. Jackpot, I thought.

Then she said, "No, I can't. Bring it tomorrow. I want to wear it to church this Sunday."

So I brought it. She started weeping right away. I felt like trash. I told her everything. I apologized, apologized, apologized. She accepted my apology and said she hoped I'd learned a lesson. She quoted something from the Bible. Just writing about it makes my stomach roil.

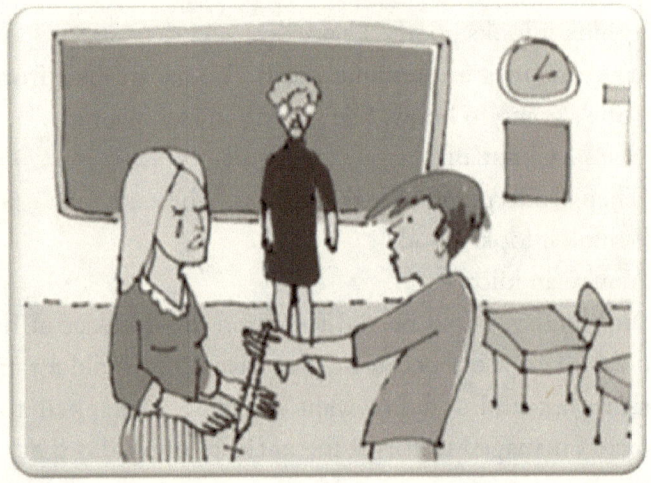

Maazel: I once told my best friend that I went into a Teriyaki Boy where all the employees were defective in some horrible way — each dragging ass behind the counter: drooling, limping, weeping. The story went on and on and climaxed with the manager of the restaurant finally telling everyone to knock it off, this wasn't fun anymore, at which point they all got normal and carried on. I made as if they were just messing with me because, after all, what's there to do at Teriyaki Boy? *Cook?*

Ohlin: I was a freshman in college, riding the 'T' in Boston with two new friends who were talking about a movie they'd both seen and loved — *Subway* by Luc Besson. One of them turned to me and said casually, "Have you seen it?" And I blurted out, "Yes." But it must not have been convincing, because he and the other friend started asking me about specific scenes in the movie. Which I then was forced to pretend I knew about, and try to add details to. I had no idea what I was talking about, but it was too late to say so. I couldn't back down. Before long both of them were in on it. Instead of busting me, they chose to egg me on with increasingly ridiculous details that, I gradually realized, were definitely not from the movie. "And that scene with the dinosaurs tearing apart the Eiffel Tower, wasn't it amazing?" *"Yes,"* I'd say. *"That was really amazing."* "And then when the moon exploded and aliens came down to earth in the form of two-headed angels, wasn't that part great?" *"Yes,"* I'd say. *"That was my favorite part."* It turned into an elaborate piece of theatre in which I wouldn't admit I was lying and they wouldn't admit that they knew I was lying and yet all of us were perfectly aware of the truth. It was a very long subway ride.

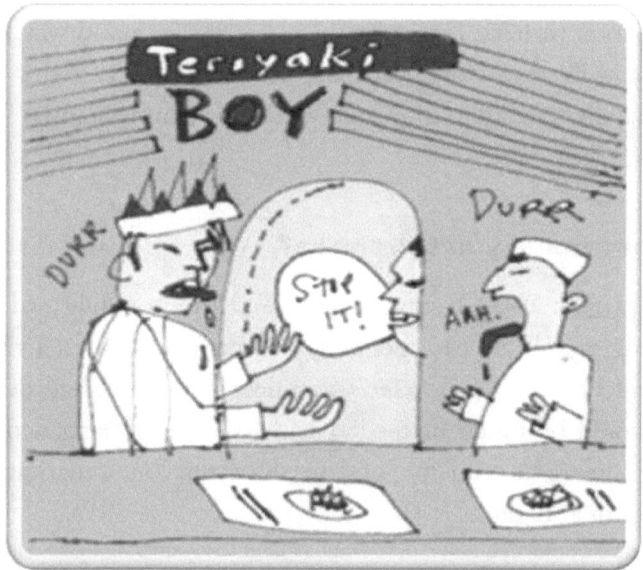

Rabb: When I was twenty-six, my father died suddenly of a heart attack. My mother had died years before that, and my sister and I inherited the house we'd grown up in. I spent a year living in the house while we settled my father's estate, and during that time, I was single and dating. Typical first date conversation:

DATE: Where did you grow up?

ME: Queens. In Sunnyside.

DATE: Oh. And you still live there? Do you live near where you grew up?

ME: Yeah, I do . . . actually . . . I live in my parents' house.

DATE: You live with your parents?

ME: No . . . they both died.

DATE (uncomfortable / sad / embarrassed / repulsed expression): Oh . . .

Then, I'd inevitably make an inappropriately cheery smile and attempt, futilely, to steer the conversation in a conventional direction.

I soon realized that there wasn't really any good way to say that you lived in your dead parents' house, so after that I answered any questions about my family by simply stating: "They live out west."

- What made you tell the lie?

Brinkman: Well, I suppose I sensed the possibility of reinventing myself. Not to mention, I desperately wanted a sibling. I'd watched the movie *Annie* countless times, and had decided life would be much better if I had someone to sing with me, and pillowfight with me, and to share the lonely darkness of my room at night.

Johnston: Is it too grandiose for me to say *'youth'*?

Maazel: I'm a compulsive liar.

Ohlin: Pride and stupidity, in equal measures.

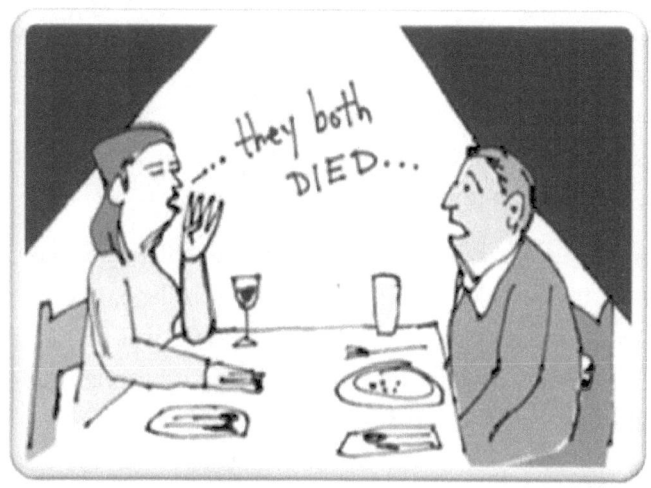

Rabb: Death is a bit of a damper on a conversation, and most people in their twenties don't have much experience with it. And apparently, mentioning you live in your dead parents' house does not make a man eager to become your boyfriend.

- What had you hoped to achieve by lying?

Brinkman: By convincing the other kids that I had a sister, my idea of a sibling became almost real. Silent, smiley Katie, while she lasted, was a brief and happy dream. For the record, I'm still an only child — a fate I've never learned to appreciate, even though my siblinged friends like to tell me how spoiled and lucky I am.

Johnston: Is it too easy to say that I wanted to protect Rebecca as much as I wanted to protect myself?

Talk Show

Maazel: I've always liked to tell stories, mostly the kind where I come off looking stupid. They are entertaining. Before I started writing in earnest, I told so many lies, I couldn't remember 95% of them. They were pointless, unmemorable — cocktail-party banter. But it made the parties fun. People laughed. After I started to write fiction with intent, I stopped telling stories and got boring real fast. If you ever see me at a party, I'm the one in the corner with nothing to say.

Ohlin: I'd just met these two other students, and wanted to befriend them. Like a lot of people in college, they seemed more sophisticated and worldly than I was. I was just some kid from the suburbs who hadn't seen very many foreign films. My only shot, as I saw it in that moment, was to fake it.

Rabb: To not feel like I was Edward Gorey in his raccoon coat, looking eccentric and kind of creepy. (Personally, I love Edward Gorey and would be entranced by anyone who showed up for a date wearing a raccoon coat, but that's just me.)

- What happened when you told the lie?

Brinkman: Katie's parents came to claim her. I was caught, and I'm sure my face turned red because I've never been skilled at hiding my shame. The other kids acted like they'd known all along. I remember one particularly ruthless comment from a girl who also must've taken notice of Katie's pink frills — "You're not even dressed nice," she blurted at me.

Johnston: Weeping, apologies, the quoting of scripture. You know, the usual.

Maazel: He laughed. Probably it doesn't sound all that amusing here, but come on: it's all in the telling.

154

Ohlin: Obviously, faking it had the exact opposite effect I'd hoped — it made me look far more idiotic than confessing I hadn't seen the movie would have. For a long time afterward, I couldn't look either of them in the eye. The one who started the whole chain of fake movie details never really warmed to me. The other person did become my friend, and remains one to this day.

Rabb: One night, I was set up with a friend's cousin who turned out to be religious, and he took me to a kosher restaurant. Under the influence of large quantities of kosher wine and his line of questioning, I embellished my "out west" story into a tale of my parents' happy existence in Colorado. I'd only been to Colorado once — but he had spent lots of time there. I kept evading his questions and, though he knew I was lying, I just couldn't break down and tell him the truth. Afterward, I never heard from him again, which was definitely for the best.

- If you could tweak the lie, how would you tweak it?

Brinkman: I don't know — I haven't grown up to become a more convincing or sophisticated fibber. Plus, such a bald-faced lie probably doesn't deserve to be tweaked.

Johnston: Honestly, I think about this from time to time, and I have no idea why I didn't simply say that I'd lost the necklace. In terms of lying options, that's certainly the one that corresponds most closely to Ockham's Razor. Why such Byzantine scheming? Rereading this now, the whole thing does smack of a bad episode of the *Brady Bunch*, probably one involving Peter or Jan. It's wholly embarrassing, as, I suppose, it should be.

Maazel: Why bother. Why look back?

Ohlin: Now that I'm older I could probably get away more easily with fudging a lie like this, saying "Oh yes, I've seen that, but it's been a long time" or something like that. But I have to say, the whole experience was so profoundly mortifying that I've rarely, if ever, pretended to see a movie or read a book that I haven't. I can't risk pretending to remember a scene with two-headed angel aliens again.

Rabb: "They live out west" was way too spartan — I should've gone all out and created a whole clan for myself with many generations of aunts and uncles and numerous siblings and cousins, modeled after *All My Children*.

Episode 14: *Generational Trauma*
with Elisa Albert, Anita Diamant, Michael Lowenthal, Askold Melnyczuk, and Jim Shepard

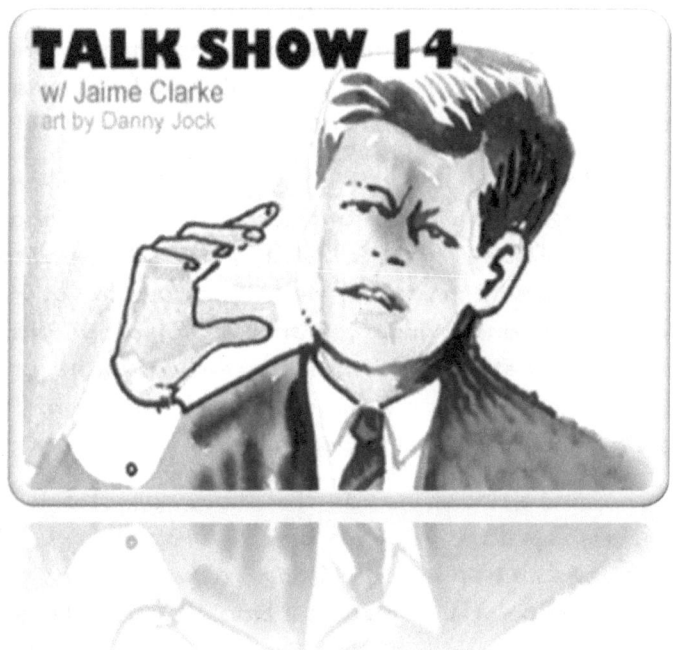

Elisa Albert's books include the short story collection *How This Night is Different* and the novels *The Book of Dahlia*, named one of the Ten best books of the year by *Entertainment Weekly*, and *The Fourth Trimester*. She is the editor of *Freud's Blind Spot: Writers on Siblings* and teaches creative writing at Columbia University.

Anita Diamant's first novel, *The Red Tent*, was awarded the Booksense Book of the Year. Her other books include the novels *Day After Night*, *Good Harbor*, and *The Last Days of Dogtown*; six nonfiction guides to contemporary Jewish life; and *Pitching My Tent*, a collection of personal essays.

Michael Lowenthal is the author of the novels *The Paternity Test, Charity Girl, Avoidance,* and *The Same Embrace.* His stories have been widely anthologized, including work in *Best New American Voices* and collections from *Tin House* and Nerve.com. The recipient of fellowships from the MacDowell Colony, the Bread Loaf and Wesleyan writers' conferences, and the Massachusetts Cultural Council, Lowenthal teaches creative writing in the MFA program at Lesley University.

Askold Melnyczuk has published four novels: *What is Told,* a *New York Times* notable book, *Ambassador of the Dead, House of Widows* and *Smedley's Secret Guide to World Literature.* He is the founder of *AGNI* literary magazine. Winner of an AWP George Garrett Award for outstanding community service in literature, Melnyczuk teaches at UMass Boston and in the Bennington Graduate Writing Seminars.

Jim Shepard's books include the story collections *Batting Against Castro, Love and Hydrogen, You Think That's Bad* and *Like You'd Understand Anyway,* which was a finalist for the National Book Award. He is the author of six novels including *Project X* (an ALEX Award winner), *Nosferatu* and *Kiss of the Wolf.* Shepard teaches at Williams College.

* * *

- Name one of the greatest traumas of your generation.

Albert: By my "generation," I assume you mean people born in the summer of 1978, right? Okay, so, I have to say that the school year of 1993/4 was pretty intensely traumatic for us. Within the span of some measly months, River Phoenix OD'd, Kurt Cobain committed suicide, and OJ (allegedly or whatever) killed his wife and a random friend of hers. This trio of mortality insanity was a lot at once, and included some powerful players in our collective cultural consciousness. It also sort of thrust the fact of violent, untimely death right up under our cushy, adolescent little noses. (That or, I suppose, George W. Bush stealing the fucking election in 2000. But I still can't deal with that one, so never mind.)

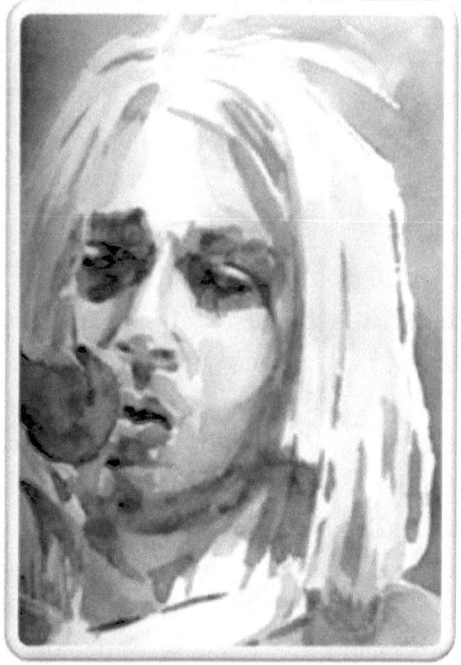

<u>Diamant</u>: The AIDS crisis of the 1980s.

<u>Lowenthal</u>: So many traumas, so little time! September 11th is the obvious one, but too much has probably been said about that already (see: Rudy Giuliani campaign, 2007). On the other end of the spectrum, the ball rolling through Bill Buckner's legs in the 1986 World Series caused its own kind of generational PTSD, at least here in Red Sox Nation. But the one I'm going to go with is George Bush's reelection in 2004. His initial "election" was trauma enough — forcing us to let go of any notion that the Supreme Court operates above political partisanship,

etcetera, etcetera — but in the wake of this utter disaster there was a sense that perhaps it was a fluke; that Bush's "Hey, let's all share some Beer Nuts" publicity machine was slick enough to have fooled America once, but not twice; and that millions of Americans, stung by Bush's illegal and immoral reign, would be more energized than ever to depose him. And so, when he managed to win AGAIN, and this time probably (though perhaps not) legitimately, even after having caused the deaths of so many Americans and Iraqis, even after having ruined America's standing in the international community, and even running against a legitimate war hero . . . well, this was just the definitive snuffing of all of our generations' hopes.

Melnyczuk: Birth is the first and greatest of traumas, of course, but we're hardly the first who've had to deal with that.

More recently, our response to the terrible attacks of September 11th is surely proof of a series of unprocessed traumas to which we have now added another chapter. Tragedy proved traumatic when the nation chose to go on the offensive, attacking a country with no clear links to the destruction of the World Trade Towers. "We" agreed to destroy Iraq in order to save it. Whenever I think of this place, "the cradle of civilization" as we were taught to call it in seventh grade World History, my heart sinks. Led by a stupid and narrow man, this country allowed itself to go berserk to appease its rage at having been caught off guard by a group of men with a long-standing grievance against the United States. Rarely have the consequences of personal grievances been so starkly evident as in the grief we have visited on millions of innocent people in Iraq and the surrounding region. I remember walking through Damascus some years ago, stunned by the number of refugees clogging its streets, and wondering how we imagined good coming out of our evil.

<u>Shepard</u>: I'm not sure whether it's my generation or not, but I still viscerally remember coming home from first grade to discover my father standing in the driveway, waving his arms to me and shouting to me before I even got into the house that President Kennedy had been shot. His shouting and arm-waving — the fact that he was evidently so unmoored by the event — floored me, and made me feel somewhat the way he did: as though someone had just pulled the rug out from under everything we believed in. So somebody — or the world — could just do *that*? Apparently they could. It was a lesson we'd have reinforced throughout the Sixties.

> "Led by a stupid and narrow man, this country allowed itself to go berserk to appease its rage at having been caught off guard by a group of men with a long-standing grievance against the United States. Rarely have the consequences of personal grievances been so starkly evident as in the grief we have visited on millions of innocent people in Iraq and the surrounding region."
> - Askold Melnyczuk

- What were you doing when this trauma occurred?

<u>Albert</u>: Variously nodding off in some obnoxious Advanced Placement high school course, cutting myself in the bathroom while my mother pounded on my locked bedroom door demanding that I turn down the *Smashing Pumpkins*, and using my '84 Volvo station wagon like a bumper car.

161

Diamant: I was working as a freelance journalist around Boston as the disease was slowly recognized, its cause identified, and then ravaged the gay community. As a straight woman, I was on the fringes of the disaster in many ways, but I wrote several stories about its devastation and how the local medical and gay communities rallied and responded. I also had a few gay friends, who were closer to the epicenter of the disaster. Eventually, it "came home" as I lost a colleague, and then a cousin.

Lowenthal: I had spent all of Election Day with my friend Jennifer Haigh, up in New Hampshire, at Kerry headquarters, phoning Democratic voters and making sure they were going to get to the polls. It felt good to be doing something concrete to help the cause, and as the party-insider info started rolling in, it seemed clear that we were going to win. We were so exhilarated! (And, in fact, New Hampshire was the only state in the country that voted for Bush in 2000 and then voted for Kerry in 2004.) At the end of the day we came home to Boston and hosted a victory party. Except that by that evening the early exit poll data had been discredited and it seemed Bush might have won. The Kerry/Edwards team had been planning their own official victory celebration downtown, in Copley Square. I couldn't persuade anyone to go with me, so I went alone. It was cold and rainy. CNN was playing on a huge Jumbotron. Ohio was going for Bush, then for Kerry, then for Bush. In the wee hours, John Edwards came out onto the stage and told us, in the most hopeless voice I've ever heard, not to lose hope.

Melnyczuk: At home, most likely watching television.

Shepard: See above.

"The fact that then-president Reagan did not utter the word "AIDS" until late into his second term was the most vivid demonstration of the way that the political establishment and lots of other people wanted to pretend it wasn't happening; that we weren't losing a generation of smart, creative, wonderful people."

- Anita Diamant

- How did those around you react this trauma?

Albert: Respectively: by blaming the victim, blaming the victim, and blaming the victim.

Diamant: It was a very bifurcated response: total mobilization or full denial. The fact that then-president Reagan did not utter the word "AIDS" until late into his second term was the most vivid demonstration of the way that the political establishment and lots of other people wanted to pretend it wasn't happening; that we weren't losing a generation of smart, creative, wonderful people. On the other hand, the gay community grew up as a response to AIDS; gay men and lesbians of my generation took action, struggled, fought, coalesced, took care of their own, built institutions and organizations, and transformed the cultural landscape forever. They fought the war on AIDS. They were helped and supported by doctors, nurses, social workers, and volunteers I met while working as a reporter; those people threw themselves into the fight against the disease — both as clinicians and as researchers and as human beings — with total dedication and passion.

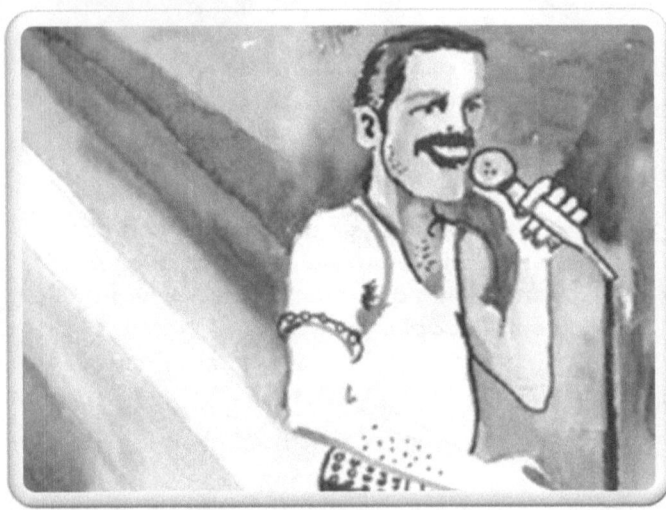

In the end, the AIDS crisis changed the way that vast segments of the straight community understood homosexuality and gay people. It was very personal, finally. The losses of brothers and sisters, children and friends helped turned the tide against homophobia, person by person, family by family. NOT TO SAY IT'S OVER. Matthew Shepard was murdered long after the disease stopped making headlines in America, long after AIDS became a chronic rather than a fatal disease for many. But attitudes were changed as a result of the public and proud acknowledgement of the presence of gay people everywhere in our culture and in our families.

Lowenthal: The crowd in Copley Square was so stunned and sad. It was as though our optimism was a beautiful creature that had been amputated at the knees. Against all our better judgment during the dark times since 2000 and Bush's stolen election, we had kept some faith in "the system" and its ability to correct itself, in truth as opposed to truthiness, in the "reality-based community." But now we seemed irreparably detached from our country and its people (and it was weird to have this happen in real time, in the rain, with John Edwards less than fifty feet away, seeming so small up there on that stage). I know many folks who gave up entirely on politics after this, who refused to read the newspapers or to vote again. Which means that Bush and his team scored their ultimate victory, far beyond this specific election.

Melnyczuk: Most of us were puzzled, unsure, confused by the information coming to us from our usual sources of information, so we watched more television.

Shepard: My family (mother, father, older brother, and me) spent the rest of the day and the days following around the television, seeing the same information over and over, until *that* changed dramatically, too, when Lee Harvey Oswald was himself assassinated in custody. Throughout all of that, the family's inability to look away, to go on to something else: that also seemed undeniable evidence that this was a massively important event.

"The majority (or, the majority of those who participate in the political process) seems to be small-minded, selfish, and fundamentally skeptical of the idea that government can be a force for good."

- Michael Lowenthal

Talk Show

- Which traumas for other generations, past and present, do you imagine are the equivalent?

<u>Albert</u>: I don't think generational trauma, by its very nature, can ever be equivalent to anything but itself. It'd be ridiculous to bring up Pearl Harbor or the assassination of JFK here, would it not? But I'd be curious to talk to someone a decade younger than myself about Britney's head-shaving and etcetera.

<u>Diamant</u>: I wouldn't want to compare this to wartime traumas, or even to other epidemics, since AIDS was/is such a loaded cultural phenomenon as well as a medical crisis. I leave it to history and historians to determine whether it was truly a "unique" moment.

<u>Lowenthal</u>: I don't know. I think of the challenges to progressive Americans' faith during the '60s, when so many bright and shining leaders were assassinated. I know these events must have been unbearably hope-crushing. But it was possible then, I imagine, to believe (and perhaps rightly) that the killings were the acts of deranged individuals, and didn't represent the will of the mainstream. Indeed, in some cases the losses may have galvanized the majority to further progressive action. In 2004, by contrast, nobody was killed, but the loss of faith was severe because it became clearer than ever that the majority of Americans — tens of millions of my countrymen and — women — was committed to taking action AGAINST progressive values. The majority (or, the majority of those who participate in the political process) seems to be small-minded, selfish, and fundamentally skeptical of the idea that government can be a force for good.

<u>Melnyczuk</u>: Vietnam, Cuba, El Salvador, Tiananmen, Palestine, Afghanistan, Guatemala, East Timor, Rwanda, the Sudanese wars, the invasion of Tibet, the Korean war, the destruc-

tion of Sarajevo, the Armenian Genocide, the Famine, World War II — depending, I suppose, on your family background.

Obviously, I'm suggesting that when a nation resorts to avoidable violence it is acting out of an earlier trauma it has not managed to examine and resolve. Consider this one statistic: at the start of the 20th century, when nations went to war, the ensuing casualties were 90% military, 10% civilian. By century's end, the ratio was reversed: now, in many conflicts, the casualties tend to be 90% civilian, 10% military. The safest place to be during a war, it seems, is in the army.

Shepard: Who knows, really? The intensities of traumas I'd assume have everything to do with individual idiosyncrasies. I'm sure I had some classmates who were more or less unfazed by the Kennedy assassination. I don't remember, now.

- How has your relationship to the trauma changed over the years?

Albert: Now I understand that women are routinely and commonly murdered by their boyfriends/ex-boyfriends/ husbands/ex-husbands, so that's not a shocker anymore. And as for River and Cobain, they've both been deified pretty thoroughly, so it's hard to imagine them living on as mere mortals. And since I'm an adult now, these tabloid horrors can seem a mite trivial. Compared to, say, GWB's stealing the fucking election. For example.

Diamant: "Crisis mode" is long past in North America. I have another cousin who is HIV-positive and has been for many years; he is healthy and thriving. The AIDS crisis rages in Africa and other parts of the world. When I read about it, I recall the sense of despair engendered by all of those death announcements in the newspaper, the ones that you had to interpret to figure out if they were from AIDS or not, and then, later, the ones that clearly stated HIV/AIDS as the cause of death. Every now and then I experience a sort of "phantom limb" phenomenon, when a name is mentioned — a choreographer, a writer, a composer, a friend's deceased lover: they should be here and they are not. We have no idea, really, what was lost. What might have been saved had the response been quicker, more compassionate, more appropriate to the threat. I suppose I'm still angry about that. But I'm also grateful for and proud of the courage and conviction of everyone — gay and straight — who fought so hard to save lives and to challenge misunderstanding of and bigotry based on sexual identity.

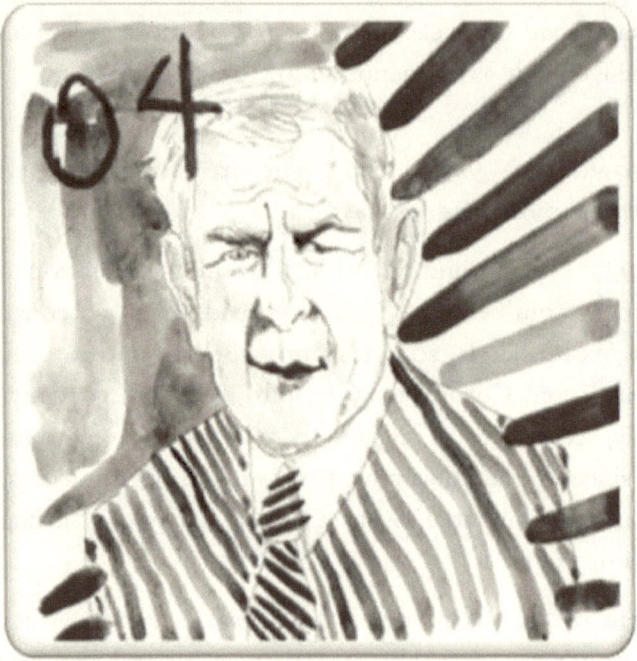

Lowenthal: I remain battered, and wonder if my faith will ever be restored. In 2000, I allowed myself to believe that Bush's election was a fluke. Now, after having lived through 2004, I think I'll consider a Democratic victory (if there is one)

to be the fluke. I'll accept it, and happily, but I won't make the mistake of thinking it betokens any kind of turn toward the better by, or smartening up of, my fellow Americans. I've become entrenched in my alienation. I recently applied for German citizenship, wanting an "out" in case our country continues to devolve. How ironic that Germany, the country from which my grandparents fled in 1939 (and from which other relatives were unable to flee), looms now as a possible haven.

Melnyczuk: The worst part of this is that we as a nation have little real awareness of the damage and destruction we've caused. We have a vague sense of our military casualties in Iraq and Afghanistan, but we know almost nothing about the ways we've destroyed the ability of millions to live what we would consider "normal" lives. Our bombs, our missiles, and our drones have killed thousands of children, women, and men over the years. Each had parents, grandparents, siblings, cousins. The consequences of violent actions tend to play out as trauma across generations — only consider how long it has taken to begin healing the wound of slavery.

My awareness of the consequences of this recent trauma remains intermittent — maybe because life would be too painful were one to inhabit it regularly and own it fully. Even those directly affected by violence — the victims and perpetrators both — want nothing more than to get beyond it. This, alas, is rarely an easy process — and yet it can be done, and is being done daily, by millions. I remember talking about this once with Susan Sontag who'd recently published a book in which she proposed a national dose of amnesia as a cure for our ills. Remember, but forgive, I argued back.

Instinct tells me that we don't dare forget what we've (often silently, sometimes under protest) allowed to happen to so many innocent people, because the consequences of an action take a long time — generations — to play themselves out. I suppose this is just the age-old argument for the importance of studying history: if you want to understand why you woke up where you did today, you have to remember where you were the night before, and so on, as far back as memory and imagination will take you.

Which gets us back to birth.

Shepard: I'm certainly, for better and for worse, now more likely to expect it.

Episode 15:
Historical Person You'd Like to Meet
with Kevin Brockmeier, Sloane Crosley, Sophie Gee, Samantha Hunt, and Melissa Pritchard

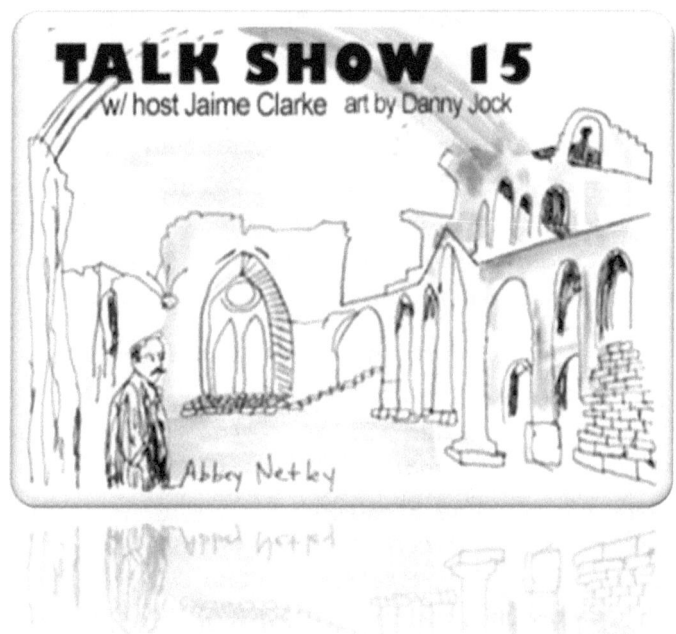

Kevin Brockmeier is the author of the novels *Illumination*, *The Brief History of the Dead* and *The Truth About Celia*; the children's novels *City of Names* and *Grooves: A Kind of Mystery*; and the story collections *Things That Fall from the Sky* and *The View from the Seventh Layer*. He was awarded a Guggenheim Fellowship and named one of *Granta* magazine's Best Young American Novelists.

Sloane Crosley is the author of the essay collections *I Was Told There'd Be Cake* and *How Did You Get This Number*. Her essays and criticism have appeared in the

New York Times, New York Observer, the *Village Voice, Playboy, Teen Vogue, Salon, Black Book, Radar* and *Maxim.* Her first novel, *The Clasp,* will be released in 2015.

Sophie Gee is the author of the novel *The Scandal of the Season,* a historical romance named one of the Best Books of the year by the *Washington Post,* and a nonfiction title: *Making Waste: Leftovers and the Eighteenth-Century Imagination.* She teaches at Princeton University.

Samantha Hunt received the Bard Fiction Prize for *The Invention of Everything Else,* a novel about the life of Nikola Tesla. Her first book, *The Seas,* was awarded a National Book Foundation award for writers under 35. She teaches at the Pratt Institute.

Melissa Pritchard is the author of four short story collections: *The Odditorium, Disappearing Ingenue, The Instinct for Bliss,* and *Spirit Seizures;* four novels, *Palmerino, Late Bloomer, Selene of the Spirits,* and *Phoenix,* as well as a biography of Virginia Galvin Piper. Her work has appeared in the *Paris Review, Conjunctions, Pushcart Prize Stories* and the *O. Henry Awards,* among other publications.

* * *

- Name a historical person you'd like to meet and why.

Brockmeier: James Agee. He wrote one of my favorite novels, *A Death in the Family,* and a few years ago, I decided to read the Library of America edition of his collected film criticism. It's a volume of great wit, passion, and clarity, as valuable (to me at least) as anything by Pauline Kael, but my enjoyment of it was hampered slightly by the fact that all of the movies Agee discusses were released decades before I was born, and roughly ninety percent of them I have never seen. I was seized by a fantasy of traveling back in time to show him some more recent films so that I could find out what he made of them. Agee, I recognize, is a relatively recent figure, and even in the circle of modern-American-literature lovers he does not have the cultural currency of, say, Hemingway or Faulkner, but I think it's fair to consider him a "historical person," insofar as history is ongoing and he's no longer in it.

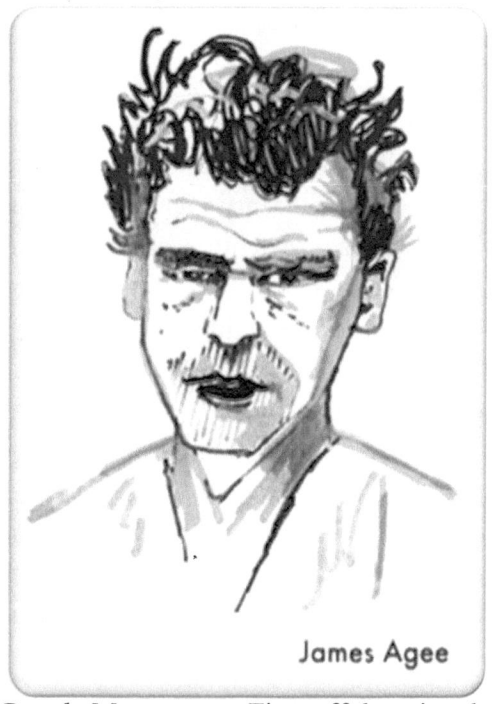

James Agee

Crosley: Guy de Maupassant. First off, he wins the award for Writer with The Most Serious Moustache of All Time. You may even be able to chop "writer" off of that distinction. Beyond that, I think it would be fascinating to meet one of the most prolific short story writers in history knowing what I/we know now: that he is most famous for a single story. And one that's probably one of the shorter tales he wrote and almost nothing like the rest in form or topic. "The Necklace" is truly amazing and ingenious; but it's also a fluke in a way, wrapped up with a heavy punch line. He's not the only writer that's ever happened to, but the irony that "The Necklace" itself is based around a simple misunderstanding . . . I just wonder how he'd feel about that, if he would see the connection or if he would have picked it out as standing the test of time. Also he grew up with Flaubert as a kindly uncle figure and led a pretty privileged life, so if I could go back in time and meet him, I'm pretty sure I'd have a nice French chateau to stay in and some great dinner companions.

Gee: I'd like to meet Lady Mary Wortley Montagu, an eighteenth century English noblewoman who ended up being one of the most brilliant and eccentric figures of all time. She was born at the end of the seventeenth century, and she could have been an idle aristocrat like other women of her class. But instead she became a celebrated intellectual, a poet and an intimate friend of Alexander Pope, John Gay and other famous writers of the time. In 1712 she eloped with a man named Edward Wortley, forfeiting her inheritance, and went to live in Turkey in 1716, where her husband was the British Ambassador. She discovered a form of smallpox inoculation already used in Turkey, and after first having her own children inoculated, she introduced the treatment into England, where she persuaded the King of England to inoculate his children. She was a brilliant, unconventional woman living in the historical period that I find most exciting. Instead of being trapped by the conventions of her social world, she defied them.

Hunt: I'd like to meet dead people from my family. I never knew my mom's dad. But perhaps that's not what you mean by historical, maybe historical has to have famous in there also. Then, the inventor Nikola Tesla. I've been writing a novel about him for four years and despite his having lived until 1943, I've never been able to find a film or recording of his voice. I'd like to hear him speak since he's been in my head for so long.

Pritchard: One name insists, that of a place, not a person: Netley Abbey, a 13th century Cistercian monastery, now a ruin, inland from Southampton Water in southern England, six miles south of the former site of the Royal Victorian Military Hospital and Lunatic Asylum, and an hour's ferry ride from the city of Southampton, former eighteenth century resort spa for English royalty, aristocracy and the likes of novelist Jane Austen, painter John Constable, poet Thomas Gray and the great Gothic aesthete, Horace Walpole, author of *The Castle of Otranto*, and his 'Committee of Taste,' all of whom paid homage to Netley Abbey. Chosen for its wild, remote location, an ascetic monastery funded by Henry III and designed by the French Gothic architect, Abbot Suger, Netley Abbey, in its near one-thousand-year history, has adapted itself, reflected and borne every human vagary and longing — for spiritual rigor, wealth, sensation, victory over death, for romance and morbid expression, for theater, paganism, reclusivity and intrigue. A shimmering timeline of English history, including its Kings and Queens, has passed through this place, originally, ironically selected for its isolation, its inaccessibility.

- Under what circumstances would you like to meet this person?

Brockmeier: Scene: James Agee steps out of a cab in front of The Nation's offices at Broadway and Fulton. He takes the elevator to the eleventh floor (he would never consider climbing the stairs). It's Friday evening, most of the magazine's personnel have already finished their work and gone home for the night. Agee is only stopping by to pick up his jacket, which he has left draped over the arm of his chair. He walks down the corridor — it's so quiet that he can hear his shoelaces brushing the carpet — and opens the door of his office. Inside he finds me waiting with a laptop computer and a stack of DVDs.

Crosley: While standing on the street and looking into the window of Cartier. I would spot his reflection in the window as he approached. And then he would say something like: "I can get it for you wholesale."

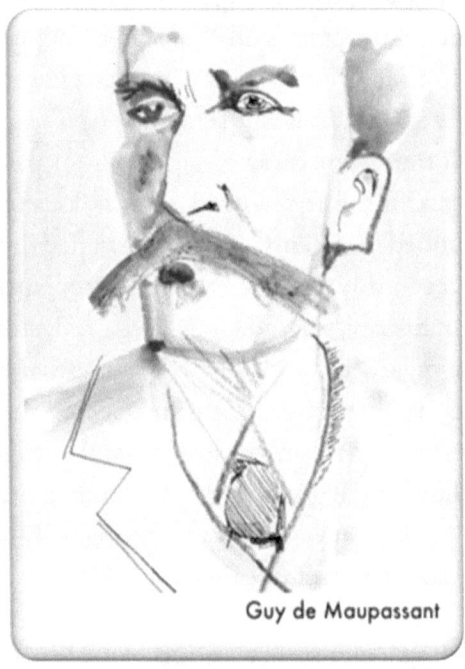

Guy de Maupassant

Gee: Since this is a game about history, of course I'd like to travel back in time to meet her. Lady Mary wrote a vivid series of letters about the years she spent in Turkey, which include a description of a visit to a Turkish bath, and the splendid meals and receptions that she was part of at the Royal Palace in Istanbul. I'd like to follow her around at those events, not just to see a historical period that has disappeared, but to see the Ottoman Empire in its full splendor too.

Hunt: I'd go back to 1893. We'd have a big dinner at the newly opened Waldorf Hotel, when it was where the Empire State Building is now. His friends Mark Twain, John Muir, Robert and Katharine Johnson would all be there. We'd eat oysters that had been pulled from New York Harbor. After dinner we'd walk slowly through 1893 Manhattan, down to Tesla's laboratory for a show of the wonders he'd been working on — wireless transmission of energy and information, oscillating resonance, flying machines, lightning.

Pritchard: 1): I'd like to be whatever bed Queen Elizabeth I tossed and turned her pale, lithesome, virginal self upon in Netley Abbey, turned grand house belonging to the Earl of Hertford, on August 13th, 1560, when she stayed the night during one of her "royal progresses." To be the straw and silk-embroidered linen beneath England's most fretful power, unable to find rest in this or any woodland sanctuary, to be that one fortunate cushion privy to a night of fierce, warring "Queenes Maiestees" thought!

2): I'd like to be that fatal stone, arch keystone of the chapel's East window, which fell upon the eminent Southampton builder William Taylor's eighteenth century head as he attempted to tear down a part of the Abbey which he had purchased for materials — after he had dreamed of this very stone, of its role in his death. Oh, to be the instrument, the gruesome stone which did Fate's bidding!

3): I'd like to be that gorgeously fleshed woman, masked, but otherwise naked, an eighteenth century reveler on a midsummer's eve, seduced and seducing in the moonlit, owl-infested Abbey ruins, counted the very next day, in Southampton, among the minor aristocracy, wondrously bejeweled, daintily dressed, demure as a nun, aloof.

- What would you say to this person, and what do expect the response to be?

Brockmeier: "Who is this odd little man," James Agee would be certain to think when he saw me, "and what is he doing in my office?" I'm sure he would be reluctant to believe me when I told him that I'd come from the future to show him some movies I thought he might enjoy. But after a few minutes of conversation any doubts he might have would begin to waver, and once I booted up the computer and loaded the first DVD, he would be absolutely convinced by my story. "No," I'd explain to him, "people in 2008 don't do all their movie-watching on these little plastic cases with the flat screens. They're portable, though, and I had no way of carrying an entire theater back in time with me. I apologize."

Crosley: I think I'd ask him which of his stories he personally got the most out of writing. I'd probably also ask him about the last days of his life, assuming that he understands me meeting him is an experiment and wouldn't be offended by me saying, "hey, what kind of torture is it to attempt to kill yourself and then die anyway a few years later?"

Gee: I'd want to ask her how an eighteenth century mother felt about her children, living in a world where childbirth was dangerous and where children might die, what it felt like traveling across Europe in a carriage, unprotected from winter weather and dangerous roads — basically what it was like to live in luxury, and yet be constantly in danger. I don't know what she'd say — these are aspects of eighteenth century life I can't get my head around.

Hunt: I certainly wouldn't tell him that I wrote a novel about him! Though perhaps I'd slip a copy under his pillow so he'd find it after I was long gone. I'd tell him that six months after he died, the Supreme Court finally ruled that he is the man who invented radio, not Marconi. I wouldn't tell him that no one pays any attention to that decision.

Pritchard: How fortunate, to have lived nearly one thousand years as a sumptuous, holy whore of English history! How I envy your chapel's very foundational stone, inscribed H: DI. GRA. REX ANGL. 'Henry, by the grace of God, king of England.' . . . envy your witness to centuries of spiritual tediums and raptures, to poetry's transcendence, to aesthetic fevers, to ambition's Machiavellian labors. You have been like the greatest of actresses, and the longest lived — you have been and you remain, the mirrored surface, the immortal fragment of glass every novelist wishes to be.

The response: a predictable, contrapuntal, maddening Silence.

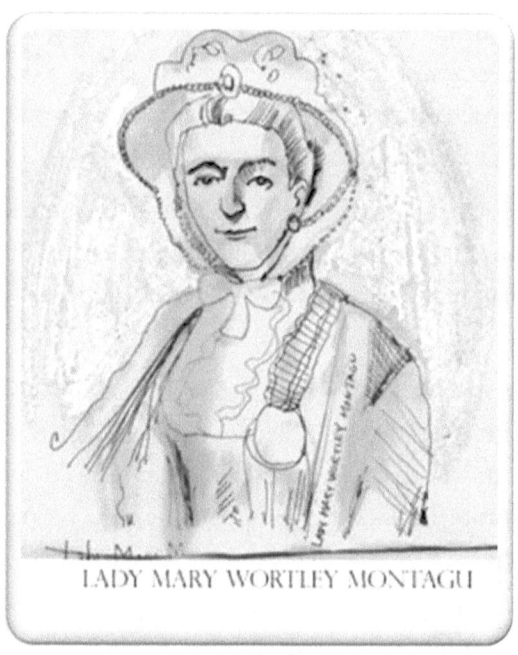

LADY MARY WORTLEY MONTAGU

- If you could tell this person something about the future, what would it be?

<u>Brockmeier</u>: The whole purpose of my visit would be to show Mr. Agee a number of modern films and listen in on his reaction to them, which is why, in my fantasy, I always find myself restricting my selection to only a handful of movies, few enough that the two of us would have time to watch and discuss them over the course of a couple of days. I imagine myself choosing a combination of critical or popular landmarks (*The Godfather, E.T., Titanic, Pulp Fiction, Groundhog Day*), personal favorites (*Ponette, Running on Empty, Crouching Tiger, Hidden Dragon*), and films that I think would particularly suit Agee's aesthetic (*Matewan, The Thin Red Line, Pather Pachali*). I'd like him to see how the art of film has developed — if not progressed — since his time, in both its narrative sensibilities and its technical capacities.

<u>Crosley</u>: I'd tell him that moustaches are going to be huge in 1970's America and that they will eventually be associated with an actor named Burt Reynolds. I imagine this would get a rise out of any Frenchman of any century.

<u>Gee</u>: The obvious thing to tell her about the future would be that immunology would turn out to be the most fundamental and life-changing medical field, and that she was one of the pioneers.

<u>Hunt</u>: Rather than telling him about the future I'd like to have him here in 2008, for an afternoon. Sitting in the middle of sunny Central Park, with no wires attached, I'd like to show him my laptop. I'd like to type his name into Google while he watches what comes up.

<u>Pritchard</u>: That your most glittering eras are passed, gone, that you can look forward to a slow dissolution back into the

very forces of quarry stone, Hampshire soil and fresh seawater that created you, but that you'll always enjoy some form of eternity. I'd also warn you of history's distortions, lapses, miscarriages of truth, stupendous errors and follied projections — that most of your stories, most of the human history you have inspired, absorbed and still draw upon to haunt, remains secret, cupboarded, subsumed.

- What warning would you give this person about his/her own historical era?

Brockmeier: I would be tempted to tell James Agee that he was killing himself with drink and cigarettes and that, in just a few short years, he would suffer a massive heart attack in the back of a taxi and die before he could reach the hospital. My sense, though, is that everyone who knew and cared for him gave him this warning, or one very much like it, time and time again, so why would he listen to me? Instead, then, I'd simply let him know how much I love his books, and afterwards I'd keep my mouth shut.

Crosley: Hmmm . . . I'd tell him to be wary of tiny emperors in big hats. Then maybe I'd explain how an indoor flush toilet works.

Gee: I don't think I could tell her anything about her historical era that she wouldn't already sense; that in spite of the confidence and excitement of the Enlightenment, she was living in precarious times. Perhaps I'd tell her that world revolution was coming, and the Europe that she had known as a noblewoman would be changed irrevocably by the French Revolution in fifty years' time. She would never see it, but massive social change was on the march. Maybe I'd tell her that the Enlightenment dream that mankind could perfect itself would turn out to be impossible. But it's hard to believe that someone of her experience wouldn't already sense that.

Hunt: Tesla lost years of work — inventions that never were — in a fire on March 13, 1895. I'd warn him about that. I'd also tell him, don't worry, Prohibition won't last. He always thought he'd live to be 125, 130 years old. He blamed Prohibition — the deprivation of his daily whiskey — for shaving years off his life.

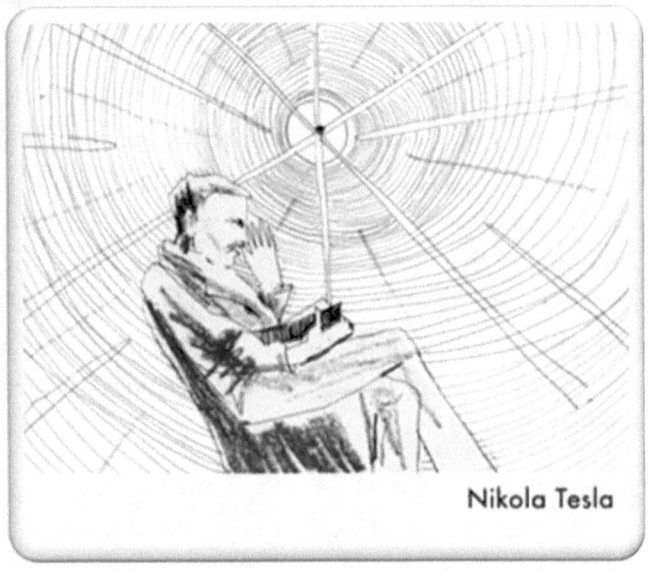

Nikola Tesla

Pritchard: Human beings understand even less than the cows and sheep wandering through your echoing, emptied, verdant spaces and broken walls, even less than the ghosts layering the air, even less than the crows skimming down from the surrounding beech and ash trees, flying through your arched, unglassed windows, that you have consciousness, that you LIVE, that you are God's own elements, shaped, trembling and finite, into man's piteous Dreams. I'd also warn you that none will every truly know you, that it is only themselves they see, seek, have ever sought, in your construction, destruction, partial resurrection.

Episode 16: *Life-changing Technology*
with Elizabeth Crane, Michael Dahlie, Tony D' Souza, J. Robert Lennon, and Salvatore Scibona

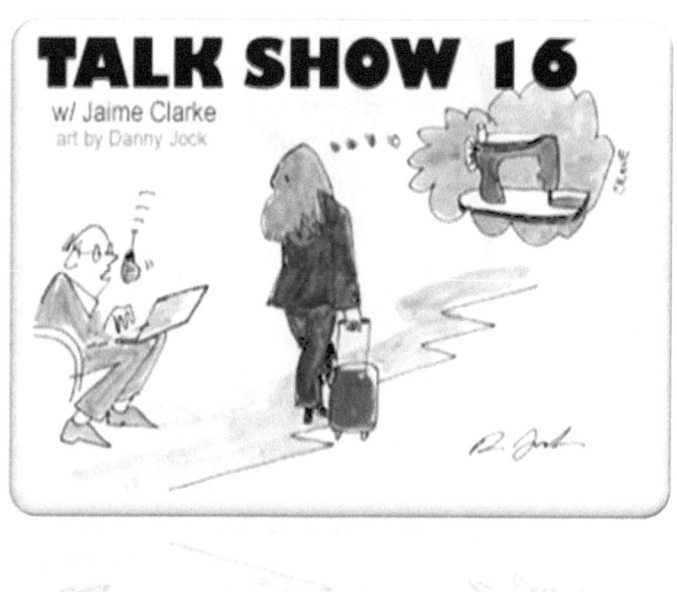

Elizabeth Crane is the author of the novel *We Only Know So Much* and three short story collections: *When the Messenger is Hot, All This Heavenly Glory* and *You Must Be This Happy to Enter.* Her work has appeared in *Washington Square, New York Stories, Sycamore Review, Florida Review, Sonora Review* and others and has been adapted for stage and screen. She is a recipient of the Chicago Public Library 21st Century Award and teaches at the University of California.

Michael Dahlie is the author of the novels *A Gentleman's Guide to Graceful Living* - winner of the Pen/ Hemingway and Whiting Awards, and *The Best of Youth.* His short stories have appeared in *Harpers', Ploughshares,* the *Kenyon Review,* and others. He is the Booth Tarkington Writer-in-Residence at Butler University.

Tony D'Souza is the author of the novel *Whiteman,* which received the Sue Kaufman First Fiction Prize from the American Academy of Arts and Letters, Best First Fiction from *Poets & Writers Magazine,* and the Florida Gold Medal for Fiction. His other books include *The Konkans* and *Mule: A Novel of Moving Weight.* D'Souza's work has appeared in the *New Yorker, Playboy, Salon, Esquire, Tin House, Granta* and others.

J. Robert Lennon is the author of a story collection, *Pieces For The Left Hand,* and seven novels, including *Mailman, Castle,* and *Familiar.* His work has appeared in the *New Yorker, Harper's, Playboy, Granta,* the *Paris Review,* and elsewhere. Lennon has been anthologized in *Best American Short Stories, Best American Nonrequired Reading,* and *Prize Stories: The O. Henry Awards.* He teaches at Cornell University.

Salvatore Scibona's novel, *The End,* was a finalist for the National Book Award, and winner of the Young Lions Fiction Award from the New York Public Library and the Norman Mailer Cape Cod Award for Exceptional Writing. His fiction has appeared in the *Threepenny Review, Best New American Voices,* the *Pushcart Prize XXV,* the *Pushcart Book of Short Stories* and others. A former Fulbright Fellow, Scibona administers the writing fellowship at the Fine Arts Work Center in Provincetown, Massachusetts.

* * *

\- Name a technology that changed your life.

<u>Crane</u>: Technology is something I think about often — my grandmother lived to be 104, and she spoke often of her memory of seeing her first car (interestingly, she never got a

license!), and it really strikes me that her lifetime was one of such extraordinarily major and rapid changes in technology that to live to see all that must have been something (although when I'd ask her, or my dad, who's eighty now, the reply was always slightly more than a shrug). Of course, I realize from my own experience that, day-to-day, it doesn't seem so rapid, but overall, there have been some pretty remarkable changes in my lifetime as well, and trying to pick one was hard! I remember when call-waiting came out — I was a typical teenager who would agonize over a possibly-missed phone call while my heinously insensitive parents were busy tying up the line, you know, the one they were paying for. And answering machines! And VCRs! Computers, obviously. I'm just old enough to have done a long stretch as a beginning writer in the typewriter era. So in trying to think of something simpler, I was really torn between two things: the wheeled suitcase (because why in hell did it take so long to figure this out?) and the sewing machine — my final answer.

Dahlie: In the late seventies, quite astonishingly, I found myself in London attending a fairly strict school where I knew absolutely none of the things I was apparently supposed to know for my age. Among my many failings, the thing that made my American ignorance entirely unbearable to the authorities was that I had horrible penmanship. They made everyone write with a fountain pen — even in math — and this was a device that I had no idea even existed growing up in Minneapolis. Every piece of paper I touched was covered with intolerable smears and smudges. The problem was that there was no way to fake it, especially since using a so-called biro (a ball point pen) was absolutely forbidden and easily detectable. And then came the roller ball, an unbelievable way to cheat since it performed without smudging but featured what the industry heralded as the "wet ink effect." Perhaps this technology is not appreciated in the US where there's no such fountain pen enthusiasm, but after the roller ball, I spent considerably less time crying over my homework in the evening.

D'Souza: The Japanese bidet-toilet, or 'Washlet.' The cover opens automatically when it senses you approaching, it's got a heated seat, and of course it washes you with warm water when you are done doing le deux. And it doesn't just wash you, but the water stream pulses and sprays, it has like three settings and it goes through all of them, like a car wash. If you want an enema, it can do that, too. All that remains is to dry off, which can be accomplished with paper or a convenient hand towel.

Lennon: I'm going to say the stompbox. For the uninitiated, this is the colloquial term for a guitar effects pedal, an electro-mechanical device that is inserted in the signal chain between an electric guitar (or other electric instrument, like a keyboard) and an amplifier, PA system, or recording device, for the purpose of altering, in one way or another, the instrument's sound. I'll admit to not particularly liking the name "stompbox": it's one of those words that describes not the object's function but the motion required to activate it (e.g., "clicker" instead of "remote" for a TV remote control). But "pedal" has other meanings in the world of rock music (kick drum pedal, keyboard sustain pedal), and "stompbox" feels good to say. So, stompbox.

Scibona: It would be imprecise to say that television *changed* my life, since it started its long campaign to smother any pleasure I might take from life before I was born. I must have heard it in utero calling to me: *"Come and be sad. Sleep restlessly. Awake stupider than yesterday. Abandon hope."* But in any case it's had a deep effect. The change came when I stopped watching it.

- How was this technology introduced into your life?

Crane: My mom, my stepmom, and both of my grandmothers were extremely skilled seamstresses, and taught me when I was in grade school.

Dahlie: I'm not sure when the roller ball was actually developed and available to the public, but I am sure that young people in London didn't generally know about it until 1979. In 1979, my class had a project involving speculations about what might happen if we were stranded on a deserted island. My essay dealt with inventive ways to catch fish, but I couldn't get through more than a few lines without an unforgivable smudge. Since the essays were to be glued to white cardboard placards and displayed for parents' night, no mistake would be tolerated. Sensing my desperation, a very unusual and deeply sympathetic teacher said she had something that might help me, namely a blue ink roller ball. It seemed impossible that such a thing would be allowed, but I was desperate, and used the roller ball to finish my work (incredibly, I was even allowed to take it home that night).

D'Souza: I just spent five months in Hokkaido, Japan, studying Ainu storytelling. My hotel in Tokyo had a deluxe Washlet, and my apartment in Hokkaido had one, too. Of the two, the one in my apartment was much better because it also had a sink at the top of the toilet. When you'd flush, the water that would refill the tank would first run down from a spigot and into this sink, which was also the top of the tank. It was a really elegant design. So you could rinse off your hands with the water that would go into the next flush. So obvious and so good for the environment. In fact, my whole toilet/tub/shower bathroom system was state of the art. My tub pre-heated my bathwater according to a timer, my shower was also a steam room, and my toilet played music. There was a little TV built into the wall with a non-steam screen. My toilet and I watched Wimbledon together like that this summer. Everything in there was made of durable plastic and everything had a digital console with a lot of buttons. I felt like I was on a space station.

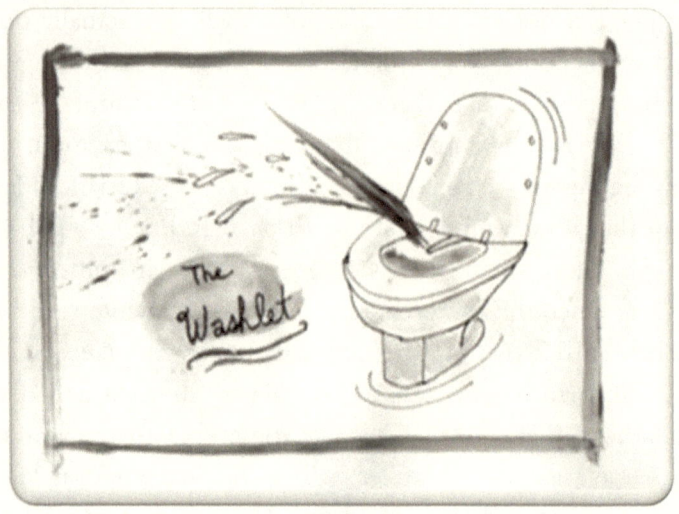

Lennon: My friend Carl, in high school, had an Ibanez Tube Screamer. This is an overdrive pedal — an effect that attempts, via solid-state technology (i.e., transistors) to mimic the sound of a tube-based amplification circuit (i.e., a tube amp, such as the Fender tweed Deluxe, aka "Tweed") in a compact, sturdy package. It sounded awesome. But for some reason, even though I desired a stompbox of my own, I resisted buying one. Somehow it didn't seem possible that I could successfully use one to enhance my own guitar playing. Also, the music I liked at the time did not feature a lot of distortion. I liked REM: jangly pop music that employed "clean" guitar sounds. It wasn't until I was in my late twenties, married and with a child, that I bought my own first stompbox: a DOD FX64 "Ice Box" stereo chorus.

Scibona: In the normal way. It perched in the corner of the living room, peering down on me and my family with "suave malice" (as I think Halldór Laxness writes of a barn cat). When it was on, it seemed like the whole living world, which would have made me, watching from outside it, dead. Right?

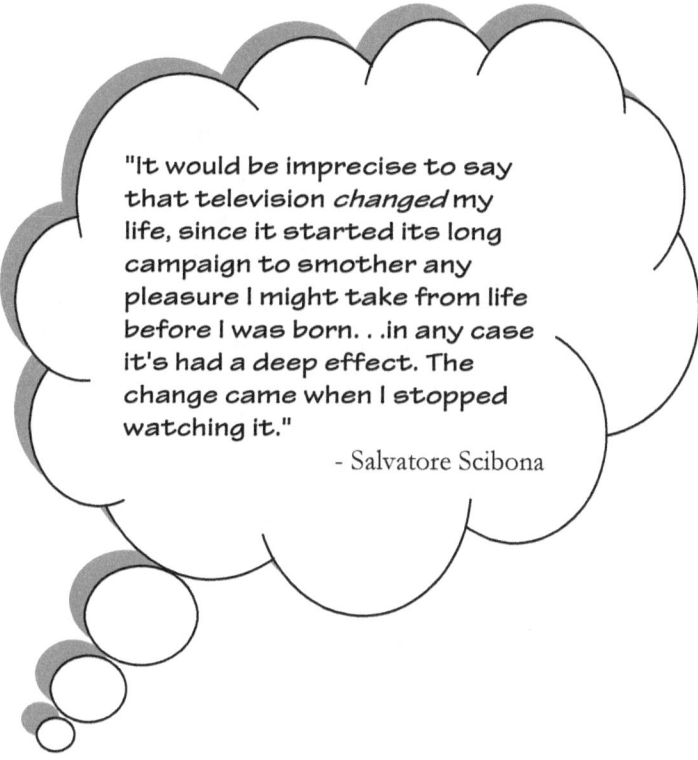

"It would be imprecise to say that television *changed* my life, since it started its long campaign to smother any pleasure I might take from life before I was born. . .in any case it's had a deep effect. The change came when I stopped watching it."

\- Salvatore Scibona

- What was the immediate impact of this technology on your life?

Crane: We didn't have a lot of money when I was young, and my mother sewed me (and my dolls) some beautiful clothes from the time I was little through maybe fourth grade — I had a lot of clothes that were of course, better than most store-bought clothes. For special occasions, she continued to sew me things as long as she was alive — my high-school graduation dress, a bridesmaid dress that eventually became my wedding dress, she even reupholstered a sofa of mine, and I continue to sew myself, on my grandmother's thirty-five-year old sewing machine, although my skills are nowhere near as advanced. I still live on a pretty modest budget, and have made curtains, quilts, and simple garments for myself frequently over the years — I enjoy it, it's practical, and it gives me a great feeling of pride.

Dahlie: These pens were actually somewhat expensive, and since I was afraid to own up to using one, I didn't ask my parents for the money. Instead, I saved a portion of my allowance for a few weeks and eventually raised the cash I needed to get one. For my in-class work, of course, it made no impact, since I couldn't be seen with such a pen. But it made a difference with my homework. I used the pen sparingly, however — a very detailed and expert inspection of roller ball handwriting would, in fact, allow a teacher to determine what I was doing, and I was always afraid of getting caught.

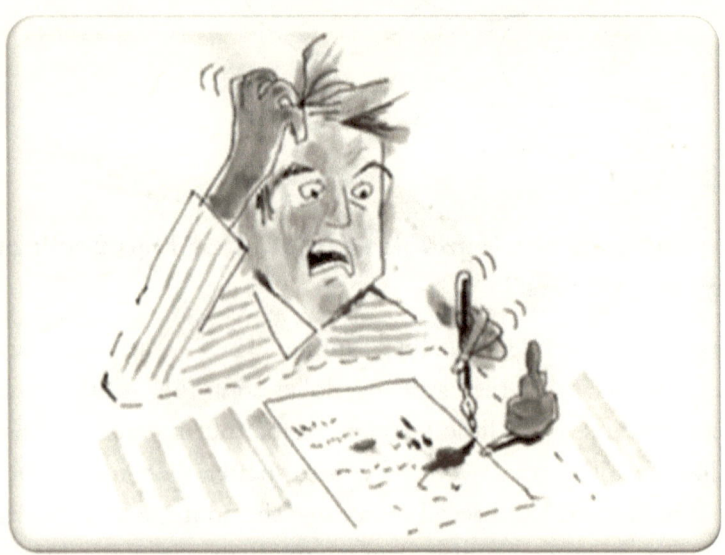

D'Souza: The first pleasure was the surprise of the warm toilet seat after a long flight and on an otherwise cold day. And the second pleasure was being washed so clean by the toilet after doing 'Number 2' that I would definitely eat spaghetti in a thick ragu sauce off of myself. Look, the point is the thing gets you clean. It just makes smearing around with paper seem so disgusting now.

Lennon: It made my shitty guitar playing sound slightly more interestingly shitty. What a chorus does is, it doubles an audio signal, then modulates the copy, then blends it back in with the original signal. The result is a kind of shimmer. Andy Summers of The Police used one, and later, Kurt Cobain of Nirvana. But in the hands of most musicians, the sound of chorus could be described as "cheesy." I played some acoustic guitar gigs in Ithaca, where I live, and on one or two songs used the chorus. It made me sound cheesy. Cheesier. I didn't know this at the time. Anyway, once I had one stompbox, I began to investigate the many permutations of the species, and pretty soon I had many, many stompboxes. I still do. The main impact of them on my life is that I now possess a lot of metal objects with knobs on them. This makes me happy, every time I lay eyes or ears on them.

Scibona: Because to watch it required sitting still and made me feel as abstracted from my mind as from my feelings, my body, and all physical sensation, it trained me to confuse sitting still with death. As I got older and was allowed to make more of my own decisions, I simply left it on all the time. Someone once told me that if you go on vacation and leave your dog with a fifty-pound bag of kibble, your dog, unable to abstain, will have eaten itself to death by the time you return. I could not stop watching — not because I was interested, but because my capacity for interest itself was being destroyed. I was experiencing veleity — volition at its most feeble. My will was poisoned.

During one junior-high summer, I would watch until five or six in the morning and sleep until one in the afternoon. Even at the time I knew there was little difference between what I was doing and a narcotic addiction.

- What in your opinion was the precursor of this technology?

Crane: Hee. Needle and thread?

Dahlie: Surely the precursor to this technology was tormented young people in Britain looking for ways to avoid punishment. I imagine that the *wet ink effect* was dreamed up by a bookish but clumsy engineer at a stationary company who was burdened by memories of being harassed at school for his poor handwriting.

D'Souza: The precursor of this technology I think is twofold. First off, I think the Washlet embodies the archetype of the clean running mountain stream. Like I think the early hominids, I think they wandered and hunted and gathered and all that and I think that eventually they came to the mountains and went up into them and they found the clear running streams. And of these they found of them pleasurable to drink, but also to wash themselves clean after answering the call of the wild. And the second precursor to the Washlet, I think, is the Japanese predilection for plastic robot type things with buttons and flashing lights that serve as surrogate friends in a dehumanized society. So we have the Washlet: it washes you, it is your friend.

Lennon: Well, the immediate precusor was the distorted guitar amplifier, which effects such as fuzz, distortion, and overdrive attempted, and still attempt, to emulate. Chorus, phaser, and flanger strove to mimic rotating speaker cabinets like the Leslie. Compressor pedals were compact versions of expensive rackmounted studio compressors such as the Teletronix LA2A or UREI 1176. And reverb and delay pedals tried to replicate mechanical spring reverberation systems, or entire rooms — echo chambers— built into the world's great recording studios. But before that, there were caves, barns, smoke-roughened voices. No sound has ever been pure. Indeed, sounds that approach purity are generally regarded as cold, emotionless, devoid of character. Human beings like fucking sound up.

Scibona: It seems to have *replaced*, to a greater or lesser degree, many things — dinner conversation, bridge, listening to your sister play the piano in the parlor, letter writing: the appetite for all these things was flattened when the television was turned on. But I think the closest technological *precursor* to the television is the novel, which, oddly, was denounced in the early days of its popularity in the same tones that television is denounced today, as an opiate.

Novels weren't always consumed silently, as today; they used to be read aloud, to the family, after supper, by the light of whale oil lamps, while snow pelted the windowpanes — that is, in a way very like television is watched at its most cozy and reassuring times. Like many American readers, I moved backwards from the descendant to the precursor: television had made me sick, and the novel, whose cultural place television had usurped, was the cure.

Around the tenth grade, I read my first adult novel. An aunt in Seattle had recommended it. I admired her. I had told her I had the blues, and she gave me a list of novels. My brother and I had inherited a black and brown polyester-upholstered couch from an uncle who had died. I lay in it, reading by the light of a bare bulb in a ceramic fixture behind my head. Felt pennants celebrating all of Ohio's major baseball and football franchises were tacked to the walls. It was a Saturday morning.

From downstairs, the television entreated through the heating register; I got up and muffled it with a copy of the *Columbia Encyclopedia* that my grandmother had given me. Then I lay down again, and I read all day long. I must have stopped for dinner and then gone back to the book.

Sometime that night, I took a minute's break to go downstairs and get a glass of water from the tap inside the refrigerator. The water was incredibly cold. It seemed to have a sweetness specific to water that I had missed in fifteen years of drinking from the very same tap. This was only one of a thousand lucid sensations that were flooding my consciousness at that moment and that, in so doing, expanded its volume in an unprecedented way.

I was awake. I had never been more awake. All of my senses were open and avid.

I knew that it was reading the novel that had done this to me. I had heard the rumor, mostly from television, that some people regarded reading literature as a sacred act, but I had never known first-hand what the fuss was. I'd spent my whole life asleep and hadn't known it until I had been woken up by reading.

- What evolution would you like to see as it relates to this technology?

Crane: Honestly, I've seen the new sewing machines and I have zero interest. They embroider, they have computers that do all kinds of things. I can embroider quite well by hand. I just need it to go backward and forward. As fascinated as I am by technology, sometimes I'm not convinced we're any better for it.

Dahlie: I'd like to see more ways for young people to resist coercion. I'm not sure what the status of the fountain pen is these days in the UK, but I can't imagine it's the same, given all the obvious changes in technology. For my part, I always hated the bizarre adult fanaticism for teaching young people to read and write, although I suppose I can see some merit in it today. All the same, I'm still not sure it was worth it in my case, especially since my penmanship remains terrible.

D'Souza: Honestly, I'd like to see the Washlet make the leap across the Pacific in a big way. Because ever since I've been back I can't get the thought out of my head, at the movies, at the supermarket, 'Everyone around me right now has a dirty asshole.'

Lennon: For a while, the trend seemed to be towards so-called multi-effects. The more the music production world came to rely on digital technology, the less necessary discrete pieces of analog hardware became. Then computer recording was introduced, and effects were rendered in software. They were entirely virtual. They were now called plug-ins and had no substance whatsoever, however good they might have sounded (and after a while, they sounded pretty good). So, I'd like to see a return to awkward, jury-rigged, weird analog technology. I want to see stompboxes with flashlights, fans, and small gas flames in them. I'd like a stompbox with a mouse in it. Or a robot. Give me weird shit in a sturdy metal housing. That's what the world of rock needs. That's what America needs.

Scibona: To this day, if there is a television in the room, it's a struggle for me not to turn it on and sit down in front of it. I can't own one.

Hotel rooms pose a special challenge: the smallest I ever stayed in — only half again as wide as the bed, and lacking a window — still had room for a color television and two dozen channels. My hope — unfair to all the non-addicts for whom an hour in front of the tube is as harmless and pleasant as a beer after mowing the lawn — is that all the televisions will be eradicated from the world.

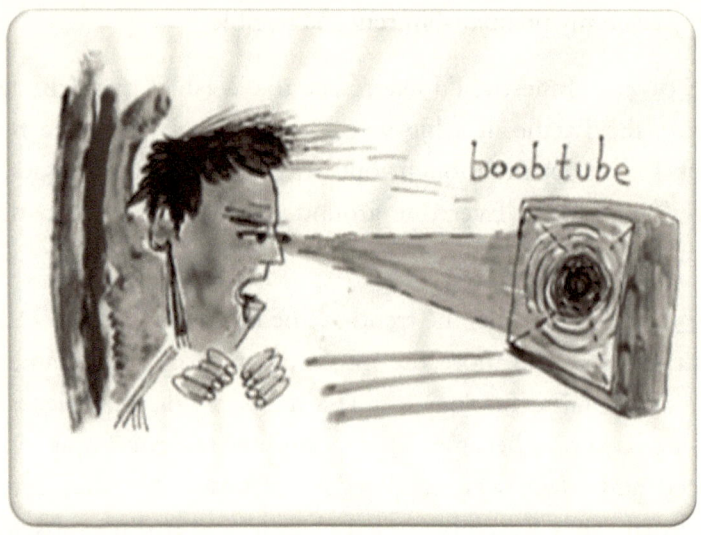

Episode 17: *Road Trip*
with Jennifer Haigh, Margot Livesey, Mark Jude Poirier, Stacey Richter, and Daniel Wallace

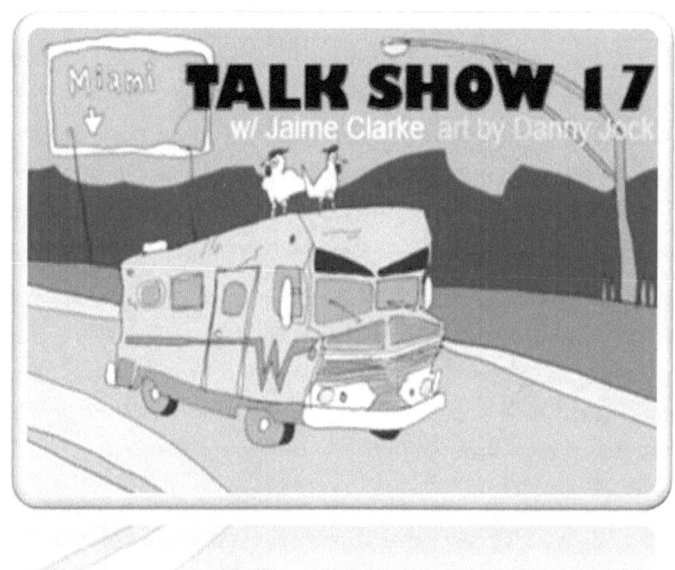

Jennifer Haigh's novels include *Faith*, *The Condition*, *Mrs. Kimble*, which won the PEN/Hemingway Award and *Baker Towers*, winner of the PEN/L.L. Winship Award for outstanding book by a New England author. Her short story collection is entitled *News from Heaven*. Haigh's fiction has appeared in *Granta*, *Ploughshares*, *Five Points*, *Good Housekeeping* and other periodicals.

Margot Livesey's first book, a collection of stories called *Learning By Heart*, was published in 1986. Since then Margot has published seven novels: *The Flight of Gemma Hardy*, *Homework*, *Criminals*, *The Missing World*, *Eva Moves the Furniture*, *Banishing Verona* and *The*

House on Fortune Street, winner of the PEN/L.L. Winship Award. Margot is currently a distinguished writer in residence at Emerson College.

Mark Jude Poirier is the author of the novels *Modern Ranch Living* and *Goats*, as well as the short story collections *Unsung Heroes of American Industry* and *Naked Pueblo*. He edited the anthology *Worst Years of Your Life: Stories for the Geeked-Out, Angst-Ridden, Lust-Addled, and Deeply Misunderstood Adolescent in All of Us*. Poirier wrote the screenplay for *Smart People* and adapted Alice Munro's short story *Hateship, Friendship, Courtship, Loveship, Marriage* for film.

Stacey Richter is the author of short story collections *My Date with Satan* and *Twin Study*. Her stories have appeared in *Zoetrope: All-Story, Tin House, Swink, Granta* and others. She is the recipient of four Pushcart prizes and the National Magazine Award.

Daniel Wallace is the author of the novels *Big Fish: A Novel of Mythic Proportions, Mr. Sebastian and the Negro Magician, The Watermelon King, Ray In Reverse* and *The Kings and Queens of Roam*. He is the J. Ross MacDonald Distinguished Professor of English at the University of North Carolina, where he teaches and directs the Creative Writing Program. Wallace's work has been translated into more than twenty-five languages.

* * *

- Name a memorable road trip

<u>Haigh</u>: The summer after I graduated college, my boyfriend, whom I'll call *J*, invited me to drive down to visit his grandparents, who had recently retired to Lake City, Florida. He neglected to tell me that we wouldn't be traveling in his car, but in a twenty year-old Winnebago camper his grandparents had left behind in Connecticut when the bank foreclosed on their chicken farm.

Livesey: The first summer I visited the States I traveled 'round first by bus and then hitching. After a rather peculiar bus trip from New York to Chicago — everyone on the bus seemed to be in flight from something — I hitch hiked alone from Dayton, Ohio — I am no longer sure why I was in Dayton — to Athens, Georgia.

Poirier: Tucson to Puerto Penasco, Mexico. (Rocky Point). 1984-1987. During those years my friends and I made this trip several times. In my memory, they all blend together.

Richter: One fall, I convinced my friend Peter to accompany me on a drug-themed road trip from California to Connecticut, where we were in college. I'd just read Hunter S. Thompson's *Fear and Loathing in Las Vegas* and was impressed by the way Thompson was committed to being fucked-up all the time, like an athlete, but of dissipation. When I brought up the idea with Peter he just said okay. This, in retrospect, seems strange. Peter was more easy-going than most of my friends, but he was also less bored and seemed to have more to live for than a lot of us (me), and what I was proposing had a sort of suicidal tinge to it. But I guess it sounded fun. And at that time, we saw no reason why we wouldn't live forever. We hadn't read the chapter on Thanatos yet.

Wallace: I took a year off between high school and college. There were a lot of good reasons to do this, but the main one was that I didn't get into any of the colleges I thought I wanted to go to: Columbia, Georgetown, Brown. I did get into my backup, Southwestern at Memphis, but I had no intention of going there. I only applied because I knew I could get in and my guidance counselor made me, suspecting, perhaps, that I was over-achieving with these other schools. I was not a good student, and, in fact, just graduated from college this year: I'm a class of 2008 University of North Carolina alumni. It feels good. Anyway, at the end of that year (1978) my girlfriend Mary and I decided to drive through America, beginning in Birmingham, Alabama where we were born and raised, and heading west.

- What kinds of preparations were made in advance of the trip?

Haigh: Nobody had driven the camper in fifteen years, but J had spent part of the summer tinkering with the engine and had managed to get it running.

Livesey: I prepared by reading Kerouac's *On the Road* and buying a map. Neither were of much help although I did encounter people who seemed very much like Kerouac characters. There were some hippies who were going to Florida in a hearse who invited me to join them several times. The fact that a mattress lay where the coffin once would have put me off.

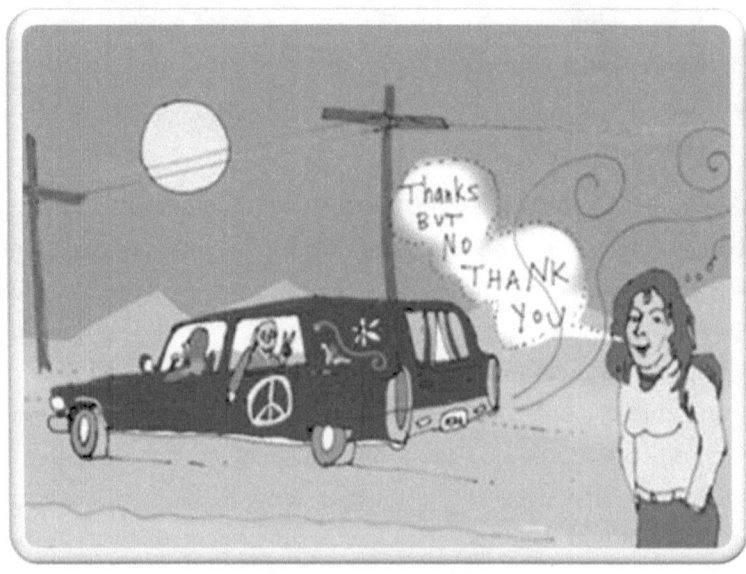

Poirier: My friend Elaine's mother threw blankets and sweatshirts into the car before we rolled out of her driveway. It was like 100 degrees, honestly, so I don't know why she insisted on blankets and sweatshirts.

Richter: We pooled all of our money and subtracted what we needed for gas and food. The rest went for the drugs. We ended up with a couple hundred bucks, which was enough for a little cocaine (entirely consumed the first night), a bag of pot, and a few doses of hallucinogenic mushrooms, which we ate at Disneyland.

Wallace: We were well-prepared. I'd been working that year, living at home, so I had nice chunk of change. We bought a tent and a stove and sleeping bags. We bought food. The car: one of the first Toyota Corollas anybody in Alabama had ever seen. What a great car that was. It had two doors, an engine, brakes, accelerator, headlamps — the essence of carness, and no more. There wasn't even a radio.

We packed and re-packed using scientific space-consolidation measures, which included removing the backseat. But there still wasn't enough room, so we had to buy a rooftop carrier. We spent a lot of time planning our route as well. Deciding whether to go south, through New Orleans, or straight across on I-40. We took I-40. We had six weeks, and we wanted to get out to California quick, take Highway 1 to Oregon, then to Montana and down to Indiana, where Mary had a friend. From there we'd go to D.C. to see my sister, and then trickle on back to Alabama. We knew where we were going to be every single night.

Of course, it didn't work out that way, but we pretended it was going to. Planning a trip is like writing a story in that way. It's good to pretend you know what you're doing.

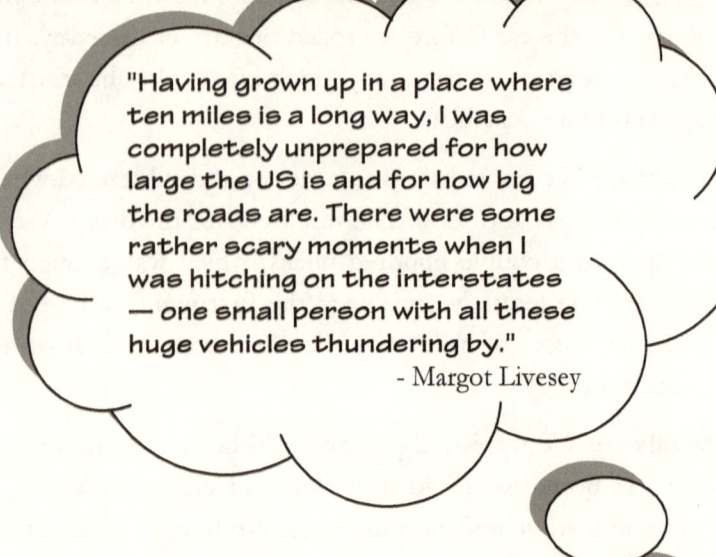

"Having grown up in a place where ten miles is a long way, I was completely unprepared for how large the US is and for how big the roads are. There were some rather scary moments when I was hitching on the interstates — one small person with all these huge vehicles thundering by."

- Margot Livesey

- What were your expectations for the trip?

Haigh: The plan was for J to pick me up at my parents' house in Pennsylvania. He'd never met any of my family, and this seemed like a perfect opportunity. My cousin was getting married that weekend, and he'd be my date for the wedding. We planned to leave for Florida the following morning. The whole trip was supposed to take a couple of days.

Livesey: Having grown up in a place where ten miles is a long way, I was completely unprepared for how large the US is and for how big the roads are. There were some rather scary moments when I was hitching on the interstates — one small person with all these huge vehicles thundering by.

Poirier: My expectations were mainly to get drunk, swim in the ocean, blob on the beach for a few days, not to think about the SATs, college admissions, or the C minus I was getting in physics.

Richter: Being high, I expected to have a more interesting, fun time than if I were not high. If I'd been paying any attention, I would have noticed the words fear and also loathing in the title and thus surmised that I might be terrified or miserable much of the time. And I was! Though Captain EO was cool.

Wallace: I don't remember what our expectations were. But it was the first time either of us had been completely on our own, far far away from our home and families. I think we expected to feel what it felt like to be free, and we did. I don't think I've ever felt that way again.

- Were there any disappointments along the way?

Haigh: J planned to arrive at my house the night before the wedding. He was often late, so I didn't worry when he didn't show up for dinner. Finally, around nine o'clock, J called from a rest area a hundred miles away. The camper had one and a half flat tires, and he was waiting for a service truck. "Can't you use the spare?" I asked him. "I already have," he said. He'd blown his first tire before leaving the state of Connecticut. I fell asleep on the couch waiting for him. A few hours later I woke to a crashing noise. J, pulling into our driveway at three in the morning, had taken the turn too wide. The noise was the camper's front fender pulling our mailbox from the ground. We set out for Florida the following morning. After J's grand entrance, my father was in a foul mood; so, we decided that J could meet the relatives some other time.

Livesey: How boring the countryside was and how similar the restaurants were. As a vegetarian I found myself eating breakfast for almost every meal. Also there were almost no places along the way where I wanted to stop and explore.

Poirier: Several. The first night, we arrived too late to find the beach where we normally camped, so we got drunk and ended up sleeping on broken glass and a community of fire ants.

Richter: Yeah. I wanted a grand adventure and this was not a grand adventure. The whole thing was surprisingly punishing — physically, emotionally, and mentally. I am no athlete of dissipation.

Wallace: There were lots of disappointments, but most of them were minor. I had never been fond of camping out, and the trip didn't make me any fonder. The idea of sleeping outside, on purpose, still makes no sense to me. The KOA campgrounds we ended up in were full of mobile home campers and sunburned kids. Mary and I fought once, I can't remember over what now, and when we stopped during the course of it so I could go into a gas station rest room she drove away and left me there. She was gone for half an hour before coming back to get me. It seemed longer.

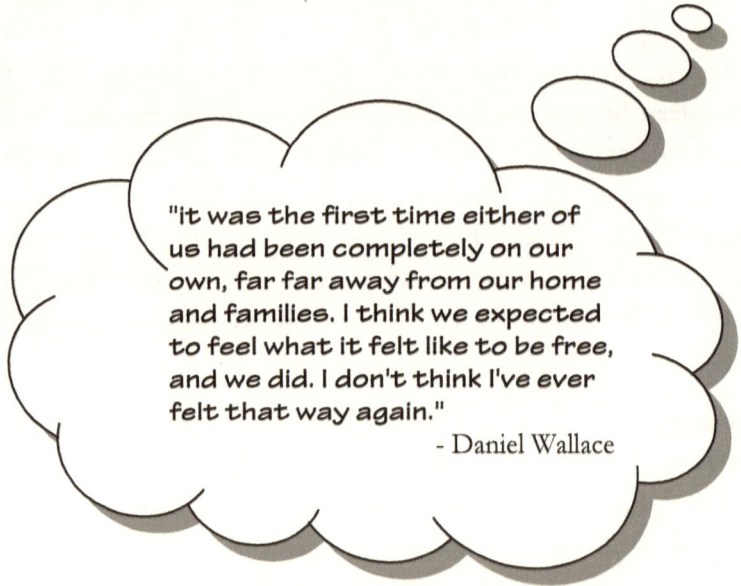

"It was the first time either of us had been completely on our own, far far away from our home and families. I think we expected to feel what it felt like to be free, and we did. I don't think I've ever felt that way again."

- Daniel Wallace

- What is your single outstanding memory of the trip?

Haigh: Our mechanical difficulties were really too numerous to mention. The Winnebago broke down, on average, every hundred miles, most notably at the bottom of an exit ramp in Columbia, South Carolina, at the height of the afternoon rush hour on the hottest day of the year. We got out and found ourselves parked at an alarming angle, leaning heavily on a dilapidated guard rail, the only thing that kept us from tipping over a steep embankment onto a busy highway below. These were pre-cell phone days, so J walked to a gas station to call for help. "Wait in the camper," he suggested. "You'll be cooler out of the sun." I did this for ten minutes, sure that at any moment a car would come careening down the ramp and into the side of the camper. Finally I climbed out and trekked a hundred yards in the hundred-degree heat, clinging to the guardrail, so overheated that my legs were dripping with sweat. I perched on the guardrail just in time to see a pickup truck roar down the ramp and into the guardrail, not two feet from the Winnebago's back end.

Livesey: How generous everyone was to me. People bought me meals, told me their life stories, advised me where to go next, asked about Scotland, gave me money, invited me to their houses. I was amazed and abashed at how open people were.

Poirier: A creepy American dude with like four teeth and scraggly hair who had been living (hiding) down there for years offered us a VCR in exchange for my friend Melissa. He was serious.

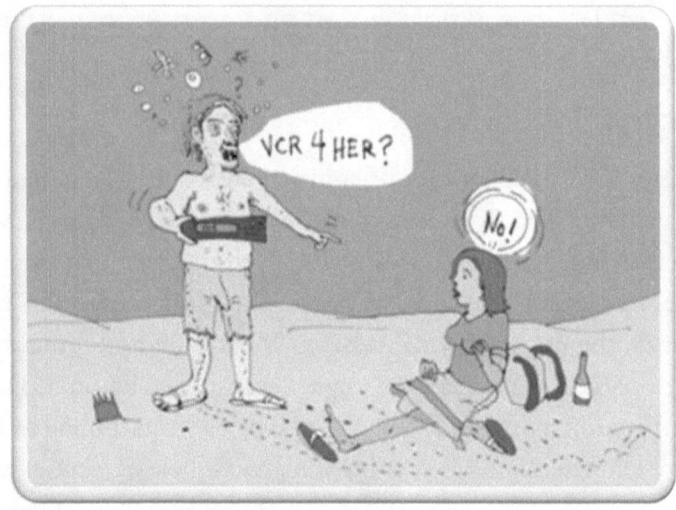

Richter: I ran into my good friend Susan at Disneyland. She's from New Orleans and neither of us lived in California. It was just the kind of utterly unlikely coincidence that can turn a little mushroom-addled co-ed to our lord Jesus. Luckily, that didn't happen.

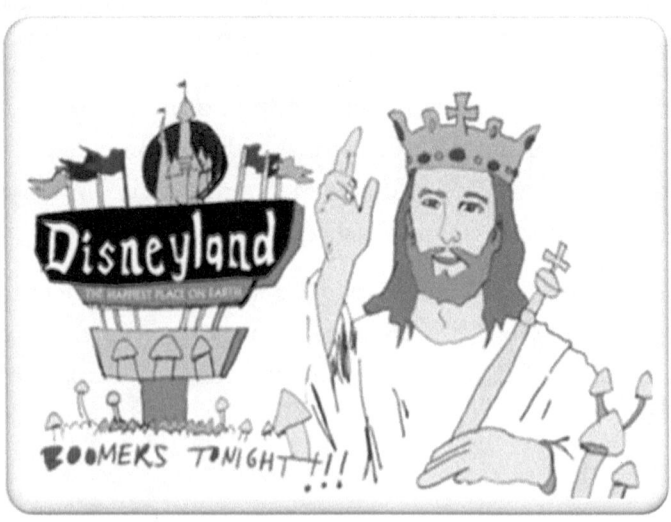

Wallace: This was in 1978, and the rock star of writing back then was indisputably Tom Robbins. *Even Cowgirls Get the Blues* and *Another Roadside Attraction* (his first book) were very, very hot. We loved his books and by extension him, so we decided to track him down. Robbins was notoriously private, however, and his book jackets said only that he lived in small town somewhere near Corvallis, Oregon. We called directory assistance of every town near Corvallis (lots of quarters), and finally found a Tom Robbins in a little town not far from Corvallis. But we didn't have an address. So like a couple of goobers we collared anyone we could and asked them if they knew where Tom Robbins the writer lived, and finally somebody did. The house was hidden in a wooden lot not far from town. Mary and I had picked a bunch of blackberries that afternoon. Mary took them and knocked on the door, and after just a moment it opened. And it was him. "We picked these for you," Mary said.

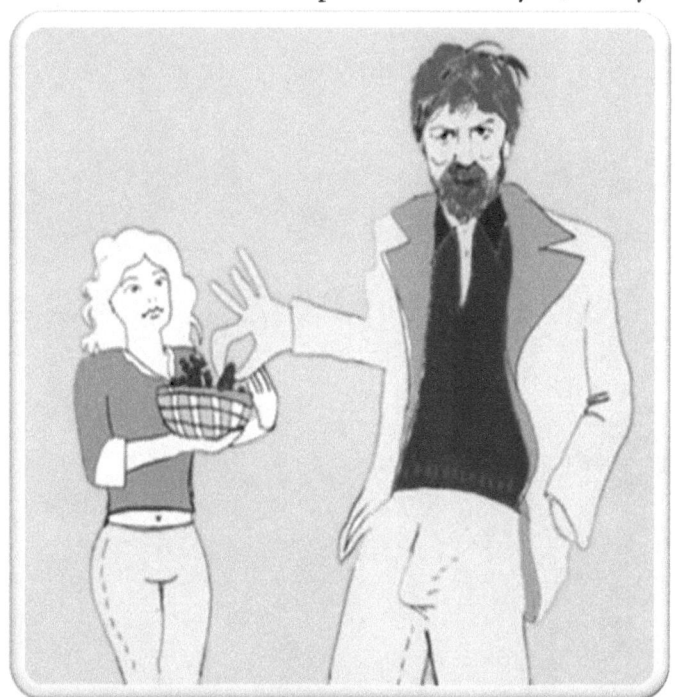

And he invited us in for dinner, just like that. He said we couldn't stay very long, though, because the next day he was going on a tour of North American roller coasters with his son. I'm not making this up. He was a very sweet, charming guy.

But I could tell that if I hadn't been there he would have slept with my Mary. In a heartbeat. Even my being there wasn't much of an impediment: when he looked at her his eyes glittered like the light from a star, and under the table I think he was touching her leg with his charming foot. Even then I wanted to be a writer. More specifically I wanted to be *Tom Robbins,* with this lovely house in the Oregon woods and about to go on a roller coaster tour of North America with the money I made selling something I'd written. I wanted to be him, but that night, for one night, he wanted to be me. After dinner we thanked him and left and celebrated by staying in a hotel. A Motel Six. It was great.

Episode 18: *First Date*
with Chris Bohjalian, Joshua Henkin,
Perrin Ireland, Aryn Kyle,
and Kelly McMasters

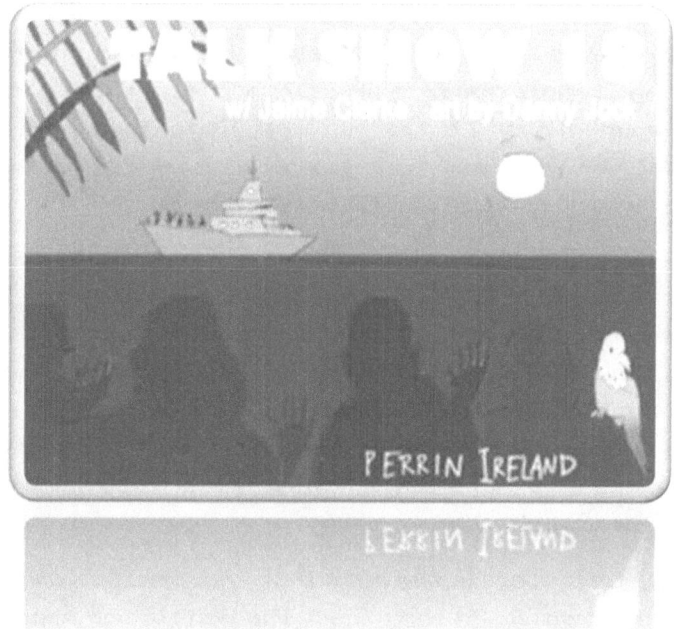

Chris Bohjalian is the author of sixteen books including the novels *The Light In Ruins*, *The Night Strangers*, *The Sandcastle Girls*, *Skeletons at the Feast*, *The Double Bind*, and *Midwives*. His work has been translated into over twenty-five languages and three times become movies. Bohjalian's awards include the ANCA Arts and Letters Award, the Saint Mesrob Mashdots Medal, the New England Society Book Award, the New England Book Award and a Boston Public Library Literary Light.

Joshua Henkin's novels include: *The World Without You*, an Editors' Choice selection for the *New York Times* and the *Chicago Tribune*, *Swimming Across the Hudson*, a

Los Angeles Times Notable Book of the Year and *Matrimony*, a *New York Times* Notable Book of the Year, a Book Sense Pick, and a Borders Original Voices Selection. He directs the MFA program in Fiction Writing at Brooklyn College.

Perrin Ireland's novels include *Chatter* and *Ana Imagined*. She was Associate Director for Drama and Arts at the Corporation for Public Broadcasting and a senior program officer at the National Endowment for the Arts. Her work has been published in *AGNI Magazine*, *The Boston Globe*, *Post Road* and others.

Aryn Kyle's is the author of *The God of Animals*, a novel that won an ALEX Award and has been translated into nine foreign languages, and the story collection, *Boys and Girls Like You and Me*. Her work has appeared in the *Atlantic Monthly*, *Ploughshares*, the *Georgia Review*, *Best American Short Stories* and elsewhere. She is the recipient of a Rona Jaffe Award and a National Magazine Award in fiction.

Kelly McMasters is the author of *Welcome to Shirley: A Memoir from an Atomic Town*. The book is the basis for the documentary film *The Atomic States of America*, a Sundance Film Festival selection. Her essays and articles have appeared in the *New York Times*, the *Washington Post Magazine*, *Newsday*, *Metropolis*, and *Time Out New York*, among others. She teaches writing at mediabistro.com and at Columbia University.

* * *

- Where did you go on your first date, and with whom?

Bohjalian: My wife and I have been together since we were eighteen years old. We met when we were just beginning the second semester of our first year of college. It was February

2nd, a Friday night. She went to Smith, a women's college, and I went to Amherst. Amherst had once been all-male but had become coeducational a few years before I arrived. Nonetheless, the college was still figuring out what it meant to be a school with women as well as men, and not merely a massive fraternity with scholarly grownups encouraging us to read a little Pushkin and Frost once in a while.

Henkin: I was in a high school graduating class of eighty, and many of us had known each other since kindergarten, and I had the good fortune, subsequently, to spend the vast majority of my years as a single person living in college towns, where people don't go on dates. You just hang out, and well . . . your intentions are made known, if often too drunkenly. All of which is to say that I've never really been on a date in my life. But if pressed, I'd say my first date took place freshman year of college, when the girl I had a crush on was brought back to the dorms by my roommate, who also had a crush on her. Trivial Pursuit was played, and deciding that I cared more for this young woman than I did for my roommate, I chose to stick around. So our first date, of a sort, was a date for three — me, my roommate, and this girl playing Trivial Pursuit (a game I hate!) in the dormitory common room. Our *real* first date (also of a sort) took place a week later when, the Friday afternoon of freshman parents weekend, I ran into her outside her dorm. "What are you doing tonight?" she asked. "I'm having dinner at Hillel with my parents," I said lamely. "I'm Jewish, too," she said. Or some such thing. So. My first date. Me, this girl, and my parents at Harvard Hillel.

Ireland: We walked to the outdoor movie theater on the naval base at Pearl Harbor where we lived. I wore a green and blue muumuu and bare feet; he wore a yellow and red aloha shirt and bare feet. He was the boy next door, or, technically, the boy one room over, since we lived in a two-family, L-shaped duplex and our bedroom windows were catty-cornered where the wings of the building met. The sounds of his wars with his younger brother offended my pacifist sensibilities.

Kyle: It was a pretty big deal: I was in seventh grade, and Randy Scotting and I met at the mall. We had a romantic dinner of Sbarro pizza and Orange Julius under the florescent lights of Café Court, then went to see King Ralph at the mall's movie theater. Afterwards, my mom picked us up in her minivan and took us to the Dairy Queen drive-through on the way home.

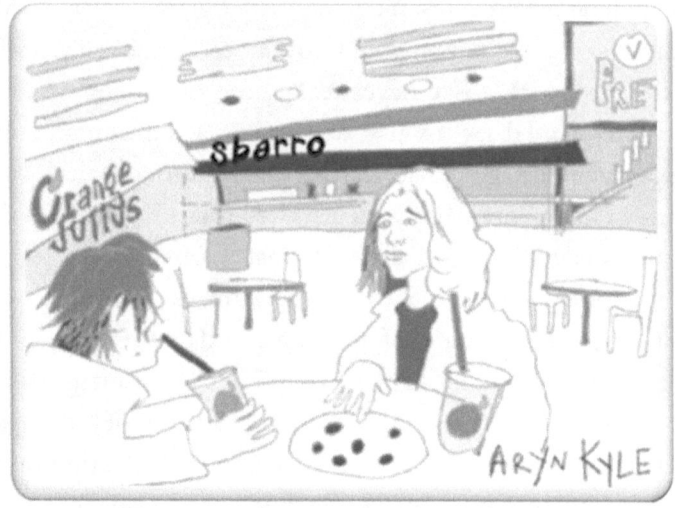

McMasters: His name was John and I can see his face perfectly. Curly black hair, brown eyes fringed with dark lashes, and translucent white skin with a smudge of freckles across his nose (funny, now that I think about it, he looked a lot like the man I married). He was a bit of a toughie, whatever that means for a third grader, and I remember clearly trying to impress him by being as much of a tomboy as possible. This included not crying when I walked straight into a steel rung on the jungle gym at recess, which cracked me so hard across the face I blacked out. Apparently, it worked. We went to the Halloween dance at our public school.

- Who asked who out, and how?

<u>Bohjalian</u>: We met at a real "Carnal Knowledge" anachronism, an honest-to-God mixer at her house (or dorm) at Smith. In theory, it was a wine tasting party. That's how old I have suddenly become: When I went to college, they actually encouraged first year students to drink. At the house, I saw a lovely blonde woman near the fireplace chatting with an acquaintance from my dorm, and he was clearly trying to pick her up. The woman was wearing a V-necked white linen blouse that fell untucked to just below the waist of her jeans, and her small feet were bare. Around her slender neck and her collarbone — a neck and a collarbone that struck me as both elegant and a just tad wanton — was an antique silver necklace with moonstones that matched her eyes. I decided I would help this fellow's cause. I put my arm around his shoulders and asked how he was doing. Before he could respond, the woman asked if the two of us were friends. I said we were. "Well, then" she observed, "you're a bigger idiot than he is if you'll admit that in public." Then she walked off. And I was entranced.

<u>Henkin</u>: Oh, who knows. Maybe she did. Except she didn't know it was a date. I'm not sure I did, either. "Hello, Mom and Dad, this is Laura. She'll be joining us now for the *motzee*."

<u>Ireland</u>: He asked his friend to ask my friend to ask me if I would go with him, and I told my friend who told his friend who told Next Door Boy, *Yes*.

<u>Kyle</u>: I'm a little fuzzy on this part. What I remember is that I thought that Randy was the cutest boy in the whole seventh grade. He played the cello and had a hyper-color tee-shirt (it

was orange, but when you touched it, it turned yellow) and when we were paired together for the dance unit in gym class, I would have had to be blind not to notice his natural abilities involving the Virginia Reel. Also, my best friend was "going out" (that's what we called it) with Randy's best friend and it seemed an obvious choice that Randy and I should "go out" as well. Our flirtation started slowly — Randy made me a Valentine out of a paper bag and I went to his house after school to jump on his trampoline. Eventually, it just seemed natural that we take things to the next level and consummate our relationship with mall pizza and Orange Julius.

McMasters: I don't remember exactly, but I imagine he must have asked me. Most of my memories with John involve me chasing after him and trying to impress him and planning out possible scenarios in my head involving things to say and do. But overall I'm sure I was pretty passive. I imagine he probably asked through a letter, since that's how most of my romances were initiated until about eighth grade, when girls and boys started actually talking to each other. John was on the macho side, usually in a sweatshirt with his sleeves rolled up to his elbows, a look I still happen to love. Based on the evidence and my foggy memories, I am guessing our love was of a very traditional flavor and he asked me.

"His name was John and I can see his face perfectly. Curly black hair, brown eyes fringed with dark lashes, and translucent white skin with a smudge of freckles across his nose..." - Kelly McMasters

- Did the date go as planned?

Bohjalian: Technically, that wasn't our first date, of course. That would occur the next night, a Saturday. We went to dinner at a restaurant in Amherst, a swank place called Plumbley's that's now long gone. The night before we had been pretty caustic with one another; later she would tell me that she had expected me to stand her up on our first real date. She worried that I had asked her out, in fact, simply so I could stand her up.

Henkin: It went as *I'd* planned it, in that once Mom and Dad were deposited at their hotel, Laura invited me to hang out at her dorm. But I have a terrible sense of direction, and a couple of hours later, when I departed, I was left to wander aimlessly around Harvard Yard, not sure how to find my way back to my dorm. In fairness, it was only October, but when I asked someone how to get to Canaday and the person wanted to know whom I was visiting, I was forced to say I *live* in Canaday, and for a second I thought the person would call the police.

Ireland: I expected to be murdered on the dark walk home beneath shadowy palms, which is why I asked my older sister to follow fifteen paces behind, but gargantuan DDT-resistant mosquitoes posed the only threat. The kiss (Big Sister hiding in the hibiscus-dripping bushes with their protruding yellow pistils) was unexpected, and led me to write *I love him* that night in my baby blue plastic diary with the raised figure of a sophisticated teenage girl on the cover.

Kyle: Pretty much. We held hands during the movie, and that was hot. Literally. Our palms were sweaty and Randy let go of my hand a few times to wipe his own on his pants. I don't remember that the movie was anything exceptional, but it hadn't actually been our first choice. We'd wanted to see something that was rated 'R,' but blew our chances by trying to get the Twelve and Under Discount.

McMasters: If by planned, you mean showing up at the elementary school gym and slow-dancing to every song and him falling madly in love with me and us fast-forwarding to our wedding day then . . . well, no, it didn't go as I'd planned. I can't remember being in costume but we must have been, which is never a good thing for a first date — that was our initial mistake. The next mistake was having his mother drive us to the dance. We both sat in the backseat of her chipping gold sedan (my mother remembers the car as green) not touching. Then when we got to the dance we immediately split up and stayed on opposite sides of the room for the whole night — boys on one and girls on the other, of course.

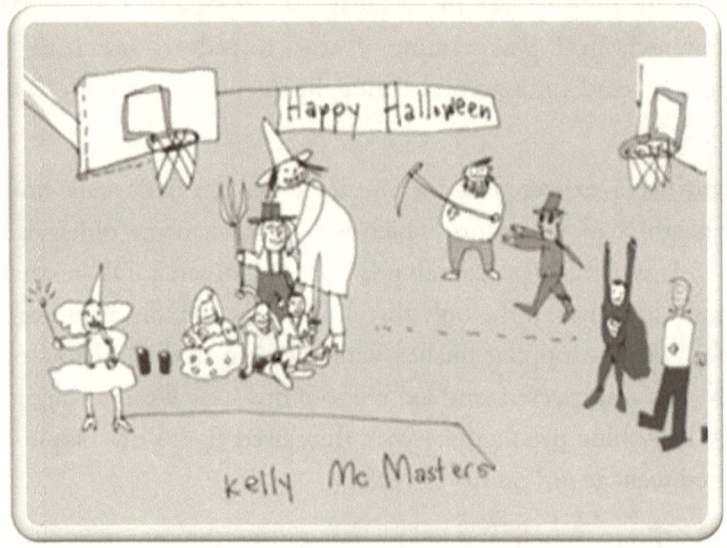

- What are your outstanding memories?

Bohjalian: At Plumbley's we were both on our best behavior. We tried to be the erudite adults we had seen around us throughout the 1960s and the 1970s — grownups pulled straight from a novel by Richard Yates or John Cheever — and so she ordered rye and I ordered scotch, and we both ordered an angioplasty-inducing death meal called the Webster's Plate: Steak and crab legs smothered in béarnaise sauce.

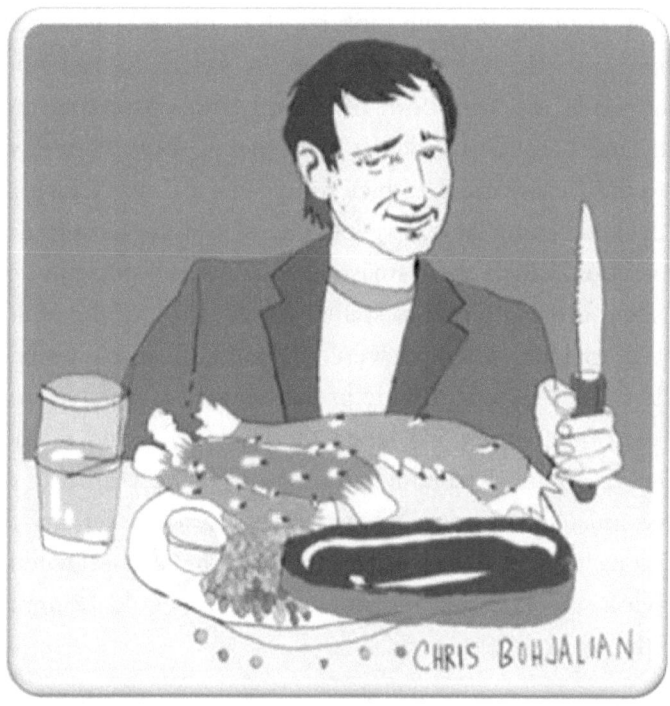

CHRIS BOHJALIAN

Henkin: Of the date itself, I remember not quite letting on to my parents that I knew this girl no better than they did. Also, I apparently made an idle comment about the comely appearance of another girl in the Hillel cafeteria, in response to which comment my father later said to me that it was impolite/unwise to say such things in front of one's female dinner guest. To which I responded that my father was backward/uncool/fifty years behind the times, all of which no doubt was true. Though it also could be argued that I was simply being a lout.

Ireland: After I closed my diary and locked it with the tiny, looks-like-gold key, returning it to its hiding place in the drawer with my retainer, I heard *The Boy* talking to his brother through the aforementioned catty-cornered bedroom window. "I kissed Perrin," he said.

Kyle: I wore my favorite pink tee-shirt and my stone-washed denim skirt, which I thought was the height of fashion and hoped made me look both older and taller. After the movie, Randy and I stood outside the mall, sharing a Dr. Pepper while we waited for my mom to pick us up. Just as I was taking a sip, Randy made some large, sweeping hand gesture, hitting the Dr. Pepper can, which then smashed into my mouth, cutting my gums and causing blood to spill down the front of my pink tee-shirt. Years later, when we were graduating from high school, I would write a note to Randy in the Senior Memory section of our yearbook, something along the lines of, "Fond memories of our first date. Remember the blood?" The yearbook committee must have thought I was referring to something more lascivious than a soda can to the mouth because when the yearbook was released, my note to Randy would be replaced with the word, "Censored."

McMasters: My strongest memory from that night is actually of John's mother. She was the kind of blonde that I would later come to recognize as out-of-a-box, and kind but hard. She was thin and a smoker and I remember her in a short skirt with tanned legs, toned from constantly being on her feet rather than jogging. She sold flowers at a kiosk in the middle of a strip mall parking lot in town near our favorite Chinese food restaurant and the Shirley/Mastic train station. I don't think there was a father in the picture and looking back I realize they were probably really struggling. When she came to pick me up John came to the door and she stayed in the car. She was distracted and John was slightly uncomfortable because she was clearly pissed in a toe tapping, wired movement kind of way. Some kids from her neighborhood had egged her car and then slathered it with shaving cream, maybe toilet paper. Some eggshells and a thin layer of grease was still visible by the time they came to get me. I didn't understand why she was so upset, although now of course I realize she was concerned because the eggs would eat at the paint on the car. This incongruity sticks in my gut — on a night when I was imagining a fairy-tale first date here was this scrappy yet still beautiful single mom dealing with more than I could have imagined at the time.

> "The kiss (Big Sister hiding in the hibiscus-dripping bushes with their protruding yellow pistils) was unexpected, and led me to write *'I love him'* that night in my baby blue plastic diary with the raised figure of a sophisticated teenage girl on the cover."
>
> -Perrin Ireland

- How did your relationship/contact with your first date end?

Bohjalian: Five and a half years later, we were happily married — and we have been ever since.

Henkin: We ended up going out for a year, arguably two, depending on how loosely one defines such things, college relationships being slippery, nebulous affairs. Suffice it to say that things turned frosty between my roommate and me, and I never spent another night in my dorm room. And since Laura was one of four suitemates living in a double, we spent the rest of freshman year sleeping on the common room floor, and woke in the morning to roommates and other strangers walking perilously close to our heads.

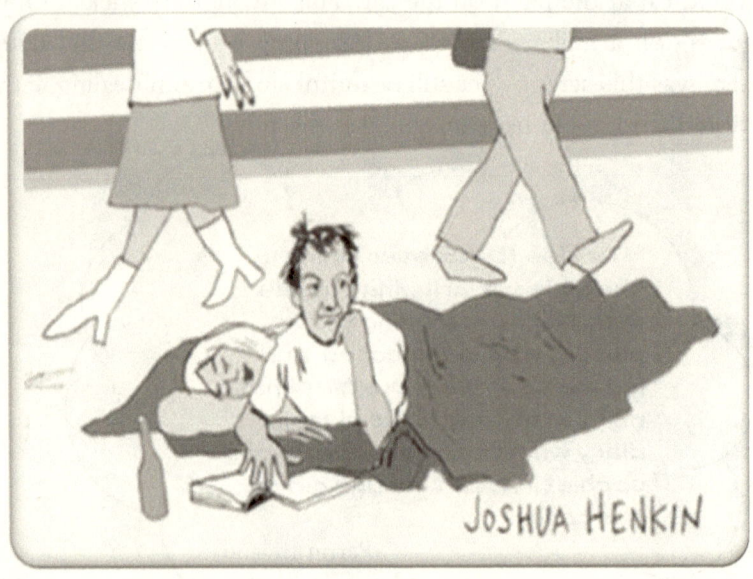

JoSHUA HENKIN

On the principle that what goes around comes around, Laura ended up marrying her roommate's ex-boyfriend a few years after graduation. The last time I saw her was at our tenth year reunion, which is eleven years ago now. Though, weirdly, I gave a reading a few months back at the Larchmont Public Library, and since Laura grew up in Larchmont, I made some off-the-cuff remarks about my own history in Larchmont — sneaking around late at night while your girlfriend's parents are asleep, setting the alarm so you're back in your designated bedroom at six in the morning. Afterward, the librarian who organized the event asked me the name of my college girlfriend, and it turns out Laura's parents are her landlords: the librarian, her husband, and their kids rent the very house I snuck around in when I was eighteen! How truly odd . . .

Ireland: Soon after, The Betrayer's family received orders back to the mainland, and I was required to attend the traditional going away party in the ship's cabin, carrying the requisite lei. I avoided eye contact, staring steadfastly at the ocean pulsing at the porthole. When it was time to go, the group stood on shore as the ship pulled out of the harbor, waiting until the vessel grew small, waving until our arms ached, waving until we no longer knew what we were waving at. I'd agreed to care for his parakeet, Kiki, until it was my turn to abandon the island. Pale blue and white, with black flecks — his beauty took my breath away.

Kyle: The relationship was, alas, doomed: I needed too much attention, and Randy was gay. At the time, though, we saw things in more complicated terms. I thought that we needed to advance beyond hand-holding to kissing on the mouth, possibly with tongues. Randy did not. We broke up over the phone and the next day in school, Andy Thatcher (a boy I barely knew) told me he was glad Randy and I had broken up because Randy was too good for me. I was devastated and rushed to the girls' restroom to weep uncontrollably while my friends fretted around me, petting my hair and promising that everything would work out okay. My friends were right, of course. In eighth grade, Randy and I would travel to Washington DC together; after high school, we would go to Italy. For a few years in college, we would live together, talking each other off various relationship-induced ledges, watching *Fame* over and over again, eating Boston cream pie on elementary school swing sets at three in the morning. And while Randy and I were never destined to have a relationship based on sharing saliva, it turned out that the kind of deep, familial love I now have for him didn't require that we ever kiss with tongues. But I still hate Andy Thatcher.

McMasters: The dance cemented our relationship as boyfriend and girlfriend. He was the first boy I held hands with and I remember them as a bit pudgy, his fingers and palms gummy as if he'd just moisturized. Later, in ninth grade, my first French kiss would be similarly jarring — again, it took place at a Halloween Dance, and my boyfriend at the time was diabetic and his tongue felt strangely swollen and soft in my mouth. Back in third grade, though, my romance with John was cut short when he moved at the end of the school year. The flower kiosk was turned into a photo hut where they sold cigarettes and film, and I never saw John or his mother again.

Episode 19: *Doubting Thomas*
with David Ebershoff, Sheridan Hay, Amy MacKinnon, Kirsten Menger-Anderson and Roxana Robinson

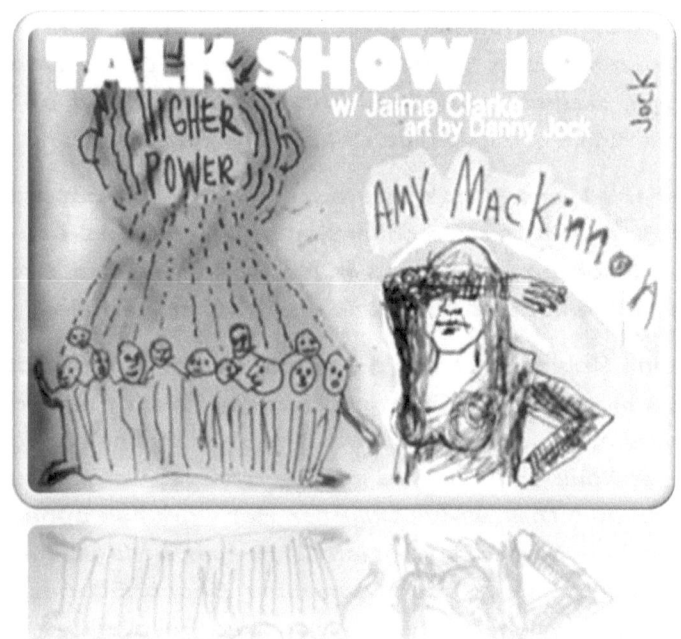

David Ebershoff's fiction includes the novels *Pasadena, The 19th Wife, The Danish Girl* and a story collection entitled *Rose City and Other Stories.* Ebershoff won the Rosenthal Foundation Award from the American Academy of Arts and Letters, the Lambda Literary Award, and the Ferro-Grumley Award for excellence in gay and lesbian literature. His books have been translated into eighteen languages. He teaches at Columbia University and is an editor-at-large at Random House.

Sheridan Hay's novel, *The Secret of Lost Things,* was a finalist for the Borders Original Voices Prize in fiction, a Barnes & Noble Discover Great New Writers selection, a Booksense Pick and a *San Francisco Chronicle* best-seller. *The Secret of Lost Things* has been translated into ten languages.

Amy MacKinnon is the author of the novel *Tethered*. A former congressional aide, she is a freelance writer whose commentaries have appeared in the *Christian Science Monitor, Seattle Times, Boston Globe, Boston Herald, Sacramento Bee, Patriot Ledger,* and on National Public Radio affiliates and *This American Life*.

Kirsten Menger-Anderson is the author of *Doctor Olaf van Schuler's Brain,* a collection of linked short stories. Her fiction has appeared in *Ploughshares,* the *Southwest Review, Post Road,* and many other journals.

Roxana Robinson is the author of nine works of fiction and a biography of Georgia O'Keeffe. Four of her books were named Notable Books of the Year by the *New York Times*. Robinson's novels include *Sparta, Cost, Sweetwater,* and *This is My Daughter*. Her work has appeared in the *New Yorker,* the *Atlantic, Harper's Magazine,* the *New York Times, Best American Short Stories* and *Vogue* and others. She has received Fellowships from the Guggenheim Foundation, the National Endowment for the Arts, and the MacDowell Colony.

* * *

- Name something others believe is true, but that you personally doubt.

Ebershoff: I don't believe the book is on the verge of extinction. That's the chatter in publishing these days: that the book is doomed. A recent newspaper story quoted an editor from a major publishing house predicting we'd all be out of business in eighteen months. After that, the industry would shut down. Last week a reporter called me. He was writing a story about the mood in book publishing these days. He asked if I was hearing any gallows humor in the halls of Random House or at lunches with agents or when gabbing with other writers. He's a good reporter, and it was an honest question. I told him I don't believe the book is going away. True, the future of the book is uncertain, but that's not the same as wheezing on life support.

Hay: Many people believe in an afterlife or, at any rate, in something other than this world. I do not. There is of course a religious sensibility that can sustain one through trials, but I'm particularly doubtful about those who speak to the dead — at least, the ones the dead "answer." I speak to my dead all the time, but the only answers they give are the same ones they gave in life. The way they "answer" me, in so far as those answers change, mark alterations in my own way of thinking. Contemplating those I have lost is a way to measure a movement away from, for example, anguish. It is my wish for them that informs my thoughts, not their imagined return. I'm particularly dubious about those with whom the dead 'communicate.' Invariably, the messages from the 'other side' are rather asinine. They are rarely illuminating or wise. Just because they're dead, I suppose, there's no reason to suggest that they're any smarter or more articulate than they were in life. But why is it that every translated report from the nether world is inevitably banal?

MacKinnon: Group thought tends to frighten me, so I often find myself at odds with the majority point-of-view on any number of truisms: religion, politics, soul mates. I yearn to believe in something, anything, that's wholly constant and omnipotent and benevolent in any of these categories. Of course the most controversial is a higher power — call it what you will, God tends to be the most common reference in these parts — but I doubt there is such a thing. I suspect it's more complicated than that. And I know the same is true for love and politics. What I do believe and try every day to practice (and fail at every day) is something that's found across the spectrum of beliefs: the Golden Rule. That alone is pretty powerful.

Menger-Anderson: I doubt that the disinfecting wipes at the front of grocery stores do any good for the average person. And while I'm on the topic, I don't believe that the pervasive use of hand sanitizer is helping society much either. And I don't believe in those "protect your baby" contraptions that nest in the folding child-seats of shopping carts like giant diapers protecting fully clothed children from the perils of what is more or less the same stuff found on playground equipment. I doubt them all.

Robinson: The green flash. I know it doesn't exist. Why would it? Why would there be a sudden streak of emerald light, flaring along the edge of the ocean horizon at sunset, in the tropics? Why on earth would that happen? Even if there were a reason, if there were some obscure scientific law governing this sort of unlikely optical event, it would still be impossible for me to believe. Because apparently it doesn't happen every evening at sunset, it only happens at certain times. But its appearance is not dependent on season or on weather. It doesn't matter if it's cloudy or clear, winter or summer. The green flash happens, apparently, only on evenings when I'm not watching. Is that a scientific explanation for anything? Is that the Eisenberg theory?

- What do you think is behind people's need to believe it?

Ebershoff: There is plenty of evidence pointing to the book's demise: studies showing Americans reading less; a flat-to-down trend in book sales; bookstores closing; the competition for leisure time coming from not only movies, television, and music, but now from the ever-expanding internet; and the emergence of the e-book, with all the dislocation it will inevitably bring to our industry. For many people, these are enough reasons to believe the book has only a few last gasps, but I don't believe that.

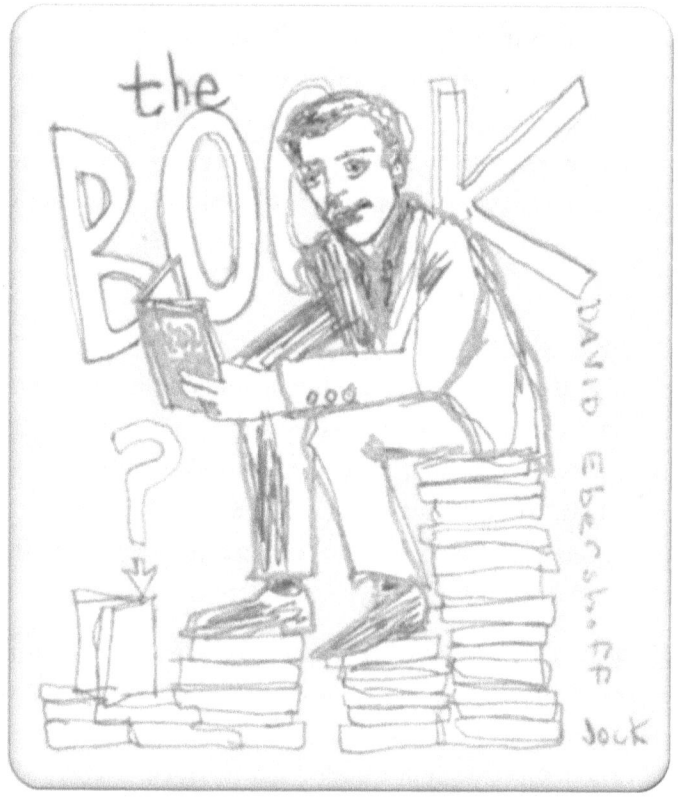

<u>Hay</u>: There is obviously a deep and inherent need to believe — to wish — that this isn't all there is. That we persist in some fashion — that there is not a limit to what we can experience. I think the fact that there is a limit to our lives, to our consciousness, is exactly what grants value to the rest. Perception

and its relation to time must be central to mortality; must be a clue to how one can "find the mortal world enough." It isn't weak mindedness that drives much of the wish to believe that something of ourselves persists beyond life. I think it is driven by a deep need to avoid pain — the pain of loss.

MacKinnon: Everyone needs to believe in something greater than themselves. I certainly do. We want to believe that if we follow the rules, we will be spared or rewarded, that our faith in the party or the god or a lover will be met with the response we seek. It's too difficult to think otherwise, too hopeless. It would be an enormous comfort to know that we were taken care of and loved unconditionally by something, that politicians truly cared about their constituents — and some do, some of the time — that true love is a state instead of a fluid state of mind.

Menger-Anderson: I think people like to believe that they have control over their environment and bodies. We like to think that we can protect ourselves and that a bottle of hand sanitizer (or a free wipe at the store) is an inexpensive way of insuring that we will not get sick. We want to believe that germs can be wiped away, that we can conquer disease before it even strikes, and that we can contribute to our own well being.

Robinson: Other people feel a need to believe in this for the same reason they believe in all beautiful otherworldly phenomena, like the Tooth Fairy. Why not believe in the Tooth Fairy, if you can? I think people simply long to see it: a vivid bloom of luminosity, mysteriously lighting up the cusp between day and night, vitality and darkness, being and non-being. Oh, you know what I mean. It's gorgeous and unknowable: of course they want to see it.

- Did you ever believe it, or did you doubt it from the beginning?

Ebershoff: I've thought a lot about it, but I have never believed the book would disappear.

Hay: I did at one time believe in the existence of some other realm. As a child, I believed I'd seen ghosts, had felt the presence of something like a spirit, even that inanimate things could speak to me. After my mother's death, I felt she kept me company as I wrote my first novel, and that my grief over her loss infused what I was writing. I heard her and felt her.

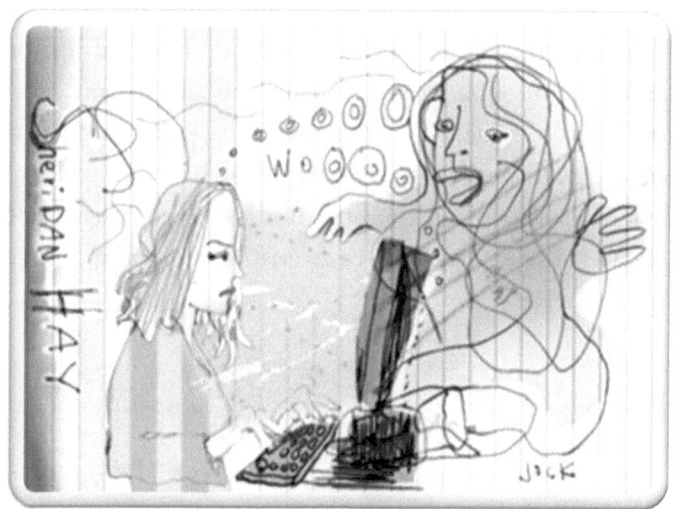

What I heard was my own wish for her return. But the memory of someone we loved deeply can be excellent company, can enliven one's imagination. Gone but not gone — memory working to make the lost person's presence more palpable than ever. Of course, we are haunted: the need for an ethereal visitation seems unnecessarily theatrical.

MacKinnon: I used to believe in everything and just about everyone. But time and experience has a way of eroding such optimism. One holdover from my youth that is pretty much unshakeable is that love and determination can change the world.

Menger-Anderson: I believe in sanitizing medical implements and I've been grateful for the hand sanitizing soap that I use when I visit the hospital. In addition, I admit to accepting hand sanitizer on two occasions: once from a good friend, whose father is a doctor, and once from a woman about my mom's age, who squirted the stuff on my hand, which I extended despite my worry that the potion would wash away my mosquito repellent and I'd end up with malaria or dengue fever (we were in a tropical rain forest at the time). In both cases, I said thank you, but I felt like I was failing to stand up for my immune system, which looks out for me all the time, not just on the occasions that I (or in these cases, other people) think to pull out wipes or sanitizer. Basically, I have always doubted super market wipes and the little bottles of sanitizer I find on the shelves. I've doubted them from the beginning. I've never given them a chance.

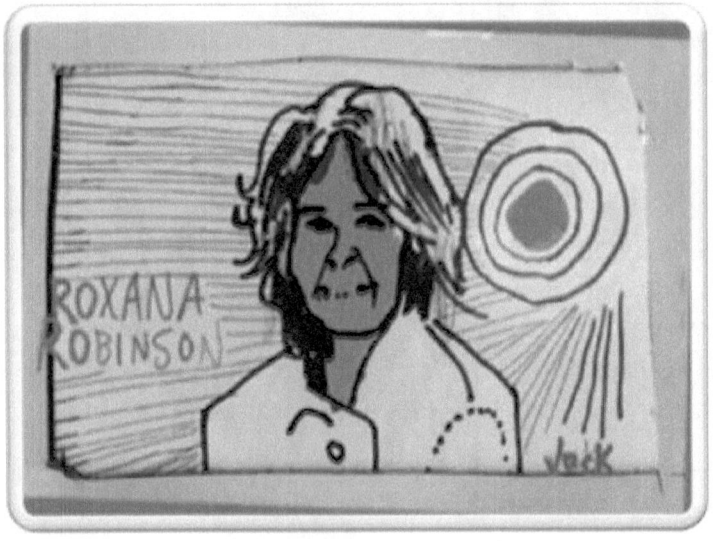

Robinson: When I was first told about it I was credulous. I believed it might exist. I was told about it by people I trusted, people who said with conviction that they personally had witnessed it. But how long can you believe in something that only happens the minute after you've gone inside to get your sweater? And whom can you trust, really?

- What is the source of your doubt?

Ebershoff: When this subject comes up — and it comes up a lot lately — we often lose sight of what we're really talking about, and therefore what we actually fear losing. We confuse the book (*an object*) with reading (*an experience*). Stripped of meaning, the printed book is merely a technology — the codex. Around the time of Christ, the codex began to replace an earlier technology, the scroll. The Roman epigramist Martial was one of the first writers to make use of this new technology. For some two thousand years, the codex, and its 2.0 release, the printed book, have served writers and readers remarkably well.

Reading, by contrast, provides an experience that humans, as far as we can tell, have always craved. Reading entails imagining, learning, and seeing what we can't see through language. If the impulse to imagine, to learn, to see the unseeable weren't vital to being human, then Homer would never have written (sung?) *The Iliad* and *The Odyssey*, and whoever bothered to pass them down through the centuries would never have done so. These great epics began their lives, of course, as songs or spoken poems, living on the tongue for centuries before Homer — or whoever — transferred them to the scroll. But just because they weren't books in the modern sense, doesn't mean that those who first heard or read *The Iliad* and *The Odyssey* experienced them in ways that are fundamentally different from how we experience them today. I have to believe that when I open my Penguin deluxe edition of the magnificent Robert Fagles translation, I experience *The Odyssey* in a way that connects me with breathtaking directness to its original audience. Despite the changes in the mode of delivery — from the tongue to the scroll to the codex to the $16.00 paperback with French flaps and a rough front — the desire to find out what happens next in Odysseus's long journey home remains constant and inextinguishable.

And so, even if the codex goes the way of the scroll, reading won't enter history's graveyard. I don't make this statement with a blithe disregard for what will be lost. Like many book people, I take great pleasure in a book that is physically beautiful and well-made. I appreciate the designers and craftspeople who, through their labors, make a book a book. I'm grateful there are so many people who have devoted their lives to designing, editing, publishing, and selling an actual book we can hold in our hands. (To say nothing of my awe for the writers who write them!) Like many others, I, too, would lament the disappearance of the thing we call a book. But even if the physical object were to disappear (which it won't in my lifetime, or yours), the impulse to tell stories through language and the impulse to understand our world through language won't expire.

As long as that impulse survives, reading, or an enhanced variation of it, will also survive. Ultimately, this matters the most. *The Odyssey* hasn't lasted all these years because of the papyrus Greek scholars copied it onto. Hasn't *The Odyssey* earned the right to say, *Relax,* I'm not going anywhere. Maybe the scrolls are disintegrating in the museum, maybe even books have begun to look a little quaint, but Homer's epics are astonishingly alive. I believe that as much as I believe anything.

Hay: It feels superfluous then, to imagine the dead floating about watching over lives when they no longer own life themselves. I've come to believe, after the deaths of other people I have loved, that the experience of mortality is transformative; that there is a more dramatic and deeper truth than the fantasy of life after death. Death transforms life — the point is that there is an ultimate limit. If life were limitless the power to be altered by loss would not exist. And I know that it does because it has happened to me repeatedly.

MacKinnon: How to explain earthquakes and pain, famine and sociopaths, the constancy of corrupt leaders and stillbirths? At its most basic level, life demands blood. One must die so another can live. That's how nations are born, sometimes children, that's the way we eat. The world is littered with omnivores.

Menger-Anderson: I don't believe that people can truly protect themselves from disease by wiping down shopping carts or occasionally dousing themselves with sanitary hand fluids.

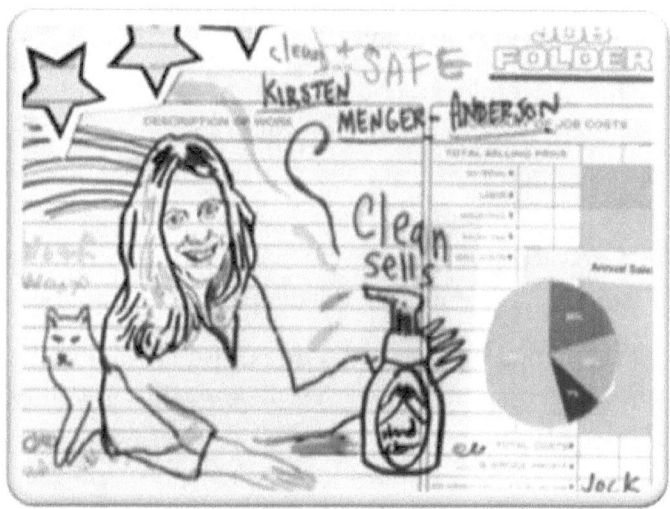

The other day, I read that most US currency has traces of E. Coli (some of which are undoubtedly harmful) in addition to cocaine (according to the cited study, U.S. currency has more cocaine on it than any other currency). My point is not that touching money directly leads to death or disease or drug addiction, or that we clutch money for as long as we do the handles of shopping carts. My point is that everything is covered in bacteria and viruses, and that as we walk through a world full of germs, wiping down a cart or applying hand sanitizer before a meal but not after we pay for it feels like the first step toward a rigid life full of hand-sanitizer application, wipes, and paranoia.

Robinson: I doubt that it exists because, although I've dedicated so much time to its research, I have never been rewarded by any evidence. I've stared deep into those tropical sunsets, over and over, I've watched the great glowing orb of the sun slip over the edge of the earth, turn molten red, the whole thing, over and over. Not a touch of green. Well, why would there be?

- What could ever convince you otherwise?

Ebershoff: Nothing, I hope. Or let me amend that: I've always thought of reading to be as magical and wondrous as time travel. I can open *The Odyssey* and find myself instantly bobbing on the ancient, wine-dark sea. So I guess I should say until we can time-travel, I don't believe the book — or whatever we will call it in the next centuries — will disappear.

Hay: Well I am convinced the dead persist, just not in the way that's regularly depicted. The myth of Orpheus and Eurydice, for example, illustrates the power of the dead over the living. The memory of someone lost is often behind imaginative and creative acts. Loss can be an opening. The dead stand in for what little knowledge we can have about time. There is a sense of liberation to be had from the experience of loss; a reminder

234

of the limit we will all come to. The dead do send the living messages — by their silence. They silently indicate that we must find freedom within the confinement of time. They tell us without speaking that the past is gone, even while they signal its value. They tell us not to be afraid of losing and they do all this while they have ceased to exist. The question is, why isn't that extraordinary and supernatural enough?

MacKinnon: Every day I'm convinced I'm wrong. Every single day I want to be proven horribly mistaken. Sometimes it happens. In terms of soul mates, there are my children, I'm convinced we were destined to be together. Politicians? I'm still skeptical. A sign from above? Well, there is this: My husband and I were shopping when I told him of this novel I'd just started, how the protagonist's name eluded me for weeks. As we walked into an antique shop, I told him that her name finally came to me: Clara Marsh. After browsing a few minutes, I spotted an old envelope leaning against a candlestick, a one-cent stamp in the upper hand corner. When I picked it up, I knew there was something more at work here, more than I was privy to. The envelope was addressed to Clara Marsh. It had to be a sign.

Menger-Anderson: If my local Safeway or Whole Foods conducted a study comparing the incidence of things like harmful E. Coli and salmonella among shoppers who use sanitary wipes on their carts and those that do not, I would consider the evidence and perhaps shift my strong and admittedly poorly informed position on this issue. Without access to such data, however, I am happy to assume that the results would show no statistically significant hand-wipe advantage (and I suspect that even if I saw hard evidence, I'd be reluctant to change my ways). Feel free to bring up my pig-headedness the next time I call in sick.

<u>**Robinson**</u>: If I saw the green flash, or the Tooth Fairy, then I'd be convinced. I'm hoping it will happen, actually, because I believe in the fantastical as a part of our lives. Look at Aurora Borealis: I believe in that. But do you want to know something? The thing is that I'm disappointed that I've never seen it. This is not a purely objective, scientific response, I know that. I'm kind of hurt, if you want to know. Because why not me? I'd be so good at watching it. I'd be riveted. I'd watch the whole thing — the sudden pale-green glow, the gradual — or swift, who knows? — fluid arrival of that wild unexpected color into the rich roseate landscape of sunset. I'd watch green flow magically into the sky, turning it into a sunset we've never dreamed of. I'd love it, I'd be spellbound. And I'd be such a proselytizer. I'd tell everyone it existed. Everyone. And I'd tell everyone to put their teeth under their pillows.

Episode 20: *Embarrassing Moment*
with Will Allison, Rebecca Donner,
Ron McLarty, and Ben Schrank

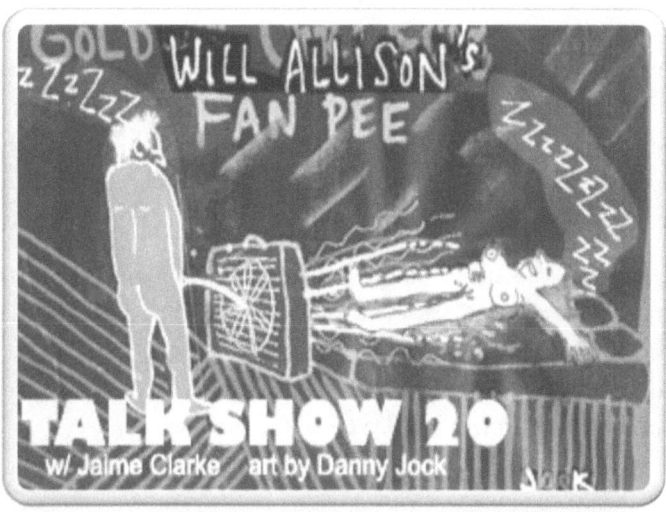

Will Allison is the author of the novels *Long Drive Home* and *What You Have Left*. The latter was named a notable book by *The San Francisco Chronicle* and was selected for Barnes & Noble Discover Great New Writers, Borders Original Voices, and Book Sense Picks. A contributing editor at *One Story,* Allison previously worked as executive editor of *Story* and editor-at-large of *Zoetrope: All-Story*.

Rebecca Donner is the author of the novel *Sunset Terrace* and, in collaboration with artist Inaki Miranda, the graphic novel *Burnout*. While enrolled in the MFA program at Columbia University, she was literary director of the KGB Fiction Series and editor of *On the Rocks:*

The KGB Bar Fiction Anthology. Her book reviews, essays, and stories have appeared in numerous publications, including *Bookforum, The Believer* and *Post Road*.

Ron McLarty wrote the novels *The Dropper, The Memory of Running, Traveler* and *Art in America*. As a veteran character actor, he is known for his many television appearances as well as his film roles and Broadway credits. McLarty's plays have been produced off-Broadway and regionally and he is an acclaimed audio book narrator.

Ben Schrank is the author of the novels *Love Is a Canoe, Miracle Man* and *Consent*. He is the publisher of Razorbill, a children's imprint at Penguin Young Readers. For several years, Schrank was the voice of "Ben's Life", a fictional column for *Seventeen* magazine.

* * *

- What would you consider one of your most embarrassing moments?

Allison: I was in grad school. My girlfriend, Melissa, and I lived in Columbus, Ohio, in a little two-bedroom apartment with no AC. In the summer, it used to get so hot that we slept with a box fan at the foot of the bed. One night, she woke me up. "Will? Will? What are you doing?" Apparently, I'd been sleepwalking. I was standing at the foot of the bed, peeing into the back of the fan, spraying her.

Donner: When, at sixteen, I stood barefoot on a cold cement floor wearing a borrowed string bikini, squinting in the glare of a spotlight as a woman flanked by a half-dozen people holding clipboards said, "Your skin, my dear, is unacceptable." She pointed her pencil eraser at my naked belly. I glanced down, and to my horror saw rivulets of sweat coursing down my bronzed skin, leaving strange, chalk-white trails.

__McLarty__: As an actor I've had plenty of these but the one that stands out and is easily my most discomfiting time in show biz was something that occurred when NBC flew me from New York to LA for a final casting call to play a regular lead in *Crossing Jordan*. This process is called 'going to network' and contracts must already be agreed upon before the biggies can consider you.

My agent called and said "They must really want you — NBC has offered a fat deal. Congratulations!"

As soon as he said that, I seemed to forget that I still had to audition. When I entered the LA casting studio, which was filled with NBC executives, producers and the head of casting,

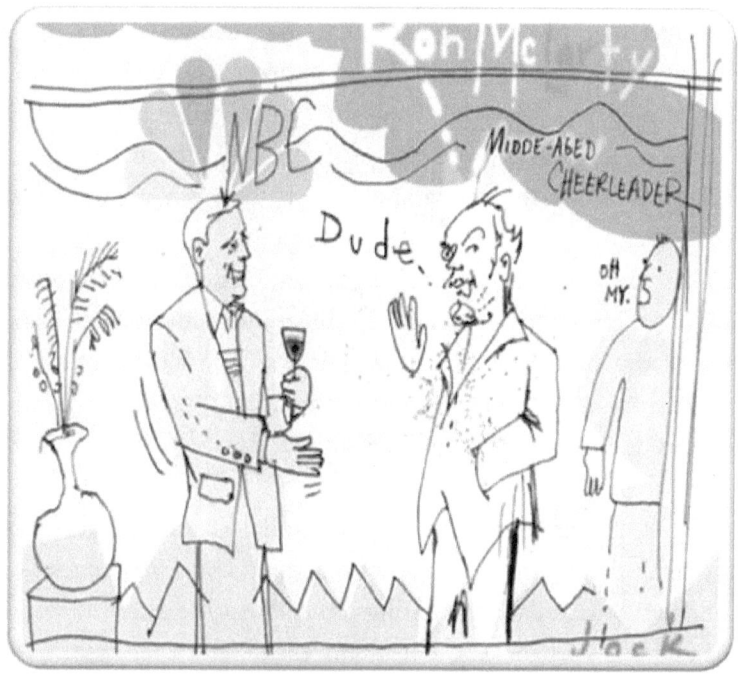

I proceeded to behave like Jack Nicholson after winning an Academy Award. I worked the room. I said things like, "Hey, doll" and "Looking good, pal" and last but not least, "Great to meet you, dude" to the president of the network. I didn't realize until the middle of the flight back to New York — when I awoke from a pleasant reverie with a start — that for the first time in my career I'd behaved like a wooly asshole.

Schrank: After midnight, on the day I turned five or six (not sure which and I'm too embarrassed to ask my mother about it), my mother and her friends snuck into my room when I was sleeping and threw confetti everywhere. I woke up at dawn and saw the confetti, climbed out of bed, and began to clean it up. I had a brown shag rug and I took a plastic ice scraper and I dragged it against the shag so that the bits of paper confetti popped in the air. Then I grabbed them in the air and put them in a pile. It didn't occur to me that our vacuum cleaner could take care of this job, or that I was supposed to enjoy the confetti. No. What I imagined was that must've been fun for my mom and her wacky college professor friends, to drunkenly make a mess of my room and use my birthday as an excuse. And I wanted the place clean, immediately.

Three or four hours later, my mom came in and found me down on my knees, wresting the blue and white bits of paper free of the shag, one at a time. The way she looked at me — the shock and awe and disappointment, adding up to the unspoken question: don't you have any idea how to enjoy yourself at all?

Well, it was embarrassing then and it's still embarrassing. I've been drunk and said the wrong thing and I've been teased in both work and school settings, and I've gone after the wrong girl and she's let me know it, many times. But that memory of cleaning up the fun is my most embarrassing moment.

"I worry about raising a kid who would behave the same way. I wish that if someone spilled something in front of me during a fun moment, I could just leave the spill lie, to laugh and spill my own drink, sing a funny song, even. But, I get up and find a rag and clean it up quick as I can, at first embarrassed and then furious with myself that I haven't let the moment run wild."

- Ben Schrank

- What was the backstory to the moment?

Allison: I thought I was in love with Melissa. We'd been together for two years, since the end of college. She was the bright spot in an otherwise confusing time. Coming out of school, I knew I wanted to be a writer, but I didn't know where to start. I ended up taking a job as the resident director of a dormitory at our alma mater, Case Western Reserve. It wasn't a real job, but that was okay, because my plan was to spend the year writing. All I wrote was garbage, though, and pretty soon I was discouraged, broke, in debt. On top of it all, some nutjob threatened me with a lawsuit over a fender bender, then my car got stolen. That's about when the sleepwalking started. The first time, Melissa found me lying naked on a mattress in a vacant dorm room down the hall. After that, she made sure I didn't get out the door.

Donner: I was at an audition for a Sunkist commercial. A friend who made a mint doing commercials encouraged me to give it a try. She was the one who had loaned me the bikini, and when I protested that my skin was fish-belly white, she produced a tube of bronzer and slathered it over my body.

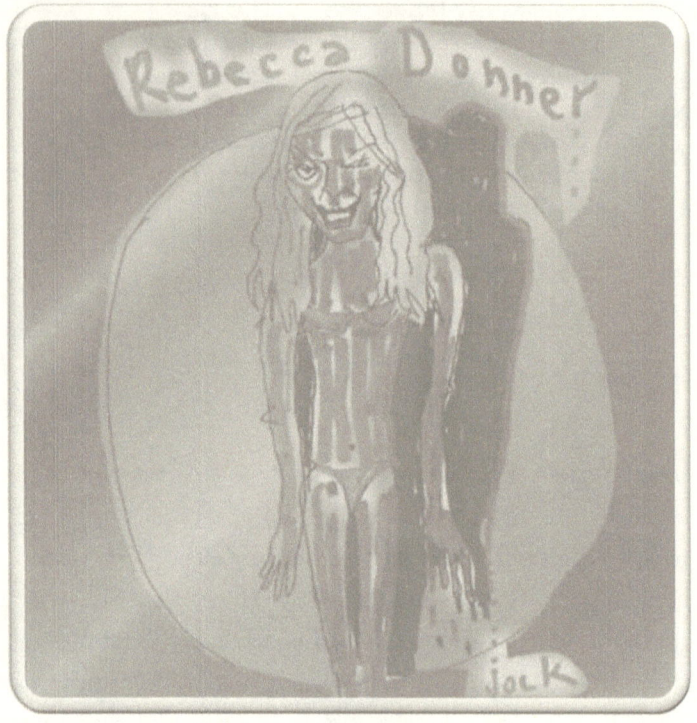

I asked her — watching my skin turn a deep, rich, (if orange-tinged) brown — if the bronzer would rub off. "Chill out, okay?" she said. "It's waterproof."

McLarty: There were a lot of factors involved in my meltdown but the big one, I think, was getting to that dangerous part of middle age where you unconsciously become your own cheerleader. When it comes to yourself, perhaps the one person who shouldn't do the evaluation is you. And also the sort of 'lottery' lure of the fat salary, which would have enabled me to retire the endless loans I'd taken to put my three sons through private school and college! The possibility of this actually happening made me cocky instead of grateful.

Schrank: My parents were divorced. I was too often a joyless fuck of a kid. I was spoiled and got everything I wanted but I didn't really understand how to have a good time. Still don't.

- What would've made the moment even worse?

Allison: If she'd accused me of subconsciously wanting to pee on her. Surely the thought must have crossed her mind.

Donner: If, standing on that cold, cement floor, I suddenly flailed my arms skyward and leaped into the air, in a poor (if earnest) imitation of a ballerina's *grand jeté*. This is what I was asked to do at the next commercial audition I went to (for Kotex Ultra Thin Pads).

McLarty: Nothing. It couldn't have possibly been worse. The casting director who walked me to my car kept asking me if I was all right. When I landed in New York, there was a message from my agent saying that I didn't get the job but ALL the people at NBC were worried about me.

Schrank: There's no way that moment could've been any worse, save child abuse. If my mother had come in and knocked me back on my ass when she saw me gathering confetti, that would have made it worse. But that didn't happen. I own what I did, as we must with all our embarrassments. And I look back with regret, because what I could've done was jumped around and smiled or lay back in bed and said yeah, it's my birthday and I am young and loved and happy.

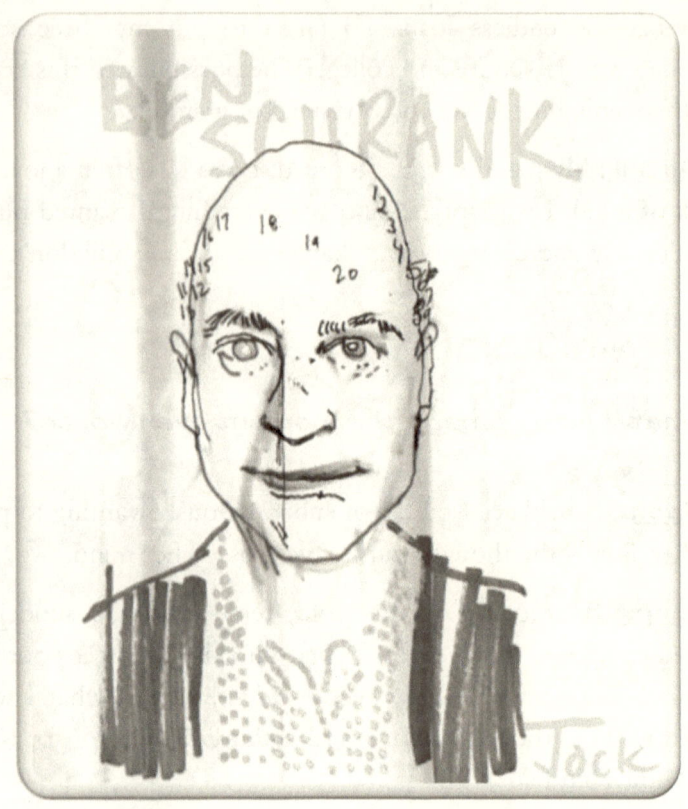

- Looking back, could it have been avoided?

Allison: Yes. We could've skipped the bars that night. More to the point, we probably should've broken up by then.

Donner: Only if one of the following events had occurred: 1): The myoepithelial cells between the merocrine gland cells and basal lamina ceased to function, thereby disrupting thermoregulation and halting all perspiration; 2): I hadn't applied bronzer.

McLarty: No. Can you avoid a crash after car is flying off the cliff? It still feels like fate.

244

Schrank: Yes. I wish my mother had recognized this lack in me and taken me to fun classes where I could've learned both fun and fun-appreciation. If I'd known how to do fun-appreciation, this memory wouldn't plague me. It needn't be innate. I like to do lots of things that I've learned, like desiring expensive watches. So that horrible birthday morning could've been avoided if I'd learned how to appreciate fun.

- Is the moment as embarrassing now as it was then? Why or why not?

Allison: It was more embarrassing then — the rudeness of it, the absurd loss of self-control. Today, it seems to me more sad than embarrassing. I ended up leaving Melissa for someone else. I think I must have already been falling in love with that someone else. But that night, Melissa and I were too tired for omens. We just changed the sheets, got into bed, and went back to sleep.

Donner: Thankfully, my high school prom provided a fresh opportunity for horror, and the humiliation I suffered with the bronzer paled in comparison. But that's another story . . .

McLarty: Strangely enough, the embarrassment has grown over the years. People I've never met before have bumped into me and said they heard the story of my immolation at a Hollywood party. Sometimes I even tell the story on myself but midway through and right before "Hey, doll," I'm sorry I started talking.

Schrank: It's worse now. Every time I pick up a newspaper and recycle it, or straighten a cushion, or wash and iron a shirt that doesn't need it, I wonder, isn't there something joyful you'd rather be doing? I worry about raising a kid who would behave the same way. I wish that if someone spilled something in front of me during a fun moment, I could just leave the spill lie, to laugh and spill my own drink, sing a funny song, even. But, I get up and find a rag and clean it up quick as I can, at first embarrassed and then furious with myself that I haven't let the moment run wild.

Episode 21: *Place and Time*
with Sven Birkerts, Lisa Gabriele,
Yael Goldstein Love, and Adrienne Miller

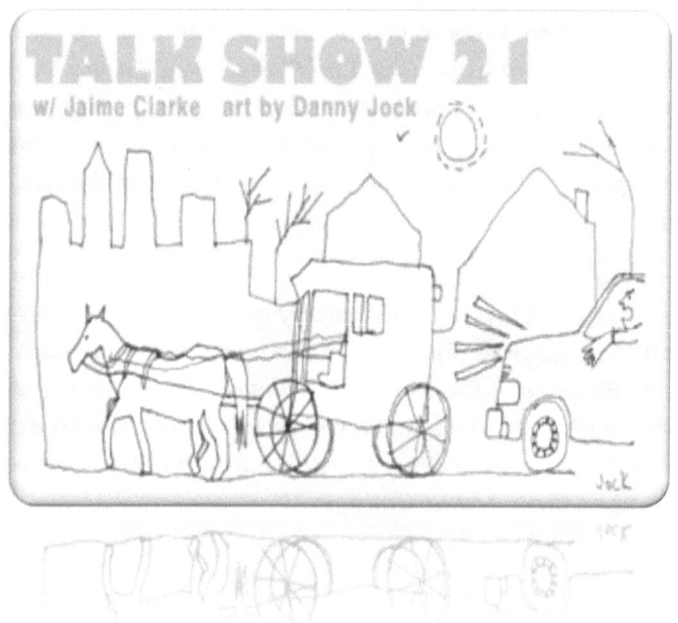

Sven Birkerts is the author of *The Other Walk, Readings, The Gutenberg Elegies, Reading Life: Books for the Ages, Art of Time in Memoir: Then, Again,* and a memoir, *My Sky Blue Trades*. His awards include a Citation for Excellence in Reviewing from the National Book Critics Circle and the Spielvogel-Diamonstein Award from PEN for the best book of essays. Birkerts has reviewed regularly for the *New York Times Book Review*, the *New Republic*, the *Washington Post*, the *Atlantic* and other publications. He is the Director of the Bennington Writing Seminars and editor of the literary magazine *AGNI*.

Lisa Gabriele is the author of the novels *Tempting Faith DiNapoli* and *The Almost Archer Sisters* and, (under the pseudonym L. Marie Adeline), *S.E.C.R.E.T.* Her writing has appeared in the *New York Times Magazine*, *Salon*, *Glamour*, *Vice*, and the *Washington Post*. Gabriele also directs and produces for television and radio.

Yael Goldstein Love is the author of the novel *Overture*, published in paperback as *The Passion of Tasha Darsky*. She is co-founder and editorial director of the literary studio Plympton. Love teaches at Grub Street and is working on a new novel tentatively entitled *Sweet William*.

Adrienne Miller is the author of the novel *The Coast of Akron*, and is the former literary editor of *Esquire*. While at that magazine she developed and edited two anthologies, *Esquire's Big Book of Fiction* and *Esquire's Big Book of Great Writing*. Miller also served as an editor at *McSweeney's* and was a visiting lecturer in Creative Writing at Bryn Mawr College.

* * *

- Name a place and time in which you'd like to have lived.

Birkerts: The question is really, for me, which novel would I most happily pull around myself? A different answer every day, but the answers are interesting. Today I'm thinking something from Balzac, Paris in the late nineteenth century, or Schnitzler, Vienna in the early twentieth.

Gabriele: I would love to have lived in the 1890s, in Dawson City, Yukon.

Love: Medieval Europe. Doesn't really matter which country or which century, but I've got to be lower class wherever I am. No noble/monastery life for me. Preferably I'd be a drudge within a noble house, but I'd take peasant, too. This is a longstanding dream. When I was four years old my favorite game was to dress up in drab-colored, raggedy clothes, fill a bucket with water, and flood the kitchen. I called this game 'scullery maid.' There's a lot of photographic evidence of this, by the way. My mother claims not to even know where I learned the term 'scullery maid' much less what attracted me to the role. She gets defensive whenever those pictures surface, and insists on pointing out that I never had chores as a child.

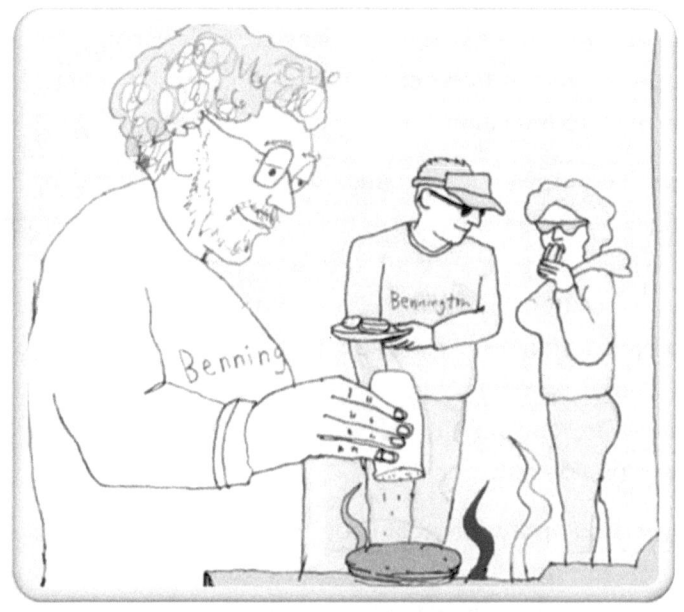

Miller: Late eighteenth-century America, probably Philadelphia.

- What about the time period attracts you?

Birkerts: What draws me is not the plumbing or the likeliness of fleas, but my fantasy of scale, of a certain immediate social density. Places big enough to support a diverse café culture, a sense of release from what Marx called "the idiocy of rural life," though on other days said idiocy exerts its own appeals.

Gabriele: I did live in Dawson in the late 1980s, almost a hundred years after gold was first found in its hills. I fell in love with the dusty ghostness of the town, like I seem to do all mining towns, from Bisbee and Jerome, Arizona, all the way up to the North American tundra line. Love them. Not sure why. I'm not a big believer of reincarnation but there's something about an old, nearly abandoned mining town that has always felt eerily, instantly familiar to me. But the period that most attracts me is the year or two of massive expansion, as Dawson grew from being a handful of filthy canvas tents inhabited by a handful of filthy men, to a teeming, cosmopolitan city of 40,000 people.

Love: The urgency that comes with a life so bound up with death. There was the constant threat of war, the constant threat of disease, and people didn't turn away from this reality. They faced it head-on, made it the center of their art, thought, and even their festivities. As a result, there's something so large and awe-embracing about what they produced — their music, art, architecture, and so on. All succeeding eras seem somehow pinched in comparison.

Miller: I do appreciate that early America was largely a ruffian culture, and that the late-eighteenth-century was a time in which people blew their noses on their sleeves, lived in log cabins, ate with their fingers, and gouged out people's eyes in tavern brawls, etcetera. But it was also the Enlightenment, and the central belief of the Enlightenment was that the world could be understood, that everything could be mastered and perfected through reason and rationality. It was a time that produced the most incredible geniuses ever to exist — Jefferson, Franklin, Mozart, Haydn, Rousseau, Edward Gibbon. To have heard the *Jupiter Symphony* when it was first performed! To have read (or at least cut apart the pages with your penknife, because that's the way books worked then) *The History of the Decline and Fall of* *the Roman Empire* when it was first published! And, oh, to have been in the Assembly Room at Independence Hall in Philadelphia at the floor debates during that intolerably hot summer of 1776, and to have seen shy, awkward young Jefferson with his flowing red hair sitting silently and lankily, and to have witnessed elderly, avuncular Franklin piping in with another long-winded story that seemed as if it were going nowhere . . . but that always ended up summing up everything brilliantly and beautifully. I'm also kind of obsessed, to the point of fetishization, with the whole Neoclassical aesthetic: give me a dome, some columns, and a Chippendale chair to sit in, and that's all it takes to make me happy.

"The urgency that comes with a life so bound up with death. There was the constant threat of war, the constant threat of disease, and people didn't turn away from this reality. They faced it head-on, made it the center of their art, thought, and even their festivities. As a result, there's something so large and awe-embracing about what they produced — their music, art, architecture, and so on."

- Yael Goldstein Love
re: Medieval Europe

- What do you imagine would be the best part of living then?

Birkerts: I like the idea of a genuine critical mass of alert humanity, rather than its virtual stand-in, and the sense, too, that the future is still vitally in formation and that the earth has not been colonized to within an inch of its life.

Gabriele: It would be amazing to watch how a city evolves, fast-forward. One day mail moves by horse and buggy, the next, a telephone line is installed. One day everyone lives by gas light, the next, electricity is strung up and pumped in. Mostly, how cool to be one of the few women who dare to venture north in search of personal fortune. I'd have done that, as, no doubt, my options would've been limited to marrying young and moving directly from my father's house to my husband's. I'd have read about the northern migration and fled home. I would like to think that I'd have been entrepreneurial, opening a sewing shop or a restaurant or a school. But the whore's money might have been too difficult to resist. Plus I'm a sucker for a corset and feathers.

Love: I think this whole 'life-with-death' mentality appeals to me primarily because I'm super-duper scared of death. I've never managed to shake that childhood awake-in-the-dark-contemplating-mortality thing that most people manage to move past (or at least healthily suppress) in adulthood. I'm still totally bowled over — and kind of affronted — by mortality. So I think the best thing about living back then would be, basically, not being like this. Being able to look at life without the terror of death mangling my view.

Miller: I must be drawn to this era in part because of the manic revolutionary fervor in the air, and because, even then, people (OK: members of the white, male gentry, but still) seemed to have understood that they were living in a remarkable time. There seemed to have been a feeling that they were living in a precedent-creating era: they were remaking and reimagining the world. Not to sound too crotchety, but how often do we look around at this shallow, frivolous, lowest-common-denominator culture of ours — not to mention our sometimes criminal government — and feel that this is the best time ever to be alive? I mean, doesn't every right-thinking person sort of have to believe that humanity has gone kind of backward? Also: late eighteenth-century clothes were super cool.

- What would be the worst?

Birkerts: The afore-mentioned fleas, still-primitive dentistry . . .

Gabriele: The smell. People reeked back then. One of the main pleasures of watching *Deadwood* was how the series accurately depicted the vile hygiene. Also bad would be the violence, especially against women. Despite my modern bravado, and all joking aside about prostitution, joining the gold rush as a woman would have been a horribly dangerous thing to do; rape was common, murder too. The overall lawlessness of an unformed society would have been stressful. But still, I'd have been game.

Love: As it turns out, I'm not actually a big fan of war and disease. I am TERRIFIED of the bubonic plague. Way more than it is reasonable to be terrified of a disease that hasn't claimed a victim in centuries. Also, I get cold really easily and I don't much like the heat either. In general, I'm not much of a trooper, physically speaking. And not being able to read. I find it hard to imagine life being all that enjoyable without books. Maybe if I could be a scullery maid in a monastery (did they have scullery maids?) and a big-hearted, forward-thinking monk could secretly teach me philosophy and theology and some alchemy for good measure at night. That sounds pretty appealing. But there'd still be war and disease to contend with.

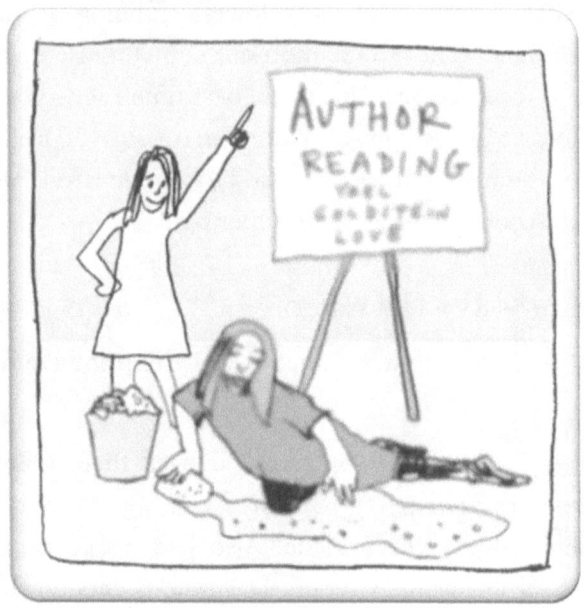

Miller: Obviously, it wasn't such a great time to be a woman. (On the upside, I would have probably gotten very good at those needlepoint alphabet primers you always see on tours of old houses.) And, boy, would it have sucked even more to be black or Native American. What else? Well, there was no anesthesia, the public hygiene was hideous, the lifespan was forty, women could almost be guaranteed an eventual death in childbirth, you were up at dawn and in bed at dusk, the last meal of the day was at 3 p.m., you ate what you grew or killed, and you were pretty much entirely self-sufficient (which might not have been such a bad thing, really). There were no pharmaceutical drugs. But there was lots and lots of alcohol. But no Stephen Sondheim. And I'm firmly of the mind: If there's no Sondheim, what's the point?

"Not to sound too crotchety, but how often do we look around at this shallow, frivolous, lowest-common-denominator culture of ours — not to mention our sometimes criminal government — and feel that this is the best time ever to be alive? I mean, doesn't every right-thinking person sort of have to believe that humanity has gone kind of backward?"

- Adrienne Miller

- **What bit of culture from today would you want with you?**

Birkerts: Certainly not television, or the internal combustion engine, or the concept of insurance, or sleep-aids, or plastic, or the camera, or cell-phones, or the internet, or the idea of the diet . . . Maybe the idea of melting cheese onto grilled meat (if that had not yet been discovered) . . .

Gabriele: My education. I think, as a woman in the late 1890s, it would help open up my options — hopefully making prostitution an unattractive alternative. Oh, and my iPod.

Love: A few years ago my husband pointed out that if we happened to be transported back to ancient Rome (we were watching the TV series *Rome* at the time), we wouldn't be able to help modernize the empire because we don't actually know how anything in our modern world works. So we decided to each learn how something really important works, just in case. I chose 'how to make penicillin' and he chose 'how to generate and harness electricity.' Neither of us has done it yet. But I guess bringing penicillin back to medieval Europe would mess up my whole life-with-death thing, anyway. Which kind of proves how stupid my medieval fantasy is. Obviously I'd rather live in a world with penicillin than one without, and I'd rather everyone else did, too.

Miller:

1. Antibiotics
2. Dental floss
3. Pilates machines
4. iPods
5. Sondheim
6. Purell. So much Purell.

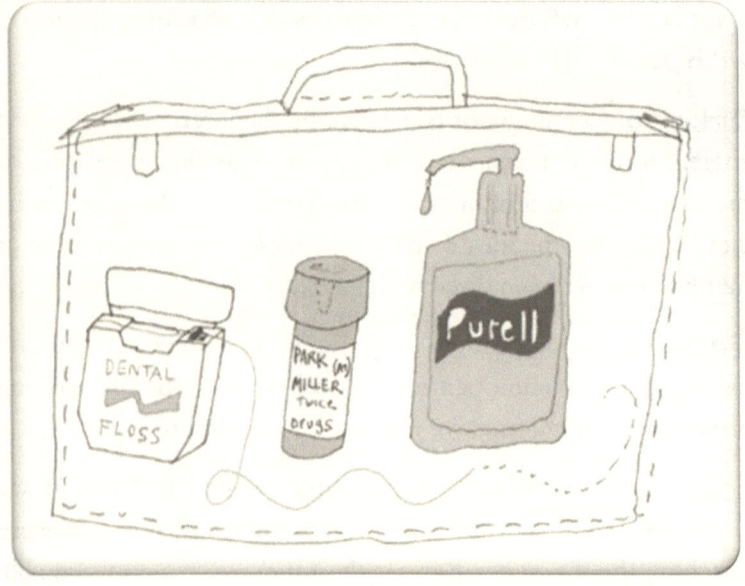

Episode 22: *Saturday Morning Cartoon*
with Allison Amend, Ryan Boudinot, Francie Lin, Ed Park, Heidi Pitlor, and Nathaniel Rich

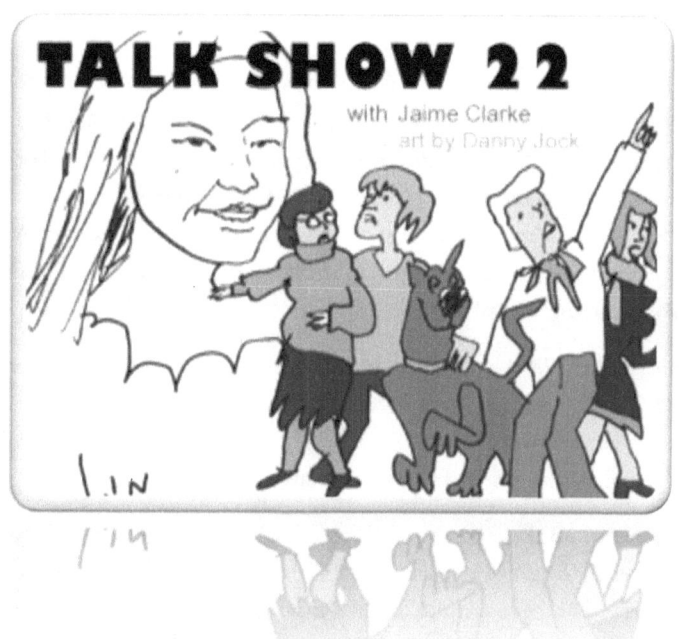

Allison Amend is the author of the short story collection *Things That Pass for Love,* which won a bronze Independent Publisher's award, and the novels *Stations West* and *A Nearly Perfect Copy.* Her work has appeared in *One Story, StoryQuarterly, Bellevue Literary Review,* the *Atlantic Monthly, Prairie Schooner* and *Other Voices,* among others. Allison teaches creative writing at Lehman College and for Red Earth MFA.

Ryan Boudinot is the author of the story collection *The Littlest Hitler* and the novels *Blueprints of the Afterlife* and *Misconception.* His work has appeared in *McSweeney's, The Best American Non-Required Read-*

ing, Nerve, Black Book and other publications. He teaches creative writing at Goddard College's MFA program.

Francie Lin is the author of *The Foreigner*, winner of the Edgar for Best First Novel. She received a Fulbright Fellowship to Taiwan and is a former editor at *The Threepenny Review*.

Ed Park is the author of the novel *Personal Days*, which was named one of *Time's* Top Ten Fiction Books. He is a founding editor of *The Believer* and the former editor of the *Voice Literary Supplement*. His work has appeared in the *New York Times*, the *Boston Globe, Salon, Modern Painters*, and other publications. Park is an editor at Amazon Publishing.

Heidi Pitlor is the author of the novels *The Birthdays* and *The Dawning*. She is the annual series editor of *The Best American Short Stories* and a former senior editor at Houghton Mifflin Company.

Nathaniel Rich is the author of the novels, *The Mayor's Tongue* and *Odds Against Tomorrow*. His essays and fiction have appeared in *Harper's*, the *New York Review of Books*, the *New York Times Magazine, McSweeney's, Vanity Fair*, the *Paris Review* and others. Rich also published a work of film criticism, *San Francisco Noir*.

* * *

- Name your favorite Saturday Morning Cartoon.

Amend: I wasn't really allowed to watch TV. But on Sundays I'd sneak downstairs before Mom and Dad were up and watch the only thing on television on Sunday mornings at 7 a.m. in 1982: *Beyond the Magic Door*, a Jewish show which I've since learned was part of the Kiruv (outreach) mission of the Chicago Council of Rabbis.

Boudinot: *Thundar the Barbarian.*

Lin: *Scooby-Doo.*

Park: Oddly, it might have been *Hong Kong Phooey*. I haven't even started to think about the cross-cultural (or in this case, "racist"?) angles to this show. Oh, man.

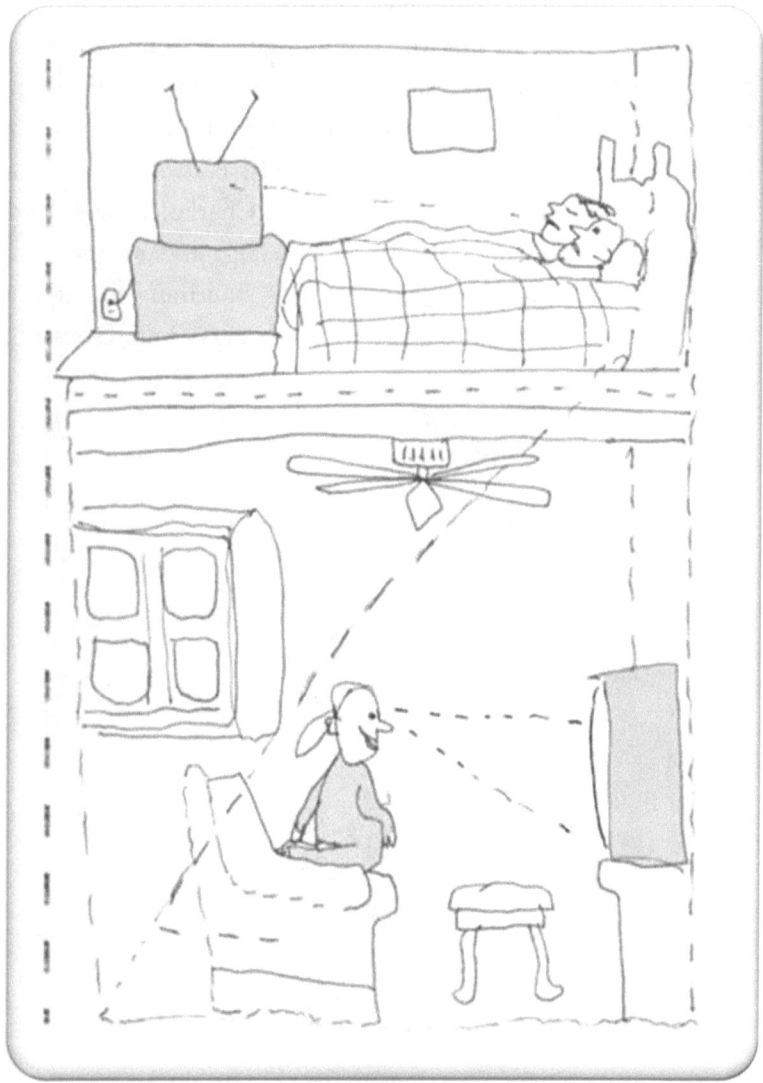

Pitlor: I think I was born a very old person who found anything too brightly colored, intrusively soundtracked or slap-
stickly humored hugely irritating. I am not and have never
been, not at three or five or ten, a fan of cartoons. I was the
only child I knew who chose not to watch *Bugs Bunny* or *Tom
and Jerry*. I distinctly remember declaring them "immature"—
and this had to be in first or second grade. It's not something
to be proud of. I've always felt left out of the national hoopla
that comes with each release of a new *Shrek* movie. A few cartoons I've found tolerable, though barely: *Peanuts* (I loved Li-
nus and Woodstock, but couldn't stand Charlie Brown's endless moping and Lucy's shrill manipulating) and *Monsters Inc.*,
though by the end of the movie, I was squirming in my seat
and desperate to look at regular human beings again. Does Pix-
ar even count?

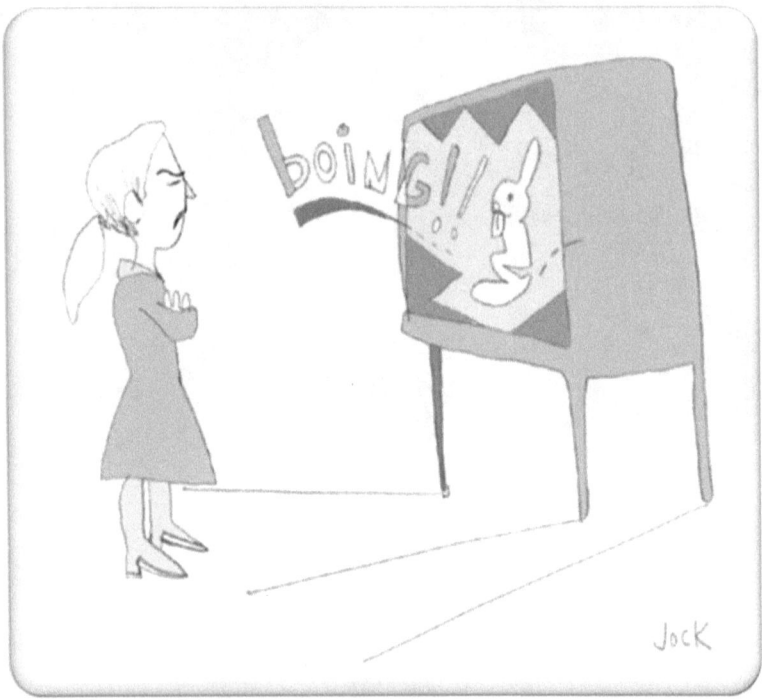

Rich: *Ren and Stimpy.*

- What are your memories of watching this cartoon?

Amend: Vague embarrassment that my religion was being paraded in front of what I assumed was the whole world, coupled with curiosity that Jews existed outside of the kids I knew from Sunday School, and compounded by boredom. I also recall, though this must be a memory that I've grafted onto that time, that the title of the show was somehow dirty . . . It strikes me now as better suited to be the title of a porn film, or the name of a Vietnamese brothel.

Boudinot: All I really remember about this show was that it took place in post-apocalyptic time. The barbarian who gave the show its title looked sort of like Conan or He-Man, and he had a number of accomplices who rode around with him on horses, fighting bad guys.

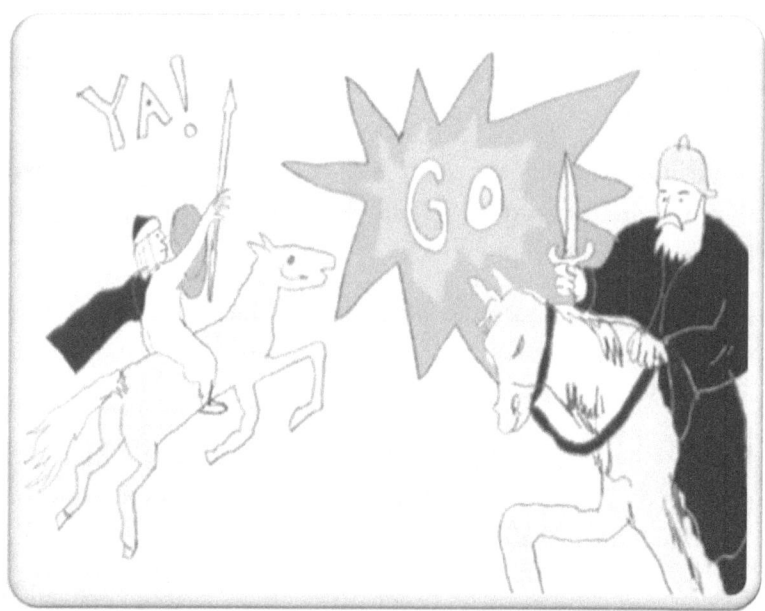

Lin: Getting up at some ungodly hour before anyone else was up to watch, and feeling panic when I missed an episode. Also,

I think I was in love with Freddy and made up lots of stories with him as the romantic interest.

Park: The secretary's nasal voice cracked me up.

Pitlor: I remember seeking out any toy, book, piece of thread, anything really with which to occupy myself while my brother or friends watched cartoons. I remember being thrilled when I learned to change the channel myself.

Rich: I remember being so excited by the idea of a pet log that I dragged in a fallen branch from the sidewalk outside my apartment and made my mother set a place for it at the dinner table.

- What was one of your favorite storylines?

Amend: They were all the same, little kids with big noses and curly brown hair danced around a living dreidel. Can that be right? Dan Castellaneta played the adult. Yes, that's right, Homer Simpson is Jewish.

Boudinot: I think the story I liked most was the one where they fought the bad guys, and the head bad guy said to his henchmen, "Seize him!"

Lin: Can't remember exact storylines — they were pretty much all the same anyway. But anything with the Harlem Globetrotters, or with Scrappy Doo, was always a treat.

Park: I have absolutely no memory of storylines. In fact, I don't even understand it: Why was it a dog who did kung fu? I'm sure there was a terrific backstory.

Pitlor: Of course in hindsight, the storylines blend together for me (slender, shrewd animal chases chubby, feckless animal. Explosives or heavy machinery involved, feckless animal turns

262

tables). But I did look forward to the *Peanuts' Christmas.* I still remember with enormous affection the little twig of a tree that Charlie Brown adopted. As a Jew, I think I sympathized with that tree each December.

Rich: *Space Madness*, which follows the adventures of Ren and Stimpy as astronauts lost in space. Here's Ren, talking to a bar of soap: *"You're not like the others . . . you like the same things I do! Waxed paper . . . boiled football leather . . . dog breath . . . "*

- Do you own any memorabilia?

Amend: Just the albatross of guilt and self-loathing that is the legacy of every good Jew.

Boudinot: Unfortunately, no.

Lin: No. Isn't that sad?

Park: No. Though my wife bought a pink *Honk Kong Phooey* T-shirt at a Target in Irvine, California, a couple years ago.

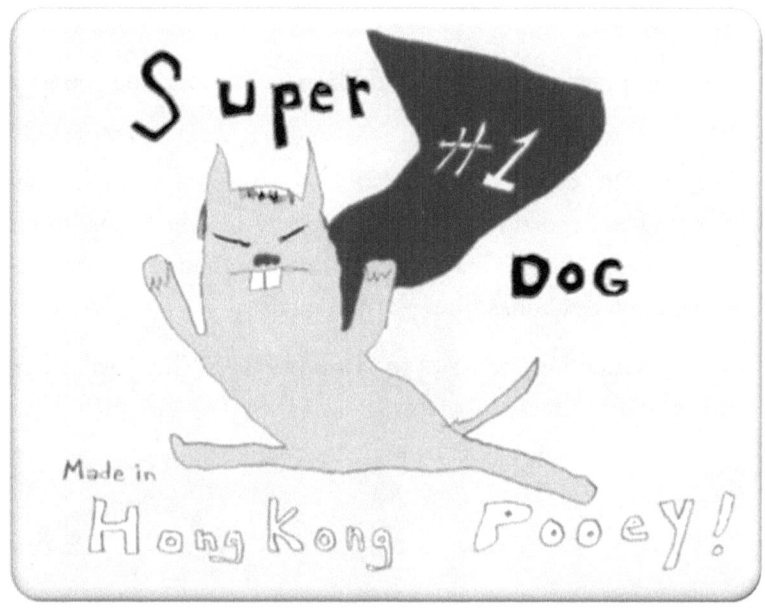

Pitlor: I don't own any memorabilia at this point, but I did have a denim jumper that was embroidered with Snoopy and Woodstock patches and I was quite proud of it. When I look at my nieces' cropped t-shirts emblazoned with glittery *Hello Kitties* or *Hannah Montana* holding a microphone, I remember my Snoopy jumper with a certain woeful nostalgia. See, I'm still a cranky old naysayer.

Rich: I wish — just the first two seasons on DVD.

— Can you remember the theme song?

Amend: Unsurprisingly, it involved the words "Beyond the Magic Door . . ." and a tiny door opened up into a large Semitic utopia. I was disappointed, many years later, when I went to Israel and it failed to look like the set.

Boudinot: Not at all, sad to say.

Lin: Of course! If this weren't an email interview I'd sing it for you now.

Park: Somewhat: "Hong Kong Phooey, number one superstar . . ."

Pitlor: Who can forget the *Peanuts* crew, arms at their sides, bouncing up and down like popcorn beside the piano to the happy, jazzy Vince Guaraldi? For me, if childhood could be distilled in a few tunes, these would qualify.

Rich: I remember the lyrics to "Happy Happy, Joy Joy." I hum it to myself in times of sorrow.

Episode 23: *Over-rated*
with Jenna Blum, Julia Glass, Nellie Hermann, Dinaw Mengestu, and Matthew Pearl

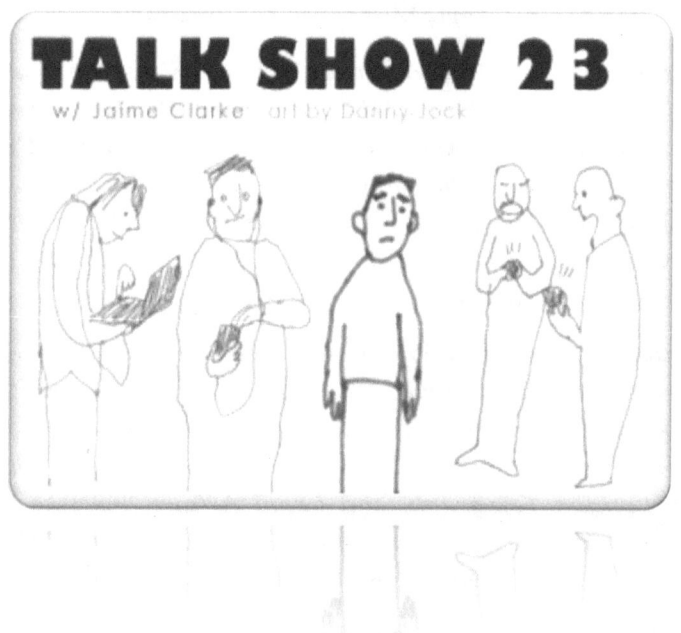

TALK SHOW 23

w/ Jaime Clarke   art by Danny Jock

Jenna Blum is the author of the novels *Those Who Save Us* and *The Stormchasers*. She taught writing classes at Boston University and currently teaches novel workshops at Grub Street. Blum writes the monthly "Writer on the Road" column for *Grub Street Daily* and was a former editor for *AGNI* Magazine.

Julia Glass's novels include *The Widower's Tale*, *Three Junes* (winner of the National Book Award), *The Whole World Over*, and *I See You Everywhere*. A recipient of fellowships from the National Endowment for the Arts, the New York Foundation for the Arts, and the Radcliffe Institute for Advanced Study, her essays have been published in numerous magazines and anthologies.

Nellie Hermann is the author of the novel *A Cure for Grief*. She is the Creative Director for the Program in Narrative Medicine at Columbia University. Her short story "Can We Let the Baby Go?" won first place in the *Glimmer Train* "Family Matters" competition.

Dinaw Mengestu is the author of the novels *The Beautiful Things That Heaven Bears*, winner of *The Guardian* First Book Award and a *Los Angeles Times* Book Prize, and *How to Read the Air*. He has written for many publications, including the *New Yorker*, *Harper's*, *the New York Times, and Granta*. Mengestu is the winner of a MacArthur Foundation Fellowship Award.

Matthew Pearl is the author of the novels *The Technologists*, *The Dante Club*, *The Poe Shadow*, and *The Last Dickens*. His nonfiction writing has appeared in the *New York Times*, the *Wall Street Journal*, the *Boston Globe*, the *London Telegraph*, and *Legal Affairs*. He has also taught at Harvard University and Emerson College. Pearl's work has been translated into over thirty languages.

* * *

- Name something you think is over-rated.

Blum: Text messaging.

Glass: Leaving aside the obvious political suspects — like, say, diamond rings and blogging — I was tempted to write about caviar or Quentin Tarantino . . . but I'll go with yoga.

Hermann: Facebook. If by "over-rated" you mean insanely ubiquitous. I'm not sure I've ever heard anyone say how great they think Facebook is with the exception of how great it is that they get to play Scrabulous (and I admit, this is a good feature) and I wonder, if given the chance to rate it, people would even rate it so highly? That's the thing — people seem to be using it all the time no matter how they feel about it. Which makes me nervous.

Mengestu: Exercise. Or to be more specific, the culture of exercise, the obsession with exercise, the wearing of exercise clothes to places that have no natural affinity with gym equipment, such as restaurants, grocery stores and classrooms. This isn't an argument for sloth, or laziness, or obesity, but a defense of what at times feels like the new "alternative lifestyle," an increasingly endangered brand of living that prefers to spend mornings shuffling in pajamas with multiple cups of coffee, and the immediate hours after work perched on or standing near a bar stool, rather than running, lifting or stretching our way to fitness.

Pearl: Everyone will be angry with me, all my friends, every other writer. But I'd say Apple, the Apple Store, i-Phone, *i*-things.

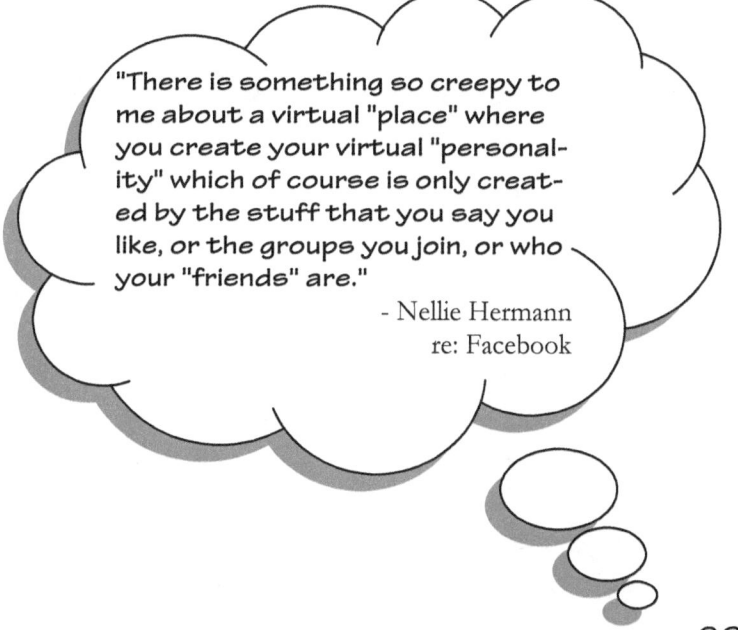

"There is something so creepy to me about a virtual "place" where you create your virtual "personality" which of course is only created by the stuff that you say you like, or the groups you join, or who your "friends" are."

- Nellie Hermann
re: Facebook

- What is your qualm with its popularity?

Blum: Texting, like IM-ing, encourages people to think in the type of abbreviations that should only be used by realtors and in newspaper ads — IMHO. Soon we'll all be communicating in scraps, *Y?* And it's annoying — like we needed yet another way for information to bombard us while we're walking down the street or driving or shopping. Whatever happened to concentrating on one thing at a time, like human beings?

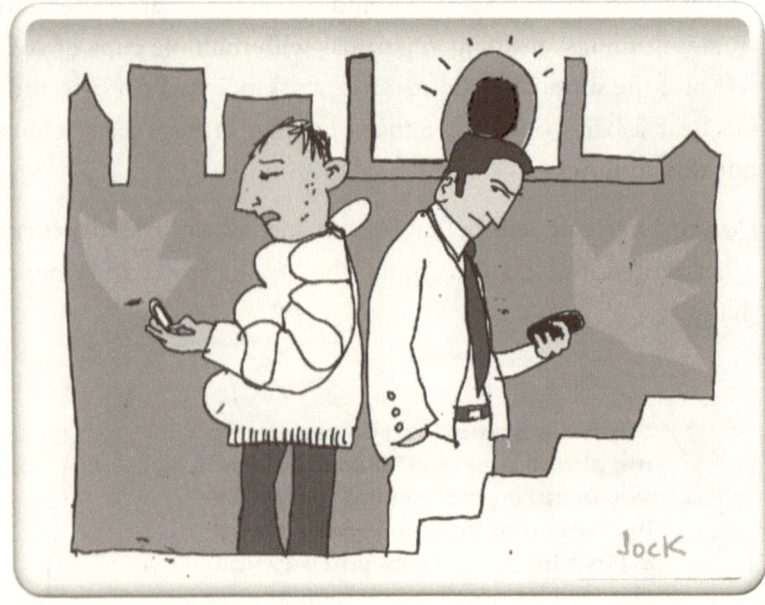

Glass: I have no qualms about yoga as a way of staying supple and physically fit, and I could probably be convinced that authentic Eastern practitioners of yoga do achieve some higher plane of mental acuity through convoluting their bodies into poses that remind me of the Twister craze back in junior high. Who am I to judge the rituals of another culture? What I find absurd, however, are the legions of modern American women who are suddenly, often aggressively, extolling the inner bliss and wisdom bestowed upon them every time they roll out a foam mat and emulate those poses. (Especially foolish are the ones who also personify our own cultural stereotypes, driving about in their big-butt cars, drinking their free-range chai, sporting their aubergine spandex capris and paisley Tevas.) Among the ersatz epiphanies proliferating everywhere, yoga-as-enlightenment may seem reasonably harmless, but anything that encourages people to mistake a hit of endorphins for an act of virtue looks sinister to me. (Perhaps I shouldn't single out women, but among the men I know who practice yoga, nobody brags about spiritual gains.) And "hot yoga"? Sounds like an engraved invitation to flesh-eating staphylococci. I know one devotee who thought it had changed her life, and it did. She developed virulent allergies to the building materials in the yoga studio where she attended classes.

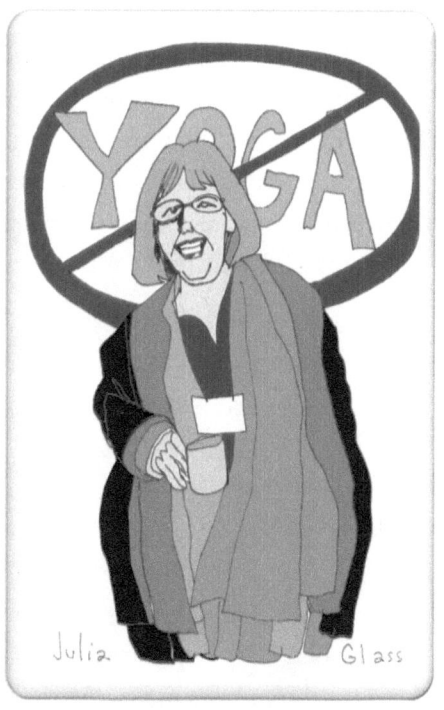

Julia Glass

Hermann: There is something so creepy to me about a virtual "place" where you create your virtual "personality" which of course is only created by the stuff that you say you like, or the groups you join, or who your "friends" are. I know I come off as some kind of old-timey crank by ranting about this, but the whole thing seems like too much posturing to me, putting up more pictures of ourselves and saying what we're "doing" at this exact moment and displaying who sent us virtual flowers. People seem to present cutesy versions of their selves, and I don't know how much honesty is involved. It also seems like Facebook is not actually interesting or worth any time unless you spend A LOT of time doing it, keeping it updated, posting clips and pictures, and then, where does your "real" personality, the more complicated one, end up?

Mengestu: I have to be honest and admit my reasons are entirely selfish. Over the years I've lost several good friends to exercise — fine, young men far from the peak of their physical form who never hesitated when called upon to have one more drink to end the night. Since they began their morning runs or trips to the gym, dinners end early; I have to stand alone, outside, with my cigarette. There are long, awkward silences that always follow the phrase, "When I was at the gym."

Pearl: It's a cult, I'm tired of being told I should have one because everyone artistic or creative does, would never use anything else, would leave the room if someone walked in with a PC. Yes, I've tried using my friends' Macs. No, I don't like the interface, I don't think it's better, I think it somehow manages to be condescending. (Plus, no right click button?) And there are no choices in products. But, worse than the computers: Apple Stores. Genius Bar. And the lines people wait on at the convention centers when new apple products are announced. Stop it. Once, I was at the movies in Los Angeles, in the row in front of us, there was a young couple. The woman had an i-Phone and couldn't stop playing with it, the guy just sat there, putting in ear plugs in preparation for the movie. I blamed the i-Phone for their existences.

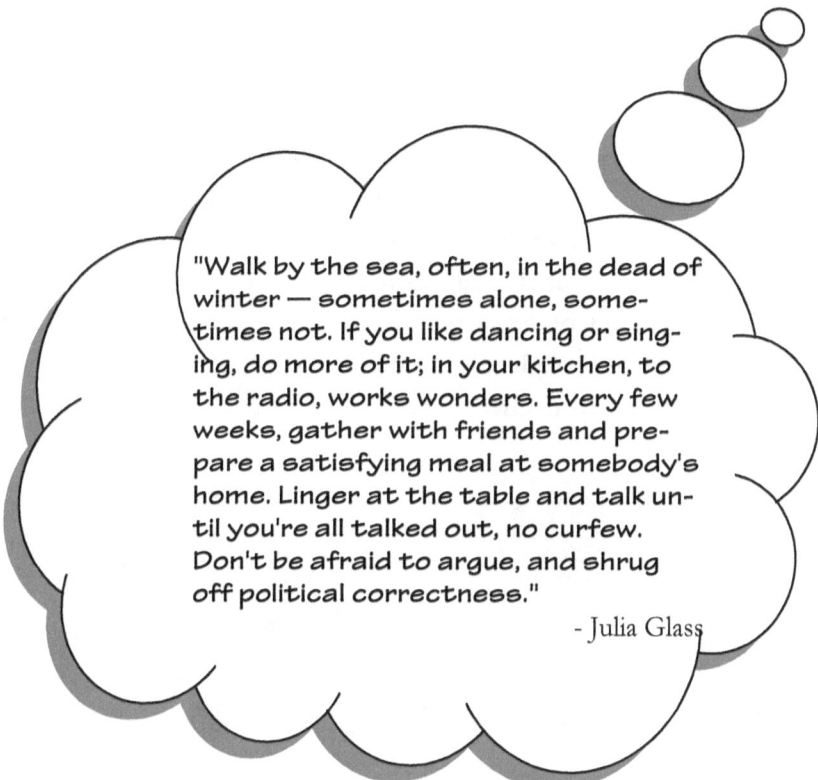

"Walk by the sea, often, in the dead of winter — sometimes alone, sometimes not. If you like dancing or singing, do more of it; in your kitchen, to the radio, works wonders. Every few weeks, gather with friends and prepare a satisfying meal at somebody's home. Linger at the table and talk until you're all talked out, no curfew. Don't be afraid to argue, and shrug off political correctness."

- Julia Glass

- Why do you think it's so popular?

Blum: Because it's there. Monkey see, monkey text.

Glass: People want to be slim, fit, and live forever; that's obvious and justifiable. But people also want short cuts to the kind of introspection and genuine humanity (empathy, humility, and fellowship) that one achieves only through positive emotional and intellectual give-and-take with friends, colleagues, family, and community — and, privately, through the contemplation of life's ordeals and the weathering of unexpected crises. Sure, everyone yearns now and then for a soul makeover. Yoga as a form of physical discipline? Admirable. As an alternative to good psychotherapy? Wishful thinking. As a mini-religion? Yikes.

Hermann: For lots and lots of reasons. I think it caters to our voyeuristic desires, and to our desire to have control over the kind of self we project to the world. I see the appeal of meeting someone somewhere and then typing his/her name into Facebook to see what kinds of stuff s/he puts out there — I'm human after all. But this can turn dangerous so fast, as in the case of a friend of mine, whose access to an ex-girlfriend's Facebook page brought him much anguish, because he couldn't stop himself from checking it all the time.

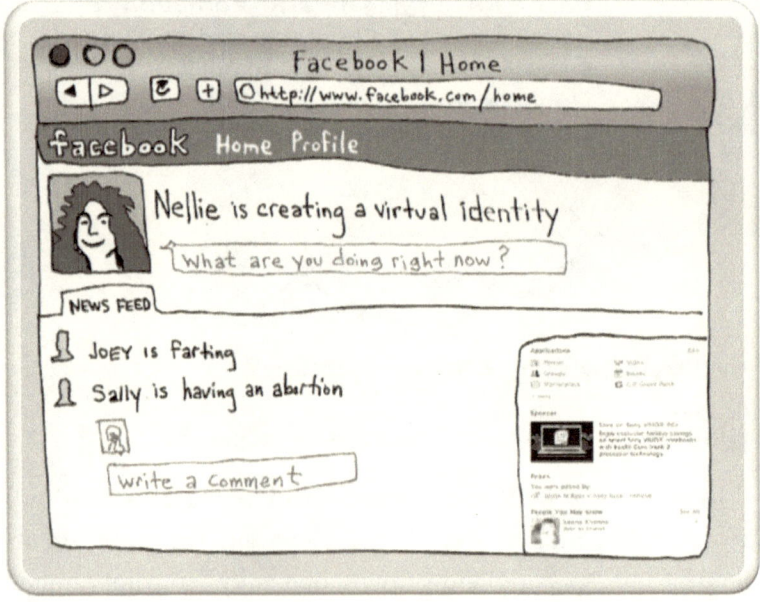

This is a serious unintended consequence, because there is a certain natural and necessary way that people come and go from our lives, and Facebook makes the disappearance a little less easy. Not to give it such power. I realize that there are plenty of people who have healthy relationships with it, and that it's possible to use it as a simple tool for connecting with people in different cities or countries, and . . . etcetera. There might be a specifically New York component to my dislike for it, because when you're only connecting to people that you live in the same city with it becomes a bit more perverted into a popularity contest of a strange sort. And don't get me started on the weirdness of the instant switch between declaring yourself "single" to "in a relationship," and the glee that I've witnessed over people making that switch and noticing that others have made that switch, and then the shame of switching it back to the dreaded "single" distinction . . .

Mengestu: Fear. Not of death, but of being left behind. Plus, who needs to get dressed up if everyone is always just coming from the gym or on the way there.

Pearl: How did Matthew McConaughey become a big movie star before he was in a movie? Somehow people were convinced that being Apple-loyal said something about one's identity. It's some kind of postmodern misplaced religious instinct. I will have no friends anymore, by the way, because of this.

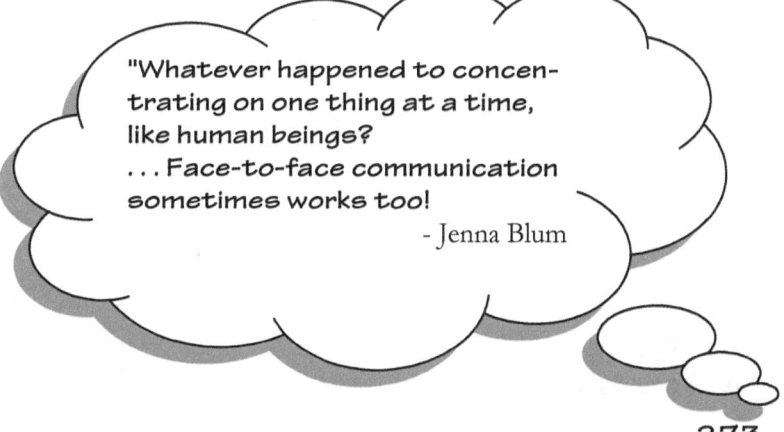

"Whatever happened to concentrating on one thing at a time, like human beings?
. . . Face-to-face communication sometimes works too!
- Jenna Blum

- **What's an under-rated alternative you'd promote in its place?**

Blum: Waiting until you get home and emailing the people you want to talk to. Or picking up the phone and calling them. I'll allow a cell. Face-to-face communication sometimes works too!

Glass: No single ritual or activity can change you so profoundly. But I have my subjective notions about what's good for the soul. First and foremost, make a habit of reading good, meaty, absorbing fiction. Read fairy tales or favorite childhood books to your kids (or somebody else's). Walk by the sea, often, in the dead of winter — sometimes alone, sometimes not. If you like dancing or singing, do more of it; in your kitchen, to the radio, works wonders. Every few weeks, gather with friends and prepare a satisfying meal at somebody's home. Linger at the table and talk until you're all talked out, no curfew. Don't be afraid to argue, and shrug off political correctness. (Park your kids in the next room, with pizza and brownies, in front of *Chitty Chitty Bang Bang* or, if they're old enough, *Lawrence of Arabia*. Let them fall asleep in their chocolate-smeared PJs.) Any or all of these things will take you deep into your better self and help you focus on the most important questions. All are potentially transformative, rejuvenating, invigorating.

Hermann: Hmm. Book groups, maybe? Sewing circles? Intramural sports teams? Conversation?

Mengestu: There are plenty of alternatives to standard exercise. Over the years I've kept my heart rate up through frantic pacing of my living room and kitchen. I've also found that if I spend hours cooking dinner for friends I'm no longer hungry by the time the food is done. Carrying home meat and alcohol from the grocery store on a daily basis has kept my arms trim.

Pearl: I use a Sony PC. But I'm not a commercial for them. That's the thing, I don't think my PC says *anything* about my identity. I don't want it to. It's just my computer. What I would like is if they stopped inventing 1/5" laptops long enough to invent a good cloth to clean my laptop screen, which gets filthy within seconds.

"This isn't an argument for sloth, or laziness, or obesity, but a defense of what at times feels like the new "alternative lifestyle," an increasingly endangered brand of living that prefers to spend mornings shuffling in pajamas with multiple cups of coffee, and the immediate hours after work perched on or standing near a bar stool, rather than running, lifting or stretching our way to fitness."

- Dinaw Mengestu

— What could convince you to join the fanfare?

Blum: Oh, I didn't say I don't text. *LOL!* But I am trying to wean off.

Glass: I tried yoga several years ago and found it physically counterintuitive — which may be the point, I know. So perhaps I quit too soon. A no-hype yoga teacher could probably recruit me again for the bodily benefits — my bones are getting too old for my running routine — but as for the rest, I'm always wary when I spot the emperor's fashion consultant cruis-

ing over the castle moat in his spiffy carriage. Call me benight-
ed, curmudgeonly, resistant, but this much I know: exercising
my imagination — as well as delving into the imaginings of
others — will always give me a spiritual workout unlike any
other.

Hermann: I admit that I've been momentarily tempted to join
under an alias just so I can play Scrabulous with a couple of
particularly wordy friends. It hasn't happened yet, and I sort of
doubt it will. If it does, I'll be the worst kind of Facebook
member, the kind that skulks around under a fake name and
makes everyone more confused about their virtual network and
who their friends really are.

Mengestu: A one-hundred percent guarantee that my life
will be substantially longer and happier, or further proof of
physical decline.

Pearl: I have an i-Pod. It was a gift.

Episode 24: *First Apartment*
with Leah Hager Cohen, Joshua Ferris,
Alice Mattison, and Ann Packer

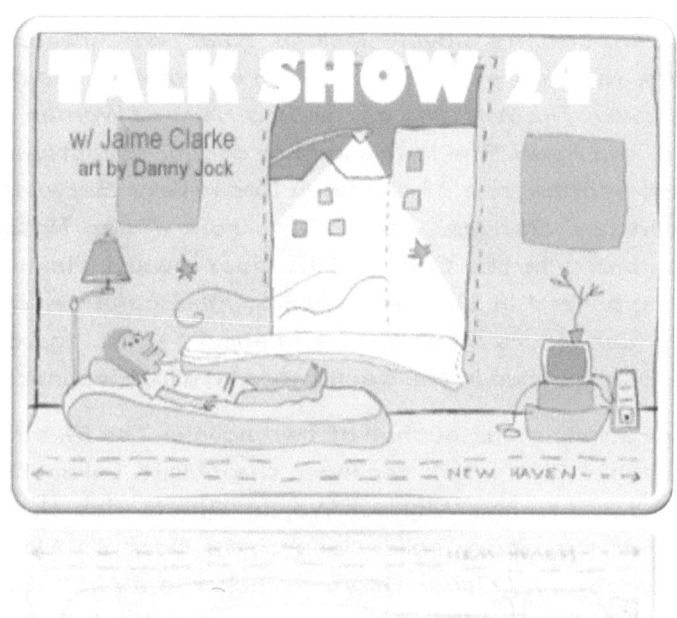

Leah Hager Cohen has written five books of nonfiction: *Without Apology; The Stuff of Dreams; Glass, Paper, Beans; Train Go Sorry* and *I Don't Know*, as well as five novels: *The Grief of Others; Heat Lightning; Heart, You Bully, You Punk; House Lights* and *No Book But the World*. Book Awards include the *New York Times* Notable Book; American Library Association Ten Best Books of the Year; *Toronto Globe and Mail* Ten Best Books of the Year; and Booksense '76 Pick. She is a frequent contributor to the *New York Times Book Review* and teaches at Lesley University's M.F.A. program.

Joshua Ferris is the author of the novels *Then We Came to the End*, winner of the PEN/Hemingway Award, and

The Unnamed. His fiction has appeared in the *New Yorker*, *Granta*, the Guardian, and *Tin House*, *Best New American Voices*, *New Stories from the South*, *Prairie Schooner*, the *Iowa Review* and others.

Alice Mattison's novels include *When We Argued All Night*, *Nothing Is Quite Forgotten In Brooklyn*, *The Book Borrower*, *The Wedding of the Two-Headed Woman*, and *Hilda and Pearl*. She is the author of four collections of short stories, one of these, *In Case We're Separated: Connected Stories*, was a *New York Times* Notable Book and won the Connecticut Book Award. Her work has appeared in the *New Yorker*, *Ploughshares*, *Best American Short Stories*, the *Pushcart Prize*, and others. She teaches in the Bennington Writing Seminars.

Ann Packer is the author of two novels: *The Dive from Clausen's Pier*, which received the Great Lakes Book Award and Songs Without Words. She is also the author of the story collections *Swim Back to Me* and *Mendocino and Other Stories*. Packer is a past recipient of a James Michener award and a NEA fellowship. Her fiction has appeared in the *New Yorker*, *Ploughshares*, *Prize Stories: The O. Henry Awards* and others.

* * *

- Where was your first apartment?

Cohen: It was on Lake Street in New Haven, just past the edge of Yale's campus.

Ferris: My mother's womb. A snug little efficiency, all utilities paid. No problem with heating or plumbing, though the landlord was a heavy smoker, to her eternal shame.

Mattison: The apartment was on Sacramento Street in Cambridge, Massachusetts. Three other women and I rented the second floor of a house that was behind another, larger house. Next to our building was the playground of an elementary school, though the school itself was across the street.

Packer: The first apartment that was mine alone was on West 10th Street in Manhattan — right in the heart of Greenwich Village, on the same block as the wonderful, quiet, literate bookstore Three Lives, where I stopped to browse two to three times per week; and the fabled gay bar the Ninth Circle, of which I was less aware, except at closing time (4 a.m.) when the party would spill raucously onto the street. Balducci's, the now much-mourned food emporium, was two blocks away, and I bought more than my share of pasta salads there, and expensive pears. This was in the early '80s, and the foodie movement didn't really have a name yet, but it was thriving on the corner of 6th Avenue and 9th Street.

The other part of the immediate neighborhood that I remember vividly is the Greek coffee shop where I bought coffee every morning on my way to the subway. There'd be a line of ten to fifteen people at all times, but it moved quickly, and within minutes of arriving it would be my turn. "Regular coffee" was my order — this meant coffee with a specific but indefinable amount of half-and-half: more than there would be in "dark coffee" and less than in "light coffee."

I'd never asked for coffee that way before, and never have since. I guess we add our own half-and-half these days, saying, "Coffee with room for cream," or even just "Coffee with room," to keep the word count low and the line moving at Starbucks.

- **Why did you rent it?**

Cohen: I was all but panting with the desire to play grown-up. That's what it felt like: I was twenty, fresh out of college, desperate to put on the clothes of independence. What to do? It was a bit like that folk song: "When I first came to this land, I was not a wealthy man. So I got myself a farm; I did what I could." Well, I got myself a job; I did what I could. That turned out to mean working at the African American Studies department and renting an apartment for $340 a month.

Ferris: I didn't have much choice in the matter, though I don't have many complaints. The smoking, as I've mentioned. But in general, the landlord was solicitous, the neighbors were supportive, the area of town secluded and warm, and there was ample space to grow.

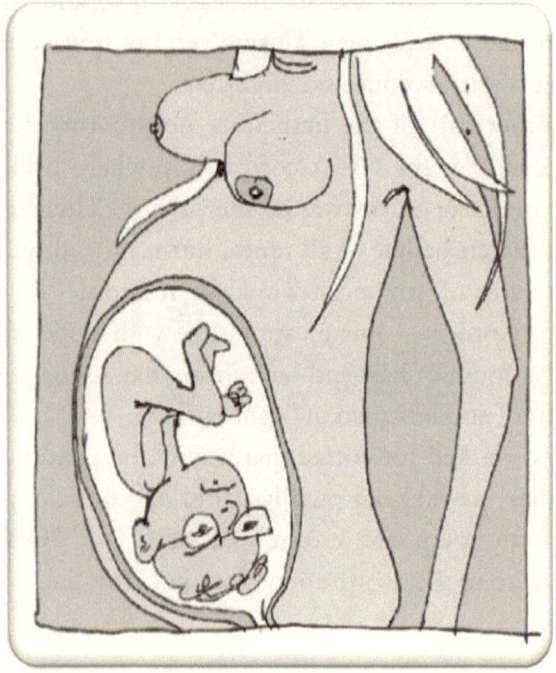

Mattison: I was in graduate school at Harvard, studying English literature and working as a teaching fellow. I'd been living in a series of university-owned buildings in which a bunch of women would each have her own room but share a living room, kitchen, and bathroom. At the end of my third year, four of us from the house decided to rent an apartment together. We wanted more independence than we had with the university as our landlord, we enjoyed one another, and I think we were ready to get past enforced friendliness with whoever else happened to be in the house with us.

Packer: There were some disadvantages to this apartment, probably the most significant of which was that it was a fifth-floor walkup, no elevator. But it had exposed brick walls and a working fireplace, and across the air shaft an apartment with a kitchen I could see into at night, to admire my unknown neighbor's collection of tiny painted animals, arrayed on every available shelf and ledge. It was in a great location, I could afford it — those were reasons aplenty to rent in Manhattan.

- What was the worst feature of the apartment?

Cohen: The worst feature was also the best, and that was the loneliness that seemed to breathe it. I had almost nothing with which to appoint the three rather generously proportioned rooms. In the kitchen, I took a door from its hinges and laid it on milk crates: that was my table. In the corner room, I spread a futon on the floor by the three large windows: that was my nest. In the middle room, I put my computer on another milk crate, and a cushion on the floor in front of it: that was my desk. I had no television, little money, no friends. I lived on peanut butter crackers, apples and milk. The time I spent drifting through those rooms, alone with my thoughts, was both maddening and glistening.

Ferris: They refused to give me a full year's lease.

Mattison: The worst feature of our apartment — which was rickety but spacious and convenient, with four bedrooms, a living room, a kitchen, and a bathroom, all off a long hallway — was that it needed to be renovated when we rented it in June, and when we returned in September, the renovation of the bathroom was just beginning. During the whole month of September, while we scrambled around trying to teach and write and study, we had a series of workmen invading the bathroom from early in the morning until night on weekdays, and for much of the month we had no shower. I remember walking into a friend's party and asking her if I could please take a shower. After a while my roommates and I talked about nothing but bathrooms. The nearest bathroom in a public building was blocks from our apartment, and we'd trek there in the morning, or take our toothbrushes and head for the library. Of my three roommates, the boldest and most elegant, Renie, perfected the art of dressing up in heels and nylons and quietly entering the school across the street to use the teachers' bathroom there. Meanwhile, a friendly but painstakingly slow series of old-world craftsmen of various nationalities glued tiles on the bathroom floor, one by one, and installed slightly nicer fixtures than had been there before.

We complained to the landlord, but it didn't help. We'd barely noticed the landlord's name when we rented the place, but we belatedly realized that he was a lesser member of an old, distinguished Massachusetts family. His brother was the governor, and his mother was a bigshot at the UN, and his ancestors had been around for centuries. At the end of the month, we had a decent though ordinary bathroom, and we felt we should pay less rent or no rent for the month, but the landlord — though we'd learned he was on the Fair Rent Commission — insisted. Renie put on her high heels again and consulted a lawyer, who said, "You mean you girls (he may even have said 'You little girls') intend to take on the Xs of Massachusetts?" We gave up and paid the rent.

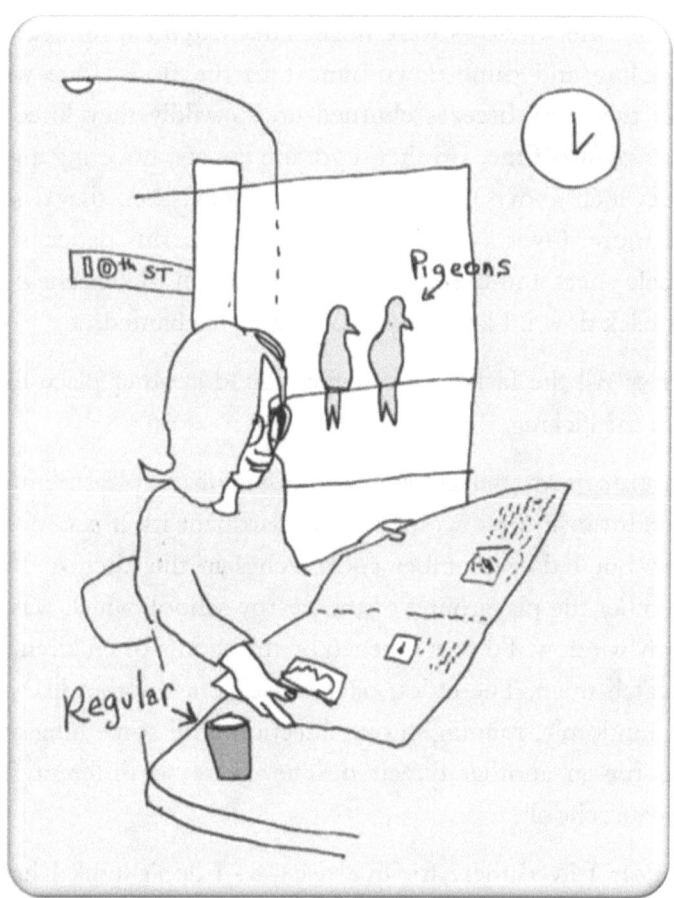

Packer: Pigeons roosted on the ledge outside my bathroom window. This window looked onto a grimy airshaft, and the pigeons were there at all times, sighing and twittering and emitting a stink that made it absolutely impossible ever to open the window. They were, in a word, gross.

- **What is your outstanding memory of the apartment?**

Cohen: I slept with the windows open. I liked the city sounds, the voices in the street, the sirens well into the night. In my memory, the windows were huge. They extended up nearly to the ceiling and came down almost to the floor. One windy night, the cross breezes churned up so wildly they lifted the covers right off me. Up they'd go, the covers, hovering a good quarter-inch above the surface of my body; then they'd settle once more. Over and over, the wind made this dance, made the pale sheet and the thin blanket levitate in the darkness and float back down. I lay awake a long time, enchanted.

Ferris: All the kicking. I've never found another place like it for all the kicking.

Mattison: My outstanding memory is of the pleasure of living with those three women. The apartment itself was nondescript, but I do remember cockroaches in the kitchen. I also remember the playground of the nearby school, which was under my window. I'd be awakened by the shouts of children, and I'd watch them. The littlest ones chased one another like puppies, randomly, running in one direction until something made them run in another direction. They were so different from graduate school!

Packer: I lived there for five years, so I don't think I have a single outstanding memory. Two images come to mind: I'm sitting at my little gate-leg table and reading the vast Sunday edition of the *New York Times*, always in the same order: Arts and Leisure first, then Magazine, then Book Review. I must've done this two hundred times. The second is cooking in the tiny kitchen. There was only just room to turn around from the stove and sink and chop or stir something on the butcher block cart I'd installed. But I threw my first dinner parties in that apartment and I remember assembling multi-course complex dinners in that kitchen, despite having to put the dirty dishes on the floor sometimes to make room for my work.

- How did your tenancy end?

Cohen: The loneliness, the self-made loneliness, began to unnerve me. My slide into an almost monkish existence came to seem like it might be an unhealthy indulgence. I picked up and moved to Brooklyn.

Ferris: In tears, heartache, superstition, anguish and death.

Mattison: At the end of the academic year, all my roommates got married. I wrote a poem I didn't show them, of which the first line was "Three roommates had I, and they all got married. . . ."

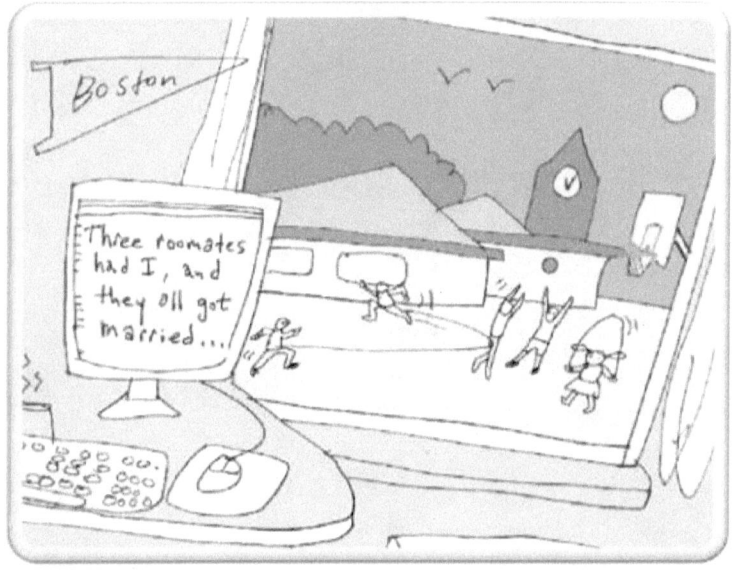

We were bridesmaids in one wedding in Kentucky, and we all went to the second one in New Jersey, but I was spending the summer traveling in Europe — which cost almost nothing in those days — and I missed the third. As they announced their engagements, one by one, I felt a little strange, but only a little. In the fall I rented a studio apartment of my own, a block away and finally lived alone.

Packer: I let go of the apartment when I decided to leave New York and enroll in the Iowa Writers' Workshop. Much of the furniture wasn't worth trying to move, so I got some friends to help me carry it down to the sidewalk. When we went back downstairs a little while later, every piece had been taken — by some recent arrival, I'd like to think, furnishing her first apartment.

Episode 25: *Irrational Fear*
with Brian Evenson, Lev Grossman, Elizabeth McCracken, Hannah Pittard, Karen Shepard, and Gary Shteyngart

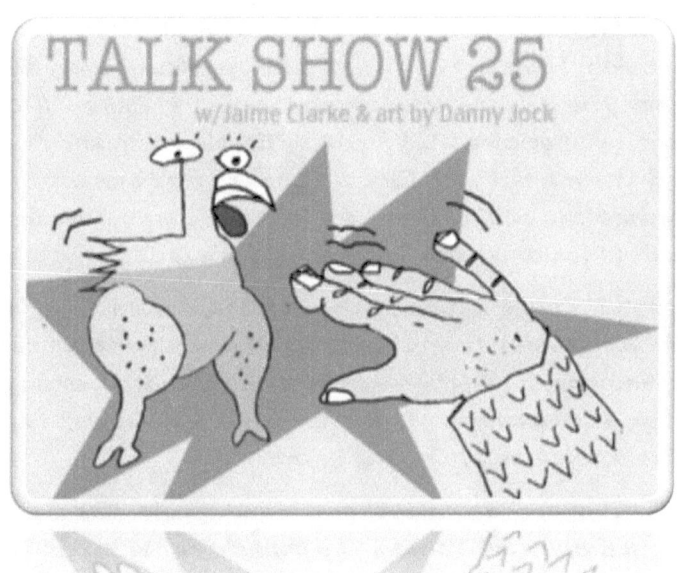

Brian Evenson's fiction includes *Last Days*, winner of an ALA award for Best Horror Novel and the collection *Fugue State*, both of which were on *Time Out New York*'s top books of the year. Other books include *The Open Curtain*, *Immobility*, *Dead Space: Catalyst*, *The Wavering Knife* (an IHG Award winner), *Dark Property*, *Dead Space: Martyr* and *Altmann's Tongue*. Evenson directs Brown University's Literary Arts Program and is the recipient of three O. Henry Prizes.

Lev Grossman is the author of *the novels The Magicians King*, *The Magicians* - named one of the Best Books by the *New Yorker*, *Codex* and *Warp*. Grossman was awarded the John W. Campbell Award for Best New Writer. His work has appeared in *Salon*, the *Village Voice*, the *Wall Street Journal*, *Entertainment Weekly*, *The Believer*, the *New York Times* and others. Grossman is the book critic at *Time* magazine.

Elizabeth McCracken is the author of the short story collection *Here's Your Hat What's Your Hurry?*, the novels *The Giant's House* and *Niagara Falls All Over Again* - winner of a L.L. Winship/PEN New England Award - and the memoir, *An Exact Replica of a Figment of My Imagination*. McCracken holds the James Michener Chair of Fiction at the University of Texas.

Hannah Pittard is the author of the novels *The Fates Will Find Their Way* and *Reunion*. She is a past winner of the Amanda Davis Highwire Fiction Award, a Consulting Editor at *Narrative Magazine*, and a MacDowell Fellow. Pittard teaches at DePaul University.

Karen Shepard is the author of four novels, *The Celestials*, *An Empire of Women*, *The Bad Boy's Wife*, and *Don't I Know You?* Her short fiction has been published in the *Atlantic Monthly*, *Bomb*, *Ploughshares*, *Glimmer Train*, *Mississippi Review*, *Southwest Review* and others. She teaches at Williams College.

Gary Shteyngart is the author of the novels *Super Sad True Love Story*, *The Russian Debutante's Handbook* - winner of the Stephen Crane Award for First Fiction - and *Absurdistan*, which was named one of the ten best books of the year by the *New York Times Book Review* and *Time* magazine. His work has been translated into over twenty languages and has appeared in the *New Yorker*, *Esquire*, *GQ*, *Travel + Leisure* and other publications.

* * *

- Name an irrational fear you suffer

Evenson: When I was young I was basically afraid of everything: I used to be intensely afraid of the dark and would wake up screaming; I refused to get out the car when we would drive through the mountains because I was afraid I might accidentally fall off a cliff. All those fears seem fairly rational to me, which is probably why they've mostly faded into the background. But I still find myself dealing from time to time with a certain fear of raw or rare chicken on the bone. I don't have the same fear of pork or lamb (which I often eat very rare) or beef (which I'm not adverse to eating completely raw). I don't mind very rare duck. I eat all kinds of sushi. I've eaten odd things like pig's ears and tripe without batting an eye. But chicken, either raw or rare, and on the bone, is almost more than I can stand. It's particularly bad when someone is separating a raw chicken into parts; the sound a chicken leg's joint makes popping out of its socket is a terrible thing.

Grossman: I have a morbid, irrational fear of the sight and sound of other people eating and drinking. I wish I were joking, but it's true. It's a phobia. I don't even think it has a cool name. When I see another person eating or drinking, I want to run away.

Pittard: To be interesting, I could lie and say Unmade Beds because I really do hate an unmade bed and am scared into making mine every morning before leaving the apartment on the off chance that I'll be killed while I'm out and that my mother will come to pack up my things and, doing so, will find my bed unmade and be forever horrified that her now-dead daughter was a worthless sloth who couldn't find time to make a bed, but the truth is that my biggest irrational fear — because I have many — is probably the most boring: Flying.

McCracken: I have a few, including dead mice, cannibalism, and amusement park haunted houses. I also have an ethnic hatred of elves. (I hate elves. But I don't fear them.) But I'm most famous among my friends for my fear of skunks. It seems a perfectly reasonable fear to me, but I've been assured otherwise.

Shepard: Every time my best friend backs out of her driveway, she is sure she's going to run over her cat. She fears she won't realize she's done this. Hours later, she will return home to discover her cat's lifeless body, flattened into her tire tracks.

She would like to buy her nephew a house, but she is afraid that he'll burn it down and die in the fire. When she hires a catsitter, she's afraid that the sitter will be raped, tortured and killed by a psychopathic intruder.

I, on the other hand, am afraid of having my belly button touched. This is one of the differences between us.

When I told her about this assignment, I said, "I'm supposed to write about an irrational fear. But I don't have any irrational fears, right?" She was silent. "Do I?" I insisted. "I'm not forgetting something, right? I just don't have them." She told me to shut up.

But it's true that if my small children, crawling all over me, get close to touching my belly button, I shudder. I'm not worried about the casual, brush touch. But that's a precursor to the firm intrusion I am worried about, the way the bad guys in the movies let you know what's coming next by brushing the blade of their knives gently against their victims' throats.

Shteyngart: I have an irrational fear of giant flying insects, such as the American water bug.

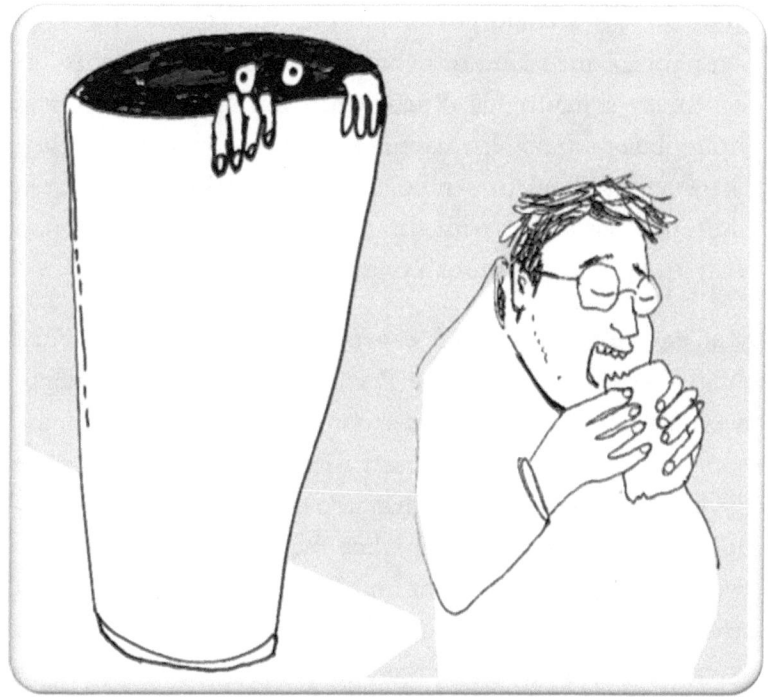

- What was the genesis of this fear?

Evenson: Probably I was told frequently in childhood that raw chicken carried disease, but I was told the same thing about pork, for instance, and am not afraid of pork, which is what makes me think the fear is highly irrational. And I don't have the same fear or reluctance with, say, boneless chicken breasts. It's something specific to the relation of the bone to the chicken. It has something to do with the way the bone itself looks and with the weird blueness you sometimes get around the joint and the way there's always a particularly disgusting vein running along the bone and the way the blood girdles the bone. It may also have to do with my mother cooking a lot of teriyaki chicken when I was growing up and with my suspicion that she never cooked it long enough.

Grossman: I could go on and on. The current thinking is that phobias are a kind of hybrid phenomenon — they're fundamentally a neurological problem, straight-up lousy cerebral wiring, but they do also have meanings associated with them. There's some kind of symbolic payload on board. I'm pretty sure mine has to do with my family. More than that I don't want to say, and you probably wouldn't want to hear.

McCracken: As far as I can remember, I was an ordinary child, able to watch *Pepe Le Pew* cartoons without breaking a sweat. (This is not true of cartoons that threatened cannibalism. You know the kind: desert island, mask-wearing natives, big iron pot — where did that iron pot come from, huh? — Bugs Bunny up to his waist while the chief mask-wearing native slices carrots into the broth.) But one summer I rented an apartment in Provincetown, a place I'd always experienced as skunk-free, and the town was crawling with them. Someone explained to me that a virus had wiped out the Cape Cod skunk population some years before this. Now the skunks were returning. I wish I could have found some romance in the notion, but instead I was scared stiff.

One late night, I looked out at the backyard and saw a dozen skunks and wondered whether I would be able to walk around Provincetown at night again. I hate skunks for the same reason I hate haunted houses: I cannot bear the feeling of wondering whether I am about to be startled. Skunks seemed horrifically unpredictable to me. My fear was made worse by all the skunk facts people passed along. Skunks, I was told, were hard of hearing, and nervous, and your best defense against them was clapping in a rhythmic, warning way. Also, they did not like the smell of dirty socks. Also, if you had been sprayed, the solution was not the fabled tomato juice, but boxed douche, like Massengill. I had a diptych vision of myself. Before: clapping, eyes darting, a gray garland of filthy tube socks around my neck. Afterwards: pulsating with stink marks at the Provincetown A & P, my little plastic shopping basket heaped up with boxes of douche.

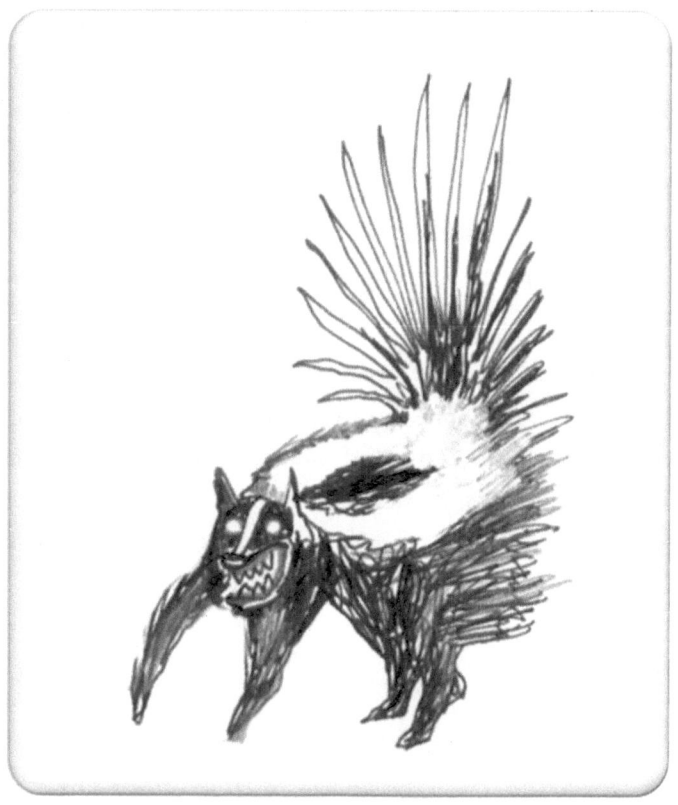

Pittard: When he's being generous, my soon-to-be husband says there's probably a biological imperative at work. But I blame my father, who is a quote-un-quote pilot in that he has his pilot's license. I remember taking off with him once and, feeling an overly strong breeze in my hair, I turned around to see that the door to the luggage compartment had been left open. I could see sky, earth, water far below us. My father instructed me to lean over and hold onto the luggage until we could land and shut the door. This, though, only *after* he'd asked me to climb back into the tiny space and see if I could reach out and pull the door in. We were 10,000 feet above land. You can imagine the trauma this caused. I was nine.

Shepard: Who knows where this fear comes from? I don't like to put my analytical mind to it, because to think about why it bothers me so much would involve thinking about the touch itself, and to do that would involve an imaginative journey that I'd prefer not to take. Instead, I wear many layers of extra long shirts. My hands hover, the Secret Service agents of my body. I grab the wrists of my husband or our children, my voice lowering to that tone of warning peculiar to mothers and wives. "Don't," I say. "I'm serious."

Shteyngart: The fear began when I was a small child. I was living in Russia and was given an illustrated children's book in which a young boy and a girl were being unprincipled communists and as punishment they were made really tiny by some party committee. Then they kept being attacked by Gigantic Flying Insects...

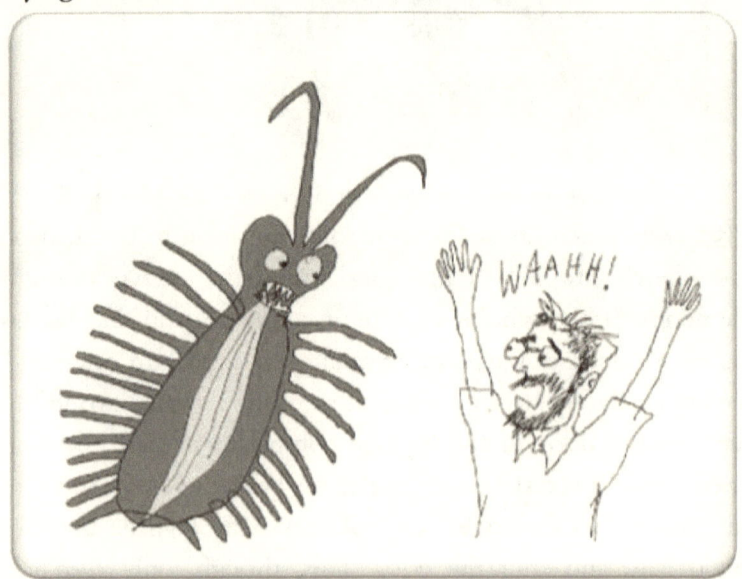

I remember at one point turning the page of the book and finding that an ACTUAL gigantic flying insect had been squished between two pages, the meat of its body covering an illustration of another such insect. I thought I was, like, going to die, you know?

"As far as I can remember, I was an ordinary child, able to watch *Pepe Le Pew* cartoons without breaking a sweat. (This is not true of cartoons that threatened cannibalism. You know the kind: desert island, mask-wearing natives, big iron pot — where did that iron pot come from, huh? — Bugs Bunny up to his waist while the chief mask-wearing native slices carrots into the broth."

- Elizabeth McCracken

- How do you manage this fear when it surfaces?

Evenson: If I can, I try to keep it from surfacing. I avoid raw chicken when I can, though sometimes, in an act of bravado, I'll actually find myself in a position where I have to roast a chicken. I arm myself with lots of paper towels and try to touch the chicken as little as possible. If I'm served under-cooked chicken at a dinner party I eat what I can and then try to figure out a way to get the bone off my plate, or position it so as to be exposed to it as little as possible. Sometimes a certain nausea starts to rise and I leave the room. At the same time, if the chicken is cooked well, even if it's on a bone, it doesn't bother me: I like to eat it.

Grossman: For the first thirty years of my phobic life I deployed a series of escalating procedures to deal with it. When confronted with somebody eating or drinking, my first line of attack would always be to flee the scene — I'd cross the street, change seats, hit the bathroom, change subway cars, awkwardly bail out of the conversation, do whatever I had to do. If I was stuck near the person eating — if I was, for example, sitting next to them on a plane, or riding in a taxi driven by them, or in the middle of negotiating a divorce settlement with them — I would engage in various "surreptitious" behaviors to try to distract myself and/or drown out the eating-noise. These would include things like listening to an iPod or sighing heavily or vigorously scratching my head and ears. Though sometimes I'd just completely lose it and cringe and cover my ears. If you ever have dinner with me you'll notice that I tend to eat my food in perfect sync with you — you take a bite, I take a bite. You sip your wine, I sip mine. That's to minimize the risk of my actually hearing or seeing you eat. Once you notice this it will probably start to annoy you, but I promise you it's necessary. We're both better off.

(I should clarify something: not every instance of somebody eating or drinking activates the phobia. There is a set of mysterious, secret (even from me) rules that govern it. I can often get away with eating in restaurants or going to dinner parties, for example; in fact going to restaurants and dinner parties is one of my greatest pleasures in life. I also love to cook. Go figure.)

Now I'm in treatment for my phobia, so I have a series of mental exercises I'm supposed to do to manage it. One of them involves envisioning the fear as a creature — it's kind of like the gremlin in the *Twilight Zone*, which only William Shatner could see. If I can control the creature — force it to obey, mentally order it to back off — the fear subsides. This actually works, sort of. Though I still wish I could just shoot the creature like Shatner shoots the gremlin.

McCracken: Well, I clap a lot. I also have a hard time walking past a spot where I have previously seen a skunk. I've not been reduced to laying in large supplies of douche just in case.

Pittard: That depends on who you ask. If you ask me, I would say, I manage just fine. I sit in my seat with my seatbelt buckled, close my eyes, and wait until we land. There are usually one or two little pink pills in my system helping me sit still. But, if you ask my soon-to-be husband, he'd tell you that I don't manage the fear when it surfaces. He says I grip the handles of the seat, over medicate, grit my eyes shut in a totally lunatic fashion, and scare the shit out of any little kids who might be on board. Sometimes I cry. Very quietly. Sometimes, if there's turbulence, I assume crash-landing position with my head between my knees. This, apparently, is what makes the little kids on board cry.

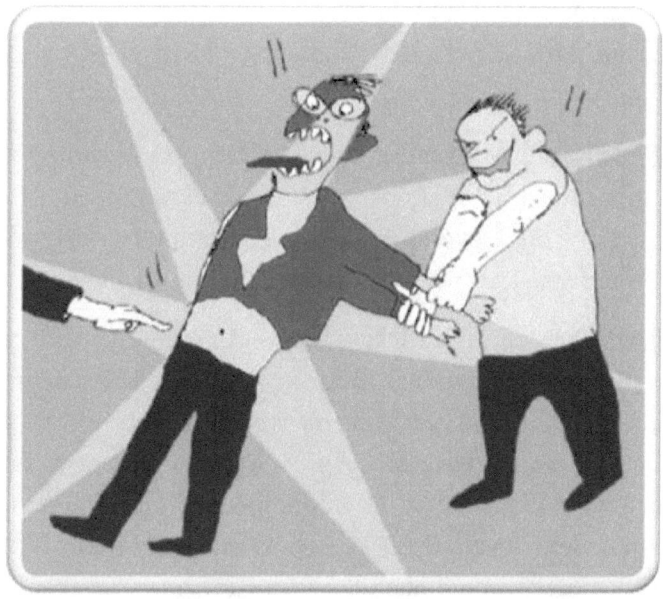

Shepard: When they gang up on me, I'm helpless. One pins my hands. Another lifts my shirt, our youngest waves one finger at me, and then presses it firmly into the folds of my inny. I writhe. I screw my eyes shut. I sweat. I'm such a freak about this that my family gives up, takes pity and leaves me to my insanity.

Shteyngart: I don't. If a water bug flies into me in an apartment I will never enter that apartment again. Some Romanians came by and sealed off my own apartment completely so that nothing can ever enter it.

- What would you give up or trade to vanquish your fear?

Evenson: This is a hard one. When it's manageable I don't think about it much. When it's not, that's the time to catch me. I've been known to give someone $5 to let me move my chicken bone onto her plate.

Grossman: What do you need? Chocolate? I would give up chocolate. Not sex, though. Something in between chocolate and sex.

McCracken: My so-called friends have, upon hearing of my fear, given me a lot of skunks — stuffed skunks, hand puppets, figurines. I would give up my entire collection. Luckily, no-one gives me elves. That would be intolerable. I really hate elves.

Pittard: See, this is a tricky question. On the one hand, yes, I know my fear is irrational. But, on the other hand, that irrationality being so ingrained in me, the fear feels sort of justified. Flying would have to be proven 100% flawlessly safe in order for me to give up the fear. So, to answer a different question: in order to have flying somehow magically become 100% flawlessly safe, I would happily give up a toe. Maybe even two.

Shepard: I would give up many things to vanquish my fear, but nothing of real value because as my best friend would be sure to point out: everyone everywhere has irrational fears worse than mine. I know this, so this is me, shutting up.

Shteyngart: I don't want to give up on this fear. It's a part of who I am.

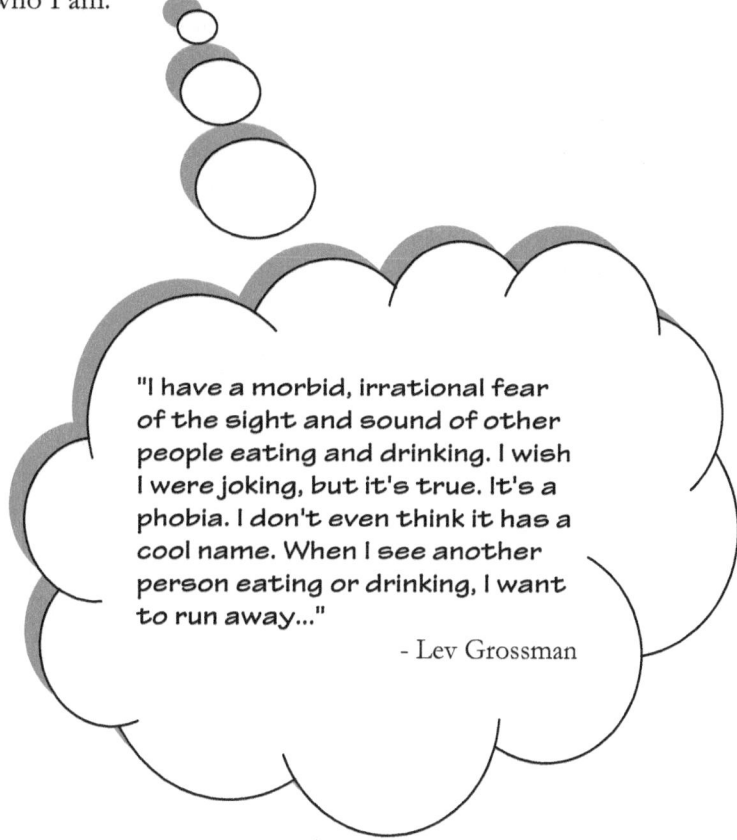

"I have a morbid, irrational fear of the sight and sound of other people eating and drinking. I wish I were joking, but it's true. It's a phobia. I don't even think it has a cool name. When I see another person eating or drinking, I want to run away..."

- Lev Grossman

- Name an irrational fear worse than yours.

Evenson: As irrational fears go, it could be a lot worse in that, unless one works for Tyson's, one doesn't have to frequently interact with raw chicken. There are a lot of fears that would be much worse. I think agoraphobia is a lot worse.

Grossman: If you have a phobia — and I'm always surprised at how many people do — then you'll have the same gut reaction I do: THERE IS NOTHING WORSE. But I know that's not true. I pull rank on people who are afraid of flying, since most of them don't fly every day, whereas I see people eat every day. But somewhere out there there's probably somebody who's afraid of breathing, or blinking, or the sound of their own heartbeat. That would be worse.

McCracken: Cats? Toddlers? Canned baked beans? Boxes of douche? Plenty, probably.

Pittard: Having dirty hands. My soon-to-be-husband can't function if his hands are dirty. I think that's kind of sad.

Shteyngart: Some people fear mammals like hamsters or beavers. Those are ridiculous fears because these are all nice animals who mean you no harm.

Episode 26: *First Favorite Album*
with Aimee Bender, David Leavitt,
Dennis Lehane, Sam Lipsyte, Peter Rock,
Dana Spiotta, and A.J. Verdelle

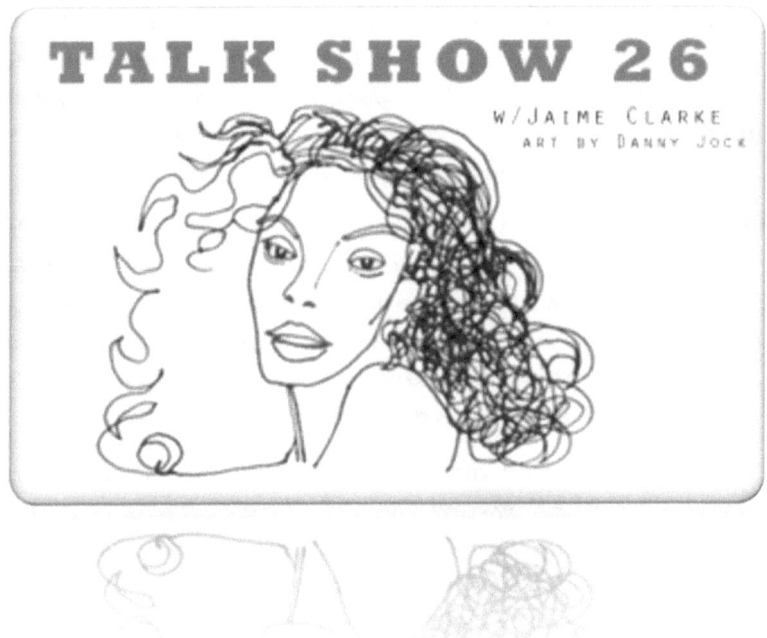

Aimee Bender is the author of five books: *The Girl in the Flammable Skirt*, a *New York Times* Notable Book, *An Invisible Sign of My Own*, a *Los Angeles Times* pick of the year, *Willful Creatures*, *The Particular Sadness of Lemon Cake*, an ALEX Award winner and *The Color Master*. Her work has been published in *Granta*, *GQ*, the *Paris Review*, *Tin House* and other publications. Bender is the winner of two Pushcart Prizes.

David Leavitt is the author several books including the novels *The Indian Clerk*, *The Two Hotel Francforts*, *The Lost Language of Cranes*. Other works include: *Arkansas: Three Novellas*, *Collected Stories* and the nonfiction work *The Man Who Knew Too Much: Alan Turing and the Invention of the Computer*. He teaches at the University of Florida and edits the journal *Subtropics*.

Dennis Lehane is the author of the novels *Live By Night*, *Moonligt Mile*, *The Given Day*, *Shutter Island*, *Mystic River*, *Prayers for Rain*, *Gone Baby Gone*, *Sacred*, *Darkness*, *Take My Hand*, and *A Drink Before the War*, and the short story collection *Coronado*. Lehane's work has been translated into over thirty languages and three of his novels have been adapted into award-winning films.

Sam Lipsyte is the author of novels *Home Land* and *The Ask* - both *New York Times* Notable Books - and *The Subject Steve*, as well as the story collections *Venus Drive* and *The Fun Parts*. His work has appeared in the *New Yorker*, the *Paris Review*, *Harper's*, *McSweeney's*, and others. He teaches at Columbia University.

Peter Rock is the author of the novels *My Abandonment* - an ALEX Award winner, *The Shelter Cycle*, *The Bewildered*, *The Ambidextrist*, *This is the Place*, and *Carnival Wolves*, and a short story collection, *The Unsettling*. His stories and freelance writing have appeared widely. Rock is a recipient of an NEA Fellowship and teaches at Reed College.

Dana Spiotta is the author of the novels *Stone Arabia*, and *Lightning Field* - both *New York Times* Notable Books, and *Eat the Document*, a recipient of the Rosenthal Award. Spiotta earned Guggenheim and New York Foundation for the Arts fellowships. She teaches in the Syracuse University MFA Program.

A.J. Verdelle's first novel, *The Good Negress*, won five national prizes. Verdelle has received fellowships from the National Endowment for the Arts, the Whiting Writers Foundation, the Lannan Foundation and Harvard University. She also received a Distinguished Prose Fiction award from the American Academy of Arts and Letters. She teaches in the MFA Program at Lesley University.

* * *

- Name your first favorite album?

Bender: The first album I remember buying for myself, with my allowance, was *Donna Summer, Greatest Hits*, 1979.

Leavitt: The Carpenters' album that was titled *Carpenters*. The sleeve was designed to resemble an envelope.

Lehane: *The Pretenders*.

Lipsyte: It's a dead (and maybe humiliating) heat: Billy Joel's *The Stranger* and Meatloaf's *Bat Out of Hell*.

Rock: *Sound Explosion*, released by K-Tel.

Spiotta: *Sgt. Pepper's Lonely Heart's Club Band*.

Verdelle: *Nina Simone*, a red album cover. A picture of her — the first head shot I ever remember seeing — took up the whole cover, and she had her hair swept up, a real do. A hairstyle that combined the American beehive and the upsweep of an African queen. Her face was almost as large as a disk — the 33 rpm size. I don't know that then, in the mid-to late-sixties, I had ever seen anyone parade their brown face without caricature, without overdone maquillage. She was bejeweled and clear-eyed, as I remember. The name of the album, I hardly noticed, hardly remembered. When I strain to recall the type on the cover, I think the album must have been self-titled. I know before I close the answers to these questions, I'll do what we do now, and go Google to supplement my memory with the name I can't recall. But for now, I will say that the title didn't matter so much. The album title did not inform about the songs the album contained, and whatever words there were on the cover were made completely insignificant by Nina Simone's proud head, her striking brown skin, her clear gaze that seemed to say, *Go ahead. I dare you. Wonder.*

– When did you first hear it?

Bender: It must've been on the radio (no pun intended, honestly). Her voice was great and when I saw the album cover I thought she was very beautiful, with that amazing long sweeping cloud-like hair. And I liked that the album cover was purple. I think I was nine years old.

Leavitt: On the Harmon-Kardon stereo that my father built from a kit.

Lehane: I heard "Brass in Pocket" on the radio and I asked for the album for Christmas, and my sister got it for me. I had zero exposure to punk at this point — I was fourteen — and "Brass in Pocket" wasn't really punk, it was more straight rock, but then I got the album and heard "Precious" and "Tattooed Love Boys" and "The Wait," and it was like somebody had lit my scalp on fire.

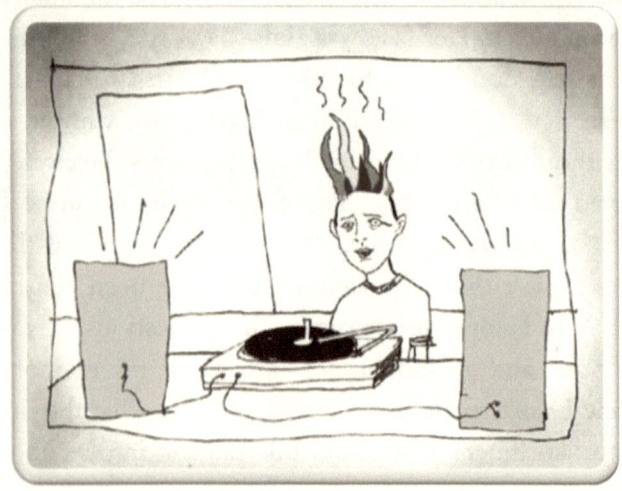

Lipsyte: It must have been the summer of 1978. I was ten. My folks had shipped me off to a summer camp in the Adirondacks. There was an emphasis on sports and sadism, best exemplified by our cruel stud of a counselor, Jeff. Jeff wore a gold chain and bragged about his expertise at drunk driving. He handed out porn mags and told us we were faggots if we didn't like them. He mocked me all the time for being a fat boy and a coward. He was so beautiful and arrogant and I loved him. I deserved to be mocked. Special days he would blast his 8-tracks. These two were in heavy rotation. So was Supertramp, but I couldn't really deal with Supertramp.

Rock: I grew up in Salt Lake City, Utah. My parents both taught school, and are both from Wisconsin, so we spent every summer in the Midwest. This meant we spent several days each spring and fall driving various station wagons across the country. Our 1976 Ford Fairmont, flesh-colored, was one of the first American vehicles with a cassette deck. Each spring, as we packed to head to Wisconsin, each family member was allowed to purchase one cassette; then, as we drove, we took turns choosing the music. One of the unfortunate influences in these choices was my older sister; first, she "helped" my younger sister and brother select their cassette to purchase, then reminded them that they wanted to choose "their" tape to be played.

Thus, a typical five (my parents counted as one person) album rotation would go:

Barry Manilow, *Even Now* (little sister's selection)

Barry Manilow, *This One's For You* (little brother's selection)*

Styx, *Grand Illusion* or Foreigner, *Double Vision* or Kiss, *Destroyer* **

Barry Manilow, *Live!* (older sister; double album counted as one selection)

Barbara Streisand or Burt Bacharach (parents)***
[repeat for 8-12 hours]

(* my brother eventually did choose for himself; in year three it was *Hotel California,* which sometimes my parents would even choose, or Billy Joel's *The Stranger* — the latter reveals Joel's many sides, and some fine whistling; the former may be the worst album ever made.)

(** This is not meant to suggest that I got more than one choice, only a few of my yearly selections — and the tapes did accumulate; at one point we probably had forty Manilow albums.)

(*** usually by day two, our parents' selection had been surreptitiously thrown out the window.)

On one of these drives we were staying with friends of my parents, in some mountain town, and we came across a jukebox in a rustic restaurant. I chose the song for its name: "Wildfire," by Michael Martin Murphy; I played it again and again, pressing my face against the scratched plastic bubble of the jukebox. If you don't know the song, and have a taste for tragedy, I commend it to you. I think Sound Explosion had stuck in my mind because "Wildfire" was one of the featured tracks, and I wanted to get back to the way that song made me feel.

Spiotta: Before I had any albums of my own, I listened to my sister's albums. She had the Beatles' "Red" album and the Beatles' "Blue" album. These were very popular *best of* albums released in the '70s. They are technically called the *Beatles 1962-66* and the *Beatles 1966-1970.* So my sister didn't actually own the original Beatles albums but these bogus compilations. I loved these records, but I was torn. I liked the way the Beatles looked on the cover of the Red album (clean cut, cheerful, young) but I preferred the music on the Blue album (intense, surreal, mature). I wasn't entirely satisfied with either Beatle product. For my maybe tenth birthday, my mother took me shopping for my very first album. I think I went straight up to the clerk and said, "Do you have any Beatles?" I was really quite clueless and I had no idea which Beatles album I should buy. I picked up *Sgt. Pepper* because I liked the look of the Beatles on the cover: half way between the Red album's chipper, almost chubby (at least John and Paul) Beatles and the Blue album's hairy, sexually threatening Beatles. On *Sgt. Pepper* all the Beatles looked great with their satin clothes and fab moustaches. Plus all the other cool stuff on the cover. And I did look at the track listing — my favorite song from the Blue album, "A Day in the Life," was on it. I had no doubt this was the album I should buy. I think it was $7.99. When I got home I was so excited I called my super-cool older cousin Chris to tell her I just bought my first album, *Sgt. Pepper's Lonely Hearts Club Band*.

My cousin instantly replied that I had bought the wrong Beatles album, I should have bought *Abbey Road*. But when I put it on the turntable, I succumbed immediately to all its quirks and pleasures. I remember leaning back on my bed and listening to it at very high volume on my headphones. I just loved how each song flowed into the next, how the album created a little world, and it was deeply engaging and mysterious. I admired how beautiful it was even as I could never really figure out exactly what the songs meant. I invented meanings for the songs that shifted as I grew older. It really is such a weird album.

Verdelle: I couldn't possibly say when I first heard this album. I believe I was listening to Nina's reedy voice, before I could register who she was, and before I could read. This is why I name this as "my" first favorite album, because although the album was my mother's, it was I who wore down the grooves.

- Where did you first buy it?

Bender: Tower Records on Westwood Boulevard was the place for record buying in those days for kids on the west side of L.A. I distinctly remember that my sisters, who were much savvier with their loves of ska and punk, scoffed at me a little for buying disco. But I didn't know it was disco or that disco was on its way out — it was just what she sounded like and how I loved the catchy songs like "Heaven Knows." It was an innocent pre-adolescent music purchase because I mainly liked to hear her sing; I was surprised to catch a sense that anyone might think otherwise.

Leavitt: At a record store in Palo Alto, California that was called "The Record Store." It was in the shape of a cube, made of sanded planks (redwood perhaps) cut on the diagonal. We called it "The Box."

Lipsyte: When I returned from camp, I begged my mother to buy them for me. We went to the local record store in our New Jersey town. I was just old enough to be embarrassed about buying a record with my mother. I remember her concern about the sign in the store window that said, simply, "Meat Loaf." She worried that immigrants would be confused and think that here was a place they could find food. I think she even got a little incensed about it all, maybe threatened to write a letter to the mayor, which was touching, and also a bit bizarre. For years I had this image of the "immigrant" staggering around town, looking for a place to buy something to fill his rumbling belly, pushing into the record store, moaning, "Meat Loaf," only to collapse from hunger as the clerk hands the album over.

Rock: 7-11.

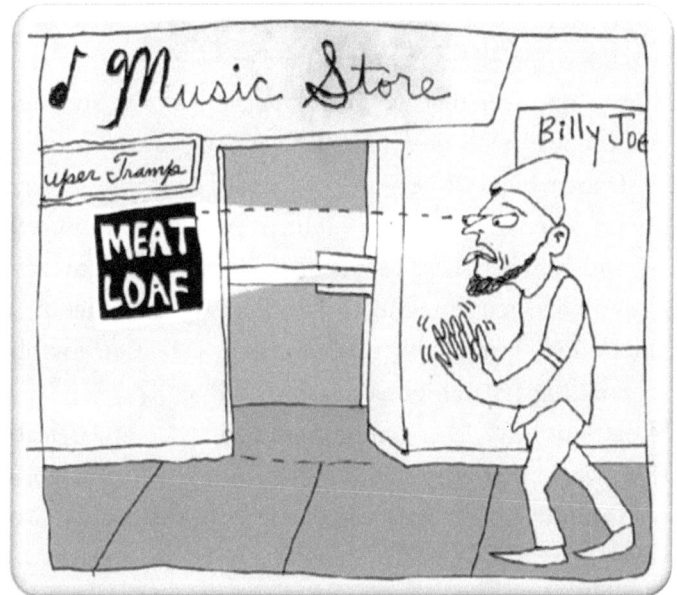

Spiotta: A Sam Goody near Glastonbury, Connecticut.

Verdelle: I first "handled" this album in the family room in the house where I grew up. And I mean, I handled it. I stared at Nina, wondered about her last name "Simone," learned later that she was born Eunice Waymon, discovered that she grew up in Baltimore, like Billie Holiday. Lingered, and lusted, over the amazing names of songs she sang, listed in light print on the reverse. "Consummation" was the most amazing of the songs, to me.

I've never bought the record myself, as an adult. In the fits and starts of researching music, I've not encountered the record in its original form. But one night, in Provincetown, Massachusetts, a friend I made in my adult life came to visit. I was in my "summer rental," high up on the third floor of painter Pat deGroot's house on the inimitable Provincetown Bay. My friend, an African American woman like me, yet unlike me, an academic dean, joined with me in an almost pre-verbal love of Nina Simone. My friend, Ngina, and I spent the whole evening singing the songs from this album, in order. We did not discuss how we knew the album, although we knew each other instantly better to discover that we both knew the album so well. We are fast friends, even now, and this evening created a plateau for us, from which we've gone on, and developed, as friends. Our lovers were appalled, that night, at how high we raised our voices, and how off-key we sounded. We likely were off-key. Nina Simone often sings in minor keys, or in other modes- Dorian, Lydian, Locrian — used primarily jazz. Our joyful imitations could not match Nina's major skill.

Nina Simone, I later learned, studied to be a classical pianist. She was either admitted, or not admitted, to Eastman, or maybe Peabody. Both well established conservatories. Maybe she went, maybe she graduated, maybe not. When she began to audition, displaying prodigious piano skills, she was told she needed to sing. She was devastated by this, but needed to make a life for herself, in music, with music. Her voice is as distinctive as handcarved sculpture. Our universe and planets and stardust are enriched and forever changed by her warbling and chanting and humming and reaching and skimming the surface of the hot center of the earth. We recognize religion and righteousness in her occasional, original, shouts. I never bought the album, but the album bought me entré into music, politics, art.

- How obsessed were you?

Bender: I listened to it a lot. I didn't understand any of the songs but I did love the idea that someone could leave her cake out in the rain.

Leavitt: I think I was seven years old. There was a song called "Hideaway" that included the line: "Where will I find another you?" My older brother drew a cartoon of a ram singing, "Where will I find another ewe?" and told me that he would send it to the Carpenters and that I would never again be allowed to buy one of their albums.

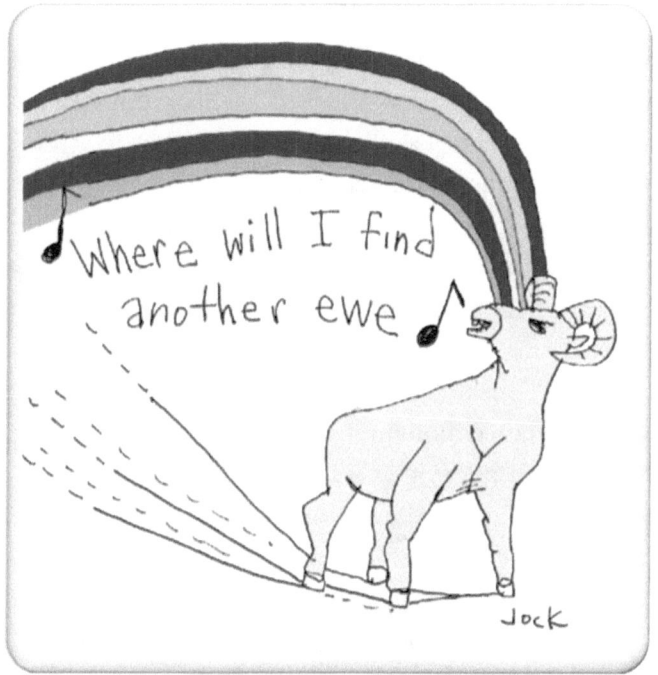

Lehane: I listened to it nonstop in my basement for a solid three months. "Precious" was the first time I'd heard "fuck off" in a song, which really left an impression, and just the whole stripped-down, tear the roof off ethos of the band was electrifying. Plus, it was a chick — a snarling, pissed off chick — who was leading this sonic revolution. Then James Honeyman-Scott, the lead guitarist, died and they never quite recaptured the sound, and I moved onto Patti Smith and The Clash but I never lost the feeling of what that album did to me.

Lipsyte: I knew every word of every song on both records. I lip-synched the songs into a hockey stick in front of a mirror every day. A few years later, at seventh grade parties, my friend Henry Kwak and I would wow the other kids with our lip-synched rendition of "Paradise by the Dashboard Light." The songs on *Bat Out of Hell* are basically show tunes, and we put on quite a show. Henry always made me do the girl part, even though I looked more like Meat Loaf. It was intense how committed he was to me doing the girl part. (Later, he became fixated on "Miami Vice" and turned his bedroom into an exact replica of Lieutenant Castillo's office. He even had the Venetian blinds and the absolutely bare desk. But that was later.) Now, we were both kneeling in the shag in somebody's rec room, both of us waving our arms and moving our mouths in perfect alignment with the voices of Marvin Lee Aday (Meat Loaf's real name) and Ellen Foley, me begging Henry to "take me away" and "make me his wife." It didn't make us popular in the ways I think we thought it would.

As for *The Stranger*, that was more of a private thing. But it seeped in very deep. Many years later, after countless hours listening to and studying the "real" stuff — The Ramones, The Velvets, The Stooges, Wire, The Birthday Party and so forth — I was recording some vocals for a project I was doing with the guitarist of one of my favorite bands, Six Finger Satellite, a brilliant and merciless noise juggernaut. After I did a few takes, trying to sound as death-savvy and unsentimental as possible, the guitarist came out of the control booth shaking his head. "What the fuck?" he said. "Did you listen to a lot of Billy Joel when you were young?" I wanted to cry, but thought that might give me away.

Rock: Lord, the damage we did to bedsprings while this LP spun in my downstairs bedroom! Jumping, I mean, from twin bed to twin bed. There was the excitement of "Sky High" and "Get Down Tonight" and the uplifting spirals of "Fly Robin Fly," the slightly forbidden "You Sexy Thing," then the sweetness of "Midnight Blue" as we began to wind down. And, yes, the windswept tragedy of "Wildfire."

Spiotta: I needed to be exclusively and obsessively devoted to something outside of my meager pre-adolescent existence. *Sgt. Pepper* was the perfect fit. This album demanded close and repeated listenings. I loved — and had never heard anything like — the moans, laughs, heavy breathing, and odd sounds that were left in or added to the ends of the songs. I loved the marginalia on that album. The little Beatle aural orgasm at the end of the cute narrative song "Lovely Rita" just killed me

To this day I get this little indelible thrill when I hear the album and feel that ingrained anticipation and expectation as each song segues to the next. The pleasure of knowing an album well (and the reprise of the song "Sgt. Pepper's Lonely Hearts Club Band" emphasizes this) and living in it, was new to me. It would be an experience — solitary, dreamy, and comforting — that I would repeat with many favorite albums throughout my teen years. But this was the first one. I dug it. No expertise required, just headphones and many, many hours of devotion.

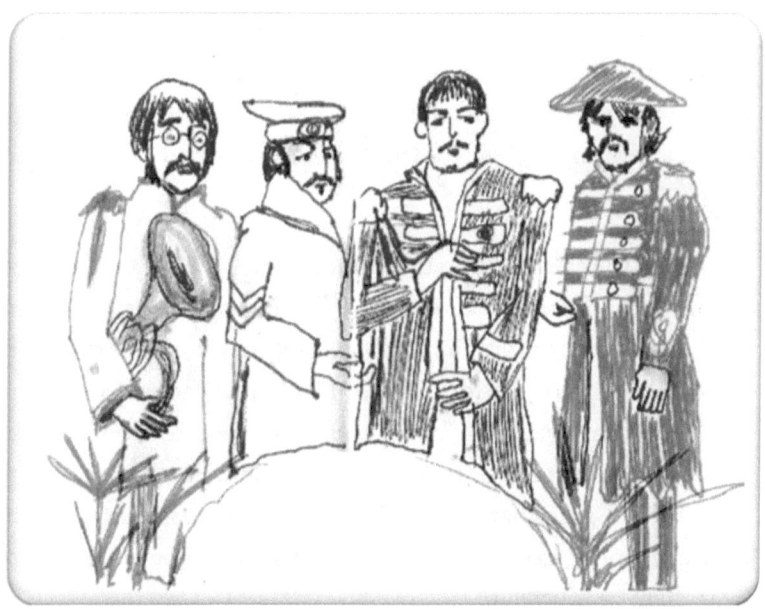

Verdelle: Extremely. She sang one song that amazed me then, and that, to this day, I can recite, and sing, asleep or awake.

This is exactly how things were when I was very young (first grade age). I, with my chocolate body and big mind, was a fascination for the few uncolored girls I knew. They liked me, and wanted to invite me to houses that were bigger than houses I knew girls grew up in. The invitations never panned out, although we talked animatedly about the good times we could have. Nina explained this to me in words my friends and I did not yet have. My situation was slightly different in that I was more likely the protector, but nothing in art is ever exact. As I recall, this song (sung *a capella*) did not seem to be listed on the album contents. I think my mother suggested that maybe the song was an interlude. I have asked many people — by way of singing — over the years whether they know this song. So few people know this song.

- Are you still a fan?

Bender: I haven't heard any Donna Summer in years but I do think some of her songs have been good covers — notably "I Feel Love" as the big Bronski Beat dance hit in the mid eighties which swept my high school and college dances.

Leavitt: Who isn't?

Lehane: Of the album, yeah. Huge. Honeyman-Scott's guitar playing is so ferocious and original, it's like a tragic gift because you only hear it on the first two albums and pieces of the third. I was listening to "Tattooed Love Boys" just the other day and some of the lyrics — "Stop sniveling—you're gonna make some plastic surgeon a rich man" or "I shot my mouth off 'til you showed me what that hole was for" — snap me to attention even now, so I can only assume how bug-eyed I was to hear them at fourteen.

Lipsyte: I'm not sure I can answer this without therapy.

Rock: Now these songs serve as a kind of historical shorthand for my sister and me. Various tragedies and complications can be understood or defused with a lyric from Sound Explosion.

Spiotta: Let's put it this way: if Paul McCartney walked into my office right now, as he is now, sixty-five or whatever, there is a good chance I would start to weep.

Verdelle: Absolutely. I met Nina Simone in person, twice. Destiny. Once at the South Shore Country Club, in Chicago. This black country club had been closed for years, and underwent a major renovation and a grand reopening. Seemed to me that Nina Simone was the first concert there, but I could be elevating what I first noticed to everyone else's first choice. She came and played riffs that us long time devotées could easily recognize. I applauded some of these riffs, almost alone, in that full house, that rapt auditorium. She responded, challenging us, playing strong as a stride pianist, "I need that applause, I need that applause."

When I went backstage that night, insistent on seeing this huge talent, this practical expatriate, up close and in-person, she asked her manager what I wanted, and when I explained to her, to him, that I just wanted to meet her, she asked him to give me tickets to her upcoming concert, in London. I was in college, at the University of Chicago. I did not have the money to go. Although I did dream about the good time I could have. I asked whether she spoke French. She told me she spoke street French. I have since learned to speak that language. She asked whether I was married. I told her I was not. She told me she'd like to be married.

The second time I met her was in New York City. She was on her way out of this life. I waited for her backstage at Carne-

gie Hall, where, by then, I could get my name on the backstage
list. Nina came in in a wheelchair, assisted, and not by the
manager with the London tickets. More than twenty years had
passed since the South Shore Country Club. Her feet were as
swollen as fresh artichokes, each one. Her tongue was slow to
move. She gave a decent concert, though the strong Nina
Simone had retired, apparently.

She said nothing to me personally, from the stage or more
directly. I followed her party to Ashford and Simpson's after-
spot; I think maybe it was called the Shark Bar. 'Can't remember. Upper West Side. She sat at a table for twelve, with people
she didn't seem to recognize. What or who she recognized —
anything or anyone — was patently unclear. I said nothing to
her personally; she seemed glazed. But I needed to see her, one
more time. Nina Simone brought me out as an artist. Her reedy
voice, her triumphs and catastrophes, her admissions and petu-
lant responses, her grand talent, her huge piano, her musical
sensibilities, her mystery, her daring. Even now, I could go on.

The name of the red album is *Silk and Soul.*

Episode 27: *Past into Present*
with Daphne Beal, Charles Bock,
Emily Chenoweth, John McNally, Irina Reyn,
and Peter Trachtenberg

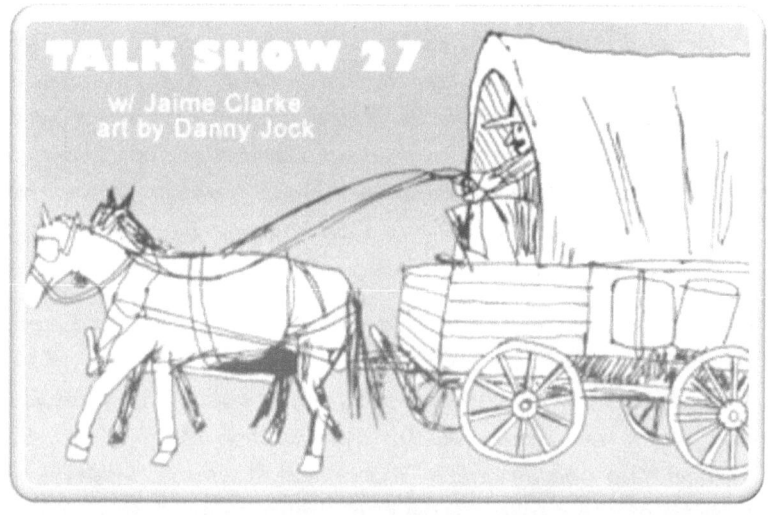

Daphne Beal is the author of the novel *In the Land of No Right Angles*. Her work has appeared in *Open City*, *the Mississippi Review*, *Vogue*, *McSweeney's*, the *New York Times Magazine* and other publications. She teaches in the Creative Writing Program at New York University.

Charles Bock is the author of the novel *Beautiful Children*, a *New York Times* Notable Book and winner of the Sue Kaufman Prize for First Fiction from the American Academy of Arts and Letters. His work has appeared in *Harper's*, *Esquire*, the *New York Times*, *Los Angeles Times*, *Slate*, *AGNI*, the *Iowa Review* and others. Bock teaches at New York University.

Emily Chenoweth is the author of the novel *Hello Good-bye*. A former fiction editor at *Publishers Weekly*, her work has appeared in *Tin House, Bookforum*, the anthology *The Friend Who Got Away*, and other publications.

John McNally's works of fiction include: *After the Workshop, Ghosts of Chicago, Troublemakers, The Book of Ralph* and *America's Report Card*. He has edited six anthologies, including *Who Can Save Us Now?: Brand-new Superheroes* and *Their Amazing (Short) Stories* (with Owen King), and written two nonfiction books: *The Creative Writer's Survival Guide: Advice from an Unrepentant Novelist* and *Vivid and Continuous: Essays on the Craft of Fiction.* McNally teaches at Wake Forest

Irina Reyn is the author of the *What Happened to Anna K.* and editor of the anthology, *Living on the Edge of the World: New Jersey Writers Take On the Garden State.* Her work has appeared in: *One Story, Post Road, Tin House*, the *Los Angeles Times*, and *Poets & Writers*, as well as other publications and anthologies. She teaches at the University of Pittsburgh.

Peter Trachtenberg is the author of *Another Insane Devotion: On the Love of Cats and Persons, 7 Tattoos: A Memoir in the Flesh* and *The Book of Calamities: Five Questions About Suffering and Its Meaning.* His work has appeared in the *New Yorker, Harper's*, the *New York Times Travel Magazine*, and others. Trachtenberg's commentaries have been broadcast on NPR'S "All Things Considered." Winner of a Whiting Writer's Award, he teaches at the University of Pittsburgh.

* * *

- Name something from the past that you'd like to bring into the present.

Beal: Chuckwagons.

Bock: The automat. I don't know if you remember these: but they started in the '50s and ran through the '70s. Basically it's a cafeteria where all the food is inside machines. You put a dollar in the machine and a slotted door opens and behind the slot is a sandwich, or an apple, or what have you.

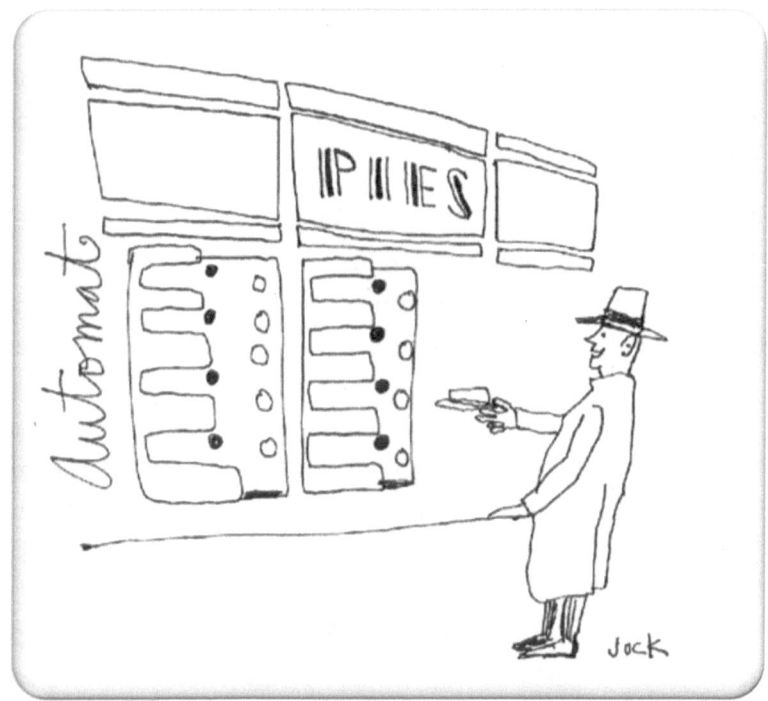

Chenoweth: I'm an indecisive person, and I couldn't pick just one thing to bring back. So here are a few: 1): the art of letter writing, 2): extended family households, and 3): the wooly mammoth.

McNally: It's high time for the typewriter to come back into vogue, much as the turntable and albums have slowly been creeping back. I learned to type on a cast-iron Royal typewriter from the mid-1940s, a machine that's heavy enough to kill someone with even a gentle whack to the head. I bought mine at a flea market in the 1970s when I was in grade school. My next typewriter was an electric Smith-Corona, the kind where you pop the big ribbon cartridge in and out from the side of it. A few years ago, a friend mailed to me an IBM Selectric, which sounds like a machine-gun when you type fast on it.

Reyn: This is more of a concept from the past (1970s and 1980s) and it's only real in the cinematic sense: I would like to yank a dinner party out of one of Woody Allen's movies and attend it in the present day.

Trachtenberg: The IWW. The International Workers of the World was a syndicalist movement founded in 1905 that aspired to serve as a single union for workers in every industry-mines, textiles, iron, timber, trucking. Its members were called Wobblies. Its program wasn't just higher wages or better working conditions but a fundamental revision of the American social contract, including the abolition of wage labor. It encompassed socialists and communists and anarchists, which was part of what made it so threatening to government and business.

Over the next twenty years the union was brutally suppressed. Joe Hagelund, or Joe Hill, was executed on a trumped-up murder charge in 1915; his death is commemorated in the song, "I Dreamed I Saw Joe Hill Last Night." In Everett, Washington at least five Wobblies were killed by a death squad convened by the town sheriff.

At its peak the IWW had 100,000 members and could call on a good 300,000 sympathizers. By the end of the 1920s, it was down to about 10,000. At present it's undergoing a small revival. It's been organizing truckers in the South, for example, and there's a chapter for employees of universities.

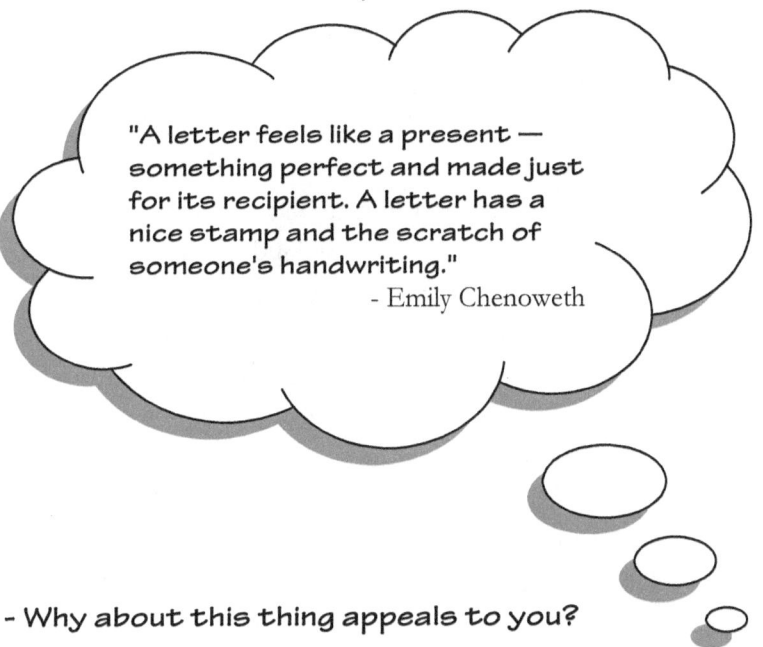

"A letter feels like a present —
something perfect and made just
for its recipient. A letter has a
nice stamp and the scratch of
someone's handwriting."
                    - Emily Chenoweth

- Why about this thing appeals to you?

Beal: While I've always had a kind of unfulfilled romance with cowboy living, my particular interest in chuck wagons has to do with the fact that I'm returning from a week in Far West Texas by myself, where I cooked most of my meals in a cast iron skillet that I bought at a cowboy supply store (the spurs were prettier but less useful). The food tasted good, and I imagine would have tasted better eaten out of doors, under the stars with family and friends. Now, traveling eastward on a plane from El Paso, I'm contemplating my return to family life in our apartment in New York City, with two children under the age of four, where mealtime will resume its usual madness. The idea that a man would pull up in a horse and wagon, portable kitchen in tow, light a fire, make fresh food, and then my family and I would all gather round for a meal with our neighbors or fellow travelers would answer oh so of our many dining issues. Also, someone else is making the coffee in the morning and doing the dishes, too.

Bock: There's something wonderfully bizarre, something almost chastely naïve in the idea behind the automat — the future is now; just press this button and, bingo, here is your tasty roast beef sandwich on white with mayo. (I remember being a kid and my mom taking me to one and the whole event was magical, even if the food actually was kind of bland). Now, the truth is, in the present day, we know too much: to be preserved like that the bread would have to be chemical-ized to death; the meat, to be warm, would have to be kept beneath a heat lamp, or else your sandwich would be cold and wrapped in cellophane and antiseptic. But the idea of an automat itself is romantic and it's vision of the world and of food has a certain wide-eyed charm to it. And, if you went to eat in an automat, you wouldn't have to give your order to someone, which is always a plus.

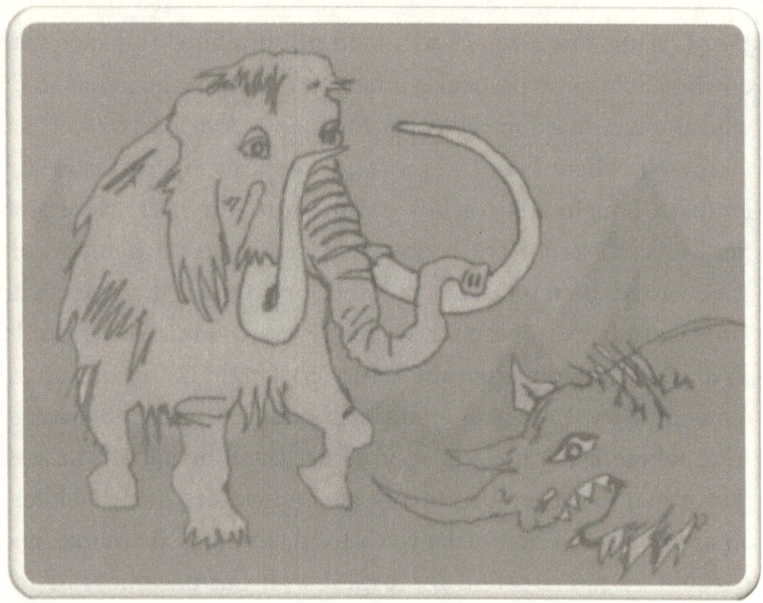

Chenoweth: 1): A letter feels like a present — something perfect and made just for its recipient. A letter has a nice stamp and the scratch of someone's handwriting.

2): I think it's too bad that people are isolated within nuclear family units. I'd like to live with/be very near my extended family because a) I love them and b) they could help me with childcare. Because playing with a ten-month-old is wonderful, but it can get pretty boring.

3): I think it'd be amazing to see a furry, eleven-foot-tall, six-ton elephant.

McNally: I miss the sounds of a roomful of people typing. You know when you hear that sound that something tangible is being accomplished, as opposed to the soft-touch keypad where someone is likely Googling themselves or updating their MySpace or FaceBook page. What I miss about the typewriter is that its purpose was singular. The only thing to do with it is type. No surfing, no Googling, no checking Amazon rankings, no looking up old enemies to see if they've self-destructed. I have great memories of sitting in front of my typewriter, working on short stories. I have no memories attached to my computers, which are as disposable as a twin blade razor.

Reyn: Partially, I would like to exorcise my slavish devotion to the lives depicted in those films. Even if the exchanges at these cinematic dinners (at Elaine's or more likely in someone's book-lined, impossibly cozy Upper West Side apartment) were often self-indulgent parodies, I would feel that I have achieved something by participating in its real, present-day incarnation.

Somehow, and perhaps this is linked to my Russian soul or growing up in Queens, I became convinced that if a wild-haired, bespectacled man in a V-neck sweater handed me a marked-up volume of *The Collected Poetry of e.e. cummings* across a food-laden table in Manhattan, it would mark me at the epicenter of intellectual life.

Trachtenberg: To begin with, the IWW is a global organization, in both senses of the word. One of the reasons the old

labor movement was so ineffectual was that it defined its interests narrowly. It was organized by industry — automotive,
film, etcetera — and its power was highly centralized, and the
result was that there was little solidarity among its individual
unions. Auto workers wouldn't mobilize on behalf of miners;
teamsters wouldn't strike in solidarity with civil servants. And
of course the more powerful the leadership grew, the more it
became like management.

In theory, at least, the IWW is an organization that recog-
nizes the common interests of everybody who works, including
the self-employed, whom the old unions excluded. What all of
us have in common is that we work for our living, as opposed
to invest or manipulate money — in the case of the banks and
brokerage houses, money that doesn't even belong to them.
Our commodity isn't money, it's ourselves, our strength, our
skill, our knowledge. And in a global economy in which corpo-
rations can hire those things more cheaply overseas with the
push of a few buttons, all of us are in the same boat. As a writer and teacher, I'm as vulnerable as anybody who works on the
line at GM.

"I miss the sounds of a roomful of
people typing. You know, when you
hear that sound that something
tangible is being accomplished, as
opposed to the soft-touch keypad
where someone is likely Googling
themselves or updating their
MySpace or FaceBook page."

- John McNally
re: bringing back the typewriter

- How do you think the present would be improved?

Beal: Instead of a lot of isolated chaos among families in separate apartments at meal time and a lot of frantic preparing of variations on salty, starchy foods and then cajoling the kids to eat, there would be mass and melded chaos among many families together. The kids who were old enough to play on their own would do so, the younger ones would have many adults to pass them around and keep an eye on them. Also, ideally the chuckwagon driver (called "Cookie") would play the guitar and sing and have a good number of tall tales to tell so there would be built in entertainment around the campfire. This sounds like a happy alternative to the whining (kids) and threatening (parents) no dessert that is our usual M.O. And then, of course, all mess would be on the ground and not all over the kitchen floor. The skillet would add a little iron to our diet, and the horses would have velvety noses, gentle demeanors, and sweet breaths.

Bock: Life would be a whole lot more fun if there were really high-end automats with walls of machines and all kinds of cool buttons and sliding doors, behind which awaited all sorts of yummy gourmet fast foods made with free range organic type ingredients. Major metropolitan areas already have such a high speed and level of automation — there's a level of popish Hong Kong-style architecture to stores now where they're basically kiosks anyway, and you get your cream puff or whatever and move along, high turnover, *bing bang boom*. At some moments, I think the automat fits perfectly with this.

Chenoweth: 1): We'd have keepsakes. We'd probably care more about punctuation and capitalization. And every day, around the time the mailman was due to arrive, we'd start to get happy.

2): We'd know more about our own histories. We could have ping-pong tournaments. If I made the soup, Grandma could make the salad and Uncle Jim could set the table.

3): We would feel awe — at the technology that brought him to life, and at the forces (climactic and otherwise) that killed him off. Maybe we'd think more about our own evolution and our own eventual extinction.

<u>McNally</u>: No longer would the computer be blamed for formatting problems or spelling and grammar errors, which, astonishingly, my students try to pawn off on the poor machine. Nope, it'll all be human error, which is the actual cause of 99% of my students' problems. No longer will I have to hear "My hard-drive crashed" or "I got the dreaded blue-screen last night, so I took my computer to IT." The typewriter is a difficult machine to lay blame on.

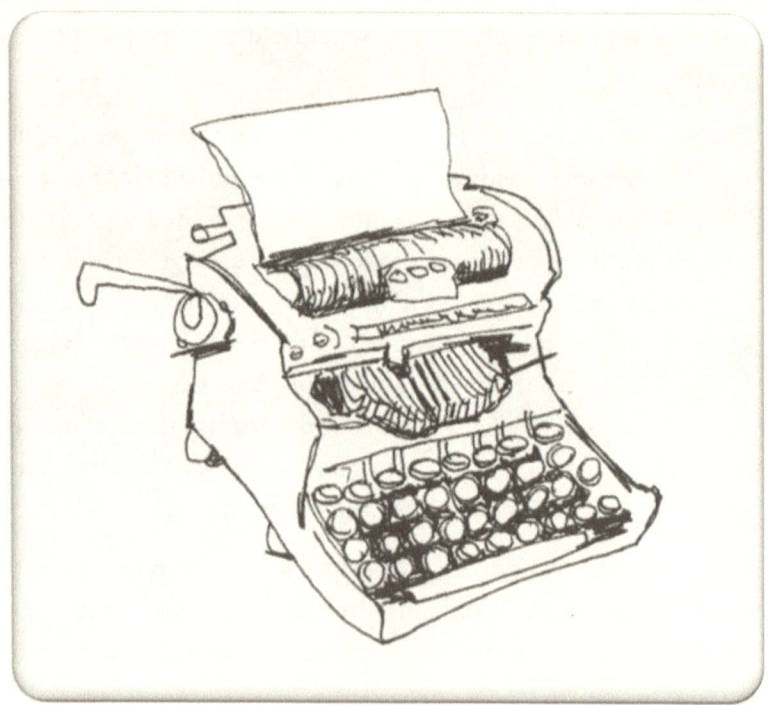

A typewriter instills discipline. I used to write longhand and then type my short stories, but I would make damned sure that each draft of a story was as good as I could make it before I began typing, because the act of retyping was so laborious. The computer has made me lazy. I can be slack on the first, second, third, fourth, and fifth drafts. Also, I've forgotten how to spell words I used to know how to spell, because I no longer need a dictionary by my side. (In truth, I do keep a dictionary nearby, but I don't open it nearly as much as I used to.) If we all had to go back to the typewriter, our days would be longer and more productive, and we'd give our brains some much-needed exercise.

Reyn: Maybe these dinner parties continue to exist among certain circles, but I have yet to be invited to the perfect one of my dreams. Okay, so maybe the present would not be entirely improved, but how bad would it be to unplug ourselves from our computers, peel ourselves away from our five-disc sets of *The Wire* or *Entourage*, and instead huddle around the table for a long evening's discussion of Kant or Ingmar Bergman or the unfathomable meaninglessness of our lives?

Trachtenberg: One, a revived IWW would have to ditch communism. If history's taught us anything, it's that Politburos are even worse than corporate boards. It would need to redefine what makes somebody a worker, as opposed to a boss, or recognize that some bosses really are workers, or have the same interests as workers. It would probably need to give up the rhetoric of 'smashing' shit. Personally, I don't care if we keep capitalism as long as no corporate CEO makes more than twenty times what the janitor does. And a reconstituted IWW should expand its constituency to include consumers. If nothing else, that would give the union much more power. If the workers at Bank of America go out on strike, how long will it take Bank of America to find new ones? But if you can get a million Bank of America credit-card holders to hold back their payment one month, you can bring down the bank.

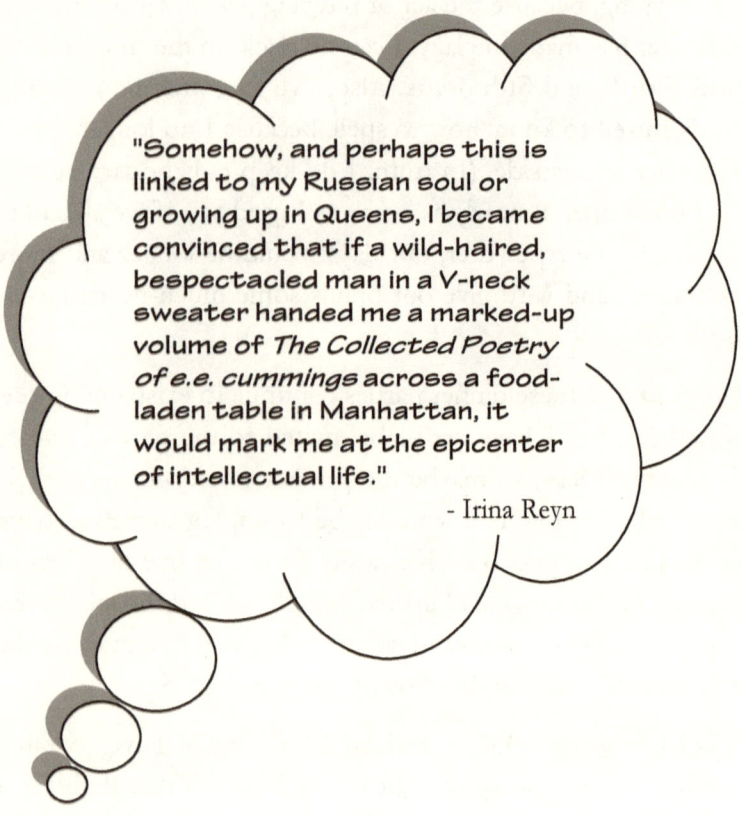

"Somehow, and perhaps this is linked to my Russian soul or growing up in Queens, I became convinced that if a wild-haired, bespectacled man in a V-neck sweater handed me a marked-up volume of *The Collected Poetry of e.e. cummings* across a food-laden table in Manhattan, it would mark me at the epicenter of intellectual life."

- Irina Reyn

- What do you imagine the present-day obstacles would be?

Beal: There are at least two obstacles that I can think of. The first was an obstacle back when there were chuckwagons, which is that the food probably wasn't all that good except for maybe the sourdough biscuits. I'm guessing on a good night it was fresh killed rabbit, some bitter wild greens collected from a ditch, biscuits, and gravy. But I bet there were plenty of times that it was all about the dried buffalo meat. (A quick Web search, a day later, pulls up "son-of-a-gun stew" and "blackbird pie." I'm not encouraged.) I'm a little more hopeful about breakfast, because my chuck wagon man would have chickens in his wagon, and we all agree on bacon around here. All the same, there would likely be a cholesterol glut and a paucity of fresh fruits and vegetables. The second problem is that chuck wagons were made for cattle drives heading west, and I live a stationary life in one of the most densely populated cities in America, where, even in the old days, there were no chuck wagons, justice-men and street carts. So not only is my fantasy anachronistic, it's totally geographically off.

Bock: I don't know that it's the kind of place that I'd want to go to alone, every day, on my lunch hour, if I was a temp in Midtown New York City — that might be a little too depressing and isolating. But then again, I might want to go every day and eat there and read. Why not? In fact, there's actually a small automat running on St. Mark's Place in New York City. You buy food like fries and hot dogs, and anything that needs to be heated, you put in a microwave. It's a nice idea and an honest attempt at bringing back this concept. Having said this, I do think we know too much about health and microwaves and preservatives for the automat, at this moment, to be much besides a cool novelty, the kind of place you see and are enchanted by and spend some money at, basically, as a lark.

Chenoweth: 1): Laziness. Email is so much easier. 2): It would be very hard to get everyone to agree to live in one place, because someone loves the Midwest and someone else can't more than an hour from the ocean, and just where is everyone supposed to find jobs, anyway? 3): Where would a mammoth live? In Siberia? In a refrigerated cage? Also, I'd worry that he'd be lonely.

McNally: No one's fingers are strong enough to make the keys of a manual typewriter work anymore. We haven't become just a fat nation; we've gone weak in the fingers. Also, we've grown accustomed to where every machine we own, including our telephone, must have the capacity to entertain us. It's hard to go back to the days when a machine performed only one function. We all need to go into technology-detox.

Reyn: Finding a date in one's schedule, an apartment on the Upper West Side that is large enough to accommodate at least ten (French Chinoiserie tapestry addressed in one corner, German Expressionist horror film in another, a heated debate about Nabokov's real-life model for *Pnin* around the center-piece), finding friends who still stay up past 11 p.m., staying up past 11 p.m. yourself, decent traveling weather to the dinner party, brushing up on Murnau and Nabokov, red wine and humble comfort food, elegant but comfortable evening wear.

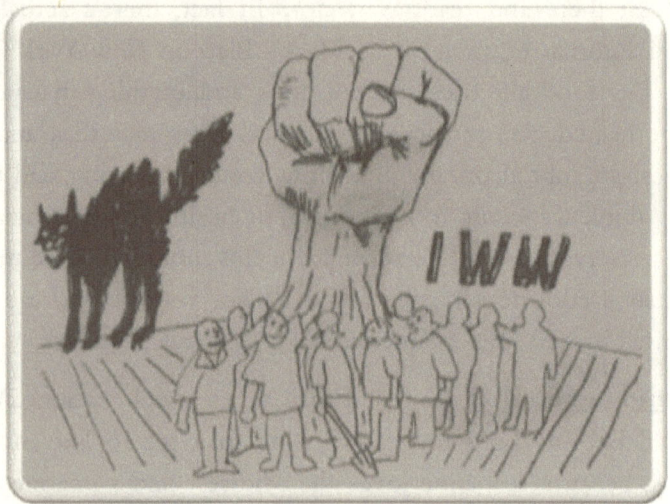

Trachtenberg: I'd say the first obstacle is that nobody iden-tifies as a worker any more. Everybody wants to be an "entre-preneur." You have the most downtrodden people in this country identifying — to an absurd extent — with the super-rich. I'm talking about WalMart clerks earning less than $30,000 a year voting against a presidential candidate who says he'll raise taxes on people who earn more than $200,000. And that's not because the clerks don't know math. It's because they think that one day they're going to make $200,000 and they're damned if they're going to pay taxes on it.

- How could these obstacles be overcome?

Beal: For the first issue, I would take up a collection among my neighbors for our chuckwagon man to do an intensive course at Chez Panisse in cooking, gardening, and foraging. We'd help him set up and tend a little garden, and we wouldn't mind if he had to pick up a few items at the deli. For the second problem, there's an empty lot nearby where we could make a fire and could tie up the horses. Either that or we're just going to have to head west ourselves.

Bock: Well, nothing is wrong with an occasional lark, for one thing. For another, there's absolutely nothing in this universe that cannot be solved by ingenuity, hard work, and a couple of hot lesbians in string bikinis making out with one another.

Chenoweth: I don't think that any of these obstacles will be overcome. In theory they could, but they won't. We'll keep moving toward virtual connections, both epistolary and familial. But maybe we could design a nice home for the mammoth, and maybe we could clone him a friend.

McNally: Calisthenics for the digits? I'm not sure. Very few of my students have ever done any manual labor. Maybe we all need to do some tasks that require pliers and a hammer, something to toughen up the fingers. I've recently begun writing longhand again, and I've brought my turntable and albums, which I haven't even looked at in over twenty years, up from my basement and dusted them all off. I spent winter break building floor-to-ceiling bookcases. Though I'm only forty-three, I'm growing increasingly tired of technology. And so, in some very small way, I'm fighting back by reclaiming those things that are disappearing from our culture. I don't want to lose books. I don't want to quit writing by hand. I don't want to waste any more days reading the opinions of people who feel compelled to express them not because they have any knowledge on the subject but because they have access to the Internet. When the end of the world comes, it won't be with a whimper; it'll be with a cacophony of ring-tones. And how depressing will that be.

Reyn: June 4th, at my friend Sonya's apartment, Red Bull martinis and Saint-Émilion, roasted chicken and *Nosferatu*. Dressed in DKNY. Anybody? Anybody?

Trachtenberg: Maybe start by inculcating Americans with the reality principle. And bring back the cool black cat emblem.

Episode 28: *Blue Ribbons*

with Thomas Beller, Joshua Furst,
Elizabeth Graver, Dave King,
and Binnie Kirshenbaum

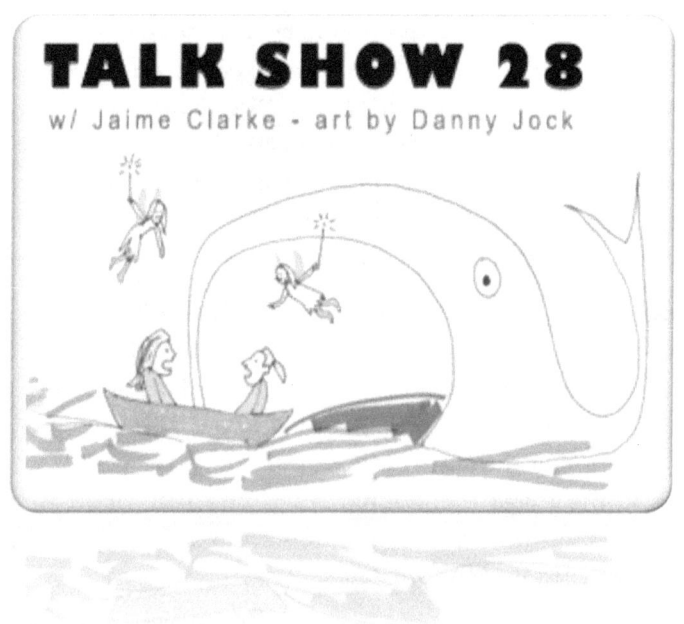

TALK SHOW 28

w/ Jaime Clarke - art by Danny Jock

Thomas Beller is the author of *Seduction Theory, The Sleep-Over Artist* - a *New York Times* Notable Book and *Los Angeles Times* Best Book - and *How to Be a Man.* He is editor of several anthologies, including *Lost and Found: Stories From New York.* His work has appeared in the *New Yorker,* the *Southwest Review, Plough-shares, Harper's Bazaar, Best American Short Stories,* the *Seattle Review and others.* Beller founded and co-edited *Open City Magazine.* He teaches at Tulane University and created mrbellersneighborhood.com.

Joshua Furst is the author of *Short People,* a collection of stories, and the novel *The Sabotage Café,* winner of the Grub Street Fiction Prize. His work has appeared in the *Chicago Tribune, Esquire, Salon,* and other publications. Furst has been awarded fellowships from the James Michener Foundation and the MacDowell Colony. He teaches at The New School.

Elizabeth Graver is the author of the novels *The End of the Point, Unravelling, The Honey Thief,* and *Awake,* as well as a story collection, *Have You Seen Me?* - winner of the Drue Heinz Literature Prize. Her work has been included in *Best American Short Stories, Best American Essays,* and *Prize Stories: The O. Henry Awards.* She teaches at Boston College.

Dave King is the author of the novel *The Ha-Ha,* named one of the best books of the year by the *Christian Science Monitor* and the *Pittsburgh Tribune-Review.* His work has appeared in *the Paris Review,* the *Village Voice Big City Lit* and others. King won a John Guare Writers Fund Rome Prize Fellowship from the American Academy of Arts and Letters and teaches at Baruch College and the School of Visual Arts.

Binnie Kirshenbaum is the author of the novels *On Mermaid Avenue, The Scenic Route, Pure Poetry, Almost Perfect Moment, Hester Among the Ruins, A Disturbance in One Place,* and the short story collections, *Married Life and Other True Adventures* and *History on a Personal Note* - a Critic's Choice Award winner. She teaches at Columbia University.

* * *

- **Name a ribbon or certificate you won in grade school.**

Beller: It was in Camp-Tennis VI. This was the highest rank of tennis accomplishment at the Cape Cod Sea Camps, which I attended.

Furst: First Place: Medley Relay Arlington County, Virginia, YMCA Intramural Swim Meet 1976. An actual blue ribbon embossed in gold.

Graver: When I was in second grade, I wrote a story called "A Moment Too Late," in which a girl and her sister go on a great ocean adventure and end up being swallowed by a whale. In the first version, fairies try to rescue the two girls but arrive "a moment too late." This — "A Moment Too Late" — was the last line of the story, as well as the title. I remember enjoying the symmetry of that. My teacher wanted me to enter the story into a children's writing contest sponsored by the local newspaper, but she strongly advised me to revise the ending and make it happy if I wanted to have a shot at winning. My story won third place for the Grades 1-3 category.

King: In third grade I wrote a Halloween story that was judged the best in our class.

Kirshenbaum: I thought for sure I must have won something in grade school; I was a good student and not the worst athlete, but if I did win a ribbon or certificate, I don't remember it, which leads me to conclude that I didn't win anything because surely I would've remembered if I had. The closest I came to an accolade, any recognition of achievement was in the fifth grade when I made the snowflakes for the Winter Pageant. On the program, at the bottom, on a line unto itself was printed: Snowflakes by Binnie Kirshenbaum.

- How did you win this accolade?

Beller: For each level, Tennis I, II, and so on, a counselor would put you through the paces on the court. You would have to hit a certain number of backhands, forehands, execute certain things. For the tennis six it was quite rigorous. I dimly recall there being a requirement for an "American Twist," serve. This involved throwing the ball above your head in such a way that you had to arch your back and give it a lot of top-spin, coming over the ball. As you might gather from the name, Cape Cod Sea Camps was focused on sailing. I did not sail. The second most intense activity at the camp was tennis, and I was into tennis. However I was a *dinker*. I fought my way up the tennis ladder by being someone who would hit the ball back a lot and, at the key moment, dink it over the net so it hit the service line and just died. It is the least graceful form of tennis. I hated myself for playing that way, but then when the competition got intense I always went to this special skill, the dink. In some ways I feel like I have been a recovering dinker ever since.

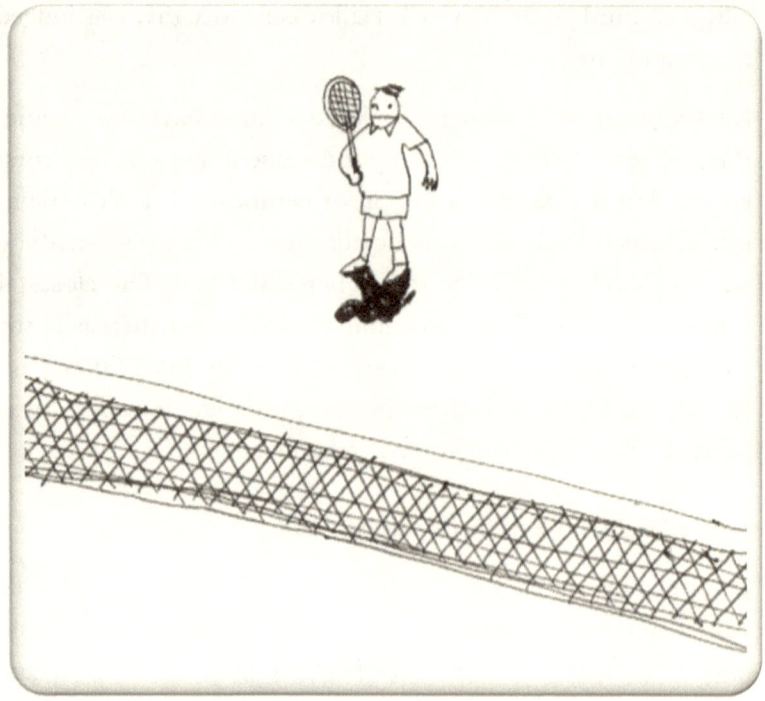

With this in mind I was not thought to be a big tennis talent and Tennis VI seemed beyond me. I had barely squeezed my way through the Tennis V test. I don't recall who administered the test for Tennis VI. I think it was a woman. I do remember thinking she was being very easy on me. At the end she said I got it. I was amazed. And here is why this is important to me — I told my friends that night at assembly. It was a special assembly where the end of the year awards were given out. I told my friend Mike Kaneb in this really low key way that I passed Tennis VI, and in his fraught but understated way, he went nuts. He had a murmurous style, but he got quite animated, he thought it was the greatest thing, he couldn't believe it, and neither could I.

But, I was already braced for the blow that was coming that night at the awards ceremony, where they handed out the prize for best this and best that. Among they prizes was best actor, or most accomplished in drama, or whatever they called it. There was a big musical at the end of camp — that year it was *Oklahoma* — and then throughout the season, there were these funny little melodramas that were put on every week. You rehearsed like crazy all week and then put on the show on Sunday. I always did these weekly things, never did the big musical, and that year I had really been on fire in those weekly shows cracking everybody up. I still recall one of my lines, I was a cop, I looked around and said, "There's something in the air!" For some reason, people really laughed when I delivered that line. But the prize tended to go to whomever had been the lead in the musical. To this day I look back at that evening and my dread of what would happen and think it anticipates some of the weird tension between short story writers and novelists — weekly play versus end of year musical. So here comes the big moment and the winner is . . . The guy who was the lead in *Oklahoma*. As I knew it would be. And yet. So for me this great peak, Tennis VI, has always been redolent of the disappointment, oddly enough, that came later that night. I should add as an addendum that before changing it to the roman numerals, above, I wrote it out as words, Tennis One and so forth, and at the end there, I wrote Tennis Sex. Make of this what you will.

Furst: By five years old, I'd risen to the rank of Sea Horse in the swim classes I took at the Alexandria YMCA. This meant that I'd mastered the rudiments not only of the crawl but also of the breast — and backstrokes. I was no longer a Minnow. I had rank and expertise. Having shown such promise at such a young age, I joined the swim club. (Was it a club or a team? It must have been a club — I'd never have made the cut on a team).

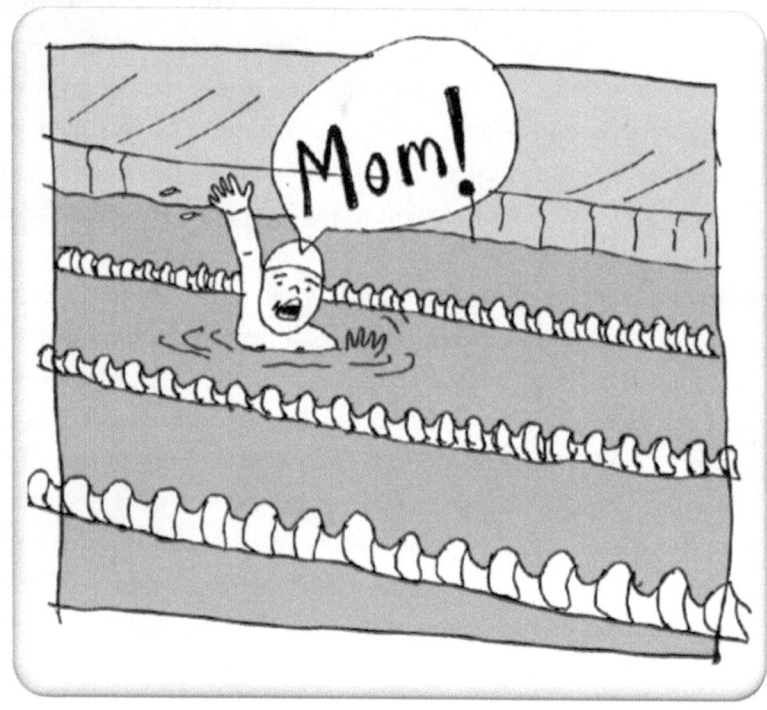

In my one and only meet, I swam the breaststroke leg of the 50-yard relay. My partners in this race consisted of two tykes like me, and anchoring us on the butterfly, a toned and powerful Dolphin (a Dolphin being someone who'd risen as high as you could go in the YMCA's system). It was an exciting day, charged with the smell of the chlorine and athlete's foot. The fold-out risers were packed with parents, mine included. When my turn came, I dove off the blocks, swam halfway across the pool and stopped, treading water as I searched the stands for my mother. Finding her, I waved with furious pride—Mom! It's me! Look! I'm swimming! Look! I'm racing! Look! Look! She waved back and the joy on her face in that moment drowned out the boos of my teammates.

Despite all this, we clobbered the competition.

Graver: I've always assumed it was because I changed the ending, but maybe the newspaper had an editor with a dark sensibility and I would have won first place if I'd stuck to my original draft. In the revised version, fairies swooped in a moment too late, as they had before, but then more fairies swooped in, a moment not too late.

It was dumb. The title no longer worked, but I kept it anyway. I didn't like the new version of the story, but I won a prize, and I liked that. Now I have a daughter in third grade. One day she came home from school saying that all stories need to have a problem and a solution, and I found myself saying (shrilly) No, *there doesn't have to be a solution; in life, there's not always a solution! Except in your life,* I added pathetically. *And your sister's.*

King: I cheated. My story had some sort of twist at the end, and though I made up my own characters and setting, I borrowed the twist from something I'd read. I think it's possible that the whole class had read the story I plagiarized, for I can recall my feelings of shock and chagrin when the winning story was read aloud on Halloween day. I hadn't bargained for that, and my classmates stared hatefully at me as it gradually became clear that a reprobate sat among them. I even wondered if the teacher had selected my story just to teach me a shaming lesson, for in those days I was still capable of attributing those kinds of motivations to adults.

Kirshenbaum: By default. In the fifth grade we auditioned for the school choir. It wasn't really an audition because the choir was the fifth grade. There were two performances of the Winter Pageant. One in the afternoon right before Christmas vacation for the younger students, and one that night for the parents and the older kids. The first week of school, the music teacher called us up, one at a time, to where she sat at the piano; we'd sing the first stanza of "Happy Birthday" and she then designated us "altos" or "sopranos." The whole *raison d'etre* of the fifth grade was the choir. The Winter Pageant was breathtakingly beautiful and now I was going to be in it, on stage, instead of part of the audience. Except when I sang "Happy Birthday," the music teacher — Miss Gilbert, her I remember — said, *No*. Neither alto nor soprano, I could not be part of the choir, I would throw everyone around me off-key, she explained. Choir practice was on Fridays mornings, at 11 a.m., and on that first Friday when everyone went to the Music Room, my teacher took me to the Art Room. There, the art teacher showed me how to fold the silver foiled paper into fourths and then again, and snip, snip, and behold! A snowflake. Every Friday, for one hour, for three months, I made snowflakes.

- Who was your closest competition?

Beller: There was no direct competition.

Furst: No one. Our Dolphin lapped everybody.

Graver: The kids who won first and second place.

King: Some kid. I doubt there was anyone famous in my third grade class.

Kirshenbaum: I had no competition. I was the only fifth grader unable to carry a tune.

- What were some of the perks of winning?

Beller: You got a patch. You got one for every level. So this was the last patch — It said "Tennis VI", and had the camp logo. I think if I had gotten it early in the season there would have been an outcry of protest that a dinker got it, but it was right before the end of camp, real life was about recommence.

Furst: A satisfying, and completely unearned, sense of accomplishment. Also, the public shame of having displayed an unseemly amount of mother-love. And then, also, the warm glow of knowing my mother knew I loved her.

Graver: I got published in *The North Adams Transcript* at the age of seven. And sold my soul. That all made an impression on me, but especially the selling your soul part. I was taken aback by being asked to change the ending, though it didn't occur to me in any serious way to consider saying no. It was an interesting introduction to the world of publishing.

King: The prize was not actually a ribbon or certificate, but a fancy die-cut model of a haunted house. It was from Hallmark, and I thought it was fantastic: incredibly intricate in all its details and in its clever use of folded cardboard. The teacher had already put the thing together, and when she unveiled it and said it would be the prize for the story contest, I knew I wanted it, whatever the cost. In fact, I'm not terribly materialistic, and this may be the incident of greatest covetousness in my entire life, so it was something of an aberration, but at the same time it was very real.

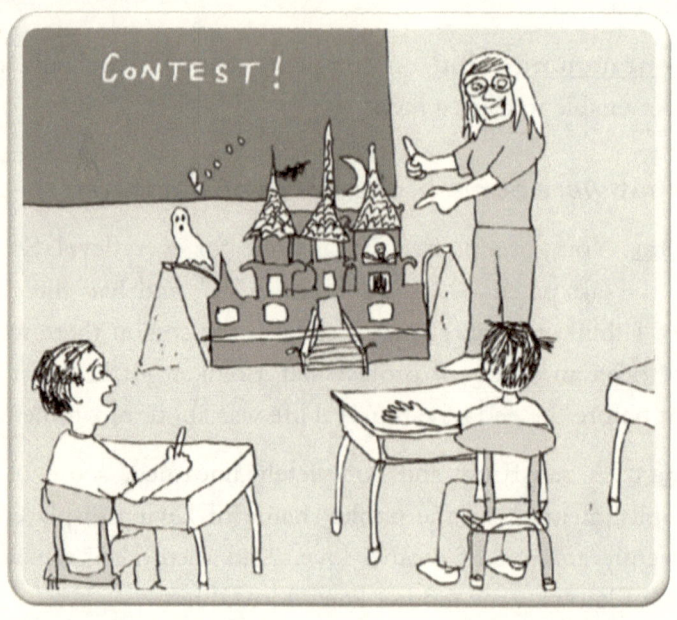

I suppose I could claim I was overcompensating because we'd just moved to that school district, and the kids in my new school had all learned multiplication, which hadn't been taught yet at my previous school; so I entered third grade as one of the dumb kids. But at the same time, I was reasonably well liked. I had friends and did Cub Scouts and for a while our family went to church. So I really can't lay this at a sense of inadequacy or social insecurity. I just had to have that haunted house. Desire's such an odd thing.

Kirshenbaum: In this case, I suppose I could say there were perks to losing. I learned to cut a mean snowflake. And I could push it and say it helped me develop a thicker skin and fostered a sense of individuality, especially when on the day of the pageant the fifth grade filed into the auditorium. We took our seats, and then after the principal made a speech, Miss Gilbert blew a C-sharp on her pitch pipe and the fifth grade rose up and took their place on the stage, leaving me in the midst of three rows of empty seats. But probably the only real perk was that I didn't have to look at that bitch of a music teacher every week.

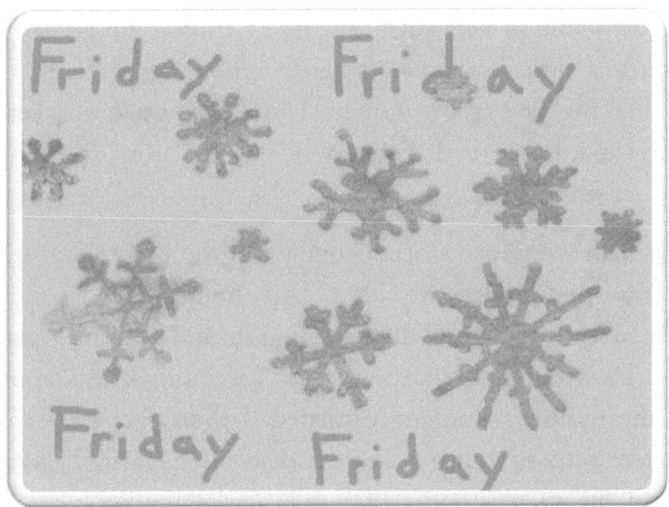

- Where do you think this ribbon or certificate is today?

Beller: I know exactly where it is, in the top drawer of a desk at my mother's house, my old desk, where I have a bunch of other childhood memorabilia. I'm glad I still have it. It's a fair, sea-gray shade of blue — a hopeful color.

Furst: In a Phillips cigar box, along with my childhood bottle cap collection, somewhere in my mother's unfinished attic.

Graver: I'd like to say I have no idea, that it's been lost in the detritus of the past, replaced by more substantial honors, or by my ability to transcend the need for them. In fact, it's on the mantelpiece in my study. For years, it was in a drawer in my parents' house, but recently I found it and took it home, sort of as a joke and sort of because . . . why? Well, it's hard to keep writing when the economy is collapsing and Americans don't read fiction and you've made the mistake of joining Facebook and can sit at your computer reading about what 150 of your so-called friends are doing right now. It's a framed certificate with my name in very nice calligraphy. Inside the glass of the frame is a little bookmark with an embroidered poem on it called "Little Things," by Grace Haines. The prize is sweet and kitschy and, because of the story behind the story, complicated — all of which I like.

King: Can we please stop talking about the darn prize? That's not the point! Because after that humiliation, everything changed for me. I wrote no more fiction, and I put on weight. I didn't learn my multiplication tables for another decade or so, and my mother's drinking escalated. I didn't get into Yale. I traveled across country and worked in a factory, loitered around the men's rooms of public parks and took acid and smoked pot. The one thing I can say is that I worked on my people skills, since it seemed that getting others to like me was my one ace in the hole. And I did fall in love. But even now, I trace every disappointment and failure I've experienced — all those nights I drank too much or too little, my tendency toward malapropisms and Freudian slips and misguided fashion choices, my failed painting career and a stammer I developed between 1996 and 1999, even the bouts of erectile dysfunction I may or may not from time to time experience — I blame all of it on the deep moral shame of October 31, 1963, and I'm still working through it. With the help of my therapist I've begun to acknowledge that the teacher may not have cared that an eight-year-old borrowed a plot point. That perhaps she gave me that prize because she liked the writing or the characters or the symbolism or the *mise-en-scène;* or because my story was the most ambitious that third grade class produced. I struggle to believe that, and I thank all the loved ones who support me in that belief. But it was only after my novel — invented, thankfully, out of my own head — won a commendation or two that I began really to heal. If, indeed, I have begun to heal.

Kirshenbaum: Indelibly etched in memory and being worked out on the analyst's couch. When I was getting ready to go to college, my mother gave me a box filled with my grade school memorabilia. I sifted through my report cards, finger painting from kindergarten, a poem I wrote in third grade, and then there was the program for the Winter Pageant: Snowflakes by Binnie Kirshenbaum. I sort of laughed and sort of didn't, and I threw it all in the garbage. So unless someone else from my fifth grade class saved their Winter Pageant program, it long ago biodegraded in a landfill somewhere.

Acknowledgments

My thanks to Benjamin Strong for bringing me into the *Fanzine* family and to *Fanzine* founder Casey McKinney for his passion and commitment to *Talk Show*. And to Danny Jock, the world's fastest mind/hand combination.

Thanks, too, to all the writers who gave their time and energy and enthusiasm to this project.

Peter Sarno's bravery made this book a reality. Thanks to his singular vision and for all he does for books.

Mary Cotton, Mary Cotton, Mary Cotton. And Max.

Jaime Clarke

Jaime Clarke is a graduate of the University of Arizona and holds an MFA from Bennington College. He is the author of the novels *We're So Famous* and *Vernon Downs* (forthcoming from Roundabout Press); editor of the anthologies *Don't You Forget About Me: Contemporary Writers on the Films of John Hughes,* and *Conversations with Jonathan Lethem;* and co-editor of the anthologies *No Near Exit: Writers Select Their Favorite Work from Post Road Magazine* (with Mary Cotton), and *Boston Noir 2: The Classics* (with Dennis Lehane and Mary Cotton). Clarke is a founding editor of the literary magazine *Post Road*, now published at Boston College, and co-owner, with his wife, of Newtonville Books, an independent bookstore in Boston.

For additional information, please visit www.jaimeclarke.com

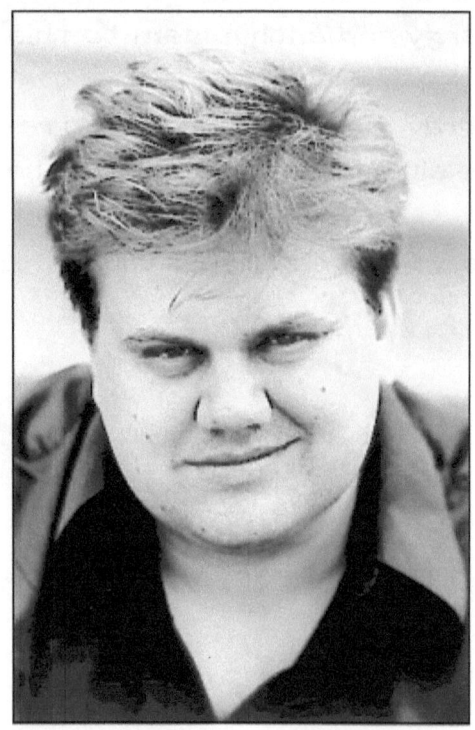

Author Photo (c) John Laprade

Danny Jock

Danny Jock grew up in Trumbull, Connecticut and graduated from The Parsons School of Design in New York City.

Jock has provided illustrations and related services to *Fanzine*, TheFix.com, BBDO, the Penguin Group, Nickelodeon and several other publications and organizations.

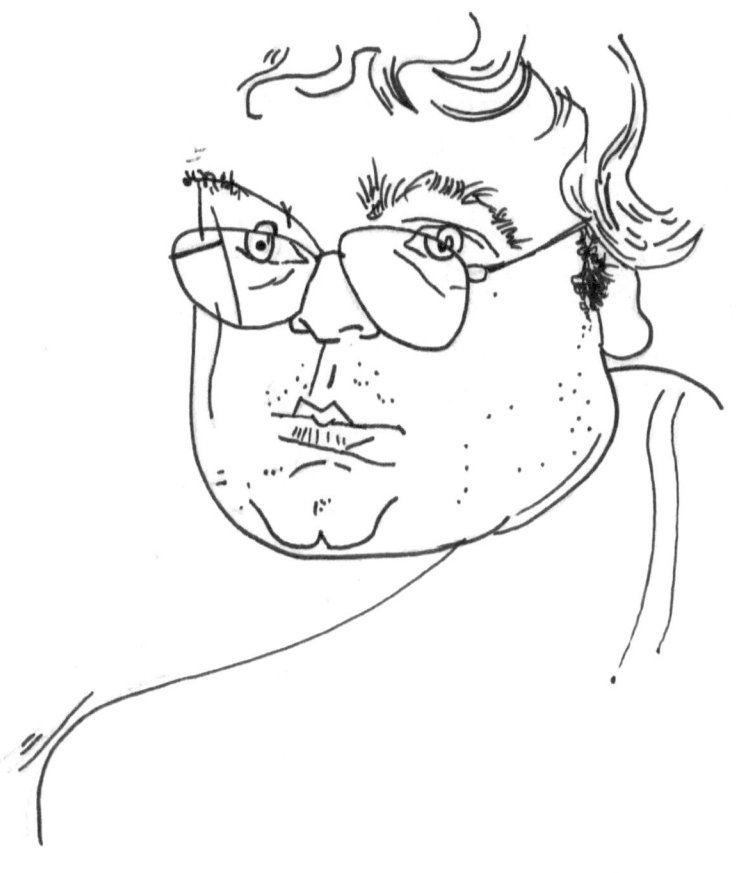

Some Other Books By
PFP / AJAR Contemporaries

Blind Tongues by Sterling Watson
the Book of Dreams by Craig Nova
A Russian Requiem by Roland Merullo
Ambassador of the Dead by Askold Melnyczuk
Demons of the Blank Page by Roland Merullo
Celebrities in Disgrace by Elizabeth Searle
(eBook version only)
"Last Call" by Roland Merullo
(eBook "single")
Fighting Gravity by Peggy Rambach
Leaving Losapas by Roland Merullo
Girl to Girl: The Real Deal on Being A Girl Today by Anne Driscoll
Revere Beach Elegy by Roland Merullo
a four-sided bed by Elizabeth Searle
Revere Beach Boulevard by Roland Merullo
Tornado Alley by Craig Nova
"The Young and the Rest of Us" by Elizabeth Searle
(eBook "single")
Lunch with Buddha by Roland Merullo
Temporary Sojourner by Tony Eprile
Passion for Golf:In Pursuit of the Innermost Game by Roland Merullo
What Is Told by Askold Melnyczuk
The Family Business - John DiNatale
"What A Father Leaves" by Roland Merullo
(eBook "single" & audio book)
Music In and On the Air by Lloyd Schwartz
The Calling by Sterling Watson